Tender | Volume II

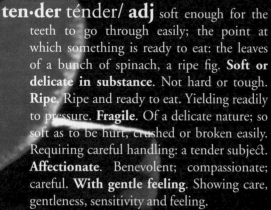

ten·der ténder/ **adj** soft enough for the teeth to go through easily; the point at which something is ready to eat: the leaves of a bunch of spinach, a ripe fig. **Soft or delicate in substance**. Not hard or tough. **Ripe**. Ripe and ready to eat. Yielding readily to pressure. **Fragile**. Of a delicate nature; so soft as to be hurt, crushed or broken easily. Requiring careful handling: a tender subject. **Affectionate**. Benevolent; compassionate; careful. **With gentle feeling**. Showing care, gentleness, sensitivity and feeling.

    Botanical. Needing protection from harsh weather, especially frost and cold.

[13th century. **Via French** *tendre* **from Latin** *tener* 'delicate, tender' (source also of English tendril).]

Nigel Slater is the author of a collection of bestselling books, including the classics *Real Fast Food*, *Appetite* and the critically acclaimed *The Kitchen Diaries*. He has written a much-loved column for *The Observer* for eighteen years and is the presenter of the award-winning BBC series Simple Suppers. His memoir, *Toast – The Story of a Boy's Hunger*, has won six major awards, including British Biography of the Year, and has been adapted into a BBC film. *Tender – Volume II* is the companion volume to *Tender – Volume I: A cook and his vegetable patch*.

Also by Nigel Slater

Tender – Volume I
Eating for England
The Kitchen Diaries
Toast – The Story of a Boy's Hunger
Thirst
Appetite
Nigel Slater's Real Food
Real Cooking
The 30-Minute Cook
Real Fast Puddings
Real Fast Food

www.nigelslater.com

Tender | Volume II

A cook's guide to the fruit garden
Nigel Slater

Photographs by Jonathan Lovekin

FOURTH ESTATE London

First published in Great Britain
by Fourth Estate
a division of HarperCollins*Publishers*
77–85 Fulham Palace Road
London W6 8JB

www.4thestate.co.uk
Love this book? www.bookarmy.com

A catalogue record for this book is available
from the British Library

ISBN 978-0-00-732521-4

Designed by BLOK
www.blokdesign.co.uk
Printed in Italy by L.E.G.O. SpA – Vicenza

Printed on Fedrigoni Freelife Cento
Uncoated recycled paper with 60 per cent
secondary pre-consumer fibre and 40 per cent
de-inked recycled wood-free FSC fibre

Mixed Sources
Product group from well-managed
forests and other controlled sources
www.fsc.org Cert no. SW-COC-1806
© 1996 Forest Stewardship Council

FSC

FSC is a non-profit international organisation
established to promote the responsible management
of the world's forests. Products carrying the FSC
label are independently certified to assure consumers
that they come from forests that are managed to
meet the social, economic and ecological needs
of present and future generations.

Find out more about HarperCollins and the
environment at www.harpercollins.co.uk/green

Introduction

And then there was fruit. I always knew that if ever I found a space in which to grow a few knobbly vegetables of my own, some of it would be set aside for fruit: fraises de bois with flowers like tiny, brilliant stars; amber and bronze apples with russet skins; dusky blueberries in old terracotta pots; maybe a blackcurrant bush or two for jam. What I had not expected was to find myself with a virtually blank canvas, an opportunity to plant not only fruit bushes but some space for trees too, a row of raspberry canes and even a vine.

Ten years on, permanently teetering on the edge of chaos, this garden creaks under the weight of my overenthusiastic planting. There is barely an inch of ground to spare. From white currants and golden raspberries to purple figs and red gooseberries, my pocket handkerchief of urban space is bursting at the seams. Give me a couple of feet more and I'll show you space for a crab apple with blossom the colour of a loganberry fool.

There is a moment, some time around the middle of September, when this garden, this diminutive *hortus conclusus* I have made in an 1820s London terrace, truly becomes the garden of my dreams. The leaves are turning from green to gold, amber and rust, the last of the fruits hang crimson and smoky blue on the trees, the pumpkin-coloured dahlias and Michaelmas daisies have collapsed like drunks across the gravel path. The garden darkens to the colour of ginger cake, here and there a shot of saffron, brilliant ochre or deepest crimson. The colours, I would guess, of the Vatican at prayer.

The last berries, apples and plums, wet and almost rotting from the late sun and autumn rain, lend a mellow, alcoholic scent to the space, like the dregs of an abandoned glass of wine. The garden is falling asleep with an air of damp tobacco and wood smoke, but it is still abundant too, with late blackberries, damsons and a grapevine at breaking point. Each year I race to get to those blackberries before the feast of Michaelmas, when the devil is said to piss on them.

Growing many, though sadly not all, of my own vegetables is a deeply pleasurable thing to do. Watering the tomatoes and the runner beans is now as much a part of my life as taking a shower, but although I produce far less of my own fruit than I do vegetables, curiously they give me even more joy. Walking round the garden late on an autumn morning, pushing past the spiders' webs that festoon the pathways and plucking those last, wine-coloured berries from their blackened canes is as good as life gets. A moment of intense wellbeing, and even more so when the time has been stolen from a busy schedule.

This space at the back of my house could so easily have been a lawn. Instead, I have ended up with a back garden laden with sensual pleasures. A bough of yellow plums the size of a blackbird's egg; an apple tree whose fruit is snow white flushed with rose pink; loganberries as dark and sultry as a glass of Pinot Noir; and grapes that hang outside the kitchen wall like bunches of jet beads. There are sherbet-sharp gooseberries and piercingly tart sticks of rhubarb; fat black figs and raspberries the colour of a glass of Sauternes. Their pleasures are brief, and yes, there is always a struggle to get there before the birds and the squirrels, but it is hard to find a mulberry more exquisite than the one you have grown for yourself, a strawberry more sweet or a fig more seductive.

Why grow your own fruit?

While I cannot imagine my little garden without its cane teepee of runner beans and their scarlet flowers, or its chipped pots of random tomatoes, it is a simple truth that more of the garden's space is given over to fruit with each passing year. The potatoes that basked in the luxury of their own bed now share it with gooseberry bushes and three crowns of rhubarb; the beetroot patch is constantly invaded by ever more varieties of strawberry; the Jerusalem artichokes have, no doubt to everyone's relief, been partly replaced by raspberry canes.

Vegetables remain at the heart and soul of this fifty-metre plot but, as the infant plums and pears mature into fully grown trees and the loganberries climb up their blue steel wires, the focus of the garden is shifting towards being a slightly more fragrant and sensual place.

The supermarkets may carry more varieties of locally grown apples and pears than they used to but they are a long way off being as interesting as a farm shop or the apple stall of a farmers' market as somewhere to pick up the week's supply of fruit. The clinical, bright aisles of even the most user-friendly chain store can never hope to approach the sight and smell of a farmers' market on a misty autumn morning.

I cannot be the only one who generally finds supermarket fruit somewhat characterless – a testament to sweetness and shelf life. By growing my own fruits I not only have the chance to grow lesser-known varieties spurned by the big boys as being unproductive, short-lived or, dare I say it, too characterful, but also that of experiencing them straight from the tree, bush or plant. But there is much, much more pleasure to growing fruit than that of a strawberry on the lips. The haunting silhouette of a bare tree against a winter sky; the first breaking buds; the childlike pleasure of an avalanche of cherry blossom and then, as the fruit ripens over the coming weeks, watching its progress like a hawk eyeing its prey. To bring a home-grown apple or a palm full of raspberries in from the garden is a different experience altogether from that of taking them off a supermarket shelf. And isn't that what we all want – food that brings us the most possible pleasure and delight?

Like interesting salad leaves and bright, vital greens, fruit is a massive part of what I eat. But, in truth, I could never satiate my need for berries and currants on my own soil alone. I wish I could. Not to mention the fact that the British blueberry, currant and blackberry season, although longer now than at any time in its history, still lasts no more than a few weeks. Where I would never touch a spring cabbage out of season or be tempted by the call of a bunch of air-freighted asparagus, I do supplement our own fruits' short seasons with those from elsewhere. As a result, I buy far more of my berries from supermarkets and greengrocers than I would like. Growing at least some of my own is, I suppose, partly a tiny attempt to redress that.

And as anyone who has dug their own potatoes from the earth or twisted a ripe plum from its stem knows, growing your own is as addictive a drug as almost anything else out there.

The trees

The fruit trees were the first to go in. My initial list, as absurdly long as a spoiled child's Christmas list, included a Nottingham medlar for which there was no obvious use and a King James mulberry from which I was told to expect no fruit for a decade. (They were right.) The others, Mirabelle de Nancy plums, Rouge de Bordeaux figs, Merryweather damsons, Vranja quinces, Durondeau pears and Count Althann's gages, were from a list made more out of romanticism than practicality. As with my first purchase of rose bushes, I bought those whose names I happened to like and the order was put together with no thought for space, pollination or correct location. I was soon to learn a hard and painful lesson.

The idea was tempting. A space at the end of the garden, past the vegetable patch with its Peter Rabbit lettuces and clumps of Joseph's coat chard, would be a small, enclosed orchard. A cloister within a cloister, if you like. Even though I knew the word orchard was a ridiculous exaggeration, I hadn't quite envisaged how I would get things so very wrong.

Trees grow. A fact that, in his over-excitement, this newbie gardener had overlooked. At first I put an apple, a plum, a damson, a quince and two nut trees in a space small enough in which to park a car. Branches tangled, blossom merged, roots entwined, the damson almost suffocated under the prolific, arching branches of the hazelnuts. The squirrels bounced from one tree to the next like kids practising parcour, taking every fruit and nut in their path.

The apple was moved, at great cost to my back, its thick roots dug out with a garden fork and the more fragile ones scrabbled out with my bare hands, to a place where it could at last spread its branches. The nuts were coppiced, their long twigs recycled as climbing frames for the runner beans; the plum was pruned to disentangle it from the nearby quince. Trees, it seemed, need to breathe just as we do.

One by one, I moved the fruit trees around the garden: a pear to one bed, a plum to another, finding each one a new home amongst the flowers and vegetables. One fig ended up in a lead-lined hole in the stone terrace, another climbing up strings nailed into the scullery wall. Within a year or so they were happy, each with a bit of space to call its own, their blossom bringing bees and butterflies to the fruits and vegetables underneath, and shade to those beds that needed it. The exception is, I suppose, the medlar whose canopy is now so thick that the bed beneath it is good only for rhubarb and gooseberries.

A garden without at least one apple tree is probably no garden at all, but one happy tree is better than several without the room to thrive. This garden has seen three. The first, a Discovery, was the first tree on my list. The young tree, barely three feet high, was planted with white phlox underneath in an attempt to realise a haunting childhood memory of the smell of ripe apples mixed with the powdery scent of fading *Phlox paniculata*. (As an eight-year-old, I would reach down through the phlox to pick up the fallen apples, and the scent of the fruit and flowers was unforgettable.) I succeeded, too: the earliest apple ripens just as the second flush of flowers starts to fade. I cannot overemphasise the effect this small success had on me. For years I had walked round with this childhood scent in my head. And now here it was in a garden of my own making.

The second, a Blenheim Orange, the apple of the Benedictine monasteries, was a more than appropriate choice as it turned out – more than one observer has described this space as having the air of a monastery garden. The blossom was exquisite, the fruit large, its skin green, orange and russet. I loved the tree's extraordinary crooked shape, like an old man in a fairy tale. I almost cried the day I returned home to find it had been ripped up, its branches hideously snapped by unknowing scaffolders who had no choice but to squeeze their long rods through my tiny orchard. (They said sorry and brought me a T-shirt.)

And then there was the Court Pendu Plat. A flat-topped apple, whose late blossom never quite coincides with that of the Discovery and so rarely bears fruit. The world of pollinators, and the idea that apple trees often need a mate, was a mystery to me in those days.

A little homework led me to choosing a pear tree with a suitable friend as pollinator. It had been suggested that rather than being home to a large tree, the garden might fare better with an espalier – a tree whose branches were carefully trained to reach out along wires attached to a wall. For once, I did things properly, getting stiff wires batoned to a south-facing wall close to the house by someone more of a dab hand than me. The tree arrived and its young, whippy branches were tied along the wires. (At first the diagrams in pruning manuals were as strange to me as those in a car maintenance book. Yet once the pruning shears are in your hand things become clearer, the diagrams suddenly start to make sense.)

My little Doyenne du Comice pear fruited within two years, and now, eight years on, has branches spreading four feet or more along the wall. The idea of espaliered trees has something of the grand kitchen garden about it, yet it makes total sense for a tiny urban garden like mine. Did I mention the garden looks much bigger in photographs than it is? Well, it does. Its mate, a Winter Nelis, has blossom like a snow flurry and, in autumn, leaves the colour of bitter orange marmalade. The pears, as hard and crisp as the Comice's are soft and luscious, and are often still hanging on the tree on Christmas Eve. They are wonderful poached slowly with maple syrup and vanilla or sliced up and dropped into mulled perry.

Of all the trees in this garden, it is the plums with which I am most enamoured. Their names are lovable – Crimson Drop, Mirabelle de Nancy, Oullins Gage and Old Transparent – but their fruit is superb too. They are worth growing for their colour alone: amber freckled with crimson; opal with flashes of mauve; Chartreuse, rust and vermilion. On a sunny day in late July they hang translucent on the tree, as if lit by a candle. Their flesh becomes soft and melting and the juice honey-sweet, a sticky golden nectar. If I could have just one tree it would be a plum.

After my Discovery apple, the second tree on the list was a damson. The trees are brittle and their growth slow. They need a firm hand with the pruning shears if they are not to run wild, but their blossom is the most delicate of all the plums, like that of a fairy's wing. I knew, even ten years ago, that cold January morning I dug the deep, wide hole for my Farleigh damson, I would never get enough fruit for more than a crumble and I still don't. No matter. The single pudding, its purple fruit bubbling up through the oatmeal crust, is as welcome as the dusky, blue-black fruit and that tissue-paper blossom each spring.

The bushes

Trees are but part of the story. The fruit bushes have been more of a success than I had ever dreamed. Any garden can squeeze in a raspberry cane or two (a friend has planted a couple just for the kids). Sadly, there simply isn't room in my patch for more than one or two of each hue of currant, or for more than two or three rows of berries. None of which seems to matter. The fruits somehow become all the more precious for their scarcity. When I was a child, there wasn't a garden on the block that didn't have a few currant bushes at the end of it. Often as not, down by the runner beans past the washing line. Mine are closer to the house, where I can keep an eye on their progress. The daily walk round the garden, pulling up the odd weed or leading a snail to a happier place, is a year-round bonus.

The day the fruit bushes arrived was one of the most disappointing of my life. At that stage, I had no idea how unpromising a young, bare-rooted plant would look when taken from its cardboard package. Wrapped in a nest of coarse, damp straw and tied in a bundle with unbreakable orange twine, they were very different from the lush bushes whose berries, hanging like jewels, I had envisaged when I placed the order. The day was bitter too, as cold as I can remember, and by four o'clock, with sleet coming sideways at me, I gave up planting my little brown sticks and toasted crumpets with ridiculous amounts of butter to make myself feel better.

Within six months my sticks had turned into a fizz of green leaves and even fruited in their first year. Not many, granted, but enough to convince me I was heading in the right direction (better gardeners would have had the sense to remove the first fruits to give the bushes a chance to build a strong root system). The raspberries were worse, a bundle of kindling that, in a final moment of disillusionment, I was invited to cut to the ground as soon as they were planted. Those Autumn Bliss raspberries have gone on to become one of the most magical parts of this little space. Huge, deep-red berries heavy with perfume (roses, Beaujolais, who can say?) hang down from late August till the first frosts. They have recently been joined by Autumn Gold, a yellow variety, and a loganberry with its prolific stems and fruit the colour of sloe gin. And yes, there are now blueberries in terracotta pots too.

I recently found that first fruit order, smudged with garden soil and yellow as nicotine, in an old box of papers. On it were the Careless gooseberry bushes that did so well for the best part of eight years. They have recently been replaced with three Hinnomaki bushes in red, green and gold. They fruited, just enough to tease, in their first year.

Fruit bushes have much to be said for them in even the smallest garden. They show off the seasons: the peaceful grey stems of winter, spring's stinging green, the spritz of those tiny summer flowers and then the fruits that slowly ripen from hard and opaque to shimmering, translucent gold.

The plants

At first I had no wish for strawberries other than the wild ones with fruit the size of midget gems. They started sweetly, a gift from a friend, and as dainty and hidden as a snowdrop, but pretty soon profligate seedlings had escaped all over the garden. Two years on from planting and I was pulling them up like weeds (to be honest, I still am). Now they are contained in a vast pot around the *Magnolia stellata*, where they grow lush, with leaves so thick they successfully hide the fruits from the blackbirds' eyes. Their spring green is one of the freshest of all, and occasionally in autumn a golden orange leaf appears.

An annual trip to the Chelsea Flower Show is never complete without the heady scent of strawberries caught in the heavy air of the Great Pavilion. Tantalising – you cannot touch them, let alone taste them – but you can still breathe in their sugary richness. A few years ago I fell for one called Florence, quite rare at the time, and ordered a dozen plants. Such a revelation was the flavour of those first home-grown strawberries that I started a small patch in the hottest of the six vegetable beds. Joined by Mara de Bois, Gariguette and later Ken Muir's Chelsea Pensioner, my little patch is now an essential part of the garden. Hiding behind the runner beans as they do, they announce their presence if not by their poster-paint colours then by the scent they give off on a baking-hot July afternoon.

The cloudberry is the one that got away. I hopefully phone the gardener in the Scottish Highlands each year, a polite enquiry, but am always unlucky. Yet again a few weeks too early or a day too late. One day I will get my hands on these beautiful berries that dot the Scandinavian countryside and make such superlative jam. They are part of my wish to bring the fruit of the hedgerow into this garden to accompany the elders and the wild blackberry. That, or I will hide some plants in my suitcase.

The vine

I have seen grapevines clamber over rickety, painted sheds on inner city allotments, dominate Victorian glasshouses on country estates and wind their tendrils over neat suburban pergolas, but it never crossed my mind to have one in my own garden.

The grapevine seems to belong to the Mediterranean. Like the olive trees on every balcony in new apartment blocks, they seem curiously out of place here. Yet we have grown vines in Britain for hundreds of years and we can make very good wine here too. I took a chance and ordered one. Well, two actually. Not interested in homemade wine, I went for the Fragola, or strawberry grape, a thick-skinned variety that has extremely juicy fruits with flesh the texture of melting jelly.

The kitchen has double doors that open flat on parliament hinges. Either side of them is a space begging for a climber. While wisteria and roses were possibilities, this bit of wall seemed perfect for a grapevine. Planted deeply, in somewhat stony soil, they couldn't be happier, and now regularly produce eighty small bunches between them. What is more, they sprout downy, rose-pink buds in early April in perfect harmony with their dove-grey stems. In autumn, although they lack the stunning colours of other varieties of vine, their fading gold leaves look suitably sombre against the matt black of the doors.

A word about blossom

My earliest memory is of blossom and staring up into branches so crammed with pink petals you couldn't see the sky. Cherry probably. One of those frilly, over-abundant varieties that are best viewed from a distance. The flowering cherry so beloved of the 1960s suburban garden, and a world away from the single, white cherry blossom I now love.

When I was a teenager, my father would take me along the 'blossom routes' that ran like maypole ribbons though the Shropshire countryside. Seeing them as vast white curds, like snow clouds resting on thick trunks, I would climb up with my head out of the 'sunshine roof' of the car, flurries of petals hitting me in the face and getting stuck to my lips. It was when he would pull up the car and we would get out and walk through the orchards that I got to admire their bent, wicked-witch shapes and lichen-encrusted branches.

There was blossom at home too. First, the three apple trees set into neatly trimmed rings in the lawn, then the orchard at the top of our new garden – plum, golden gage, pear, damson and wonderful, crisp apples. When I first drew the London garden out in my notebook, a spectacular show of pure white blossom in April and May was just as much my aim as the fruits that followed. Blossom is all about hope – a promise of good things to come.

A half-century on from that first pink cherry tree, I am obsessed by the flowers of the fruit tree. I seek out the fragile, butterfly-wing petals, from the sloes in the hedgerows around Sissinghurst to the wild apricots that grow on the hillsides outside Kyoto. Where orchids and lilies are the ultimate blooms for some, the sight and scent of frost-white plum blossom against a grey branch is what sets this heart racing.

Buying fruit trees, bushes and plants – a few notes

I must say that I have found fruit specialists to be more rewarding hunting grounds than garden centres. They tend to hold more interesting varieties and often have wise proprietors and staff who are generous with their advice. If you have the transport, you can often go and choose your tree; if not, they will send them by post.

Be warned that it is the least interesting trees that are sent by post, the sort whose branches will fit neatly into their uniform packaging. They obviously need to pick trees that won't get damaged in transit. If you want something with a bit of character, you might do better to go there and pick one out for yourself.

Buying by mail order has its advantages, and I have had both surprises and disappointments. My first blueberry plants were lanky and unpruned, I would never have bought them had I seen them first, but a fig tree was unexpectedly fine, its branches held secure on canes and even a few infant fruit in place.

I can read a specialist's fruit list like a novel, but we should be careful not to get carried away. Evocative, poetic names are infinitely tempting. Curled up by the fire with a catalogue, I would sometimes imagine a larger garden altogether, a place with room for a Michaelmas Red apple and a D'Arcy Spice, a Peasgood's Nonsuch and a Nutmeg Pippin; not just a Careless gooseberry but a Catherine and a Keepsake too, not to mention a Floribunda crab apple and a Jules Guyot pear. Oh and what about that Sanctus Hubertus plum or a white-fleshed pear called Moonglow? Imagine biting into that one freezing, starlit night in the garden.

My advice, as with ordering vegetable seeds, is to make your list at night but do not send it. Look at it again the following day when you can delete your wilder flights of fancy. A loquat? What was I thinking?

And, just as this book went off to press, I heard that finally, after years of searching, I had secured six little cloudberry plants from Scotland.

Fruit and cooking

The recipes

Just as savoury dishes made up the bulk of the recipes in Volume 1, baking, cakes and desserts form the heart and soul of this second part of *Tender*. This is as it should be. Fruit has an inherent sweetness that makes it more appropriate for sweet recipes than for savoury ones. But just as we dipped our toes into the world of beetroot cakes and pumpkin scones in the first half, this second part has a host of savoury dishes too – a pan-fry of venison with blueberries, pork with pears, and spare ribs with a cooling lime and peach salsa, to name just three. There is duck served with damsons, lamb stewed with quinces and quite a few recipes for rabbit, pheasant and partridge.

That said, you should find nothing to raise an eyebrow in this collection, no flights of fancy, no strawberry sauce with chicken to upset the family at suppertime. Despite many an enthusiast's insistence that rhubarb works in a beef stew or that peaches make a nice sauce for chicken (and I am sure they do), I have generally kept away from fruit's more unusual applications. Some may say that I haven't been experimental enough and I take that accusation on the chin, but I wanted to produce a collection of recipes that were useful and delicious rather than extraordinary and seasoned with the zeal of the evangelist. I hope I have the balance right.

Where I have used fruits with meat or very, very occasionally fish, then I would like to think it is because the inclusion was relevant rather than revelatory. I will leave it to you to experiment further.

Meat and fruit

The meat dishes of the Middle East have long been sweetened or given bite with appropriate fruits: a casserole of lamb that benefits from the sweet acidity of the apricot; quail roasted with a scattering of jewel-like pomegranates; sizzling beef steak cut into strips and tossed with tart green grapes; roast duck smeared with golden quince paste. Classical French cooking includes a sauté of chicken with apples, cream and Calvados, the famous porc aux pruneaux and the much derided but oh-so-delicious duckling à l'orange that can be so good when made with the correct bitter Seville fruits.

In autumn, Scandinavian cooks feast on salads of bacon and plums, veal with rhubarb and the ever-popular meatballs with a compote of lingonberries. Only the Italians resolutely refuse to mix fruit with meat on a regular basis – apart of course from the ever-present lemons – until you get further down south into Sicily, where oranges and raisins appear as a matter of course. It is worth remembering, however, that their beloved tomatoes and zucchini are both fruit.

British cooks, once happy to serve fruits with their main-course meats (Elizabethan cooks made much use of them), have become a little wary. Where a sharp apple sauce has always been welcome with pork and sometimes gooseberry too, it has taken a long time to get our collective palate to accept that there is more to rhubarb than fool.

If I am unsure whether a particular fruit will work with meat or game, I apply a simple rule. If the two regularly share a landscape, then maybe the combination is worth trying. The chances are that grouse, deer and partridge will have eaten the wild berries that pepper the hedges and

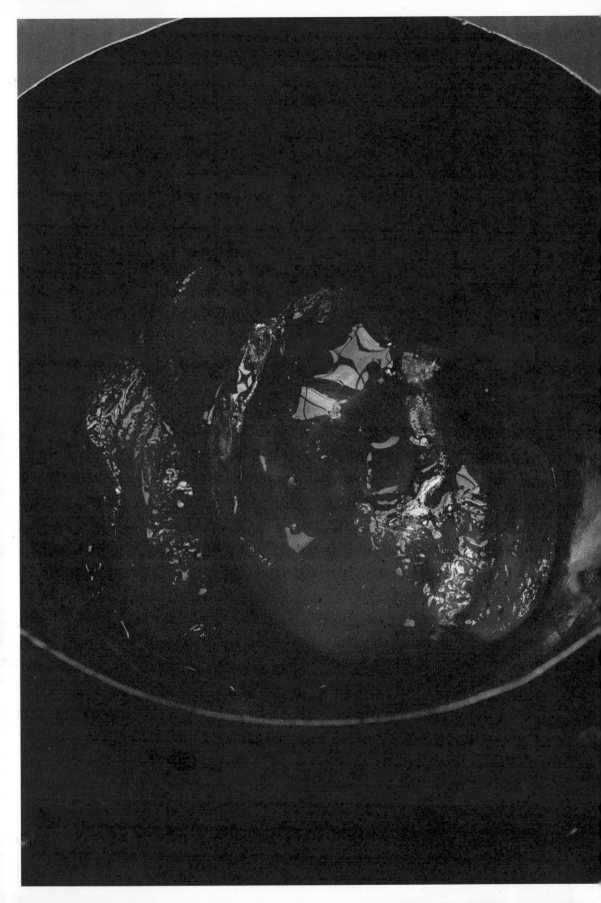

moors that are part of their habitat. Most game birds are happy to indulge themselves on elderberries, just as pigeons do on my plums. If the idea of adding fruit to a recipe sounds plausible, then I am happy to explore it. There have been some wonderful surprises, such as the venison and blueberries on page 784.

The marriage of fish and fruit is generally too controversial even for me. I just don't get it. Sole with bananas simply doesn't do it for me. But cut the fattiness of a marinated herring with a crisp, wincingly sharp apple salad the way the Swedish do, or fry mackerel with rhubarb or gooseberries to slice through the oily flesh, and then I think we could be on the same page. But I freely admit to being less happy with the marriage of fruit and fish than some more open-minded cooks.

Ten years ago, finding myself with an unwanted lawn, I set about digging it up with the hope of growing some of my own fruits and vegetables. Five years later, shortly after *The Kitchen Diaries* was published, I set out to chronicle what I grew and to learn more about the possibilities that can arise once you stick your trowel in the soil or push a seed into a pot.

In that short time my tiny plot has established itself as a place that, whilst coming up laughably short of the self-sufficient, nevertheless enriches my life and wellbeing more than this book can ever tell. Not just when I twist an apple off the tree on an autumn morning or get pink-fingered from picking raspberries on a July afternoon; not only when there is a dish of roast tomatoes with my own-grown garlic and thyme in the oven, or when I ladle out a bowl of carrot soup, but in myriad other ways too. The enrichment of my life that comes from watching a pear slowly ripen on the branch, the bud of a potato opening to reveal a fragile flower of the softest lilac, or when the greens of the garden turn from gold to amber and darkest bronze. I have always said that the joy of food should go way beyond the plate and it does.

Now I couldn't imagine life without some sort of allotment, a window box or a few pots in which to plant something, however small. What I grow here is a drop in the ocean of my daily needs, but you know what? I really don't care. The pleasure I get from growing a crisp, white-tipped radish in a pot is pleasure enough for me.

As I sit here now at the summer solstice, watching my little patch of strawberries ripen, the still-green Crimson Drop plums swelling on the trees and yet another sowing of beans pushing their swan's necks through the soil looking hopefully for one of my rickety cane affairs, I have to say that I am probably closer to my food, and more respectful of it, than I had ever thought possible. The pleasure, let me tell you, is immeasurable.

Apples

The most interesting apples are probably to be found in private gardens, farmyards and monasteries, their skins a tapestry of moss green, sage and amber, their flesh crisp, acid-sweet and full of character. Perhaps they will be copper or deepest crimson, or etched here and there with a web of russet as rough as a farmer's hand. They may be known as Christmas Red or D'Arcy Spice, Fenouillette Gris or Peasgood's Nonsuch, or maybe their names have been lost in time. The trees will be loved too, for their lichen-encrusted branches, tissue-frail blossom and quiet benevolence.

The apples of commerce can be good too, but I have had more fun at farm shops and farmers' markets than at neon-lit superstores. I prefer to rummage through wooden crates for my Pippins, happy to go home with bags of misshapen fruit of all sizes: plump ones for breakfast, majesties for baking and a few the size of baubles for snacking on.

Apples lack the seductive qualities of the peach and the mystery of the pomegranate but they make up for it in no-nonsense appeal. I have never met anyone who doesn't like an apple. Yet from early spring till late summer I rarely touch them, except in a sugar-crusted pie or a slick of sauce to cut the richness of the Sunday roast. From the first Discovery in August to the last of the Cox's in February, I eat an apple every day, sometimes two, three even – tiring only once I have seen the pink and white froth of blossom of the new year's growth.

I was brought up with munificent Bramleys and reliable Cox's, but took them for granted. Only when I got my own garden and planted first a rose-hued Discovery, then a Blenheim Orange and an ancient and late-flowering Court Pendu Plat did I appreciate their finer qualities, the possibilities of flavour – strawberry, walnut, nail varnish – and the satisfaction of picking the right variety for the right job.

There is probably an apple for every occasion: the Ribston Pippin for an aromatic crunch, the russet-skinned Ashmead's Kernel to munch with a wedge of Cheddar, an Emneth Early for a frothy pudding and an Orleans Reinette for an open tarte fine. There are apples with subtle hints of pineapple, raspberry or hazelnut and others with the pronounced astringency of a pear drop. Some could probably charm their way into our shopping bags by their names alone: Michaelmas Red, Pig's Nose and Cornish Honeypin. Others still by their looks, such as the Christmas Pearmain or the extraordinarily apt Catshead.

An apple's character is prone to change as the season progresses. Many deepen in flavour after picking, as their starch turns to sugar and their notes of nutmeg, aniseed or pineapple come to the fore. Others simply become soft and woolly. I have had more than a few of those. A fruit that disappointed on the tree may, by Christmas, be sublime, with all its credentials on show – the Pippins and the honey-scented Cornish Gilliflower being cases in point.

An apple in the garden

The apple tree originated in Central Asia, and its wild ancestor is found in the mountains there to this day. Many a tree will fruit within a year or two of planting, and they are well suited to a domestic garden – some take up barely more space than a revolving washing line (and the blossom is prettier than even your fanciest pair of smalls). Thanks to Barrie Juniper at Oxford University and DNA analysis, we know that our domestic apple probably originated from a single species still growing on the north slopes of the Tien Shan mountains in northern China. This perhaps explains why I prefer apples from a cold climate.

The apple is part of Norse mythology, a gift to the gods for eternal youth, and has long been associated with fertility. This, of course, is the tree of life, but to Christians it is the tree of the Knowledge of Good and Evil (mala, the Latin plural for apple, is identical to that for 'evil'). Not for nothing, then, is this the forbidden fruit.

Apple trees for the garden come as dwarf and standard, fans and espaliers, cordons and bushes, and a few sizes and shapes in between. There are some 7,500 known cultivars, though the choice at the garden centre will not be large. Specialist nurseries are the places to look for the older, often more interesting varieties. They send out young trees in the dead of winter, the perfect time to plant, before the sap rises.

My semi-dwarfing (M26 rootstock) apples were a wise choice for a small town garden, though more by luck than good judgement on my part. They stand at roughly my height, their silhouettes twisting against the winter sky. These are not the large, uniform trees of commercial orchards but interesting trees with branches that curve and twist.

An apple tree in blossom is a magical sight in any garden – the petals getting caught on the breeze and occasionally falling in flurries, like snow. Apple blossom and the young leaves burst early, and can occasionally be caught by frost, but look enchanting against the grey bark and silver skies of early spring.

A tree will often need a friend if it is to bear fruit, and, more importantly, a compatible variety that flowers at around the same time. I have the earliest and latest of varieties at home, which is probably why my crop can be hit and miss. Wise cooks will plant more than one variety to keep them going through the autumn.

An apple in the kitchen

Once we take an apple into the kitchen – for a pie, perhaps – its flavour becomes only slightly less important than that of an apple eaten straight from the tree. You might lose the very top notes, the subtlest hint of raspberry, say, or nutmeg, but the backbone of sharpness or intense sweetness will remain. It may even sing louder than in the raw fruit.

It is worth considering which might be the best apple for the job. A slice of pork crackling needs a sharp bite to offset its rich fattiness; a dish of poached apples will possess an extraordinary elegance when made with a batch of early Discovery; a baked apple needs plenty of acidity to balance the brown sugar and vine fruits with which it is traditionally stuffed. But what is most important to the cook is whether an apple is the sort to keep its shape or not. Will the fruit stay in one piece or will it expand in a balloon of snowy bubbles?

Talk of 'cookers' and 'eaters' is confusing and full of anomalies. Many varieties cross over between dessert and cooking. A crisp Howgate Wonder, for instance, is as happy with cheese as it is under the crust of pie. You can cook with any apple, but whether it is a wise choice is another matter. I tend to think of *Malus domestica* as dividing into two kinds – those that will look good in soldierly slices under the glaze of a fruit tart, and those that will melt into a sweet, fragrant slush.

Varieties

We have grown well over 2,000 varieties of apple in this country. I would dearly like to list the characteristics of each deserving one but that would constitute a hefty book in its own right (I occasionally have to remind myself that whatever else it may be, *Tender* is principally a cookery book). For a full discussion of apple varieties, you cannot do better than Joan

Morgan and Alison Richard's *Book of Apples* (Ebury Press, 1993). It barely leaves my side in autumn, and it is here that I check the history and tasting notes of, say, Hoary Morning or Mrs Wilmott. It is a directory, but this is also where you will find out that D'Arcy Spice is traditionally picked on Guy Fawkes Day and that the Norfolk Beefing was dried in bread ovens and used by bakers. An extraordinarily detailed and important work.

The internet, too, has rich pickings. Where else would you learn that you have been looking in the wrong place for the Manaccan Primrose (it is found almost exclusively around the Lizard in Cornwall) or that, despite its delicious name, Buttery d'Or (or Buttery Door or Buttery Dough) is best as a cider apple?

I have instead split the most popular apple varieties (and those we are most likely to come across during the Apple Day celebrations around the 23rd October each year) into what I feel are the most useful categories for the cook – apples that hold their shape, those that froth and those that have a unique affinity for eating as they are, or with cheese.

The frothing apples

A baked apple, its skin split, the top half rising like a beret, is best achieved with an acidic variety. The list includes Golden Noble, Kentish Fillbasket, Emneth Early, Monarch, Charlotte, Newton Wonder, Lord Derby and the Carlisle and Keswick Codlins. Most of these I have met at some point in my cooking life; others, such as Edward VII and the Eynsham Dumpling, I have never even seen on sale, let alone poured custard over. Then, of course, there are the seedlings: Bramley, Dumelow's and Pott's.

If you are in Cornwall with nothing much to do on an October afternoon, you might like to go in search of the Colloggett Pippin. You will be in with a good chance if you pronounce it Clogget and are within sight of the Tamar. The Cornish have a habit of shortening place names the way children shorten those of their best friends.

An apple that will bake nicely without collapsing is the Grenadier, but it carries a hefty dose of sweetness too. My own reverence is kept for Peasgood's Nonsuch, a generous, beaming apple with the geniality of a pumpkin. Handsome, striped and slightly russetted, it combines cloud-like froth and deep flavour. Frustratingly difficult to find, it leaves the Bramley standing.

Keeping their shape – apples for an open tart or a good, stiff purée

The variety of apple we use is, of course, a matter of taste, but occasionally the choice can be crucial. Attempt to make a tart in the French manner, with fine pastry and overlapping slices of fruit, using a frothing apple such as Bramley and you will fail. A fruit that keeps its shape when cooked is essential if the characteristic neatness of classic French pâtisserie is to be preserved. French pastry chefs don't really do wobbly. That means a Charles

Ross, James Grieve, Gravenstein or, if you find one, a Cravert. A Granny Smith will behave well too, and its lack of sweetness will balance the fruit jelly you will inevitably use as a glaze.

The drier the flesh of an apple, the more likely it is to retain a semblance of its shape. Annie Elizabeth, still popular in the Midlands, is just about perfect for this, but I wish you good luck in tracking her down. Golden Pippin will work, though my own pick is Blenheim Orange, with its lightly flattened top and flushed skin the timid orange of an October sunset.

Firm, creamy-yellow-fleshed fruits are also worth a thought as stewing apples, becoming tender, almost canary yellow, when simmered with a little sugar, whilst not exploding into a mass of foam.

An apple for cheese

Away from the stove, there are apples to be chosen to eat with cheese, which can be a lifelong and pleasure-filled hunt. The marriage of fruit and cheese is a very personal one, and only you can say whether Adam's Pearmain is the one for a wedge of Cheddar, or the Beeley Pippin works better with a six-month-matured Caerphilly than it does with a newly made goat's cheese. As with pairing food and wine, there is no right and wrong.

A lump of cheese and an apple is a regular lunch in our house; more often than not with a bowl of soup – a mildly spiced parsnip soup, a jagged lump of Cheddar and a Cox's being a favourite January lunch.

I tend to prefer the aromatic apples with cheese – those whose notes may include a subtle breath of hazelnuts, aniseed, pear drops or a faintly herbal inflection. Aromatic apples are not the easiest of fruit to find, being mostly older, less sweet varieties. With the exception of Ashmead's Kernel, which I have occasionally spotted in supermarkets, these are farm-shop varieties, or ones to jostle for, elbow to elbow, at the farmers' markets. Cornish Gilliflower, Alfred Jolibois, Ribston and Beeley Pippins, Carlswell's and Ellison's Orange, D'Arcy Spice, Orleans Reinette, Easter Orange (though I have yet to taste it), Jupiter and Suntan are what I call cheese apples.

Apples and...

Fennel Both the bulb and the seeds will introduce a welcome breath of aniseed to an apple salad.

Cinnamon The knee-jerk spice for apples it may be, but with good reason. Any dessert application will benefit from a generous pinch of the ground spice, particularly where brown sugar is involved.

Nutmeg Just the most diminutive grating will lend a homely warmth to a sweet recipe.

Dark sugars The butterscotch notes of light muscovado and the treacly tones of molasses sugar marry well with the sharper varieties of apple.

Berries The sharper fruits such as blackcurrants, elderberries and loganberries are better partners for the apple than sweet strawberries or raspberries.

Blackberries Apple and blackberry is probably the ultimate pairing of fruits. A partnership that feels like part of our national identity.

Honey Use to brush an apple tart after baking or instead of sugar when sweetening stewed apples.

Maple syrup Pour over baked apples or blend into a purée. Use to glaze wafer-thin apple tarts straight from the oven.

Brandy I am not one for including much alcohol in recipes, but brandy with the fruit of the apple tree is an exception. A very successful match.

Cheese I have gone into detail about this masterful match elsewhere, but a highlight of any Saturday shopping trip in autumn is when we buy a bag of apples from the farmers' market, then try them out with different cheeses. This is the way I discovered the delights of munching Discovery and goat's cheese and Egremont Russet with a piece of Double or (very rare) Single Gloucester. It's a good family-round-the table game.

Nuts The nut family is never happier than when in the presence of apples, especially in cakes. Hazelnuts, almonds and walnuts are more successful than brazils or pistachios.

Butter The preferred cooking medium with this ingredient, though if oil is a necessity, then use groundnut, hazelnut or walnut rather than olive or sunflower.

Dried fruits Slices of yellow Russet and a lump of British cheese on a piece of raisin-freckled fruit bread is a great mid-morning pick-me-up and much better for us than tiramisu.

Pork Any sharp apple will cut the fatty notes of pork, but the silkiest sauces tend to come from the large fruit such as Grenadier, Peasgood's and the like.

Sage A difficult herb to marry with fruit, but apples and sage get on well. A couple of leaves tucked into the filling of a pie with a cheese crust is worth a try.

* The fatty qualities of roast pork are best balanced with a dab of sauce made from the Bramley-style fruits, but other meats will benefit too: duck, goose and pork sausages take on a lighter feel in the mouth with a smear of apple purée.

* Apple and game is well worth trying, especially pheasant and mallard. Apples flatter the dark character of venison too, particularly if you stir a spoonful of rowan or redcurrant jelly into the gravy.

* Mackerel, grilled till its skin crisps, is just as happy with apple sauce as it is with gooseberry.

* Most varieties can be used as a flavouring in a sausage hotpot, but only as a gem to find hidden in the rich gravy, not as a main ingredient, where their effect would be too sweet.

* Try a couple of 'cookers' in a pork casserole, cut into thick slices and added half way through cooking.

* The wedlock of apples and ham works in many ways. An apple jelly makes a fine accompaniment for cold honey-baked ham; thinly sliced Russets are refreshing in a ham sandwich made with Granary-style bread; a piercing purée of Bramley-type fruit will enliven a plate of warm poached ham; gammon steaks become infinitely more interesting with the addition of a spot of apple sauce.

* Some varieties store more comfortably than others. Nothing quite beats the traditional slatted wooden storage racks, but then, few of us have the room nowadays. Wrapping them in newspaper seems to succeed, as does nicking a few polystyrene apple trays from your greengrocer (it works well enough for his crummy old imports). The crucial point is to prevent the fruit touching one another. Apart from the risk of bruising, if the skins are nestling too close to each other a single bad apple will spread like wildfire through the whole box.

* Any type will keep better under refrigeration. I have kept even the most temperamental apples in a plastic bag in the bottom of the fridge for weeks. To avoid loss of flavour, bring the fruit to room temperature before eating.

* When deciding which apple to use for which job, check its sugar content. The sweeter the apple, the more likely it is to keep its shape. The sharper the apple, the more likely it is to collapse.

Pheasant with apples and cider or verjuice

The sharp character of some of our apples (Grenadier, early Worcester, Peasgood's Nonsuch and, of course, the Bramley) offers a knife-edge with which to cut the rich, fungal taste of game birds. Pheasant, partridge and wild duck are all flavours that benefit from the bite of damsons, sour cherries, bitter oranges or a good sharp apple.

As a teenager, I probably ate more pheasant than I have ever done since. We lived in deepest Worcestershire, Dad was a good shot (he trained as a gunsmith) and the birds would often loiter on the lawn, a shimmer of bronze in the autumn light, asking to be lunch. The traditional way to get round the lack of natural fat in game birds is to cover their breasts with fatty bacon, so it melts and bastes the birds as they roast. But moisture in the pan can work too, in the form of wine or stock, so that the air inside the oven is moist.

To this end, I find a batch of small apples tucked around the bird can help. The fruits split and froth up in the pan, issuing sweetness and, hopefully, a shot of cider-spritz into the juices present in the roasting tin (there are often onions and bacon in there, too). To the pan, I add liquid such as cider or, just as suitable, a glass of verjuice – the light, fruity liquor ('tain't wine, 'tain't vinegar) made from unfermented grapes. It can be difficult to find, so I buy two bottles when I see it. Its extraordinary mellow-sharpness, if there can be such a thing, feels as if it were invented for the lean meat of the pheasant.

> *enough for 2*
> medium onions – 2
> unsmoked streaky bacon rashers – 4, cut into short lengths
> a little butter
> sage leaves – 3 or 4
> verjuice, dry cider or white vermouth – 250ml
> a pheasant
> bay leaves – 2
> small, tart apples – 4–6

Peel and roughly chop one of the onions and put it into a roasting tin with the bacon and a little butter. Leave to cook over a moderate heat until the bacon fat has turned opaque and the onion is starting to soften. This is a ten-minute job. Add the sage, then pour in the verjuice, cider or vermouth.

Whilst the bacon is cooking, set the oven at 220°C/Gas 7. Rub the pheasant all over with a little butter, salt and black pepper. Cut the remaining onion in half and tuck it inside the cavity with the bay leaves. Place the buttered bird on top of the softened onions; slit the apples around their middles, then tuck them around the bird and roast for fifteen minutes.

Lower the heat to 180°C/Gas 4 and continue cooking for thirty to forty minutes, depending on the bird's size. It should be juicy, very slightly pink inside, and the skin should be amber-gold. The aromatics in the tin should have the deep, appley scent of autumn, especially if you have used cider for want of verjuice.

To serve, I tend to put the bird on the table in its roasting tin, deal out the apples, bacon and onion, carve the bird as best as I can – usually something of a hatchet job – then spoon over the thin, flavoursome juices from the tin.

Black pudding with apple and mustard sauce

A properly made black pudding is a fine thing if you can find one: coarse, soft and silky. If soft, hand-made black pudding escapes you, then head for a boudin noir, the French version, which has the necessary open texture and generous seasoning.

> *enough for 2, maybe with a crisp cabbage or celeriac salad*
> a little oil
> black puddings – 2, weighing about 200g each
> bacon rashers – 4
> small sweet apples – 2

Heat the oven to 200°C/Gas 6. Pour a thin film of oil into an ovenproof pan. Put in the black puddings, bacon and the whole apples. Roll the puddings in the oil, then bake for twenty minutes or so until they are meltingly soft inside and the apple has fluffed up. Serve with the mustard cream sauce below.

A quick mustard sauce

Warm 150ml cream in a small saucepan with a couple of sprigs of thyme and 2 teaspoons of grain mustard. When the sauce is thoroughly hot but not boiling, add a palmful of chopped parsley. Season carefully and serve with the black pudding and apple above.

Pot-roast guinea fowl with sausage and apple

The guinea fowl, the intruder alarm of the farmyard, is not a large bird. I usually count on one being enough to serve two, with some left for picking at the next day (good with a crisp apple salad). Add a few substantial bits and pieces – sausages maybe, a few onions – and you can stretch it to three.

enough for 2–3
medium onions – 2
butter – a thin slice
olive oil – 2 tablespoons
thick butcher's sausages – 4
medium potatoes – 2
a large guinea fowl
apples – 3 (about 600g)
bay leaves – a couple
brandy – 25ml

Set the oven at 200°C/Gas 6. Peel the onions and cut them in half, then into thick segments. Put them in a large, heavy casserole – one to which you have a lid – with the butter and olive oil and leave to colour over a moderate heat. Slice the sausages into three and add them to the pan, then stir from time to time to stop them sticking. Peel the potatoes, cut them into large chunks and add them to the pan. Continue cooking until the onions are soft and golden, the potatoes are pale gold and the sausages have coloured nicely. Push everything to one side of the pan, put in the bird, breast-side down, and let it colour briefly, then turn it over and do the other breast and the underside.

Meanwhile peel the apples, core them and cut them into thick chunks. Drop them into the pan, then season with the bay leaves and some salt and coarsely ground black pepper. Tip in the brandy and leave to bubble furiously for a minute or two. Cover with a lid and put in the oven. Leave for forty minutes, then remove the lid. The fowl should be golden on all sides. Check that it is ready by inserting a skewer deep into its thigh. If the juices run clear, then it is done. If there is any sign of blood, then put it back in the oven for a few minutes.

Pork chops for an autumn night

Magic tends to occur when French cooks get their hands on apples, pork and the cream jug. Though in fairness, they usually resort to a slug of Calvados too, the intense, almost bitter apple brandy that has been part of Normandy cooking since the sixteenth century. Usually not one for cream with red meat, I am nevertheless fond of a dish of pork that has been roasted or sautéed till its sugars – the ones that have caramelised on the surface of the pan – are sticky like toffee and can be stirred into cider and thickened with cream. On the side, you need nothing more than watercress and a few pale potatoes, boiled till their cut edges start to fray.

enough for 2
thyme – leaves from 4 bushy sprigs
black peppercorns – 6
olive oil – 2 tablespoons
pork chops – 2
large, sharp apples – 2
butter – a thick slice
sugar – a scant tablespoon
cider – 200ml
double cream – 150ml

Strip the thyme leaves from their stems and chop them finely, then tip them into a mortar together with the peppercorns and half a teaspoon of sea salt. Pound with the pestle, slowly mixing in the oil until you have a loose paste.

Scrape this marinade into a shallow dish and turn the pork chops in it until they are coated on both sides. Leave them to marinate in a cool place for a good hour – longer if you have it.

Peel the apples, remove the cores and cut the flesh into large dice. Melt the butter in a shallow pan and add the apples and sugar, leaving them to cook till golden and approaching tenderness. It's worth turning them now and again with a spoon, gently, so they do not crush, and letting them take on an even colour. Lift them out and set aside.

Return the pan to the heat, lower in the chops and their oil and let them cook over a moderate heat till they are done to your liking (probably about five minutes on either side) and have formed a slightly sticky, golden residue on the surface of the pan. Lift them out and keep warm. Pour the cider into the pan and stir to dissolve the pan-stickings. Leave to bubble and reduce till there are just a few tablespoons left – a matter of three or four minutes or so.

Pour in the cream, whisk lightly to mix it with the cider and let the mixture bubble briefly. Return the chops and apples to the pan. This is not a thick sauce, but one that will soak neatly into the accompanying boiled potatoes.

Stuffed pork belly with apples

Belly pork, with or without its wide, flat bones, is a regular in my kitchen. It is one of the cheaper cuts and roasts more successfully than the bargain cuts from other animals tend to. As I was buying a piece the other day, my butcher, Mr Godfrey, suggested I stuff it with apples and sausage meat. I did, and the result was sumptuous.

enough for 6
pork belly – 1.5kg, boned and scored
plump, herby butcher's sausages – 5
a large, sharp apple
small sage leaves – 6
a little oil or pork dripping
a large glass of cider

Set the oven at 220°C/Gas 7. Lay the pork belly flat on a work surface. Remove the sausages from their skins and put the sausage meat into a bowl. I am tempted to suggest a little more salt and black pepper, but you alone will know the seasoning of your butcher's best. Peel, core and roughly chop the apple, then stir it into the sausage meat with the whole sage leaves (the leaves are cooked whole so they add a subtle note and you can remove them as you carve).

Put the sausage meat down the centre of the pork, then roll the meat up to form a thick cylinder. Tie with kitchen string down its length to secure the stuffing. Unless you are very professional at tying meat up, it will bulge out here and there, but no matter. Lightly oil the base of a roasting tin, lay the rolled pork in the tin and season the skin thoroughly with salt and pepper. Roast in the preheated oven for twenty minutes, then lower the heat to 200°C/Gas 6 and continue cooking for forty to fifty minutes, until the juices run clear.

Remove the meat from the tin and keep warm. Pour off much of the fat from the roasting tin (there will be quite a lot) and put it over a moderate heat. Pour in the cider and bring to the boil, scraping at the pan-stickings and stirring them to dissolve them into the cider. Check the seasoning. Carve the pork and serve with the hot pan juices.

A casserole of apple and rabbit

A sweet, apple-rich stew for a cool autumn evening – mild and soothing to the point of verging on the soporific.

enough for 4
dried flageolet or haricot beans – 250g
olive oil – 3 tablespoons
rabbit pieces on the bone – 8
butcher's sausages – 4, cut into quarters
medium onions – 2
dessert apples – 400g
rosemary – 3 sprigs
plain flour – 2 tablespoons
a bay leaf or two
cider, stock or, at a push, water – 500ml
double cream – 3 tablespoons
cider vinegar – a tablespoon (or more, to taste)

Soak the beans overnight in cold water. Drain and bring to the boil in fresh unsalted water. Let them simmer for approximately forty minutes, checking their progress now and again. How quickly they are ready will depend on the age of your beans. Drain and set aside.

Set the oven at 190°C/Gas 5. Warm 2 tablespoons of the olive oil in a shallow ovenproof pan, add the rabbit pieces and the sausages and let them colour nicely on all sides. Whilst the rabbit is cooking, peel and roughly chop the onions, core and chop the apples, and remove the rosemary needles from their stems and chop them.

Remove the meat to a plate and add the onions to the pan, letting them soften. Introduce the apple, allowing it to colour on all sides, adding the remaining oil if necessary. Stir in the chopped rosemary, flour, bay leaf and some salt and pepper. Continue cooking for a few minutes to cook out the raw taste of the flour, then pour in the cider or stock. Let the liquid bubble for a couple of minutes, stirring to dissolve any crusty bits from the pan. Stir in the drained, cooked beans.

Cover with a lid, place in the oven and bake for forty-five minutes to an hour. Check the meat is tender, then stir in the cream and cider vinegar. The sauce should be quite sweet, but if it is too much so, then add more cider vinegar. Check the seasoning, adding more salt, pepper and vinegar as necessary. Serve in shallow bowls.

A hotpot of sausage and apples

A rich and heart-warming supper for a freezing night. I tend to go for a
fairly plain pork sausage here, just a plump, good-quality banger, but a
slightly garlicky one might work too. Any apple will do, but a dessert apple
is less likely to collapse than a 'cooker'.

enough for 4
dried flageolet or haricot beans – 250g
onions – 3
olive oil – 2 tablespoons
large garlic cloves – 3
fennel seeds – 2 small pinches
bay leaves – 2
thick, nicely seasoned pork sausages – 8
large dessert apples – 2
plain flour – 2 tablespoons
Madeira or medium dry sherry – a glass
stock – 1 litre
grain mustard – 2 tablespoons

Soak the beans overnight in cold water. Drain and bring to the boil in fresh
unsalted water. Let them simmer for about forty minutes, checking their
progress now and again. Drain and set aside.

Peel the onions, cut them in half, then cut each half into six or so thick
segments. Warm the olive oil in a casserole over a low to moderate heat. Put
the onions in the pan and leave them to colour lightly, stirring them from
time to time so that they don't stick or burn.

Whilst the onions are cooking, peel and finely slice the garlic, then add
it to the onions with the fennel seeds and bay leaves. Push the mixture to
one side of the pan (if your pan is on the small side, then remove the onions
and return them later). Cut the sausages into short lengths, add them to the
pan and lightly brown them on all sides. Meanwhile, peel, core and quarter
the apples. Cut them smaller if you wish, but be mindful that the smaller
they are, the more likely they are to break up. Mix the sausages with the
onions (if you removed the onions, return them to the pan now), then stir
in the flour and the apples. Cook for five minutes or so, then gradually
pour in the Madeira or sherry and stock, stirring. Add half the mustard,
season and leave at a low simmer for a good twenty-five minutes.

Add the beans to the sauce, season with salt and black pepper and
simmer the mixture gently for twenty to twenty-five minutes. It is ready
when the sausages are fully cooked and much of the liquid has evaporated.
Stir in the second spoonful of mustard and continue to simmer for a minute
or two, remembering that mustard loses its interest if cooked for too long.

Cheese and apple puffs

There are some who might call these pithiviers aux pommes et au fromage. Well, they are cheese and apple puffs to me. Shop-bought pastry is fine here, though a homemade version could be even better. One per person is enough for a light lunch. But I think they need a salad to offset their richness; something with the bitterness of chicory or watercress would be perfect. You could use pretty much any cheese here, but the blues from Strathdon or Lanark would be more than worth a try. I used Bramleys for this because that is what I had around, but I see no reason why a sweeter apple couldn't be good too.

enough for 4
puff pastry – 500g
apples – 400g
the juice of half a lemon
blue cheese, such as Gorgonzola – 175g
an egg

Set the oven at 200°C/Gas 6. Roll the pastry out thinly. Using a bowl or small plate as a template, cut out eight discs and put four of them on a baking sheet. Put the others aside.

Peel and core the apples, then slice them thinly, dropping them into the lemon juice as you go. Cut the cheese into small cubes and toss it with the apple slices. Season with salt and pepper, then divide the mixture between the four pastry discs. Lightly beat the egg and brush the edges of the pastry.

Roll the remaining circles of pastry out just a little more, then lay them over the apples and press tightly to seal the edges together. Brush with beaten egg and bake for fifteen to twenty minutes or until the pastry is deep gold. Leave them to settle for a few minutes before eating.

Rollmop herrings with beetroot and apple

The acid crunch of a green apple sits well with vinegary rollmop herrings. A mouthful as refreshing as being splashed by a wave. A Russet would work well here with the slightly sweet dressing, of which there may be a little left over for the next day, but it is difficult to make less.

enough for 2
cooked beetroot – 2 (about 200g)
medium apples – 2
soused herrings (rollmops) – 4
small spinach or chard leaves – 4 handfuls

for the dressing
white wine vinegar – a tablespoon
olive oil – 3 tablespoons
chopped dill – a tablespoon
double cream – a tablespoon
grainy mustard – a teaspoon

Cut the beetroot into thin wedges. Thickly slice and core the apples. Unroll the herrings and cut them into quarters across their length to give short, fat pieces. Wash the spinach or chard leaves thoroughly, tear them up into manageable pieces or shred them with a large knife, then add them to the beetroot, apple and herring.

Make the dressing by dissolving a pinch of salt in the vinegar, then whisking in the olive oil, dill, cream and mustard. A little black pepper won't go amiss.

Gently toss the salad ingredients and the dressing, avoiding the temptation to over-mix, then serve.

Apple rabbit

Welsh rarebit – or rabbit, call it what you will – is traditionally made with ale. I like a lighter, non-alcoholic version for this recipe, where I have hidden some fried apples under the blanket of melted cheese. The classic recipe is served after a meal as a savoury, but to my mind this also makes a very fine light lunch, served with a crisp, wintry salad on the side (frisé, chicory, watercress) and maybe some fruit to follow.

enough for 2 as a light snack, 4 as a savoury
large apples – 2
butter – a thick slice
farmhouse cheese – 75g
double cream – 6 tablespoons
grain mustard – 2 teaspoons
bread – 4 small slices

Halve the apples, remove the cores and cut the fruit into thick segments. Warm the butter in a shallow pan and, once it starts frothing, lower in the slices of apple. Leave them to cook till they are golden and thoroughly tender. Remove and drain on kitchen paper.

Meanwhile, grate the cheese coarsely, put it in a bowl and stir in the cream, mustard and a light grinding of salt and pepper. I always take care not to over-mix at this point. The cream and cheese mixture can easily 'seize' with too much stirring.

Toast the bread lightly on both sides, so that it is gold rather than brown. Distribute the apples over the bread, spoon over the cheese sauce, then place under a hot grill till bubbling.

I find Welsh rarebit always tastes best when the edges of the toast are slightly burnt. The mixture of creamy cheese, mustard and crisp, black-edged toast is sublime.

A mildly spiced apple sauce

You could serve this with pork or eat it with yoghurt, at breakfast.

half a cinnamon stick
cloves – 2
juniper berries – 4
a strip of orange zest, about 4cm long
unfiltered apple juice – 400ml
fairly tart apples – 1kg
light brown sugar – 3 tablespoons
a knob of butter

Put the cinnamon, cloves, juniper berries and orange zest in a muslin spice bag or a piece of thin cotton and tie with string. Bring the apple juice to the boil, lower the heat and add the spice bag. Allow to simmer for half an hour or until it has considerably reduced. Remove and discard the spice bag. It has done its work.

Peel, core and roughly chop the apples, then add them to the reduced apple juice. Add a grinding of salt and the sugar, cover and simmer until the apple is soft and slushy. Taste and add a little more sugar if you wish. Stir in the butter and serve.

The classic apple sauce

A slush of sharp apples is still the finest accompaniment for roast pork and its crackling. At least, I have yet to find anything more appropriate.

> large, sharp apples, such as Grenadier, Peasgood's Nonsuch or
>   one of the Seedlings – 3 or 4
> caster sugar – 2 tablespoons
> juice of a lemon

Peel, core and roughly chop the apples. Put them in a medium-sized enamelled or stainless steel pan with the sugar, lemon juice and a tablespoon or two of water. Let them cook down, covered by a lid and stirred regularly, till soft and fluffy. Check them for sweetness; they might need a little more depending on the season. Beat with a wooden spoon till no lumps remain, then serve with pork.

Apple sauce with clove and orange

Make the classic sauce as above but add a couple of cloves to the apples as they cook, then a fine grating of orange zest once they have started to soften.

Apple and horseradish sauce

I first came across this in Sweden, sharing a plate with some grilled herring. Fabulous.

> *enough for 6 or more*
> large, sharp apples – 3 or 4
> the juice of half a lemon
> caster sugar – 2 tablespoons
> a small piece of horseradish root, to give 2 tablespoons grated

Peel, core and roughly slice the apples. Put them in a medium-sized enamelled or stainless steel pan with the lemon juice, sugar and a couple of tablespoons of water. Let them soften over a moderate heat, covered by a lid and stirred regularly till they have fallen into a pale golden slush. Stir in the grated horseradish and beat with a wooden spoon till no lumps remain.

Apple and rhubarb purée with almond brittle

An invigorating start to an icy morning. The brittle is quite optional but
its crunch makes a satisfying contrast to the silken purée.

enough for 4

for the purée
rhubarb – 400g
caster sugar – 2 tablespoons
orange juice – 3 tablespoons
sweet apples, such as Cox's – 500g

for the brittle
skinned almonds – 75g
caster sugar – 75g
water – 5 tablespoons

Heat the oven to 200°C/Gas 6. Cut the rhubarb into short pieces and put it
in an ovenproof dish. Scatter over the sugar, then add the orange juice and
bake for twenty to twenty-five minutes, till it is soft enough to crush (you
could cook it over a moderate heat, if you prefer). Mash with a fork. While
the rhubarb is cooking, peel the apples, core them, and cook with a couple
of tablespoons of water, no sugar, over a moderate heat. Crush to a purée
with a fork.

To make the brittle, tip the nuts into a shallow pan and toast over a high
heat for a minute or two, till golden. Put the sugar into a small, heavy-based
saucepan with the water and bring to the boil. Leave to bubble fiercely,
without stirring, until the syrup changes to a rich brown. Tip in the toasted
nuts, then pour the mixture carefully on to a lightly oiled non-stick baking
sheet and leave to harden.

Smash the brittle into small pieces and set aside. Serve the two crushed
fruits mixed together, scattered with broken almond brittle.

A deeply appley apple crumble

Any apple is suitable for a crumble. A dry variety such as a Russet just needs some moisture – a splash of apple juice, perhaps, some lemon or a spot of brandy. Others will collapse into a frivolous cloud under the sand and pebbles crust, some will keep their shape.

A sublime crumble is probably one where the fruit lies somewhere between thick juice and soft nuggets of flesh. For me, the filling should be a mixture of barely recognisable chunks on the verge of collapse and a sort of sweet slush the texture of melting snow. This is easier to achieve with the larger apples, such as Howgate Wonder, Peasgood's, Lord Derby and Gravenstein. Blenheim Orange works well if still young and juicy, as does Suntan, a cringeworthy name for a fine cooking apple. Bramleys will do.

I can't begin to imagine the number of apple crumbles I have made over the years, the first aged nine, while my mother ironed my winceyette sheets on the other side of the kitchen (if heaven has a smell, then it is that of warm ironing and apple crumble).

Part of the deep, toe-tingling pleasure of cooking is that of constantly tweaking a much-loved recipe, and none more so than the apple crumble. My latest move on the classic instructions has been to caramelise the fruit lightly in a frying pan before I cover it with the sweet rubble of butter, flour and sugar. It's a worthwhile step forward. The flavour seems all the more pronounced for that bit of caramelisation. If the apples are tight and not producing much juice, then you know you need to add something in the way of moisture before you cover them with the crumble. The result will be less of a gamble.

I like a crust of mixed texture – a little sand, some gravel-sized lumps and some larger, crumbly, buttery pebbles. This is easily achieved by scattering a spoonful or two of water over the crumble mixture and shaking it back and forth. The crumble will form clusters of different-sized grains. Another method is to squeeze the crumbs together in your hands before you scatter it.

And no, I'm not sure the world needs another recipe for apple crumble either, but it is something I have worked on repeatedly over the years and I want to share it with you. There is much, much pleasure to be had in a simple thing, perfectly made.

enough for 4

for the filling
cooking apples – 850g
half a lemon
golden caster sugar – 75g
butter – 30g

for the crumble
butter – 95g
plain flour – 150g
golden caster sugar – 45g

Peel and core the apples, cut them into plump chunks (about 2cm on each side) and toss them with the juice of the lemon half and the caster sugar.

Melt the butter in a shallow pan over a frisky heat. When it starts to sizzle, tip in the apples and sugar and let the fruit colour lightly. It is essential not to move the apples around too much. Let the sugar caramelise here and there, so the fruit is golden in patches. There should be a faint smell of toffee. Stir them gently.

Lift the apples out and put them into a baking dish, about 1.5 litres in capacity, together with the pan juices. If there are any sticky bits in the pan, add a dash of lemon juice or water and stir till they dissolve. Tip amongst the apples. Set the oven at 180°C/Gas 4.

Make the crumble by rubbing the butter into the flour with your fingertips (you could happily use a food processor here). When the mixture looks like fine breadcrumbs, stir in the sugar. Add a tablespoon of water, shake the crumble mixture till some of it sticks together in gravel-sized lumps, then tip it over the apple. Bake for forty-five to fifty minutes, till lightly coloured.

Early autumn apples on hot toast

You could feel it: something wonderful was happening. The air had a cider-like note, part sweet, part rotten. Shoppers hugged knobbly brown paper bags to their chest. I felt the need to hurry in case I missed something. Around the corner, outside the cheese shop, customers jostled around a stack of open wooden crates. The first of the autumn's apples had arrived.

A sucker for a Russet, I buy them by the bagful. Any will do: Egremont, Ashmead's Kernel or St Edmund's Pippin. Rosemary Russet is a treat and a half. The aniseed notes of its flesh flatter a lump of Gloucester or a jagged crumb of Caerphilly. Heat will sometimes bring out a hidden waft of orange. I roll them over and over in my hand too, rubbing their scabby roughness with my thumb.

I arrived home with a mixed bag of early Russets, some deeply craggy early Cox's, two-mouthful Worcesters and a handful of the regrettably named Scrumptious. After I had crunched enough, I sliced yet more of them up, keeping their skins intact, and let them soften in a pan with enough butter and sugar to give them a thin coating of caramel. Then I tipped them on to fresh toast and spooned unpasteurised yellow cream over them.

> *makes 2 rounds of toast*
> small dessert apples – 4
> a little lemon juice
> butter – 50g
> golden caster sugar – 2 lightly heaped tablespoons
> a handful of raisins or sultanas
> a knifepoint of ground cinnamon
> 2 slices of toast, made from brioche, nut and raisin bread or a milk loaf

Quarter the apples, core them, but leave the skin on. Slice the apples thickly, then toss them with a little lemon juice. It will stop their flesh browning and balance the sugar you are going to add.

Melt the butter in a shallow pan. Before it froths, stir in the sugar and leave to bubble for a minute or two. Introduce the apples, letting them cook for five minutes or so over a moderate heat till soft. Stir in the raisins or sultanas and cinnamon.

Have the toast ready. I like it to be hot and lightly crisp. As soon as the apples are soft and lightly coated in caramel, tip them over the toast. A tub of cream, thick and yellow, would be quite wonderful here.

An apple crisp

A lighter crust, more open and less rich than that of a crumble, can be achieved using breadcrumbs instead of flour. It will also suit those who have convinced themselves they can't make pastry.

A couple of years ago, on finding myself with a batch of less than fresh bread in need of a home, I took the step of reducing all except the crusts to coarse breadcrumbs, packing them loosely into plastic freezer boxes (I seem to remember they were old yoghurt tubs) and keeping them in the freezer. Throughout the next month or two, I would dip into this squirrel store of breadcrumbs to mix with a stuffing or to make fishcakes or gremolata, and on a couple of occasions to top a crumble. Storing breadcrumbs is a habit I have slipped into, and one I recommend to anyone whose heart sinks when they see the line '50g fresh white breadcrumbs' in a recipe.

enough for 6
sharp apples such as Bramley or Peasgood's Nonsuch – 1kg
a knifepoint of ground cinnamon
soft white bread – 125g
light muscovado sugar – 75g
butter – 75g
double cream, to serve

Heat the oven to 190°C/Gas 5. Peel and core the apples and cut them into thick slices. Drop the fruit into a buttered pudding basin or shallow casserole and toss very gently with the ground cinnamon. Please don't overdo the cinnamon, otherwise your crisp will taste like a sticky bun.

Whiz the bread to rough crumbs in a food processor. I like them not too fine – more of a soft rubble than a fine sand. Mix the breadcrumbs and sugar and cover the apples loosely with the mixture. Melt the butter in a small pan, then pour it over the crumbs, making certain to soak them all. Bake for thirty-five minutes, till the apples are soft and melting and the crumbs on top are golden and crisp.

Serve with double cream.

A deep cake of apples with cinnamon and nutmeg

We could fall out debating whether this is a cake or a pie. Whatever we
decide to call it, the result is extraordinarily deep. The recipe needs a little
care: the pastry is extremely fragile and you will feel as if you are peeling
apples for England. But the finished cake is truly splendid. Just the thing
to make on a wet autumn day.

enough for 8 at least

for the pastry
butter – 200g
golden caster sugar – 200g
a large egg
plain flour – 400g
baking powder – a heaped teaspoon
a little milk and sugar, to finish

for the filling
sweet dessert apples – 1.8kg
a lemon
golden caster sugar – 2 tablespoons
a knifepoint of ground cinnamon
a little grated nutmeg

cold double cream, to serve

To make the pastry, cut the butter into chunks and put it in a food mixer
with a beater attachment. Add the sugar and beat till pale and creamy. Break
the egg into a cup, mix it gently, then add to the butter and sugar, mixing
thoroughly. Mix together the flour and baking powder, then add carefully
and slowly to the butter mixture. Stop as soon as the flour is incorporated.
Remove the dough, put it on a lightly floured board and roll into a fat
sausage. Wrap in greaseproof paper or cling film and chill for half an hour.

Meanwhile, peel the apples. As you finish each one, drop it into a
bowl of cold water in which you have squeezed the juice of half the lemon.
Quarter the apples, then core and thickly slice them, dropping them back
into the acidulated water as you go. Drain the apples and put them into
a large, heavy-based saucepan with the sugar, cinnamon, nutmeg and the
juice of the remaining lemon half. Bring to the boil, then turn down to a
simmer and continue till the apples are tender but still hold their shape –
about ten to fifteen minutes over a moderate heat with the occasional stir.
Leave them to cool.

Very lightly butter a 20cm loose-bottomed cake tin. Remove the pastry from the fridge, cut off a little less than a third of it and return that to the fridge. Cut thick slices from the large piece of pastry and use them to line the base and sides of the cake tin, pressing it firmly into the corners and patching any tears or cracks. The pastry should be quite thick. Chill for twenty minutes. Set the oven at 200°C/Gas 6.

Line the cake tin with a sheet of greaseproof paper or baking parchment and half fill with baking beans. This will keep the pastry in place. Put a baking sheet in the oven and, when it is hot, put the lined cake tin on it (the heat will help the pastry cook underneath). Bake for fifteen minutes, remove and leave to cool slightly, then remove the paper and baking beans. Take care not to tear the pastry. Return the tin to the oven for five minutes without the beans and paper. Remove and leave to cool down a little. Turn the oven down to 180°C/Gas 4.

Fill the pastry case right up to the rim with the apples, holding back as much of the liquid as possible. Roll out the remaining pastry to fit the cake and place it over the top. Patch any holes and gently press the raw pastry on to the edges of the cooked. Cut three slits in the top of the pastry to let out the steam (though they will close on cooking). Brush the top with a little milk.

Bake on the hot baking sheet for forty-five minutes, till the top is nut brown. Remove from the oven, dust with a little caster sugar and leave to settle down for a good fifteen minutes. Run a palette knife round the edge to free the pastry from the tin, but leave the cake in place for now. When the cake is thoroughly cool, carefully remove from the tin. You will need a sharp knife and a jug of cream.

Wholemeal apple and marmalade cake

A good, reliable cake that will keep for a day or two, the sort you find on village-fête cake stalls.

enough for 8
butter – 220g, at room temperature
light muscovado sugar – 210g
eggs – 4
wholemeal flour – 250g
baking powder – a lightly heaped teaspoon
ground cinnamon – half a teaspoon
apples – 200g (peeled weight)
golden sultanas or raisins – 100g
orange marmalade – 125g
finely grated zest of an orange
demerara sugar

Set the oven at 160°C/Gas 3. Use baking parchment to line a 20cm round cake tin with a removable base. Beat the butter and sugar together in a food mixer until light, fluffy and pale coffee coloured. Meanwhile, lightly beat the eggs with a fork. Sift together the flour, baking powder and cinnamon. Core and roughly chop the apples. They should be under 1cm square. Toss the chopped apples with the sultanas or raisins and stir in the marmalade and orange zest.

Add the beaten eggs a little at a time to the creamed butter and sugar, introducing a spoonful of flour if the mixture starts to curdle. Gently but firmly fold in the rest of the flour. Fold in the fruit and marmalade mixture. Spoon into the prepared cake tin, scatter a fine layer of demerara over the top and bake for an hour and fifteen minutes or until a skewer comes out moist but without any cake mixture sticking to it. Cool before serving.

A cake of apples and courgettes

enough for 8 at least
butter – 200g
caster sugar – 200g
eggs – 2
courgettes – 150g (about 2 small ones)
a small apple
plain flour – 200g
a pinch of salt
½ teaspoon baking powder
a pinch of ground cinnamon
pecans – 60g
sultanas – 80g

Preheat the oven to 180°C/Gas 4. Butter and line the base of a loaf tin measuring 20cm x 12cm x 9cm deep.

Cream the butter and sugar until light and fluffy. Lightly beat the eggs and beat them in a little at a time, making sure each bit is fully incorporated before adding the next. Coarsely grate the courgettes and apple. Squeeze them with your hands to remove any excess moisture, then add to the mixture. Mix the flour, salt, baking powder and cinnamon together and gently fold them into the mixture. Stir in the nuts and sultanas. Transfer to the lined loaf tin and bake for about an hour, until golden and firm to the touch. Allow to cool in the tin before turning out.

Marmalade apple tart

As much as I like contemporary eating, I warm to the tastes and smells of food from other times. This sticky open tart, like oat flapjacks and pea and ham soup, smells of a different era. Appropriately enough, you will need an old-fashioned pie plate for this, with a rim around the edge, the sort ironmongers still sell.

enough for 6

for the pastry
butter – 75g
golden caster sugar – 75g
an egg yolk
plain flour – 150g
a little milk

for the filling
sweet dessert apples – 850g
half a lemon
golden caster sugar – a tablespoon
marmalade – 250g

double cream, to serve

To make the pastry, cut the butter into chunks and put it in a food mixer fitted with the beater attachment. Add the sugar and beat till pale and creamy. Mix in the egg yolk. Add the flour carefully and slowly to the mixture, stopping as soon as it is incorporated. Check the texture of the dough, adding a very little milk if necessary to bring it to a nice rolling consistency. Remove the dough from the bowl, put it on a lightly floured board and shape it into a fat sausage. Wrap in greaseproof or cling film and chill in the fridge for half an hour.

Meanwhile, peel the apples. As you finish each one, drop it into a bowl of cold water into which you have squeezed the lemon half. Roughly chop them and put back into the acidulated water as you go.

Drain the apples, put them into a large, heavy-based saucepan with the sugar and bring to the boil. Turn down to a simmer, and cook till the apples are tender and have all but lost their shape – about twenty or thirty minutes over a moderate heat with the occasional stir. Leave them to cool.

Very lightly butter the pie plate. Remove the pastry from the fridge, cut it into thick slices and use them to line the tart tin, pressing the dough firmly into the corners and patching any tears or cracks. The pastry should be quite thick. Prick it lightly with a fork, then chill for twenty minutes. Set the oven at 200°C/Gas 6. Place a baking sheet in the oven.

Put the chilled pastry case on the hot baking sheet and bake for twenty minutes, until lightly biscuit coloured. Remove from the oven and turn the heat down to 180°C/Gas 4. Fill the tart case with the apple purée. Warm the marmalade in a small pan, then spoon it on top of the apple and return to the oven for thirty to thirty-five minutes. Serve warm, with cream.

Apple custard tart

Those cartons of ready-made custard come in two sorts: one full of sugar, colouring and thickeners, the other, marginally more expensive, that is simply eggs, sugar, cream and vanilla. Go for the latter if you want to make this heavenly pie. You could make your own custard, of course, but I am not sure it is worth the trouble in this instance, where it is essentially hidden.

> tart 'cooking' apples – 1.15kg
> butter – 75g
> ready-rolled puff pastry – 375g
> ready-made custard – a 400g tub
> a large egg yolk, beaten
> milk – 2 tablespoons
> caster sugar, for dusting

Peel, core and thinly slice the apples. Melt the butter in a shallow pan over a moderate heat, then toss the apples in it. As the apples start to soften – a matter of five or six minutes – remove them from the heat and leave to cool.

Preheat the oven to 200°C/Gas 6. Put a baking sheet in the oven. Unroll the pastry and cut it into two, one piece slightly larger than the other. Roll out the smaller piece and trim it into a 28cm circle. Lay this in a floured deep metal tart tin, 24cm in diameter. Roll out the second piece of pastry into a 32cm circle and set it aside.

Pour the custard on to the apples and toss gently. Pile the mixture on to the pastry in the baking tin in an even mound. Brush the edge of the pastry with the beaten egg yolk. Lay the second piece of pastry over the apples, then pinch the edges together firmly all the way round. There will inevitably be some leakage but it will be contained in the dish.

Mix together the milk and the remaining beaten egg yolk and brush the pastry with it. Scatter caster sugar over the top, cut a small hole in the centre to let the steam out, then place the tin on the hot baking sheet and bake for about forty-five minutes to an hour, until golden brown.

Treacle tart with russet apples

Warm treacle tart – the deep, stick-to-your-spoon variety – remains on my list of desert-island dishes. I experiment with the basic recipe, sometimes making a humble, tin-plate-style tart (for which see *The Kitchen Diaries*) and on other occasions producing a thicker version such as the one here.

The unrelenting sweetness of the genre needs something cold and sharp alongside. I serve mine with ice cream or crème fraîche, or a big jug of double cream. But in the depths of autumn, when this sort of pudding is almost compulsory, some brightly flavoured apple, cooked till soft and sticky, is a pleasing change of step. Needless to say, I do serve both the apples and the crème fraîche.

enough for 8

for the crust
vegetable shortening – 35g
butter – 35g
plain flour – 150g
water – roughly 2 tablespoons

for the filling
golden syrup – 675g
the zest and juice of a small lemon
fresh coarse white breadcrumbs – 270g

for the apples
medium Russet apples – 4
a little caster sugar
cloves – 2

Make the pastry in the usual way, rubbing the fats into the flour with your fingertips until the mixture resembles rough breadcrumbs, then bringing it together with a little water to form a soft ball of dough. Alternatively, mix the ingredients together in a food processor.

Roll the pastry out, using a little flour so it does not stick, and use it to line a deep-sided 20cm tart tin with a removable base. I always take great care to push the pastry deep into the corners. Put on a baking sheet and in the fridge to chill.

Set the oven at 200°C/Gas 6. Pour the syrup into a saucepan over a moderate heat. It takes an age to empty a whole tin, so I tend to write my name with the golden syrup at this point. Stir in the lemon juice and breadcrumbs, then pour into the uncooked pastry shell. It should come almost to the rim. Slide the tart into the oven and bake for fifteen minutes.

Turn the heat down to 180°C/Gas 4 and continue cooking for a further fifteen to twenty minutes, till lightly firm.

While the tart is cooking, cut each apple into six or so pieces, removing the core as you go. I leave the skin on, but it is up to you. Put the apples in a pan with a little sugar, the cloves and a couple of tablespoons of water, bring to the boil, then lower the heat so the apples simmer to an all-over softness. Stir from time to time and add a little more water if necessary, until the fruit is sticky and golden. Remove from the heat and put aside to cool. Serve with the tart.

A tart of mincemeat and apples

A simple tart, yet one that is also thoroughly festive. I serve this as a Christmas dessert, with cream, but it works as a cake too. In which case I would serve it strudel-style, with coffee and whipped cream on the side.

enough for 6
cooking apples – 400g
caster sugar – 2 heaped tablespoons
puff pastry – 500g
mincemeat – 400g
beaten egg

Peel the apples, core them and cut them into small, thin slices. Put into a wet saucepan with the sugar and leave to simmer gently till the sugar has melted and the apples are tender but not quite collapsed. Set the oven at 200°C/Gas 6.

Cut the pastry in half and roll out each piece to measure 36 x 16cm. Place one half on a non-stick baking sheet, or one lined with baking paper, then place the mincemeat in a wide line down the centre of the pastry, leaving a margin around the rim. Place the apples on top (any juice should be left in the pan), then brush the edges of the pastry with some of the beaten egg. Lay the second piece of pastry on top, pressing the edges firmly to seal. Trim any ragged edges, crimp them with a fork if you wish, then decorate with any trimmings of pastry if the mood takes you. Brush with more of the beaten egg, cut four or five small slits in the top of the pastry and bake for twenty to twenty-five minutes, till golden and crisp. Serve warm, with cream.

Apfelstrudel

There is apple in neat, thin slices, golden sultanas the size of pistachios, the warm Christmastide note of ground cinnamon and drift upon drift of snow-white icing sugar. There are crisp leaves of pastry and, should I feel the need, a little pot of whipped cream at its side. As I press my fork down on the folds of crackling pastry, the scent of late autumn slowly fills my corner of the room. I have coffee too, in a tiny, thick-sided cup, and a newspaper on a stick of which I can read barely a single word.

I have a love of Europe's timeworn cafés. Those hallowed rooms heavy with the scent of chocolate, cinnamon, burnt sugar and marzipan. The tables that are just that bit too small, too dinky; the long, white aprons and fraying leather purses of the waiting staff; the creaking chairs and well-trampled wooden floors. Each has its speciality – a deep apple cake in Stockholm; cheesecake in Budapest; chocolate cake in Vienna; and in Berlin the mother and father of apfelstrudel. Believe me when I say I will be happy to die with a pastry fork in my hand.

In Germany and Austria I have been offered cream, custard and ice cream with my hot strudel. It's a hard decision to have to make. I generally take it without any accompaniment, then regret it, wishing I had gone for the vanilla ice cream. The addition of a little apricot jam in the filling is purely mine and not at all traditional.

enough for 6

for the filling
sweet apples – 800g
the zest and juice of a lemon
apricot jam – 3 tablespoons
caster sugar – 50g
a pinch of ground cinnamon
golden sultanas – 50g
flaked almonds – 50g

for the pastry
butter – 150g
fresh white breadcrumbs – 80g
filo pastry – 10 sheets
icing sugar, for dusting

Peel, core and quarter the apples, then cut each quarter into very thin slices. Toss them with the lemon zest and juice, the jam, sugar and the cinnamon. Add the sultanas and flaked almonds. Set the oven at 200°C/Gas 6.

Melt the butter in a small frying pan, then pour a good half of it into a small bowl. Add the breadcrumbs to the butter remaining in the pan and fry them till they are golden and crisp. Tip them out on to a piece of kitchen paper.

Place a large sheet of greaseproof paper or a clean tea towel on a work surface. Place two sheets of filo side by side, long sides slightly overlapping. Brush with some of the melted butter and scatter over two heaped tablespoons of the toasted breadcrumbs. Place another two sheets of pastry on top but in the opposite direction. Brush them too with butter and breadcrumbs and continue, alternating the direction of the pastry each time, until all ten sheets are used up. Scatter any remaining breadcrumbs over the top sheet of pastry.

With the long edge of the pastry nearest you, pile the apple filling on to the nearest third of the pastry. Make sure the edge is well buttered, then roll up the pastry into a fat sausage, keeping the filling in place as you roll. Squeeze the open edges together to seal the filling inside. Slide it on to a flat baking sheet. Brush with butter and bake for thirty minutes or so, till the pastry is thoroughly crisp. Dust with icing sugar and serve.

Warm rice with cinnamon, apple and maple syrup

A pudding as comforting as an old teddy bear.

enough for 4
Arborio, Carnaroli or other risotto rice – 150g
water – 500ml
full-cream milk – 500ml
a good pinch of ground cinnamon
a large apple
caster sugar – 3 tablespoons
maple syrup

Put the rice in a small pan and cover it with the water. Bring to the boil, then simmer until the water has almost entirely evaporated. Keep an eye on it. Pour in the milk, bring back to the boil, then turn down to a simmer and partially cover with a lid. Leave for about fifteen minutes, stirring regularly and keeping a watch on the liquid level. It should still be very creamy at the end. Stir in the cinnamon, adding more to taste if you wish.

Grate the apple, peeling it if you wish, then stir it into the rice together with the sugar. Leave for five minutes, during which time some of the remaining liquid will be absorbed, then serve, pouring the maple syrup over as you go – at least two tablespoons each.

Baked apples with apple ice cream

Baked apples, originally cooked in the fading heat of a wood-fired oven, are almost unique to the northern hemisphere. We have a history of growing the varieties whose acid flesh rises, soufflé-like, from their skins: Howgate Wonder, Dumelow's Seedling, Bramley. Generously proportioned apples, with skins tough enough to hold back the billowing froth that peeps at their brim.

We have stuffed their chiselled hollows with mincemeat, buttered breadcrumbs and syrup or turned them into deep wells of molten honey. We wrap them in pastry and call them dumplings. Wise cooks score around the apples' tummies, so that rather than exploding, they emerge from the oven with beaming smiles, their contents intact. A jolly pudding for a bitterly cold night.

Any apple will bake – a Russet can be deeply aromatic when stuffed with a walnut of butter and a clove or two – but the drier and more yellow the flesh, the less likely it is to puff up. Cox's have a tendency to explode.

It is, I find, not easy to know when to serve a baked apple. Too often they appear at Sunday lunch, a dish slid into the oven when the roast comes out, a meal unlikely to leave any of us needing more. In our house, the baked apple, with its blackened skin and snow-white froth, tends to appear after a bowl of thick soup, possibly of white beans or pumpkin, most usually on a short, frosty day with a sulphurous sky.

My mother offered cream with her baked apples, her replacement Bird's custard. My own preference is for ice cream, a shocking contrast to the searing heat of the apple's flesh. Vanilla works in its usual calming manner, and praline made an interesting change, but in the autumn of 2007 I made an ice cream from the apples themselves. The result was delicate and full of warm bonhomie.

enough for 4, with more than enough ice cream for later

for the ice cream
sharp apples – 1kg
golden caster sugar – 200g
single or whipping cream – 400ml
egg yolks – 4

for the baked apples
large dessert apples – 4
a little butter

To make the ice cream, peel the apples, core them and cut into thick slices. Put them in a heavy-bottomed saucepan with half the sugar and let them stew slowly over a moderate to low heat (they need no water, but keep an eye on them so they don't burn). Once a little juice has formed in the bottom of the pan, cover with a lid and leave to simmer gently for twenty minutes or so, stirring from time to time, till the apples are fluffy. Mash with a fork and leave to cool.

Bring the cream to the boil. Beat the egg yolks and remaining sugar in a heatproof bowl till thick, then pour in the hot cream and stir. Rinse the saucepan and return the custard to it, stirring the mixture over a low heat till it starts to thicken slightly. It won't become really thick. Cool the custard quickly – I do this by plunging the pan into a shallow sink of cold water – stirring constantly. Chill thoroughly, then mix with the cold mashed apple. Pour into your ice-cream maker and churn according to the manufacturer's instructions. It will seem quite a thick mixture. Scoop into a plastic, lidded box and freeze till you are ready.

To bake the apples, set the oven at 200°C/Gas 6. Remove the apple cores with a corer if you don't wish to do battle with them at the table. Score the fruits round their tummy with a sharp knife. Put them into a small roasting tin or baking dish in which they will fit snugly. Drop a knob of butter into each hollow and bake for forty to fifty minutes, till the apples are puffed up and golden. Serve with the ice cream.

Baked apples with mincemeat and brandy

Apple brandy has been made in this country since the 1700s and of late has been undergoing something of a revival. It is my first choice for adding to baked apples, or indeed any apple recipe that might benefit from a touch of alcohol, if for no other reason than that it feels right. Of course, French-made Calvados, or even an 'ordinary' cognac, is fine here too.

enough for 4
4 very large or 8 smaller apples
mincemeat – 6–8 tablespoons
apple brandy – 6 tablespoons

Set the oven at 200°C/Gas 6. Score each apple lightly round its tummy with a sharp knife. You want to split the skin so the apple doesn't explode in the oven. Remove the core of each apple with an apple corer or a small knife. Put the fruit in a shallow baking dish or roasting tin. Mix the mincemeat with 2 tablespoons of the apple brandy, then spoon as much of the mixture as you can into the hollows in the fruit. If there is any mincemeat left over, put it into the roasting tin. Pour in the remaining brandy and bake till the apples have puffed up and started to split open, revealing a fluffy interior of baked apple. This will take about forty-five minutes to an hour, depending on the variety of apples.

Judging a baked apple for doneness is best accomplished with the eye rather than by the clock. A baked apple ready to eat will have risen so much that its skin has split open into a wide smile and the interior is turning to fluff and frothing round the edges.

An apple in the hand

Lastly, a fruit not to trap between two layers of pie crust, fold into whipped cream or nibble with a piece of Wensleydale, but a fruit to eat for its own sake. This should be a very special apple, one whose flesh packs as much acidity as sweetness, whose notes are complex and come at us in waves. An apple so good you could eat its core.

For me, there has to be an ice-like crunch, followed by an element of sharpness and that slight acidity that gets you at the corner of your mouth as you take the first bite. I am in the minority. The ancient sharp apples are considered of little interest commercially, with North Americans and Europeans supposedly preferring sweet, dull-tasting fruit with no apparent flavour other than that of sugar. It is interesting that these modern flavourless apples are also those that perform well in terms of high yield, having a tolerance for storage and long transport, a uniform shine and an unchallenging character. In other words, manna for the supermarket chains. So perhaps it is not what we want to buy that ensures the popularity of mediocre fruit so much as what they wish to sell us.

Each to his own, but I would like to put in a word for the Russets. The web of rough skin that sits like fine sandpaper on the surface of the apple, softening the rusts, umbers and crimsons of the skin, offering an extra texture to delight the hand and the tongue. Blenheim Orange, Braddick's Nonpareil, Claygate Pearmain, the Egremont and Golden Russet, Ribston Pippin, Ross Nonpareil, St Edmund's Pippin and Tydeman's Late Orange can usually be relied upon and, in season, are not impossible to find. Beyond the lacework of rough skin will be apples of extraordinary interest, with hints of nut and spice.

Each season, an apple passes my lips that I insist is the best I have ever tasted. It could be a late Cox's Orange Pippin, a particularly honeyed Pitmaston Pineapple, a Christmas Pearmain with its dusty crimson skin or, more usually, a frustratingly anonymous apple from someone's fruit bowl. At that moment it is the perfect apple, the one I have been looking for all my life. Until, that is, I find the next one.

A few quick ideas

A salad of black pudding and apple

If you have a lovely black pudding, then you might like to use it in an autumn salad. I did this the other week, marrying the savoury pudding to crisp young Cox's.

Cut the pudding into fat chunks, about 4cm long. Get a trace of oil hot in a shallow, non-stick pan and brown the pieces nicely all over. Remove them to a warm plate, covered with foil, as they become ready or push them to one side of the pan. Add a little more oil or some butter to the pan if necessary, then add slices of apple, cored but not peeled, and let them colour nicely.

Have ready a bowl of spinach and watercress leaves, rinsed and shaken dry. Mix a dressing of groundnut oil, smooth French mustard and cider vinegar and toss gently with the leaves, apple and hot black pudding. A more robust alternative could use shredded and lightly cooked Savoy cabbage. I might save that one for the colder weather.

Vanilla ice with hot mincemeat and apple sauce

If there is one sensation I love, it is hot sauces over cold ice cream. Great favourites are coffee over vanilla and hot chocolate sauce over coffee ice. This is a Christmas version of that marriage.

Core and roughly chop three small apples. I prefer not to peel them for this recipe. Put them into a small pan with a couple of tablespoons of brandy or Calvados and warm over a low heat till the apple has softened. If you cover the pan with a lid, this will take about eight to ten minutes, but it is a good idea to check regularly that they are not boiling dry. When the apple is very tender, stir in 425g mincemeat and bring almost to the boil.

Put two or three small balls of ice cream into each of four dishes and pour over the hot mincemeat sauce. Serve immediately.

A cinnamon crème fraîche for baked apples

Set the oven at 180°C/Gas 4. Score four apples round their tummies, cutting just through the skin. Put them in an ovenproof dish. Wet the fruit with a tablespoon or so of water, then scatter a little sugar over them and dot with butter. Bake for forty minutes or so, depending on the size of the apples.

Just before you remove them from the oven, put 200ml crème fraîche in a small non-stick pan, add two level tablespoons of golden caster sugar and a knifepoint of ground cinnamon and bring almost to the boil. As soon as the sugar has dissolved, remove from the heat and serve over the apples.

Stewed apples with blackcurrants

Perhaps my favourite use for a blackcurrant compote is to fold it into stewed apples. First peel and core five large apples, slice them thickly, then let them cook over a low heat with a couple of tablespoons of sugar and barely two tablespoons of water. When they start to froth, switch off the heat and leave to cool. Chill thoroughly.

Divide the apples between four dishes and fold in a small amount of stewed blackcurrants, so that it leaves a purple ripple running through the apples. Pour over cream or yoghurt and serve.

Apricots

A fine apricot, rich, intense, fragrant, is perhaps the rarest of all fruits. So rare, in fact, that I briefly considered its exclusion in this collection, but to have done so would have been to give up on what can be a sublime and memorable fruit. This is a fruit as soft and tender as a baby's cheek, with a scent that is part honey, part almond. A fruit whose flesh has notes of peach, brown sugar and orange blossom and an opportunity for pleasure that is too good to miss. Coupled with the new popularity of apricot cordons being bought for the home garden, and a slowly warming climate, *Prunus armeniaca* has secured its place in these pages.

But note that I said 'a fine apricot'. You know, apricots have been spoilt by commerce, with its need for a lengthy shelf life and its constant obsession with size and sweetness. I know of no fruit or vegetable whose character and reputation has been so spoilt by the greed and ignorance of commercial growers and the supermarkets they supply. I am not as critical as some of modern commerce but in this instance it deserves it. Even a trip to France to witness at first hand the progress of the modern apricot industry did not convince me. My idea of progress was very different from theirs.

Anyone who has given up on the modern apricot, with its heart of watery cotton wool, would be heartened at coming across the real thing. A fine apricot will have a cluster of dots, freckles of ruby, rust and chocolate, around its shoulders. It may have a patch of rough skin the size of an old sixpence. Within its velvet skin, it will glow a deep, intense orange, as if lit by a candle flame. You will be able to tease the two halves apart with a single pull, at which point it will almost certainly lose a bead or two of juice. The flesh will be soft and sumptuous, very different from the hard, modern apricot with its sunset blush that so often leads us up the garden path.

The apricot came to us from China, and was probably cultivated well before 2000 BC. Its name, *Prunus armeniaca*, is understood to have come from the Greeks, who supposed, incorrectly as it turned out, that the fruit originated from Armenia. The word apricot is linked to the Roman *praecocium*, meaning precocious, referring to the fact that it ripened so early. It is this early ripening that is the cause of so many of the fruit's problems. Such early blossom and fruits are truly at the mercy of the weather.

The reason this exquisite fruit is here at all is down to Henry VIII's gardener, who brought it from Italy in 1542. Although grown throughout Iran, China, Japan, America and southern Europe, it will, given a warm wall and a bit of luck, do rather well here too.

An apricot in the garden

Just one more wall. That is all I ask, a wall on which to train the branches of an apricot tree. A wall that is in full sun, sheltered from early frosts yet open enough for the blossom to tempt the bees. They can be grown as large trees, but training against a wall is a more popular method, providing reflected warmth and making for easier picking.

Apricot blossom is pure white and comes in March, three weeks or more before the leaves open. A roll of horticultural fleece will prevent the frost doing its worst to the buds. Keep an ear open for the weather forecast. The fleece should be removed during the day to allow pollination to take place. That said, it is still very early in the year and many insects are yet to get out of bed, so pollinating by hand is wise. I have seen it done and it is not difficult.

An apricot will not bear fruit on new wood; it must be one or two years old. They can be pruned in spring and summer. Choose a dry day (winter pruning may result in diseased wood, as it does in plums and damsons). In most cases this will be to remove any growth that cannot be tied neatly back against the wall in an open fan shape.

The fruit is best ripened on the tree if possible, which will mean keeping the birds at bay. Like apples, apricots are ready when they can be removed from the twig with one firm twist. Should they refuse, hold fire a day or two. Although they are some of the earliest stone fruits on the market, British-grown varieties tend to appear in late summer.

Varieties

The varieties named on supermarket packages are often modern hybrids suited to the climate of South Africa, Chile, France or wherever they are grown. I list the most successful for growing in our climate.

Moorpark The most popular variety here, Moorpark is happy in our hit-and-miss climate and can generally be relied upon. Ripening in early August, it has a good colour with plenty of red freckles. Likes a south-facing wall.

Blenheim A pale-fleshed but deeply flavoured variety first grown at Blenheim Palace in the 1840s. Best grown in plenty of sun, this is often thought of as our finest variety. August ripening.

Isabella A chance find in Gloucestershire, hardy and apparently of good colour and flavour (I have yet to taste this one).

Golden Glow A pale-yellow apricot discovered in 1985 growing on the Malvern Hills, not far from where I spent my childhood. It is said to be very hardy and a good cropper.

Gold Cott I am less than impressed with this vigorous modern variety, but it has been bred for our climate and is generally reliable.

Hemskirke Rather like Moorpark but less prone to die back. Bright-orange flesh with a reddish blush; the fruit should be ripe by late July.

Petit Muscat Small fruits of an intense flavour.

An apricot in the kitchen

The apricot is one of the more successful additions to savoury recipes. More versatile than the plum, the fig or even the pear, its lack of sugar and faint back-note of acidity give a lot more scope for mixing with meat and game. Lamb, duck and pork are especially comfortable with apricots, and for once we have a fruit that appeals with rice, couscous and lentils, though I would keep it well away from fish.

Middle Eastern cooking is rich in apricot recipes. I had a heady lamb tagine in Marrakech, thick with golden sultanas, mint and pickled lemon. A French version, with rosemary and garlic, is surprisingly satisfying too. A slow-simmered casserole of duck and apricots makes a welcome change from the more usual oranges, while a salad of duck skin and blood orange will brighten up a winter's day.

In desserts, the apricot excels where the peach fails, having a snap of acidity missing in the sweeter fruit. Where a peach tart may cloy, one of apricots will shine brightly in the mouth, always offering a note of freshness to balance the buttery pastry. An apricot puff pastry tart is one of the most enduring pieces of pâtisserie, but it also works in a more homely crumble.

A warm couscous, comforting, frugal, grounding, is infinitely more interesting when it contains a few apricots. I would include pistachios, sultanas and sometimes mint, too. Apricots also work in a rice salad, which cannot be said of many fruits, especially if you have some caramelised onions in there for balance.

Wherever possible, I keep the stone in. Not in a tart, where its presence would intrude, but whenever I poach the fruit for a compote, and I always leave a few in when making jam. The stone is the heart and soul of the fruit and its faint almond note seems, like cooking a piece of meat on the bone, to work a little magic.

Apricots and...

Rice No fruit works so well with the nutty flavour of rice. Use apricots fresh in a rice salad with mint and sultanas or add the poached fruits to a rice pudding.

Pistachios The apricot's natural affinity for this mauve and green nut can be exploited in a rice pilaf or by scattering the chopped nuts across the glaze of an apricot tart.

Almonds A marriage of antiquity and quiet perfection. A tart with a heart of ground almonds; a Danish pastry with flaked nuts on its glacé icing surface; a single kernel floating on an apricot compote. The almond and the apricot are as true a culinary friendship as you will ever find.

Cinnamon A dusting of ground cinnamon is worthwhile on a dish of baked apricots, as is a whole quill tucked into a dish of the poached fruit.

Honey Despite, or perhaps because of, the apricot's honeyed tones when truly ripe, a spoonful of the real thing is a successful sweetener in place of sugar. Try a trickle over the fruits before you bake them.

Lamb Perhaps the most welcome of meat and fruit partnerships. Tuck fresh or dried apricots into a lamb casserole or tagine, or offer a salsa of the chopped fruit with mint and watercress to serve with grilled chops. Used as a stuffing, the fruit will work with pork or turkey too.

Brandy I'm never one to use many spirits in the kitchen, but the apricot does nevertheless like a drop or two. Sprinkle over apricots for baking or add to the sugar and water when stewing.

Yoghurt The apricot feels much more at home with yoghurt than with cream, as you might expect of something with such a heritage.

* Unlike some soft fruits, apricots will go on to ripen after picking, though there may be a small loss of flavour. Ideally, though, we should leave them to ripen on the tree.
* Apricot kernels, the 'stone within the stone', add an almond note to cooked apricots and jams. Use only one or two per recipe. In large amounts, the prussic acid they contain can be poisonous.
* Apricot jam is the correct one to use in a classic Sachertorte.
* The distinctive flavour of the crisp, light amaretti di Saronno comes from ground apricot kernels.
* Apricot leather is a Middle Eastern speciality, rather like fruit-flavoured jelly. You can melt it down for a tart glaze.
* To make a glaze suitable for fruit tarts, warm the apricot preserve in a small pan with a squeeze of lemon juice or a spoonful of brandy, then push it through a sieve. Apply with a pastry brush.
* The smartest way to gauge an apricot's flavour is by smell rather than colour. The more headily fragrant the fruit, the more chance of it being what you are hoping for.

An apricot pilaf

The scented steam emerging from white basmati puttering in a covered pot; the homely note of warm, sweet spices; the top notes of fresh, clean mint. If ever smell alone could bring us to the table, then this is it. Add to that the sharp, fruity note of fresh apricots and you have an olfactory feast of the first order. I have eaten this as a side dish to lamb cutlets from the grill and as a quietly pleasing main course.

enough for 4 as a side dish
white basmati rice – 200g
butter – 50g, plus an extra knob
bay leaves – 3
green cardamom pods – 6, very lightly crushed
black peppercorns – 6
a cinnamon stick
cloves – 2 or 3, but no more
currants – 50g
apricots – 200g
spring onions – 4
mint – 2 or 3 sprigs
flaked almonds – 2 tablespoons

for the yoghurt sauce
chopped mint – 2 tablespoons
a pinch of ground cinnamon
thick, natural yoghurt – 200g
olive oil – 2 tablespoons

Wash the rice three times in a bowl of cold water, moving the grains around in the water with your fingers. Cover with fresh water and set aside for ten minutes.

Melt the butter in a saucepan, then add the bay leaves, cardamom pods, peppercorns, cinnamon stick, cloves and currants. Stir them round in the butter for a minute or two, until the fragrance wafts up. Drain the rice and add it to the warmed spices, then pour in a centimetre's depth of water and bring to the boil. Season with salt, cover with a lid and turn the heat down to a simmer. Stone and roughly chop the apricots. Trim and finely slice the spring onions. Chop the mint.

After ten minutes, remove the lid and gently fold in the chopped apricots, spring onions and mint. Replace the lid and continue cooking for a further two or three minutes, until the rice is tender and all the water has been absorbed. Leave, with the lid on but the heat off, for two or three minutes. Toast the almonds in a non-stick pan till golden.

Remove the lid and add the knob of butter and the almonds. Fluff gently with a fork.

For the yoghurt sauce, mix the mint, cinnamon and a little salt into the yoghurt, then stir in the oil. Spoon the sauce over the pilaf and serve.

Spiced apricot couscous

The apricot takes nicely to a little spice, and not just the sweet cinnamon stick and pinks-scented clove but the cardamom pod and chilli too. All the flavours it was brought up with.

I like apricots in a couscous, fat nuggets of fruit flecked through grain as soft and comforting as a cashmere blanket. This is something to sit beside lamb that you have cooked slowly till its fibres fall grainily from the bone, or peppers that have been stuffed simply with rice and herbs.

enough for 8
large banana shallots – 2 (or a medium onion)
butter – a thick slice
half a cinnamon stick
green cardamom pods – 6
dried chilli flakes – a good pinch
apricots – 200g
sultanas – a handful

for the couscous
couscous – 150g
olive oil – a tablespoon
hot vegetable stock – 250ml
harissa paste – 2 tablespoons
a preserved lemon
coriander – a small bunch

Peel and chop the shallots, then cook them in the butter over a moderate heat for ten minutes or so, till soft and golden. Stir in the cinnamon stick, cardamom pods, chilli flakes and a grinding of salt and black pepper. Halve, stone and chop the apricots and add to the pan with the sultanas and a cupful of hot water. Leave to simmer gently for ten to fifteen minutes, till the apricots are truly soft.

Put the couscous in a heatproof bowl with the olive oil. Pour over the hot stock and cover with a lid. Leave for ten minutes, then fluff up the grains with a fork, stirring in the harissa paste and the finely chopped skin of the lemon (you can discard the inner pulp, if you wish). Fold the cooked, apricots into the couscous, then chop the coriander and fold it in too.

A tagine of lamb with apricots

Of all the fruit and meat marriages, this is the one that appeals to me most. Meat, spices and apricots probably work better together than any combination since roast pork and apple sauce.

enough for 4
diced lamb shoulder – 1kg
ground cinnamon – 2 teaspoons
ground cumin – 2 teaspoons
ground turmeric – 2 teaspoons
sweet paprika – a tablespoon
hot paprika – a teaspoon
olive oil – 2 tablespoons
onions – 3
garlic cloves – 4
sultanas – 60g
honey – 2 tablespoons
saffron stamens – 1 teaspoon
stock – 750ml
chopped tomatoes – two 400g cans
apricots – 350g
a preserved lemon
coriander leaves – a handful
mint leaves – a small handful

Toss the cubed lamb in half the ground spices and leave for at least four hours. Overnight would be ideal.

Set the oven at 160°C/Gas 3. Warm the olive oil in a deep, heavy-based casserole and add the seasoned meat in small batches. Remove when it is browned nicely on all sides. Peel and roughly chop the onions, then peel and finely slice the garlic. Add to the pan with the remaining spices and allow to soften and colour lightly. Stir regularly over a moderate heat so that the spices flavour the onions but do not burn.

Add the sultanas, honey, saffron stamens, stock, tomatoes and apricots, then return the meat to the pan. Bring to the boil, season with salt and black pepper, then cover with a lid and place in the oven. Cook for two and a half hours.

Cut the preserved lemon in half and discard the interior pulp. Finely chop the skin and stir into the tagine. Lift out the meat with a draining spoon and boil the sauce over a high heat till it is reduced and thick, then stir in the roughly torn coriander and mint leaves. Return the meat to the sauce and serve.

A 'Frenchified' casserole of lamb, apricots and rosemary

enough for 4
olive oil – 2 tablespoons
butter – a thick slice
cubed shoulder or leg of lamb – 1kg
pancetta or bacon, in the piece – 150g
onions – 2
carrot – a smallish one
garlic cloves – 2
tomato purée – a tablespoon
plain flour – a tablespoon
white wine – 2 glasses
bay leaves – a couple
rosemary – 4 short, bushy sprigs
a strip of orange zest from half an orange
small apricots – 12

Warm the olive oil in a large, heavy-based casserole. The heat should be quite high. Drop in the butter and, when it starts to froth, add the cubed meat. Let the meat brown a little on each side, then remove it to a dish with a draining spoon. Whilst the lamb browns, cut the pancetta or bacon into small cubes, peel and roughly chop the onions and carrot and peel and slice the garlic.

Tip the bacon into the pan, let it cook over a slightly lower heat till the fat turns gold, then add the onions, carrot and garlic. Let the vegetables cook until they are just lightly coloured, then stir in the tomato purée and flour. Leave for three or four minutes, with the occasional stir, then pour in the wine. Bring to the boil, scraping at the base of the pan with a wooden spoon to dissolve the pan-stickings (so much flavour there), then add the herbs and orange zest. Return the meat to the pan, turn the heat down, season with salt and black pepper and leave to simmer, partially covered by a lid, for an hour, with the occasional stir.

Halve and stone the apricots and add them to the pot. Continue to simmer for thirty minutes. The casserole is ready as soon as the meat and apricots are tender, but it would taste even better the next day.

Guinea fowl with apricots, orange and Szechwan pepper

The lean, slightly gamey meat of the guinea fowl has an affinity with fruit – it is very successful with apples and Calvados, and with plums too – though the addition of apricots here was done at a whim. One of those thoughts you wish you had had earlier in life. The hint of acidity in the apricots is good with this dark, rich meat.

enough for 2
butter – a thin slice
olive oil – 2 tablespoons
a large guinea fowl, about 1.5kg
medium onions – 2
medium carrots – 2
celery – a stick or two
a clove of garlic
Szechwan peppercorns – a teaspoon
plain flour – a heaped tablespoon
stock – 600ml
orange zest – 4 long strips
bay leaves – a couple
star anise – 3
apricots – 8

Set the oven at 200°C/Gas 6. Melt the butter in the oil in a large, deep casserole. Cut the guinea fowl in half through the backbone, salt and pepper it, then colour it lightly on both sides in the butter and oil. Remove and set aside.

Peel the onions and cut them in half and then into thick segments. Put them in the pan in which you browned the guinea fowl and leave to colour over a moderate heat. Scrub and roughly chop the carrots, trim and roughly chop the celery, then add them to the onions. Peel the garlic, crush and add it. Toast the peppercorns in a dry frying pan, then crush or grind fairly finely and add them to the pan together with the flour. Continue cooking for three or four minutes, then pour in the stock.

Bring to the boil, then turn down to a simmer. Season with salt, pepper, orange zest, bay and star anise. Return the guinea fowl to the pan. Halve, stone and chop the apricots, then slip them into the sauce. Cover with a lid, transfer to the oven and bake for fifty minutes. Serve the guinea fowl surrounded by its sauce and vegetables.

Roast pork, apricot and pine nut stuffing

A boned shoulder is an economical cut of pork and a sound candidate for stuffing and roasting for a Sunday lunch. I get the butcher to remove the bones (you can put them in the pan with the roast, if you wish; it will lead to tastier pan juices). I also ask the butcher to score the fat for crackling. Spinach is the vegetable for this one, and maybe a leafy summer salad with which to wipe up the juices from your plates.

enough to serve 6 generously
a boned shoulder of pork – at least 2.5kg, skin scored
rosemary – 3 sprigs
apple juice – 200ml
stock – 200ml

for the stuffing
butter – a thin slice
a medium onion
apricots – 8
pine nuts – 3 heaped tablespoons
rosemary – a tablespoon of chopped needles
lemon zest – a tablespoon
fresh white breadcrumbs – 60g
egg – 1, beaten

Make the stuffing: melt the butter in a large pan, peel and roughly chop the onion and fry it in the butter for ten minutes, until soft and pale gold. Stone and roughly chop the apricots and stir them into the onion with the pine kernels, rosemary, lemon zest, breadcrumbs and the beaten egg. Season with salt and pepper, then set aside. Set the oven at 220°C/Gas 7.

Put the pork shoulder skin-side down on a large chopping board. Spread the stuffing over the surface (you might have a little left over, in which case cook it in lumps around the roast). Roll the meat up as best you can, tying it securely in several places with kitchen string.

Place in a roasting tin, tucking the rosemary underneath, then rub the skin with salt. Roast for twenty-five minutes, reduce the heat to 160°C/Gas 3 and cook for a further two hours.

Remove the pork from the tin, put it on a warm dish and cover it loosely with foil (covering it too tightly will soften the crackling). Pour most of the fat from the roasting tin, leaving the darker juices behind (there won't be many). Put the tin over a moderate heat and pour in the apple juice, scraping away at any crusty bits on the tin as it bubbles. Pour in the stock, let it boil and reduce by half, then season and pour into a warm jug.

Carve the meat and serve with the apple gravy.

Baked apricots with cream cheese

There was an unforgettable afternoon last summer when a dish of sugared apricots, still warm from the oven, was passed round the garden table with a plate of small, snow-white fresh cheeses. We sat, barefooted on the searing hot stone, scooping up the warm juices with our spoons.

enough for 4
apricots – 12
golden caster sugar or vanilla sugar – 3 tablespoons
soft, fresh cheeses, such as Petit Suisse, mascarpone, caprini freschi
  or fromage frais

Heat the oven to 180°C/Gas 4. Halve the apricots and discard all but one or two of their stones. Lay the fruit snugly in a shallow baking dish, dust with the sugar, then tuck in an apricot stone or two. Pour over just enough water to wet the sugar, then cover with a lid of some sort. Bake for an hour or until the fruits are soft and deeply coloured.

Serve them warm, in small dishes, with a little soft fresh cheese.

Grilled apricots with mascarpone

Ripe fruits of deepest orange are the only ones to use here.

enough for 2
seriously ripe apricots – 6
mascarpone – 80g
caster sugar – 4 tablespoons

Get an overhead grill really hot. Cut the apricots in half and remove their stones. Place them hollow-side up on a grill pan lined with foil. Spoon the mascarpone into the hollows, spoon half of the sugar on top and place under the grill. Leave for four or five minutes, then add the remaining sugar.

Return them to the grill till the mascarpone has melted and the sugar has formed a partial crust. Eat immediately.

Slim apricot tarts

At the height of summer, we often eat around the zinc table in the garden. Whilst everyone is wiping the roasting juices from their plates with a few soft salad leaves, I sometimes take the opportunity to slip a tray of paper-thin apricot tarts into the oven. It's a feel-good moment, partly because for once I feel like an organised cook. True, a certain amount of prep is required: the apricots need to be cooked and left sleeping in their syrup; the pastry has to be cut; the oven has to be on. Yet it is a rather wonderful moment, bringing to the table a tray of warm, slim pastries, their crusts holding a handful of melting apricot halves.

enough for 2
apricots – 8
sugar – 2 tablespoons
puff pastry – 200g
apricot jam – 4 tablespoons

Put the apricots into a small saucepan, add the sugar and enough water just to cover the fruit and bring to the boil. Lower the heat and simmer for ten minutes or until the fruit is soft and tender. It must be soft enough to crush between your fingers. Drain, halve, and discard the skin and stones. The skin should slide off effortlessly. Heat the oven to 220°C/Gas 7. Place a baking sheet in it to get hot.

Roll the pastry out to 3mm in thickness, which is thinner than you would normally expect. Cut two rounds of pastry approximately 15cm in diameter. Score a wide rim around the outside of each one, about 1cm in from the edge, taking care not to cut right through the pastry. Place the apricots flat-side down on the pastry, steering clear of the rim of each tart.

Lift the hot baking sheet from the oven, lift the tarts on to the baking sheet with a large, flat fish slice and bake for ten to twelve minutes, till the pastry is puffed and golden. Warm the apricot jam in a small saucepan and brush it over the tarts. Eat warm or cool.

An iced apricot and blackcurrant terrine

You could get away with using shop-bought meringues for this, but if you wish to make your own, then use the recipe for rosewater meringue in the Blackcurrants chapter. Ideally, omit the rosewater and bake the meringue on a lined baking sheet as six or eight individual meringues; that way you will have a good balance of crisp shell and gooey middle. You will need 200g of them, so keep the remainder for another day.

enough for 6
blackcurrants – 200g
caster sugar – 2 tablespoons
water – 2 tablespoons
ripe apricots – 4
double cream – 500ml
meringues – 200g

You will need a plastic or metal freezer box approximately 24cm x 12cm by 7cm deep, lined with cling film.

Pull the blackcurrants from their stems and put them in a small saucepan with the sugar and water. Bring to the boil, leave to simmer for five minutes, until the fruits start to burst, then boil hard for two minutes, until the liquid has reduced a little. Remove from the heat and allow to cool.

Slice the apricots in half, remove the stones and chop the fruit into small pieces. Whip the cream until it is thick but stop short of whipping it so far that it will stand in peaks. It should still be able to slide very slowly from the whisk. Crumble the meringues in small chunks – not to a fine powder – then fold them gently into the whipped cream with the chopped apricots. Pour into the lined dish. Pour the blackcurrants on top, then gently swirl them through the mixture. Fold the overhanging film over the top and freeze for at least four hours.

To serve, cut into thick slices with a sharp knife.

Apricot betty

The hot pudding has a place in summer as long as it contains fruit – at least that is my thinking. Classic winter recipes are worth trying with summer ingredients, such as steamed pudding with damsons, rice pudding with blueberries or, in this instance, a betty made with summer fruits. This is even better with a little cream to flatter the hot, crisp crust and meltingly tender fruit.

enough for 4
ripe apricots – 750g
caster sugar – 2 tablespoons
butter – 25g

for the crumb layer
butter – 75g
golden syrup – 2 heaped tablespoons
soft white breadcrumbs – 125g
light soft brown sugar – 100g

Set the oven at 180°C/Gas 4. Cut the apricots in half and remove the stones. Lightly butter a pudding basin, add the apricots and sprinkle lightly with the sugar. Add the butter, cut into small cubes.

To make the topping, put the butter and syrup into a saucepan and let them melt slowly. Mix the breadcrumbs and sugar together. Pour over the melted butter and golden syrup, then pour this mixture over the apricots. Bake for thirty minutes, till the crust is crisp and the fruit is fully tender.

Classic almond apricot tart

A classic from the pâtissier's window. Some cream – thick, yellow and unpasteurised – is needed here. Or possibly crème fraîche. Either way, it should be offered with generosity.

enough for 6

for the filling
apricots – 6
caster sugar – 180g, plus 2 tablespoons
sherry (dry or medium dry), or marsala if you have it – 2 tablespoons
butter – 180g
large eggs – 2, lightly beaten
plain flour – 80g
ground almonds – 150g

for the pastry crust
cold butter – 150g
plain flour – 250g
caster sugar – 2 tablespoons
an egg yolk

Halve and stone the apricots. Put them in a bowl and add the two extra tablespoons of sugar and the sherry or marsala.

For the pastry, rub the butter into the flour with your fingertips or in a food processor. The mixture should resemble fine, fresh breadcrumbs. Stir in the caster sugar, egg yolk and a tablespoon or two of water to bring the mixture to a firm dough. Pat into a ball, flatten with a rolling pin, then roll out on a floured work surface. Use to line a loose-bottomed 24cm tart tin, trim any overhanging pastry, then leave to chill in the fridge for thirty minutes. Set the oven at 200°C/Gas 6.

To make the filling, cream the butter and sugar together till smooth and pale. Add the lightly beaten eggs a little at a time, adding a tablespoon of the flour if there is any sign of curdling. Mix in the ground almonds and flour.

Remove the pastry case from the fridge, line with greaseproof paper and fill with baking beans, then bake for fifteen to twenty minutes, until the edges are dry and pale. Carefully lift out the paper and beans and return the pastry case to the oven for five minutes, until the entire surface feels dry to the touch. Turn the oven down to 180°C/Gas 4.

Spread the almond paste over the base of the tart case. Arrange the apricots evenly on the almond paste (they will sink as they cook) and bake for twenty-five to thirty minutes. Allow to cool a little before attempting to remove the tart from the tin.

A simple apricot jam

A fresh-tasting jam that is best kept in the fridge.

enough for two 500g jars
apricots – 1kg
granulated sugar – 750g
juice of half a lemon

Halve, stone and quarter the apricots. Break open a couple of the stones and extract the small, bitter kernel within. Put the apricots into a large steel or enamelled pot, add the sugar and bring to the boil. Turn down the heat and let the fruit and sugar simmer enthusiastically for twenty-five minutes, until the fruit is soft. Skim off any foam that rises to the surface and discard. Test to see if the jam is ready by dropping a small spoonful on a fridge-cold saucer and placing it in the fridge. If a skin forms within a minute or two, it is ready. Stir in the lemon juice, add the two apricot kernels and transfer to Kilner jars. Seal and store in the fridge.

A few recipes for canned and dried apricots

When apricots are halved, stoned and dried, they take on an intense flavour with a welcome edge of acidity. Rather than becoming a shadow of its fresh self, a dried apricot develops true character and is often used in place of the fresh fruit in pastries and cakes. No inferior ingredient this, but rather a hint of what the fresh fruit was like before it had the life bred out of it. I can eat dried apricots like sweets. I include a couple of recipes for them without apology.

Turkey with pistachio and apricot stuffing

I suggest you order the turkey leg a couple of days before you need it. Ask the butcher to bone it and remove the sinews. A large leg should weigh about 1.8kg, and when stuffed will feed six.

enough for 6
a small to medium onion
fresh white breadcrumbs – 150g
soft dried apricots – 75g
shelled pistachio nuts – 45g
interesting sausages – 350g
thyme leaves – a tablespoon or so
grated zest of a small lemon
parsley leaves – a handful, chopped
a large turkey leg, boned, sinews removed, ready for stuffing
olive oil
vermouth – a glass

Peel the onion, chop it finely and put it in a mixing bowl. Stir in the fresh breadcrumbs. Chop the dried apricots and the pistachios, then add them to the bowl. Slit the sausage skins and peel them away, then mix the meat in with the other ingredients. Add the thyme, lemon zest and parsley, then season thoroughly with salt and a little pepper.

Set the oven at 160°C/Gas 3. Put the turkey leg skin-side down on the work surface and bat out the meat with a rolling pin or cutlet bat to roughly 1cm thick (there will inevitably be holes and tears). It needs to be thin enough to roll into a thick sausage when stuffed. Spread the stuffing over the meat, pushing it almost to the edge. Roll up the meat to give a long, fat sausage, then secure with string at 3cm intervals.

Place the meat in a roasting tin, moisten with olive oil, cover with foil and roast for two hours. It is done when the juices run clear when tested with the point of a skewer.

Remove the meat to a warm place to rest (such as the switched-off oven), covered with foil, and tip most of the fat from the roasting tin, leaving behind the darker residue and any crusty pan-stickings. Put the roasting tin and its juices over a moderate to high heat, pour in the vermouth and stir to dissolve the gooey flavours stuck to the pan to make a thin, delicious gravy. Simmer for a few minutes, taste for seasoning and pour into a warm jug.

Put the meat on a carving board, slice thickly on to warm plates and serve with the hot pan juices.

A cake for midsummer

Raspberries and apricots are rippled through the soft, almond-rich crumb of this pretty cake. The very essence of summer. I sometimes add a few rose petals and an extra handful of raspberries at the last moment, or perhaps a light scattering of icing sugar.

enough to serve 8–10
butter – 175g
golden caster sugar – 175g
ripe apricots – 200g (4 or 5)
eggs – 2
self-raising flour – 175g
ground almonds – 100g
milk – 2 tablespoons
raspberries – 170g

Line the base of a 20cm loose-bottomed cake tin with baking paper. Set the oven at 180°C/Gas 4.

Cream the butter and sugar together in a food mixer till pale and fluffy. Halve, stone and roughly chop the apricots. Beat the eggs lightly, then add to the creamed butter and sugar a little at a time, pushing the mixture down the sides of the bowl occasionally with a rubber spatula. If there is any sign of curdling, stir in a tablespoon of the flour.

Mix the flour and almonds together and fold in, with the mixer on a slow speed, in two or three separate lots. Add the milk, and once it is incorporated add the chopped apricots and the raspberries.

Scrape the mixture into the cake tin and bake for an hour and ten minutes. Test with a skewer; if it comes out relatively clean, then the cake is done. Leave the cake to cool for ten minutes or so in the tin, then run a palette knife around the edge and slide it out on to a plate, decorating as the fancy takes you.

Apricot almond cake with apricot purée

An endlessly useful cake, shallow like a single layer of sponge, for use with poached fruits or a plate of strawberries. In summer, I serve it in slim slices with a purée of fresh apricots and an egg-shaped scoop of crème fraîche.

enough for 10–12
butter – 250g
caster sugar – 250g
ground almonds – 75g
plain flour – 100g
soft dried apricots – 100g
large eggs – 4, beaten
the grated zest and juice of an organic or unwaxed lemon

for the apricot purée
ripe apricots – 400g
granulated or caster sugar – 100g
a lemon

Line the base of a shallow 23cm cake tin with baking parchment or greaseproof paper. Set the oven at 180°C/Gas Mark 4.

Beat the butter and sugar together in an electric mixer until white and fluffy. Mix the almonds and flour together. Whiz the apricots in a food processor until they are very finely chopped. They must be finer than candied peel – almost, but not quite, a purée.

Add the eggs to the butter and sugar mixture a little at a time, with the beater on slow. Turn the machine off and add the lemon zest and a third of the almonds and flour, then turn the mixer on slow until the dry ingredients are incorporated. Add the second and then the third lot of almonds and flour, switching the machine off each time. If you do this too quickly you will end up with a heavy cake.

Lastly, the machine still on slow, mix in the lemon juice and the apricots. Using a rubber spatula, transfer the mixture to the lined cake tin and bake for thirty-five minutes. Run a palette knife around the edge of the tin, turn the cake out on to sugared greaseproof paper and leave to cool.

For the purée, put the apricots in a saucepan with the sugar and 4 tablespoons of water. Bring to the boil, turn down the heat to a simmer and leave to cook for twenty minutes, or until the fruit is very soft. Pour into a food processor and blitz to a smooth purée, or push through a sieve. Sharpen with lemon juice to taste and leave to cool. Serve with the cake.

Apricot and pistachio crumble

I have tried fresh, dried and canned apricots for this sumptuous pudding and have come to the conclusion that canned, with some of its silky syrup, beats everything else hands down. A pinch of ground cardamom in with the apricots or the crumble topping would be wonderful.

enough for 4
apricots in syrup – three 425g cans
a knob of butter for the dish

for the crust
shelled pistachio nuts – 125g
cold butter – 150g
plain flour – 300g
Demerara sugar – 175g

Set the oven at 180°C/Gas 4. Grind the pistachios to a point somewhere between the fineness of ground almonds and the coarseness of chopped nuts. They should resemble fine gravel. Rub the butter into the flour till it resembles fresh breadcrumbs, then stir in the ground pistachios and the Demerara sugar.

Pile the apricots and 4 tablespoons of their syrup into a buttered baking dish, tucking a few whole pistachios in, if you wish. Tip the topping on to the fruit and bake for thirty to thirty-five minutes, till the crust is crisp and golden, the fruit soft and tender. Take care that the crust doesn't burn (nuts always burn easily) – cover with foil if necessary. Serve hot, with cream.

Baked apricots with lemon tea

One of the most reliable plants in my garden is the lemon verbena bush, coming back from its winter dormancy every May with its slender, rough, lemon-scented leaves. I use them for tea mostly, but occasionally find a use for them in the kitchen. They have much to contribute to a dish of poached fruits, particularly peaches and apricots.

enough for 4
fresh apricots – 500g
a handful of lemon verbena or 2 verveine tea bags
sugar – 2–3 tablespoons
star anise – 2
a vanilla pod

Set the oven at 180°C/Gas 4. Wipe the apricots, cut each one in half, twist them apart and discard the stones. Lay the halved fruit in a shallow dish, tucking them together snugly.

Put the kettle on, and when it boils, pour enough water into a heatproof measuring jug to come up to 750ml. Drop in the leaves or tea bags and leave them for five minutes, then fish them out and throw them away (I put mine on the compost). Stir the sugar into the tea until it has dissolved, then pour it over the apricots, tucking in the star anise and the vanilla pod as you go.

Bake the apricots for about forty minutes, until they are tender. Remove and allow to cool before chilling thoroughly.

Blackberries

Of all of the blossom that fills this garden in the spring, the blackberry's is the most fragile. A stiff breeze or an April shower will destroy in a heartbeat the tissue-paper-white petals with their faint purple blush.

The blackberries are not officially mine, but cascade over the garden wall and its thick covering of ivy courtesy of a generous neighbour. They produce enough fruit for a pie or two, sometimes a crumble as well, ripening gradually from mid July till the first frosts. Picking a late blackberry on a misty November morning is one of the great pleasures of the British countryside. In my patch they are no trouble, except when I snag my arm on their vicious thorns as I walk past on my way to pick a pear or to take something up to the compost heap. If there are not enough for a pie, then I throw them in the breakfast muesli, where they stain the goat's yoghurt a romantic purple.

Archaeologists have proof of *Rubus fruticosus* having been eaten for at least 2,000 years. The blackberries in the shops are now both earlier and juicier than I remember them. I knew them as an autumn fruit, ripening around the annual return to school, the berries a temptation on the long walk back home from where the school bus dropped its lone, last passenger. The fruits were sharp, juicy and tightly packed. Today I see locally grown fruit in the shops at the same time as black and redcurrants, many three times the size of those I picked as a kid, and fatter too. (Had it come earlier in the season, I might have questioned whether the tiny berry of my childhood was in fact the similar, but smaller, dewberry.) The fruit of commerce – strawberries, raspberries, redcurrants, as well as this one – will continue to get sweeter and larger until someone finally realises they are diluted beyond recognition; but why those grown in the wild are also larger nowadays is a mystery. I remember them as the odd, sharp cluster of berries that you tipped into an apple pie, a few berries intense enough to flavour even the largest quantity of apples. I don't recall them being something plump and sweet enough to put in a bowl and eat with cream. We are lucky we have both at our disposal.

With each acre of green land that disappears under new and doubtless necessary housing estates, the remaining brambles become all the more precious. Collecting berries, with a wicker trug for the regulars, plastic bags for the unprepared, has been a late-summer pastime here for centuries. It may not be the most valuable of our wild food, nor as exciting as finding a cluster of apricot-capped chanterelles, but it is the most common and probably the most appreciated by all the family. Though how many of those bags of purple squish ever become a pie one can only speculate. But the art of reaching over the mounds of thorns and scratchy leaves to get at the fattest berry ('just one more, then I'll go home') is a pleasure in itself. We should probably continue to do it whilst we can.

There is a little myth and superstition to the bramble. Brave is he or she who picks a bag of blackberries once Michaelmas has passed. It is then, we are told, that the devil is supposed to piss on them. The facts back this up. The cooler weather permits the growth of Botryotinia, which can occasionally be mildly poisonous. So once again, an 'old wives' tale' proves true.

Blackberries in the garden

Botanically this is not a berry but an aggregate fruit made up of numerous drupelets. Well, it looks like a berry to me. Deer are especially fond of their leaves, while bees dote on their nectar-rich flowers. I rank them as one of my favourite fruits. The blackberry's natural habitat is woodland, meadows and waste ground, with many plants forming part of our hedgerows. I found some last year in the back lanes of a north London housing estate, together with rusting prams and car tyres. A wild feast just waiting to be picked. Blackberries will do very well in the average garden, taking up only as much room as you allow them to. They will climb a hedge or ramble over an unsightly garden feature. 'Scrambling' is probably the best description for this perennial's growth, like that of a particularly vigorous climbing rose (the bramble belongs to the family Rosacea). The plants are not even remotely fussy about their soil and will happily form dense thickets even on wasteland. Like the lemon, the bush has both blossom and ripe fruits at the same time.

You should really get new plants going in the autumn, but a winter-planted one will survive. I have said they will grow anywhere, but they won't complain if you give the ground a little manure as a housewarming present. Those long stems with their powerful thorns that are produced in the first year are generally fruitless, but flower buds will follow in the second year. They like a good winter, by which I mean a long, cold one. It encourages bud production.

Blackberries need some sort of support to scramble up. A makeshift structure knocked up from a couple of poles and horizontal wires will work, or you could train them over a rustic arch. Thornless varieties will save scratched arms and legs, but you can train the long shoots up trellis and pergolas to make their picking more manageable. Mine just fall in great skeins over the hedge. As soon as you get the plants in, cut the canes back to the second visible bud.

They will over-winter in that dormant way that fruit canes do (you will probably think you have killed them), then in spring will send up the first of the new shoots. As these grow, keep tying them in by folding them around the wires or trellis by hand or securing them with pieces of string. When the second winter approaches, ruthlessly cut back all the side shoots on each of the major canes. Come spring, the plant will send up a whole new batch of shoots from ground level. Tie these in as soon as they are long enough.

Varieties

Sylvan Large fruits on a very thorny and vigorous plant. Ripens mid summer.

Loch Ness A very popular variety, with a long season from late summer onwards. Should keep you supplied with large, richly flavoured berries throughout the autumn.

Fantasia Another widely grown variety with a long season. Will keep fruiting until the first frosts.

Oregon Thornless A compact variety, good for the smaller garden. Not overly large, the fruit has a good flavour, approaching that of the wild. Ripens from late August onwards and offers pleasing autumn foliage.

Waldo Needs a bit of protection from high winds, but produces good-quality fruits on disease-resistant plants.

The hybrids

The loganberry (*Rubus x loganobaccus*) is a cross between the blackberry and the raspberry. A closer look suggests it may have been the Aughinburgh blackberry and the Red Antwerp raspberry. The deed was done in the late 1880s in Santa Cruz by the horticulturalist James Logan. Legend has it that the fruit is a result of an accident when he was trying to cross two varieties of blackberry. It was introduced into Europe in 1897.

Deep burgundy red in colour and less seedy than the blackberry, it is said that the loganberry has a little of both berries in its flavour and I think that is a fairly accurate description. But it also has a vinous quality that makes it richer than both. It makes a particularly sumptuous jam. Slightly earlier than the blackberry, it should be picked from July to September, the fruits ripening in slow succession rather than all at once. They have a habit of hiding under their leaves.

The tayberry is a further cross between the loganberry and the raspberry.

The boysenberry is the result of a threesome between the logan, the raspberry and the blackberry.

Blackberries in the kitchen

The difference between the wild and cultivated blackberry is extraordinary. The berry you pick from a country lane invariably has the truest flavour, sweet but sharp, wine-like and heavy with the warm glow of nostalgia and berry-gathering trips past. The cultivated berry is good enough, plump and handsome, yet sweeter and somehow flat tasting in comparison. While the flavour of a wild berry will linger in the mouth long after the berry itself has gone, the pleasure of the cultivated fruit is short lived. Rather than thinking of the cultivated as an inferior form, I treat it as a different berry altogether, perhaps one to eat with yoghurt rather than to be mixed with apples for a pie or eaten from the container on the way home.

Scrumping aside, we are more likely to cook with blackberries than to eat them raw. It is unusual to sit down to a dish of them with cream as we might strawberries or raspberries, though one can. There is a quiet beauty in the sight of a pile of blackberries in a celadon blue bowl.

Good though the raw berry can be, they really appreciate warmth, and the addition of cinnamon and brown sugar. Most of all, it is their partnership with apples that is worth exploration. It is rare for a fruit to be so comfortable in the presence of another, but blackberry and apple is one of the great food marriages. A sharp apple is my first choice here, but they all work well enough once the heat gets going and the tree-fruit starts to soften. It is best to introduce your berries only once the apples have softened. Add them too soon and they will overcook. Once the two have been brought together, breathe in, dream of more carefree times, then use them to start the day, in a crumbly-crusted pie, a turnover or as a filling for the easily shattered crust of a strudel. You can stuff them into a suet crust, tuck them beneath a layer of crumble or use them to fill pancakes. The mixture likes custard as much as it does cream. And what sight is more tempting on a Sunday afternoon than that of translucent apples, their edges tinged with rich pink, being spooned out of a sugar-dusted pastry crust?

The marriage is partly seasonal and partly an attempt to make a small haul of berries go a long way, but more importantly it is the little explosions of rich, wine-like berries amongst the mass of mildly flavoured apple that make this such an enduring partnership.

I like forager Mike Irving's idea of adding a little wild mint to a dish of blackberries. In the past I have also had much pleasure from introducing blueberries, whose musky mildness seems to heighten the wild berries' flavour. Blackberries, particularly the slightly tart ones, are gorgeous with ripe melon – the green varieties in this case being even more appealing than the orange-fleshed.

Blackberries and goat's milk yoghurt remains a favourite breakfast. They are the second berry I add to my morning smoothie (the blueberry being pretty much essential in this house). Few fruits are quite so uplifting at 7am, though grapefruit comes pretty close. Which reminds me to suggest you take a look at the grapefruit tree in Chelsea Physic Garden if ever you are passing. Sheltered by high walls, it is often loaded down with its crop of golden orbs.

Blackberries and...

Game Only dark-fleshed game works with blackberry. Pheasant, venison, grouse, partridge. Add a few berries to the pan juices when making a game roast, or serve a puddle of sieved berries. Blackberry jelly is rather fine with cold roast pheasant.

Red wine The inkier the better. Simply anoint the berries with a splash of particularly fruity red wine. A little sugar is needed too.

Melon Sweet melon salad, especially Charentais, appears all the sweeter for the inclusion of a few juicy blackberries.

Apple One of the best marriages of all, especially when sheltering under a pastry crust.

Cream The richer and yellower, the better.

Pastry crusts The copious juice of the blackberry sinks delectably into the underside of the crust, giving a slightly moist piece of pastry soaked in juice. I find this the best bit of any fruit pie.

A textured fool of blackberries and apples

The charm of a gooseberry fool – pure, calm, gentle dessert that it is – relies on its smoothness, but other fools can delight by having a small amount of the fruit left whole amongst the softly whipped cream. Raspberry, rhubarb and blackberry all seem to be improved by a ripple of lightly crushed but wholly identifiable fruit in their midst.

The apple and blackberry fool that follows came about by happy accident as late as last autumn (my breakfast poached fruit folded into whipped cream as an emergency pudding). So pleasing was the result that I now make it from scratch but this is also a kind end for that cold baked apple from the fridge that no one could manage.

enough for 2–3
dessert apples – 3 large
water – 3 tablespoons
double cream – 240ml
blackberries – 150g

Peel the apples, core them and slice them thinly. Put them into a small pan with the water and bring to the boil. Turn down the heat and simmer gently until the apples are tender. They must be completely soft. Leave to cool.

Whip the cream in a fridge-cold bowl till it is just thick enough to hold its shape (I usually stop once it starts to feel heavy on the whisk and it will lie in soft folds).

Crush the apples to a coarse purée with a fork. Lightly crush the blackberries. Fold the fruit into the cream very lightly, so that it is still visible. Pile into glasses.

A salad of blackberries and golden melon

You look at a bowl of jet-black berries and melting, orange-fleshed melon and instantly know the time of year. If the melon is truly ripe and fragrant and the berries are not too sweet, such a dish is a delight for the senses.

Roast partridge with blackberry pan juices

A plate redolent of autumn if ever there was one. The toasted bacon, golden-skinned bird and glossy, berry-stained juices make this a gorgeous treat to behold.

> *enough for 4*
> young, plump partridges – 4
> thyme – 6 bushy little sprigs
> juniper berries – 12
> butter – 100g
> green bacon – 8 thin rashers
> blackberry, redcurrant or rowan jelly – 2 tablespoons
> blackberries – 100g
> Madeira or dry marsala – a wine glass

Inspect the birds for any stray feathers. Set the oven at 220°C/Gas 7.

Using a pestle and mortar, mash the thyme leaves with the juniper berries, butter and a hefty pinch of sea salt and black pepper. Spread the butter all over the birds but particularly on their breasts.

Place each bacon rasher on a chopping board, then stretch with the flat of a knife blade to give a longer, thinner rasher. Wrap the rashers round the birds and place in a roasting tin. Roast for twenty minutes, then peel off the bacon, setting it aside if it is crisp enough or leaving it in the roasting tin if not. Return the birds to the oven for ten minutes.

Remove the tin from the oven and set the birds somewhere warm (I use a large warm plate for this with an upturned bowl on top). Put the roasting tin over a moderate flame, drop in the jelly and blackberries and let them soften for a minute, then squash the berries lightly with a fork. Add the Madeira or marsala, stir to dissolve the pan crustings and season with salt and black pepper. Bring to the boil, put the birds on to warm plates, then spoon over the blackberry gravy.

Roast duck legs with squash and blackberry and apple sauce

Duck legs are something I tend to eat far more often than a whole bird. They have a neatness to them, and often seem to work out to be better value. You need just one leg apiece. Recipes for pot-roasting them are rare, but cooked that way the results can be tender in the extreme and a pleasant change from the usual crisp-skinned roast bird or grilled breasts. Soft, moist flesh is the goal here, with the squash soaking up some of the herb-seasoned fat.

enough for 4
small sprigs of thyme – about 8
sea salt
whole black peppercorns
plump duck legs – 4
a small squash or pumpkin
bay leaves – 2
blackberry and apple sauce – overleaf

Pull the thyme leaves from their branches (you could leave some stems whole) and pound them with half a teaspoon of sea salt and the same of black peppercorns. I use a pestle and mortar, but a wooden rolling pin in a bowl works too. Season the duck legs generously.

Put the legs in a deep casserole with a heavy base. Place the casserole over a moderate heat and quickly brown the duck pieces on both sides. The skin should colour to a pale amber; the fat should melt to form a shallow film in the pan.

Halve, peel and deseed the squash, pulling away and discarding any coarse fibres from the centre. Cut the flesh into thick chunks.

Tuck the pieces of squash alongside the duck legs with the bay leaves, turning them in the seasoned fat as you go. Cover with a lid, then turn the heat to low and leave for forty-five to fifty minutes or so, until you can pull the flesh easily from the bones with a fork. You shouldn't expect the skin to be crisp, but soft, fragrant with thyme and meltingly tender. The squash should be at the point of collapse.

Transfer the duck legs and squash to warm plates and serve with the blackberry and apple sauce that follows.

A blackberry and apple sauce for pork or duck

Apple sauce is something I make in any number of ways: with 'cooking' or 'eating' apples either in a shallow pan with a little water; or by baking the apples whole. The last method, useful if the oven is on for the Sunday joint anyway, seems to give a deeper, more concentrated flavour. The quantity of sugar you add is dependent on the sweetness of the apple variety.

enough for 4
Bramley-type apples – 4 large
blackberries – 150g
a little icing sugar

Score the skin of the apples round the middle (so that they don't explode) and put them in a baking dish. Bake them at 180°C/Gas 4 (or whatever temperature your roast is on) for a good forty minutes or so till they have puffed up and the apple is soft and frothy.

Put the blackberries into a small pan, add a tablespoon of stock or water and bring to the boil. Crush lightly with a fork.

Scrape the flesh from the apples' skin into a bowl. Using a small whisk or fork, beat in the sugar. Stir the crushed blackberries through the apples and serve with the duck above or with a roast shoulder or loin of pork.

Deep-dish blackberry and apple pie

It is almost impossible to think of a dish that so accurately expresses the glories of the British countryside in autumn as a vast, sugar-dusted blackberry and apple pie. It is everything we do so well: apples, wild berries, pastry crusts and comfort food. Far from what you could call an anglophile, I suddenly feel like waving a little flag.

enough for 6–8

for the pastry
plain flour – 250g
butter – 75g, cold from the fridge
lard – 75g, cold from the fridge
ice-cold water
a little milk, for brushing

for the filling
Bramley-type apples – 6 large
caster sugar, to taste
blackberries – 2 or 3 large handfuls

double cream, to serve

You will need a traditional 2-litre oval pie dish that measures about 32cm in length.

Put the flour into a large mixing bowl with a small pinch of salt. Cut the butter and lard into small chunks and rub into the flour with your thumbs and fingertips. You could do it in a food mixer but I can't really see why. It only takes a minute by hand. To bring the mixture to a rollable dough, add a little ice-cold water. Start with a tablespoonful, adding it gingerly (too much is difficult to correct), and draw the dough in from the sides to form a ball. You may need a couple of spoonfuls. You are looking for a dough that is firm enough to roll but soft enough to demand careful lifting. Set aside in the fridge, covered with a tea towel, for thirty minutes.

Set the oven at 200°C/Gas 6. Roll the pastry out to fit the top of the dish. You need enough extra pastry around the edge to be able to cut off and cover the rim of the dish (plus a few scraps to make some leaves, if you like that sort of thing). The simplest way to do this is to turn the dish upside down on the pastry and score around the top, then score a second line around the outside as wide as the rim.

Peel, core and quarter the apples, cut them into thick slices or chunks, then put them into the pie dish. Taste them to gauge their sweetness. I like my fruit fairly tart, so add just a surface sprinkling of sugar. The sweet of tooth may want to use anything up to a tablespoon per apple. Add the blackberries and toss them with the apples and sugar. Wet the rim of the dish – water will do – then fix the outer rim of pastry to it, cutting and pasting to fit. Wet it with water or beaten egg. Lift the pastry on to the pie, pressing the edge firmly on to the pastry rim. Crimp it with your thumb and first finger to seal or by pressing down with the prongs of a fork.

Cut two or three short slits in the centre of the pastry to let out the steam and, if you wish, decorate the pie with scraps of pastry cut into leaves. Brush with a little milk and dust with caster sugar. Bake for forty to fifty minutes, until the pastry is crisp and pale gold, covering it as needs be to stop it browning. Serve with double cream.

Little turnovers of blackberry and apple

These sweet little turnovers are good hot or cold. Rather than put sugar in the pastry crust, I have used a traditional pasty pastry recipe but added a wafer-thin crust of sugar as they come out of the oven.

makes 6 small turnovers

for the pastry
lard – 55g
butter – 55g
plain flour – 225g
cold water

for the filling
cooking or dessert apples – 1kg
sugar – 4 tablespoons
blackberries – 150g

a little beaten egg and milk for glazing
an egg white
caster sugar
cream or custard, to serve

Put the lard and butter into the freezer for an hour. Grate the fats into the flour and add enough water to make a firm dough – about five tablespoons. Rest for twenty minutes.

Peel the apples, discard their cores and cut into small chunks. Put them into a saucepan with the sugar and a couple of tablespoons of water and cook over a moderate heat, stirring regularly, until they start to soften. Tip in the blackberries and set aside. Set the oven to 200°C/Gas 6.

Divide the pastry into six pieces. Roll each into a disc about 12cm in diameter, using a saucer as a template. Brush the edges with beaten egg and milk, then put a small heap of the apple filling on each disc. Fold the dough over to make a semi-circle and press hard around the edges to seal.

Transfer the pastries to a baking sheet lined with baking parchment. Brush all over with beaten egg and milk. Cut a couple of steam holes in the top of each pasty to prevent them bursting. Bake for about forty minutes, till golden.

Lightly beat the egg white with a fork till it starts to froth. Brush lightly over the hot pastries, then scatter with caster sugar and return to the oven for three or four minutes. Eat warm with cream or custard.

Little fig and blackberry pies

Here is the softest pastry for the juiciest of fruit pies. Don't be tempted to roll it thinly. Cut the pastry into four and pat each piece out lightly, pushing it into the corners of the baking tins. Spoon in the filling, then fold the pastry lightly over the top. Sharp cream or thick yoghurt on the side would be appropriate but not necessary.

enough for 4

for the pastry
plain flour – 230g
butter – 140g
icing sugar – 50g, plus a little for dusting
a large egg yolk

for the filling
blackberries – 250g
large figs – 4
blackberry or redcurrant jelly – 4 tablespoons, melted
juice of half a lemon
ground hazelnuts – 60g

You will need four deep tartlet tins about 9cm x 4cm.

Put the flour into a mixing bowl and rub in the butter with your fingertips, then mix in the icing sugar and the egg yolk. Bring the dough together and squeeze it into a round, then roll it into a short, fat log before putting it in the fridge for half an hour to chill. I find this pastry works well in the food processor too; first blitz the flour and butter, then mix briefly with the sugar and egg yolk.

Set the oven at 200°C/Gas 6. Rinse the fruit, roughly chop the figs, and toss with the melted jelly, lemon juice and ground hazelnuts.

Cut the pastry into four. Flatten each piece on a floured board and use to line the tart tins, leaving the excess pastry overhanging the edges. Pile the filling into the tart cases, then loosely fold over the pastry. It should not meet in the centre, but instead leave a gap through which the fruit is visible.

Place the tarts on a baking sheet and bake for thirty to thirty-five minutes or so, till the pastry is dark biscuit coloured and the fruit is bubbling. Dust with a little icing sugar and eat warm or cool.

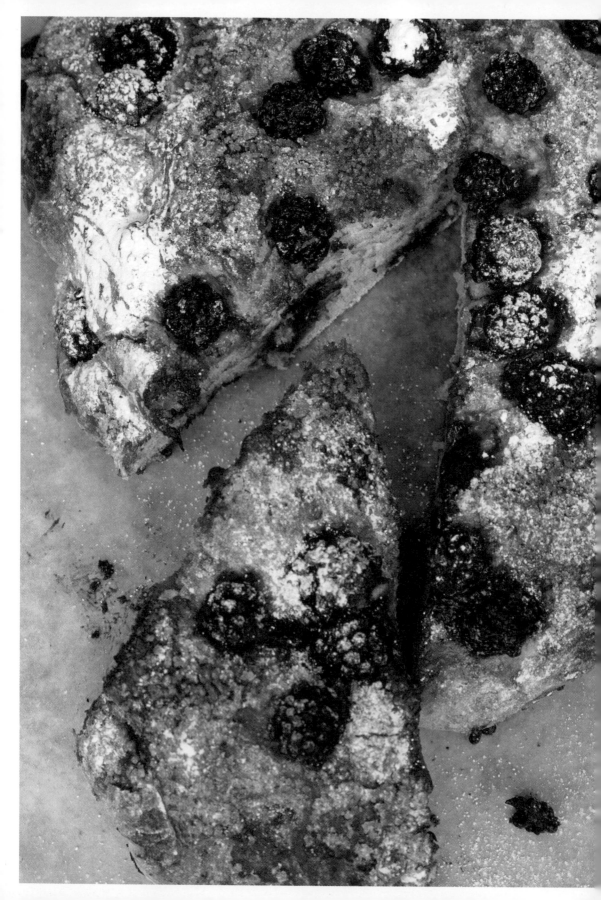

Blackberry focaccia

A dough speckled with fruit. It is difficult to know exactly when to eat such a treat – it's too substantial for dessert, so maybe we should file it under tea.

enough for 8
strong white flour – 450g
easy-bake yeast – 1 sachet (7g, 2 teaspoons)
sea salt – 1 teaspoon
caster sugar – 1 tablespoon
warm water – 350ml

for the topping
blackberries – 250g
olive oil – 2 tablespoons
caster or demerara sugar – 2 tablespoons
icing sugar for dusting

Put the flour in a large bowl, add the yeast, the sea salt (if you are using coarse salt, crush it finely first), then the sugar and warm water. Mix with a wooden spoon, then turn the dough out on to a generously floured board and knead lightly for five minutes or so. You need not be too enthusiastic. A gentle pummelling will suffice.

Once the dough feels elastic and 'alive', put it into a floured bowl, cover with a clean cloth or cling film and leave it somewhere warm to rise. It will take approximately an hour to double in size. Once it has, punch it down again, knocking some of the air out. Tip it into a shallow baking tin about 30cm in diameter. Gently knead half the blackberries into the dough, scattering the remaining ones on top. Cover the dough once more and return it to a warm place to rise.

Set the oven at 220°C/Gas 7. Once the dough has expanded to almost twice its size, drizzle over the olive oil, scatter with the sugar and bake for thirty-five to forty minutes, till well risen, golden brown and crisp on top. It should feel springy when pressed. Leave to cool slightly before dusting with icing sugar. Cut into thick wedges and eat whilst it is still warm. It will not keep for more than a few hours.

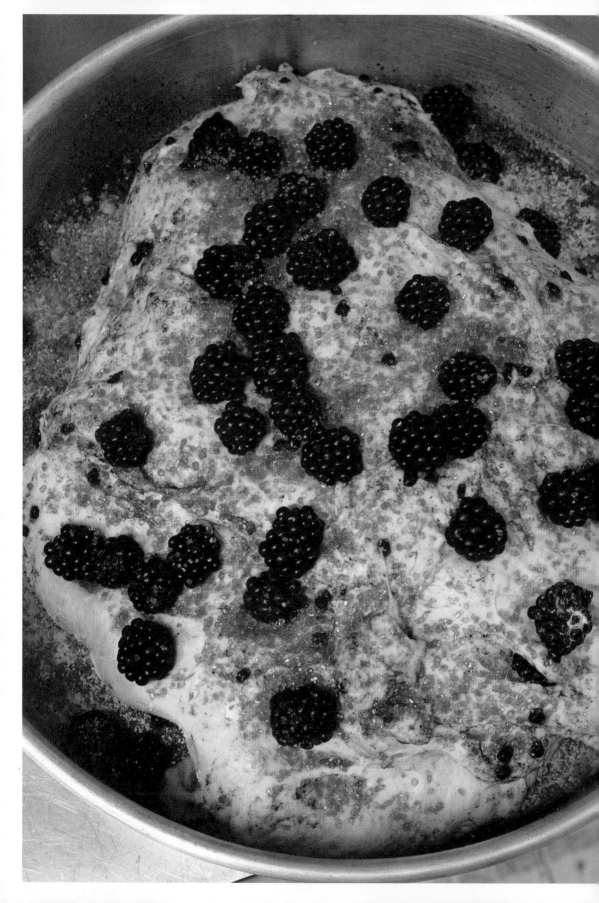

Blackberry bread and butter pudding

Autumn is bread and butter pudding season, for no other reason than it feels right. I will occasionally add a spreading of apricot jam or a handful of blueberries – even, on one occasion, some broken pieces of chocolate. Best of all, I find, is the addition of large, ripe blackberries. The custard around them curdles slightly, and those that float to the top can catch a little in the heat of the oven, but overall I feel they are a good thing, adding a touch of tart fruitiness to the bland and comforting bread and custard.

enough for 4
white bread – 9 small slices
soft butter
egg yolks – 4
milk – 300ml
double cream – 300ml
golden caster sugar – 100g
a drop or two of vanilla extract
blackberries – 200g
a pinch of ground cinnamon

Set the oven at 160°C/Gas 3. Butter the bread on one side and cut into thick soldiers. Beat the egg yolks gently in a bowl and then add the milk, cream, sugar and vanilla.

Lightly butter a medium-sized baking dish. Place the bread hugger-mugger over the dish, scattering the blackberries as you go. Pour over the egg custard and then finally add a mild dusting of cinnamon over the surface. Lower the dish into a roasting tin and pour in enough hot water to come half way up the sides of the dish. Carefully place in the oven. Bake till the custard has set and the bread is golden, about forty-five to fifty minutes. Take great care removing the tin and its hot water from the oven. Leave to settle down before eating.

Blackberry and apple betty

A betty is a crumble made by pouring melted butter and syrup over
a mixture of sugar and breadcrumbs. I find it possibly the most endearing
name for a pudding. All is well with a world where there is a betty on
the table.

enough for 4
Bramley apples – 1kg, peeled and cored
butter – 30g
blackberries – a couple of large handfuls

for the crumb layer
soft white breadcrumbs – 125g
light soft brown sugar – 75g
butter – 75g
golden syrup – 4 heaped tablespoons

Set the oven at 190°C/Gas 5. Cut the apples into large chunks, put them in
a pan and toss with the butter and a couple of tablespoons of water over a
moderate heat. When they start to soften but are still keeping their shape,
drop in the blackberries, then tip the fruit into a 1.5 litre baking dish.

Mix the crumbs and sugar and cover the fruit loosely with the mixture.
Melt the butter and syrup in a small pan, then pour them over the crumbs,
making certain to soak them all. Bake for thirty-five minutes, till the apple
is soft and the crumbs are golden and crisp.

A moist cake of apples, blackberries,
ground hazelnuts and cinnamon

The weight of autumn fruit is inclined to make this gorgeous cake sigh
a little in middle. If you are the sort of tightly-wound cook who thinks a
sunken cake is a failure then turn away now. We will eat this supremely
moist, cinnamon-scented wonder without you.

The first time I made this cake I used whole hazelnuts which I skinned
and toasted before grinding. The roasting gave the cake a deep, nutty
warmth and I recommend it if you have an extra twenty minutes to spare.
Failing that, toast the ground hazelnuts under a hot grill before you fold
them into the cake mixture.

enough for 4–6

for the cake
small dessert apples – 2
half a lemon
blackberries – 150g
butter – 150g
caster sugar – 75g
dark muscovado sugar – 75g
eggs – 3 large
plain flour – 85g
baking powder – 1½ teaspoons
ground hazelnuts – 100g

for the crumble
cold butter – 50g
plain flour – 50g
Demerara or golden caster sugar – 60g
rolled oats – 2 heaped tablespoons
ground cinnamon – a knife point

You will also need a deep loaf tin approximately 22cm x 12cm

Set the oven at 180°C/Gas 4. Line the loaf tin on the bottom and sides with baking parchment. It will stop the cake from sticking. Cut the apples into quarters, core them, then cut into thin, but not paper thin, slices. Squeeze a little lemon juice over them, then mix lightly with the blackberries.

Put the butter, cut into small pieces, in the bowl of a food mixer together with the sugars and beat till light, smooth and pale coffee coloured. Break the eggs into a small bowl and whisk them lightly with a fork to break them up. Add them, a little at a time, to the mixture, beating all the time.

Sift the flour and baking powder together, followed by the hazelnuts, then add in two or three lots to the mixture. Transfer to the lined cake tin. Scatter the apples and blackberries over the top and push some of the fruit lightly down through the mixture with your finger.

Make the crumble by rubbing the butter – cut into small pieces – into the flour, either with your fingertips or using a food processor. Stir in the sugar, rolled oats and cinnamon. Scatter over the top of the cake and bake for about an hour, till a skewer or knitting needle inserted into the centre of the cake comes out moist but relatively clean.

Leave the cake to cool completely before removing from its tin. The cake will improve if wrapped in foil and stored overnight before cutting. But either way you will end up with a moist, crumbly cake that is the very essence of autumn.

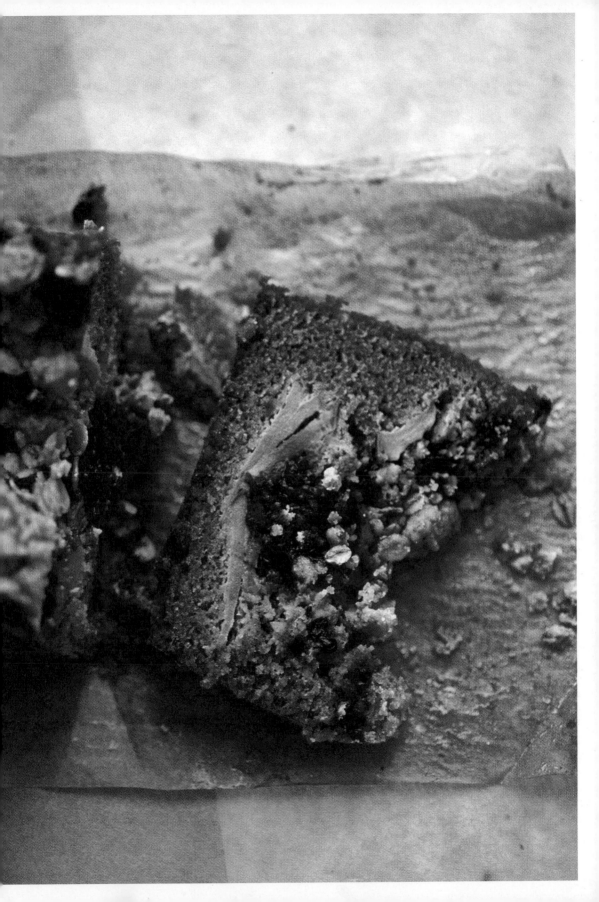

Blackcurrants

Without heat, there is little point to the blackcurrant. Along with the other kitchen fruits, the dusty purple damson and the hard, green gooseberry, the blackcurrant needs to be cooked to render it a pleasure. Once warmed, the dull black fruits have an incomparable intensity of flavour. But it is a flavour that must be sweetened if it is not to pucker the lips as tight as a cat's bottom.

There is no gloss to this fruit. It does not sparkle on the market stall like its red and white sisters. There is little clue for the nose or eye that this is the most vivid-tasting fruit of all. An early-eighteenth-century writer insisted they smelled of bedbugs. I am not sure I would know, despite confessing to a romantic predilection for seedy Parisian hotels.

Currants bring back memories like those of no other fruit. They provide, by their flavour and the scent of their pruned wood, a clearer memory of my childhood than any photograph album ever could. Their smell – musky, sour, almost fetid – reminds me of my first bid for freedom, a school holiday job in the fruit fields of Worcestershire, picking tray after tray of small fruit, much of which ended up, apparently, as cordial. Ninety per cent of the country's harvest is made into Ribena. My parents were happy for me to drink gallons of the stuff, watered down with lemonade, which to this day I find a refreshing drink with much ice on a blistering summer's day. As a child, I ate them raw, as I do now, towards the end of August when they are plump from the rain.

Our modern, warming climate is not good for this berry, which needs a snap of frost to stimulate its growth. New varieties appear from time to time and it is hoped breeders will come up with one that can thrive in the warm. As fruit goes, the blackcurrant is a recent arrival. I can find no mention of it before the late 1700s. Herbalists welcomed the tar-black berries for their ability to soothe a sore throat – they are still used in cough pastilles.

A currant is cooked when its skin splits. The chemistry of burst currants, sugar and heat will give a thick, rich syrup to garnish a vanilla ice, lubricate a piece of sponge cake or supply a base for a powerfully flavoured sorbet. Such intensity is exploited in crème de cassis, the suave, deep purple liqueur made in Burgundy and used for the most part to jolly up a glass of white wine for drinking outdoors.

It is possible, I suppose, to have too much flavour. A bowl of stewed currants, all purple and punch, is too forceful for some. Temper its power with cream, or with bland stodge in the form of a suet crust, bread or pastry. A more delicate version of summer pudding, where the fruit is supported by slices of brioche, is a modern answer. I have made many a summer pudding with blackcurrants instead of red. It works as long as you are the sort not afraid to indulge in the cream jug.

A mouthful of tart black fruits and crumbly pastry is bliss to me. Pastry that will soak up some of the juice, a deep crumble topping or an American-style thick cobbler crust has more point than a sweet, thin pastry case. The juice-soaked crust is, at least to my taste, the reason for this fruit's existence.

A blackcurrant bush in the garden

Once the lawn had been removed and the six soil beds dug and manured, I planted fruit bushes. Ben Lomond is the blackcurrant I grow, and has fruited exceptionally for nine years. The fruits are plump even in a dry year, and stay in good condition on the branch for up to four weeks. They last better there than in the fridge, if they are shaded and you can keep the birds away. A net will help, but you can get into a right old tangle trying to take it off after the stems have inevitably grown through.

Currants love rich, damp soil and a regular dose of manure. The black will tolerate shade, unlike the red, but are not fond of wind. Blackcurrants fruit on old wood. This means careful pruning if you are not to end up with either no fruit (over pruning) or an untidy bush (under pruning).
No one wants an untidy bush. I prune out some of the older, weak-fruiting branches or those that cross one another as soon as the fruit has finished in September. This way there are always some old branches for next year's berries and space to allow new growth next spring.

Varieties

I have seen small currants *(Ribes nigrum)* growing wild in Scotland and it is certainly where the cultivated strains do well, though they can still be found in woodland in Cumbria and Yorkshire. Damp is no problem to this fruit. They do very well on the wet side of my garden. There may be as many as 150 varieties all told, but few are ever seen beyond the much-loved and tough-skinned Baldwin and the modern 'Bens' – an assortment of cultivars named for the Scottish peaks, Ben Nevis being taller than most.

Baldwin An old variety, vigorous, with sweet, late fruit.
Ben Alder Late flowering, a heavy cropper with juicy fruit.
Ben Lomond An early 'Ben' and still fruiting copiously.
Ben Nevis A tall, upright bush with large, late fruit.
Ben Sareck A small variety, good for compact gardens.
Ben Connan Large, juicy berries that will stay on the bushes in good condition for a couple of weeks.

Blackcurrants in the kitchen

The fact that the blackcurrant is essentially a cook's fruit, of no interest in the fruit bowl, is partly why I have such affection for it. Actually, it is more like an obsession. I applaud the fact that its appeal isn't instant, like that of a peach or a nectarine. It is part of why I am a cook.

As soon as I see them in the market in their green cardboard punnets, round about the second week in July, I start a sort of personal homage to this fruit. First it's a handful of raw berries on the way home; then a compote of eye-watering richness; then a crumble, a pie, a soggy dome of summer pudding; a potent jam for plain scones or to hold together a buttery sponge; best of all is a shallow pie, its pastry pale and glistening with sugar, its filling hot, velvety, sour. At that point I reach for the cream.

Its short season through July and August can often end in a glut, and you would be wise to freeze a punnet or two. Their rich, startling taste will not seem out of place in a winter pie. Robust flavours for cold days.

Once cooked, the blackcurrant has the most strident flavour of any fruit save the damson. You will need a little patience to pull the pearl-sized berries from their stalks. Even more if you are the fastidious type who likes to remove the dried flowers as well. I am not sure it makes enough of a difference to bother. A cook's tip is to run a fork down the stem to remove the fruit but, being a hands-on kinda guy, I prefer holding the end of the stem and plucking at the fruit with my fingers. Blackcurrants are often dusty from the open transport along farm tracks and may need a gentle rinse.

It takes barely five minutes to cook a currant. They need just a little water to stop them burning before their skins pop: three tablespoons per 400g currants is about right. Once their juice has mingled with the necessary sugar they are ready. Boil any longer and you will have jam.

This particular member of the currant family occasionally turns up in savoury recipes, especially with game. If it must, then let it be with the darker meats, venison or pigeon perhaps, the fruit squished into the pan juices with the back of a wooden spoon.

Well worth trying for its subtlety is a quivering lump of blackcurrant jelly left to dissolve in the roasting juices after you have taken the meat out to rest. You can make the jelly at home using the recipe later in this chapter. It is also very good just as it comes, with venison steaks or partridge.

The ubiquitous crumb-edged cheesecake with its thick layer of blackcurrant jam, seen on the counter of virtually every delicatessen in the 1980s, was a clue to how effective this fruit is in the presence of dairy produce. Its mouth-puckering sharpness deals instantly with the cheesecake's tendency to cloy. A modern interpretation might be the cherry cheesecake on page 809, served with a slick of the indigo compote below.

An early-autumn pudding made with an equal mixture of blackberries and currants will quell the currants' strength. A jam of the fruit is easily set, and is possibly the best thing you can do to a rice pudding. A purple-black sauce is very sexy on a snow-white ice cream. Or on top of a meringue, when you can pull your fork through the cream to make vibrant, Hodgkinesque swooshes on your plate.

Blackcurrants and...

Mint Odd but true. Add a few finely chopped leaves to a blackcurrant purée or to a fruit salad in which very ripe blackcurrants are included.
Vanilla ice cream Spoon a purée of the fruit over vanilla ice or stir it into home-made vanilla ice cream after churning and just before it goes into the freezer.
Pastry Where a pastry or crumble crust will do nothing for a red or white currant, they have a certain affinity with the blackcurrant. Use them in a pie, a crumble or an American-style cobbler. They are the only currants that work in a pie.
Cream and cream cheese If there is a more suitable topping for a cheesecake than a layer of blackcurrants I have yet to find it. Although cream and the poached fruit can curdle on meeting one another, the flavours work together in surprising harmony. Blackcurrant jam is my favourite of all preserves for piling aboard scones and clotted cream.
Oats A layer of blackcurrant jam is generally a welcome thing to find in the middle of a thick oat flapjack. A dollop on an oatcake spread with curd cheese is more of a luxury than it sounds.

A summer pudding of blackberries and currants

For years I have gorged myself on Christmas pudding in winter and summer pudding as soon as the currants and berries are ripe. They both have some magic attached to them that takes them far beyond the sum of their ingredients.

I make the classic summer pudding but generally stray off the beaten track (always a good idea with classics, since you may discover something you like even more) by adding blackcurrants to the more regular mix of raspberries and redcurrants. I like their richness and breathtaking fruitiness.

As the summers have gone by, the redcurrants in my pudding get fewer, so that it is now virtually all blackcurrants – too strong until the fruit meets the cream jug. Last year I introduced blackberries into the recipe. I suggest you start with half and half, then keep tweaking until the mix suits you.

> *enough for 6–8*
> mixed blackcurrants and blackberries – 850g
> white sugar – 3 tablespoons
> firm, good-quality white bread – 7–8 slices,
>   cut about as thick as your little finger
> cream, to serve

Sort through the fruit tenderly, picking out any that are unripe or mouldy. There's nearly always a few, especially if the weather is damp. Pull the currants from their stems, then put them, with the blackberries, in a stainless steel saucepan over a low heat. Taste the fruit for sweetness and add sugar accordingly. For commercial, sweet blackberries and slightly tart currants, I add three tablespoons or so. Sometimes you may need slightly less if they are very ripe, or more if your blackberries were tart and from the hedge. Use your own judgement, bearing in mind that the finished pudding should have a bit of sharpness to it. Pour in a little water, a couple of tablespoons will do, then bring it to the boil. The currants will start to burst and give out their juice. They need no longer than three or four minutes at a cautious simmer. The fruit should be shiny and there should be much magenta juice in the pan. Turn off the heat.

Cut the crusts off the bread. Set one piece aside, then cut the rest into 'soldiers' – that is, each slice of bread into three long fingers. Push the reserved piece into the bottom of a 1-litre pudding basin or dish, then line the inside of the basin with the strips of bread, pushing them together snugly so that no fruit can escape, keeping a few for the top. Fill the bread-lined basin with the fruit and its juice; it should come almost to the rim. Lay the remaining bread on top of the fruit, tearing and patching where necessary so that no fruit is showing.

Put the basin in a shallow dish or bowl to catch any juice, then lay a flat plate or small tray on top with a heavy weight to squash the fruit down. Some juice may escape, but most will soak into the bread. Leave overnight in the fridge (you may have to remove a shelf, depending on how deep your fridge shelves are).

Remove the weight and plate, then slide a palette knife around the edge, pushing carefully down between bread and basin so as not to tear the bread. Put a plate on top, then, holding the plate in place, turn quickly upside down and shake firmly to dislodge the pud. It should slide out and sit proud. Pass a jug of cream around – it is an essential part of the pudding.

A fabulous jam

I love jam. I love it more than treacle, much, much more than honey and only slightly less than marmalade. It is not just the preserve itself that appeals but the tubby little pot on the table, its contents glistening as you twist off the lid. The way the fruit and syrup fill the spoon as you push it ever downwards, and that sticky dribble that hangs, jewel-like, on the rim of the jar.

The jam I use to measure all others was made by the late Dorothy Carter – a glorious jam, the most memorable of which was her blackcurrant, a soft preserve that glistened on the spoon. When Miss Carter died, the company survived briefly but the magic seemed to go with her. Miss Carter's extraordinary preserve aside, there are some very good jams made both commercially and by artisan cooks. Village fêtes, farm shops and charity stalls are good hunting grounds.

Gooseberry, loganberry and plum appeal to me more than the sweeter preserves such as strawberry. But the pinnacle of jam-making for me is blackcurrant, and with good reason. The sharpness of the blackcurrant makes it one of the very few fruits that can cope with the copious amount of sugar in the average jam recipe. That and the way it glistens as you spread it across the rough furrows of a warm scone or a triangle of seedy brown toast.

Blackcurrant slightly bucks the trend when it comes to sugar-to-fruit ratios, because of the currant's supreme acidity. The recipe that follows is for a softly set jam with a deep flavour of the fruit that glows deepest purple-black on your spoon.

makes 2 jars
granulated or caster sugar – 900g
blackcurrants – 600g
water – 560ml

Warm the sugar slightly in a low oven. Pull the currants from their stalks. Put the fruit into a large saucepan with the water and bring to the boil. As the mixture starts to bubble and the currants burst, tip in the sugar and let it dissolve without stirring. Once the sugar is completely dissolved, turn the heat down slightly so the jam simmers enthusiastically, stirring briefly. Leave to cook for ten minutes, then switch off the heat.

Have two 500ml preserving jars or four or five smaller jam jars ready. They should be spotlessly clean, sterilised with hot water from the kettle and dried. Spoon in the jam right to the top and seal.

A rice pudding to show off a fruit compote

I rarely sully the warm, ivory purity of a rice pudding. I make an exception for a compote of currants, though. I never stir, preferring to take a small amount of the glistening compote on the spoon with a larger amount of rice. Should you stir, you risk ending up with a pudding the colour of a bruise.

enough for 4
pudding rice – 70g
full cream milk – a litre
butter – 30g
caster sugar – 2 tablespoons
a vanilla pod

for the currant compote
blackcurrants – 250g
sugar – 2 tablespoons
water – 2 tablespoons

Set the oven at 140°C/Gas 1. Put the rice, half the milk, the butter, sugar and vanilla pod into an ovenproof dish. Slide it into the oven and leave to get on with things quietly for an hour. Lift the pudding out of the oven and pour in the remaining milk, stirring gently. Leave to cook for a further hour and a half.

Rinse the currants and pull them from their stalks. Drop them into a stainless steel or enamelled cast-iron pan and add the sugar and water. Bring to the boil over a low flame, taking care that the fruit does not burn. Lower the heat and allow to bubble gently for five minutes or so, until the currants have started to burst and you have a small quantity of deep purple juice. Switch off the heat.

Serve the rice pudding in all its simplicity or with a spoonful of the warm currant compote. A dessert to bring peace and calm to all who eat it.

A rosewater meringue with blackcurrants and cream

Meringue is always easier to make in large quantities (the same goes for mayonnaise, in my experience). You will find you have a few meringues left over for the next day. They will keep quite well in an airtight container. The idea of warming the sugar before adding it to the egg whites is new to me, a tip picked up from Yotam Ottolenghi, but I find it produces the stiff, glossy meringue that has previously evaded me.

enough for 8–10

for the meringues
caster sugar – 300g
egg whites – 5
a few drops of rosewater

for the blackcurrant sauce
blackcurrants – 300g
caster sugar – 3 tablespoons
water – 2 tablespoons

double cream – 300ml

Set the oven at 180°C/Gas 4. Make the meringues: scatter the sugar over a baking sheet, put it in the oven, then leave for ten minutes or so, until warm. Whip the egg whites with an electric beater till firm and fluffy, then fold in the warm sugar and the rosewater. Keep beating with the electric beater for a good five minutes, until the meringue is shiny. Place large, heaped spoonfuls of the mixture on a baking sheet lined with baking parchment, leaving room for the meringues to spread and puff. Put it in the oven and immediately turn the heat down to 120°C/Gas ½. Bake for about an hour, turning down the heat if they are browning too much – you want them to be a pale honey colour. When the meringues are crisp on top, let them cool. The ideal is for them to remain fudgy inside.

Pull the blackcurrants from their stalks. Put them into a stainless steel saucepan with the sugar and water and bring to the boil. As soon as the berries start to burst and the juice turns a dramatic purple, remove from the heat and set aside. Leave to cool, then chill.

Whip the cream till it will just about keep its shape; it shouldn't be so thick that it will stand in peaks. Press the centre of each meringue with the back of a spoon so that you make a hollow. Pile the cream inside. Serve the sauce in a jug to pour over as you eat.

Blackcurrants under an oat and almond crust

A blackcurrant purée, sorbet, even a compote, can be too highly flavoured for some. It requires tempering. A dear friend, who died last year, got round the currants' overpowering strength by adding an oat crust – a sort of oaty, nutty rubble. This was one of his favourite puddings and I think of him, dear, lovely man that he was, every time I eat it.

enough for 4

for the filling
blackcurrants – 500g
caster sugar – 3 heaped tablespoons

for the crumble
butter – 100g
plain flour – 150g
ground almonds – 75g
Demerara sugar – 60g
rolled oats (or barley) – 75g
water – 2–3 tablespoons

Set the oven at 180°C/Gas 4. Top and tail the blackcurrants. Rinse them under cold water and tip, still wet, into a 1-litre ovenproof dish. Scatter over the caster sugar and toss gently. The sugar will stick to the berries like frost.

With your fingertips or using a food processor, rub the butter into the flour until it resembles coarse breadcrumbs. Stir in the almonds, Demerara sugar and rolled oats. Shake the water over the crumble mixture, then jiggle the bowl so that a few small, pebble-sized lumps are formed. This will give a delightful assortment of textures to the crumble.

Tip the crumble over the sugared fruit. I leave it just as it falls out of the bowl, to lend a looser texture to the crumble. I never pack it down. Bake for fifty minutes to an hour, until the fruit bubbles through the crust.

A quivering jelly

I find it slightly amusing that I am now the sort of person who makes jellies and jams. The process is relaxing and somehow good for my wellbeing. Twenty years ago I would have laughed at the idea of ever pouring cottage garden fruit through a jelly bag, let alone labelling my own jars of jam. Getting older isn't all bad.

It is useful to have a side-of-the-plate accompaniment for roast partridge, lamb, rabbit or pigeon that will also add a mild sweetness when melted into their cooking juices in the roasting tin. Such a clear jelly will also make a discreet glaze for sweet tarts of raspberry, blackberry or strawberry and is simple enough to make by simmering the fruit with an almost equal quantity of sugar, then sieving it to remove the skin and pips.

I have always liked this shimmering jelly with roast meat, even at that early stage in my life when anything on the side of the plate – mint sauce, mustard, horseradish – was unwelcome. The homemade version has a sparkle to it, and is more lightly set than the stuff you buy from the shops.

redcurrants – 450g
a small handful of blackcurrants
white sugar – 450g

Put the fruits, still clinging to their stalks, into a deep, stainless steel pan. Pour in the tiniest amount of water, barely enough to cover the bottom of the pot, then add the sugar. Stir from time to time and boil for eight minutes – no longer or the flavour will spoil – then pour through a fine sieve, or a jelly bag if you have such a thing, set over a wide jug. Leave until all the juice has dripped through. It is a mistake to press the fruit in the hope of producing more juice. Ultimately, you will cloud the jelly.

Pour into clean jars you have sterilised with boiling water from the kettle and dried, preferably in the oven or at least with a spotless tea towel. A lack of scrupulous cleanliness at this point will impair the jelly's keeping potential (it will be mouldy within a month). Cut discs of greaseproof paper to fit over the preserve. I think it is worth being neat, it will only take a minute, then cover tightly with a screw-top lid. Store in a cool, dry place.

Blueberries

The blueberry pie, its dusky berries and their purple juice held under a soft, sugar-dusted crust, is reason alone for the fruit's inclusion in this book. That and the botanical fact that the modern berry is a descendant of the diminutive and enchanting wild bilberry of British heath and moor – a forager's fruit – and one that deserves every bit of praise we can throw at it.

At first, I didn't 'get' the cultivated blueberry. It lacked the sensual qualities I look for in a fruit – that rich, heady fragrance and the pinprick of sharpness that makes a berry interesting. Where, I wondered, was the gorgeous arterial juice of the logan; the wine-like scent of the raspberry; the tempting gloss of the bramble or the charm of the wild strawberry? The fact that I first met it as part of a pavlova didn't help: the deep clouds of snow-white sugar-cake need a fruit with a sting in its tail (the Antipodeans are bang on with their inclusion of passion fruit) if the dessert isn't to cloy.

Whilst I sometimes still find its flavour a little shallow, the fruit has slowly but surely grown on me. The powdery, violet-grey bloom, the neat little crown, its inky-blue skin and purple juice have gradually seduced me. Once you see the blueberry growing on its short bushes and witness the bell-shaped flowers in their shades of green and apple-blossom pink, it is difficult not to fall in love.

Its mild, dusky flavour, the gentle sweetness, and the way its skin bursts in the mouth to reveal its pale-green flesh only add to its charm. If you eat it with thick yoghurt or crème fraîche or add a squeeze of lemon juice, the flavour will sing a little louder than it does with sweet cream.

The modern blueberry, *Vaccinium corymbosum* (a cluster of fruits), is related to our smaller, native bilberry, the bush fruit that grows wild on moors, heaths and oak woodland in southern England, Scotland, Lancashire, Yorkshire, Wales and the southeast. The Scots know it as the blaeberry or whinberry for its habit of growing amongst 'whin' or gorse. In parts of the south, the berries are known as whorts. The wild fruit has not just the purple skin of the cultivated blueberry but purple flesh too. Its flavour is deeper, sharper and more intense.

The blueberry is revered in North America – 90 per cent of the world's production comes from there – and it is to them we owe both our own blossoming blueberry industry and much of our year-round supply. The fruits we have now are the result of years of work by North American fruit breeders, who have given us a berry that is, unsurprisingly, bigger, sweeter and with a longer shelf life – a berry more suited to big commerce. The search for a bigger berry that can be mechanically harvested, will sit on a supermarket shelf for days and impress with its size is bound to result in a fruit very different from the charming, richly flavoured berries I have occasionally picked from the wild, but it is an ingredient I would hate to be without. I admit to buying long-haul imports in a way I would never think of with a raspberry or strawberry. Once the American harvest is over, those of New Zealand, Poland, Mexico and Chile come on line. Our own harvest appears in July and August, my favourite variety being Herbert.

The blueberry is rich in tradition and folklore. Just as the Scots gathered the wild fruit from the heaths, so the Native Americans picked it from their forests and bogs. The calyx forms a five-pointed star, which the elders believed was a sign that the fruit had been sent by the Great Spirit to halt famine. Tea was made from its leaves and used to strengthen the blood, while its juice was used as a cough medicine. All this before we knew of the blue pigments – anthocyanins – so rich in anti-oxidant properties. Most importantly, blueberries were dried and stored for winter food. The dried blueberry can be used in place of currants, if a little expensively. But it has a distinctive sharpness and I like it as part of a breakfast granola. I cannot remember a day when I did not eat at least a handful of these little blue berries.

Blueberries in the garden

Blueberries thrive on the acid soils also loved by other members of the Ericaceae family – heathers, azaleas and rhododendrons. An alkaline soil will send them into a deep sulk. You can change the soil around them for an ericaceous one or add pine needles and sulphur to your existing soil, but they might do better in a pot, where you can easily control the pH levels.

The bushes demand not only a low-pH soil (5.5 or below) but plenty of sunshine to ripen and more than a little water. And not just any old water either. Tap water is too alkaline for them; only rainwater will do. These needs met, the bushes will reward you handsomely throughout late summer. Deciduous and woody stemmed, the blueberry is generally one of the longer-lived fruit bushes.

The blossom, bell shaped and similar to that of heather, is often flushed with rose pink and appears in early spring. Like some apples and cherries, many varieties need a suitable mate and a good local bee population if they are to produce fruit. You can expect somewhere between 120 and 150 days from blossom to ripe fruit.

We have grown the fat blueberry in the UK since it was introduced from Canada in the 1930s, a 'highbush' variety easier to harvest than the very hardy low bushes. A couple of bushes in pots outside the back door won't keep you in pies but are enough for a late-summer treat, at least that's what mine are.

Varieties

All need a wet, acidic soil of pH 4 to 5.5. You can check this with a little device available at most garden centres.

Berkeley An early- to mid-season berry with large fruits and plenty of flavour. The colour is pale and rather elegant. You will need another variety to ensure pollination.

Bluecrop Possibly the most popular variety in the world. A vigorous, upstanding bush producing light, medium-sized fruits for a total of five or six weeks.

Coville Moderate yields from a large bush. A favourite of blueberry specialist Jeremy Trehane, who describes its flavour as 'perfumed'.

Duke Short bushes, large fruit, a little late and great flavour. A very popular and vigorous variety with the supermarkets because of the firmness of its fruits, this one often does well in the north.

Early Blue One of the earliest to ripen, producing large, softly hued berries on upright bushes. Best in a protected site to reduce the risk of damage from early frosts.

Bluetta Compact bush with early blossom. Few varieties can be relied on for an earlier crop.

Chandler A vigorous variety producing heroically large fruits.

Herbert An exceptional large, late berry and one of my favourites.

Nelson Hardy and self-fertile. Well flavoured.

Top Hat A short, squat, late-cropping bush with glorious autumn colour. Unusual in that it is self-fertile and doesn't need a mate.

Spartan A useful variety that doesn't mind the cold, has large fruit of good flavour and attractive autumn foliage.

Blueberries in the kitchen

To look across the undulating surface of a blueberry pie, its swollen tump, its edges oozing violet juice, is to witness one of the glories of home baking. I have used the fruit in a crumble too, where they make a lavish gesture though never quite hit the heights of one made with gooseberries or sharp plums.

This is the fruit with which to make a rib-sticking cobbler. The scone-like crust of sugar, flour, butter and soured cream sits biscuit-like on the surface, whilst underneath collecting the vivid juice like a sponge. Less successful in fools and syllabubs because its mildness just cannot do battle with the cream, this diminutive fruit works admirably in the cosseting crumbs of a cake. I toss them into muffins too, and cupcakes, and make a thick sauce for cheesecake.

The little baubles tend to collapse in a pie, and a tender pastry crust, so fragile it crumbles with the merest pressure, seems more appropriate than a crisp one. That said, a flaky strudel pastry can be pleasing, even more so if you can keep the bottom layer crisp (getting your baking sheet hot in the oven before sliding the raw strudel on to it is a good start).

Blueberries take very little time to cook. In a pan with sugar and a spoonful of water they take less than ten minutes to reveal their treasure. Under a crust, they will be soft long before the pastry is the colour of a biscuit. As soon as the skin bursts, you get a clearer understanding of what this once-wild berry is all about.

It is in those moments when my blood sugar drops that *Vaccinium corymbosum* truly comes into its own. A fat handful in the blender with a dollop of goat's yoghurt, a scoopful of whey protein and enough goat's milk or water to produce a result thin enough to find its way into a glass will produce a smoothie to save your life.

Blueberries and...

Yoghurt Sharp dairy produce such as natural yoghurt and crème fraîche will bring out the flavour more successfully than sweet double cream.
Cream cheeses and mascarpone Can be used as a base for blueberry cheesecakes or in a frosting for cupcakes.
Oats Oatmeal and rolled oats have an affinity with both the cultivated berry and particularly the sharper wild berries. A warm oatcake spread with cream cheese and a scattering of berries is a snack that works on many levels.
Lemon juice Even the smallest amount will make the berries' flavour shout a little louder.
Game Pigeon, pheasant and partridge are appealing with a little puddle of blueberries that have been cooked with sugar and a dash of lemon juice. Or try adding them to the pan juices when you make the gravy.

* Avoid adding manure around the bushes as it may scorch their roots.
* Never let the plants dry out, especially when they are grown in pots.
* Blueberries often have a slight flash of olive green to them, and will darken and wrinkle as they age.
* This is one of the very few fruits I freeze. Whizzed with yoghurt, the straight-from-the-freezer berry makes a glorious breakfast smoothie.
* In 2010 supermarket sales of the blueberry overtook those of the strawberry for the first time.
* Blueberries are just plain wrong with fish of any sort. Whatever anyone says.

Venison with blueberries

I like game birds and venison with berries. The addition is a mild one, yet entirely relevant. The birds may well have eaten wild blueberries, or blaeberries as they are sometimes known, and their dark, woodsy flesh works well with the sweetness of the berries. This is one of the few savoury uses of the blueberry I have enjoyed.

enough for 2
black peppercorns – 12
thyme – the leaves of 3 small sprigs
a little olive oil
venison steaks – 4
port – 75ml (you could use Madeira or dry marsala instead)
blueberries – 150g
redcurrant jelly – 2 heaped tablespoons
butter – 30g

Roughly crush the peppercorns and thyme leaves with a pestle and mortar, add half a teaspoon of salt and just enough olive oil to form a rough paste, then rub into the venison. Get a shallow pan hot. Lay the oiled venison in the pan and leave for four or five minutes. Turn over and cook the other side. Ideally, the venison should be nicely browned on the surface and rare within. Remove to warm plates.

Pour the port into the pan, stirring in any crusty or sticky bits left by the meat. Let it boil down by half, then add the blueberries and the redcurrant jelly. Continue boiling till the fruits start to burst and the pan juices turn purple. Stir in the butter, taste for seasoning, then spoon the sauce over the venison steaks.

Cassis jelly with blueberries and crème fraîche

Cassis has always been my favourite of the fruit liqueurs – uplifting, rejuvenating, a sort of adult Ribena. We make a good version in Britain, too. As with most of my jellies, this is designed to be soft, and tends to slouch rather than stand to attention on the spoon. Don't even think of putting it in a mould.

enough for 4
leaf gelatine – 12g
fruity red wine – 400ml
cassis liqueur – 200ml
sugar – 2 tablespoons
blueberries – 200g
crème fraîche and more blueberries, to serve

Put the gelatine, sheet by sheet (rather than in one solid block), into a bowl of cold water and leave to soften. It should be ready in about five minutes.

Pour the wine into a small stainless steel saucepan and stir in the cassis and sugar. Place over a low heat and stir till the sugar has dissolved. Don't let it boil. Lift the gelatine from the water and drop it into the warm wine, stirring gently until it has totally dissolved. Put the blueberries into four small glasses, pour over the jelly and set aside to cool, then refrigerate till set (about four hours).

Serve with a small bowl of crème fraîche and another of blueberries.

Blueberry pie

When you push the soft crust with your knife, the purple juice gushes to the surface like blood from a deep cut, staining the sugar-frost coating. The flavours here are untaxing, a different thing altogether from a blackcurrant pie with its loud, piercing ring. I choose a soft pastry, too tender to transfer from tart tin to plate in one piece. More of a shortcake really.

enough to serve 6 generously

for the filling
blueberries – 500g
lemon juice – 2 tablespoons
cornflour – 1 generously heaped tablespoon
redcurrant jelly – 1 heaped tablespoon

for the crust
butter – 150g
golden caster sugar – 150g, plus a little more to scatter over the top
plain flour – 250g
baking powder – 1 teaspoon
an egg, beaten
a little milk, or beaten egg and milk, to finish

Set the oven at 180°C/Gas 4 and put a baking sheet in it (this will help keep the base of the pie crisp). Lightly butter a 24cm shallow metal pie plate. Put the blueberries into a bowl with the lemon juice, cornflour and redcurrant jelly. Toss gently to mix, then set aside.

Cream the butter and sugar in a food mixer till pale and fluffy, pushing the mixture down the sides of the bowl from time to time with a rubber spatula. Sift the flour and baking powder together. Incorporate the egg, a little at a time, into the butter and sugar mixture, adding a little flour if it starts to curdle. Mix in the flour and baking powder to form a soft dough.

Flour the work surface generously. Bring the dough together to form a ball, then knead lightly for a minute. Cut into two equal pieces and roll one out to fit the base of the pie plate. Line the dish with the pastry, taking care to push the dough well into the corners and to leave some overhanging.

Add the filling. Roll out the remaining pastry. Brush the edge of the pastry lining the dish with a little milk or beaten egg and milk, then lower the pastry lid on top. Press the edges to seal, trim any overhanging pastry and cut two small holes in the top (if you don't, the pastry may split). Brush with a little milk or beaten egg and milk and scatter lightly with sugar.

Bake on the hot baking sheet for forty minutes or so, till golden. Allow to calm down a little before serving.

Blueberry batter pudding

Batter pudding, the French clafoutis, is one of the few hot puddings that are acceptable in high summer. Possibly because, like quiche, it is traditionally served warm rather than hot. Though cherries are more traditional, I find this pudding works exceptionally well with blueberries, their tart purple-blueness seeping into the quivering egg custard.

Blueberries

788

> *enough for 4–6*
> eggs – 4
> plain flour – 75g
> caster sugar – 80–90g
> single cream – 250ml
> full-cream milk – 225ml
> blueberries – 300g
> icing sugar and cream, to serve

Set the oven at 200°C/Gas 6. Butter an ovenproof dish about 25cm in diameter.

Whiz the eggs, flour, caster sugar, cream and milk together in a blender or food processor, or beat them all together with a hand-held whisk. Tip the fruit into the dish, pour over the batter, then bake for about forty minutes, till the batter is lightly risen, golden and just firm to the touch. Dust with icing sugar and serve with cream.

Blueberry yoghurt smoothie

An alternative and slightly more substantial version of this can be had by adding a couple of scoops of whey protein in place of the banana.

> *enough for 1*
> blueberries – 100g
> a medium-sized banana
> yoghurt – 5 tablespoons
> juice of an orange

Drop everything into a blender and blitz till smooth. You can add ice cubes, if you like, to make a longer drink.

A quick blueberry fool

Sometimes fools can be almost as simple as stirring fruit into cream.

enough for 4
blueberries – 300g (plus some for decoration)
caster sugar – 3 tablespoons
double cream – 200ml
thick yoghurt – 150g

Put the berries in a small pan and add the sugar and 2 tablespoons of water. Put over a low heat and simmer for five minutes. Crush the berries with a fork, then let them cool.

Whip the cream till thick, then gently fold it into the cold fruits with the yoghurt. Leave to settle in the fridge for an hour or so, then serve decorated with blueberries.

Little blueberry pies

Again, the softest pastry, but this time for little pies. Sharp cream or thick yoghurt on the side would be appropriate.

makes 4

for the pastry
butter – 140g
plain flour – 230g
icing sugar – 50g, plus a little for dusting
a large egg yolk

for the filling
blueberries – 300g
redcurrant jelly – 3 tablespoons
juice of half a lemon
ground almonds – 60g

You will need four tartlet tins with removable bases, about 8cm in diameter. Rub the butter into the flour with your fingertips, then mix in the icing sugar and egg yolk. Bring the dough together and squeeze into a round, then roll into a short, fat log before putting it in the fridge for half an hour to chill. I find this pastry works well in the food processor too: first blitz the flour and butter, then mix briefly with the sugar and egg yolk.

Set the oven at 180°C/Gas 4. Rinse the fruit and toss it with the redcurrant jelly, lemon juice and ground almonds.

Cut the pastry into four. Flatten each piece on a floured board and use to line the tart tins. Leave the surplus pastry overhanging the edges. Pile the filling into the tart cases, then loosely fold over the overhanging pastry.

Place the tarts on a baking sheet and bake for twenty-five minutes, till the pastry is biscuit coloured and the fruit is bubbling. Dust with a little icing sugar and eat warm or cool.

Blueberry pancakes

Thick, soft pancakes about the size of a digestive biscuit and mottled with the juice of the warm blueberries.

enough for 4
ricotta cheese – 250g
caster sugar – 4 tablespoons
eggs – 3, separated
finely grated zest of an orange
melted butter – 2 tablespoons plus a little extra
plain flour – 50g
blueberries – 100g

In a large bowl, mix the ricotta, caster sugar and egg yolks together. Grate the orange zest into the bowl and stir it in gently with the melted butter. Sift in the flour and carefully fold in.

Beat the egg whites with a balloon whisk in a large bowl till stiff, then fold them lightly into the ricotta mixture. It is important not to knock the air out. Carefully fold in the blueberries.

Warm a non-stick frying pan over a moderate heat, brush it with a little butter, then place a heaped tablespoon of the mixture in the pan, followed by another two or three depending on the size of your pan. Let them cook for a minute or two till they have risen somewhat and the underside has coloured appetisingly, then, using a palette knife, flip them over to cook the other side. Do this as if you mean it, otherwise they will collapse as you turn them. A further couple of minutes' cooking, then serve immediately, hot from the pan.

Meringue with warm berry compote

An extravagant dessert for a special occasion. The inclusion of blackcurrants is to act as a contrast to the cream. I feel it is a necessary addition. Pour the fruits over at the very last minute before serving.

enough for 8–10
large egg whites – 5
golden caster sugar – 300g
white wine vinegar – a teaspoon
cornflour – 2 heaped teaspoons
vanilla extract
whipping or double cream – 400ml

for the fruit compote
a mixture of blackcurrants, blueberries and blackberries – 300g
sugar – 2 tablespoons or so, depending on the sweetness of your fruit

Set the oven at 180°C/Gas 4. Lightly oil a non-stick, loose-bottomed 20–21cm cake tin with almond oil, if you have it. If not, then use something similarly flavourless like groundnut. Dust the tin lightly with flour.

Beat the egg whites with a metal whisk until they stand in billowing, shiny folds. The easiest way is to use an electric food mixer with a whisk attachment. Beat in the sugar in two or three lots. Scatter over the vinegar and cornflour, then add a couple of drops of vanilla extract and fold in gently with a large metal spoon. Don't over-mix.

Scoop the lot into the prepared cake tin, smooth the top level and put straight into the oven. Immediately turn the heat down to 150°C/Gas 2. Leave the meringue to cook, without opening the door, for a full hour and ten minutes. If the top is getting brown, turn the heat down a little further. It should be a pale honey colour. Turn off the heat and let the meringue cool without opening the door. The marshmallow centre will sink and leave high, crisp sides.

Check the fruit over, removing any leaves or stems, put it in a stainless steel saucepan with the sugar and bring slowly to the boil. You shouldn't need any liquid, but if the fruit looks as if it is starting to stick, then add a tablespoon or two of water. When the fruit starts to burst, remove from the heat and allow to cool a little.

Beat the cream in a cold stainless steel bowl till it sits in soft folds. Pile it on top of the meringue. At the last moment, just before serving, spoon the fruit compote over the top.

Spelt and blueberry 'muffins'

Muffin makers will quickly spot that my blueberry muffin is a muffin only in looks, and bears little resemblance to the traditional recipe in either method or ingredients. In some ways, it is more like a cupcake (the butter and sugar are creamed together here, rather than the butter being melted and added at the end) and contains yoghurt rather than the more usual milk or buttermilk. The result is softer and slightly richer, and without the taste of raising agent that is a feature of many more traditional recipes. Enough pedantry. These are delightful little cakes, easily made and quick to bake.

makes 12
plain flour – 125g
wholemeal spelt flour – 125g
baking powder – 1½ teaspoons
bicarbonate of soda – ½ teaspoon
salt – ½ teaspoon
butter – 55g
golden caster sugar – 125g
large eggs – 2
vanilla extract – a teaspoon
yoghurt – 110g
blueberries – 220g
Demerara sugar and a few spoonfuls of rolled oats

Preheat the oven to 190°C/Gas 5. Place twelve paper muffin cases in a muffin tin. Sift together the flours, baking powder, bicarbonate of soda and salt.

Cream the butter and sugar together until pale in colour, scraping down the sides of the bowl with a rubber spatula as you go. Lightly beat the eggs and add slowly to the butter and sugar mixture, beating thoroughly. Add the vanilla extract, then mix in the yoghurt.

Gently add the sifted dry ingredients and continue mixing thoroughly. Fold in the berries. Drop the mixture into the paper cases, then scatter the tops with a little Demerara sugar and a few rolled oats.

Bake for twenty to twenty-two minutes, until a metal skewer or knitting needle inserted in the centre comes out clean. Let the muffins cool briefly in the tin, then place them on a cooling rack.

Cherries

Cherries bring with them a certain frivolity,
a carefree joy like hearing the far-off laughter
of a child at play. Their appearance, in deepest
summer, comes when life is often at its
most untroubled. A bag of cherries is a bag
of happiness.

Britain has always had wild cherry trees, the
'geans' and 'mazzards' much loved by the birds,
but it is only since the sixteenth century that we
have enjoyed the rich, black-skinned cultivated
fruits we have today. The British cherry season
lasts for six weeks at the height of summer, the
first appearing in the markets in late June with only the very late varieties
still around in the second week of August. Before and after this, our supplies
come from Turkey or the United States.

I often have a brown paper bag of cherries on my desk, picking at
them absentmindedly as I type. They provide an accompaniment to my
writing throughout July, like the slow ticking of a clock in the still heat of
the day. My heart gently skips when I find a pair joined at the stalk, like a
kid who has just been handed an ice cream. It is their crispness that makes
them so full of joy – that and their brilliant carmine juices that stain their
surroundings like blood splatter.

Cherries are perhaps at their most tempting when they come as a mixed
bag: the hue of canary feathers with the pink of seaside rock; deepest saffron
with cheeks of dark maroon; tarty scarlet; burgundy; inky purple-black. Yes,
the flavour is more upfront in the darker fruits, but too many at once can
cloy. The pale Rainier varieties have a more complex flavour, unmasked by
the heavy sugar of the blackest varieties. They have a freshness to them and
you are thankful for their lack of sweetness.

We probably have the Romans to thank for the cultivated cherry,
though it was Henry VIII's fruiterer – one Richard Harris – who established
the Kentish orchards and thus started the English cherry industry. At its
height in the 1950s, there were 7,000 hectares of cherry orchards in the

United Kingdom. Thirty years later, there were under 400. But there is the occasional ray of sunshine: horticulturists have recently bred trees on smaller rootstock, allowing the tall, inaccessible trees of the past to be replaced by shorter, more easily managed stock with fruit less precarious (for which read expensive) to harvest. That, and a concentrated media campaign to restore our interest in locally grown fruit, may ensure a future for the industry yet.

The sudden sight of a cherry orchard in flower, perhaps as you turn a corner on a twisting country lane in Kent, can take your breath away. The delicate blossom, all marshmallow froth, with petals fluttering butterfly-like in the breeze, is one to awake the child in us, like seeing poppies in a field of corn. Fuller than that of plum and damson, and occasionally a little saccharine in quantity, cherry blossom is one of the glories of the English countryside in April.

A cherry tree in the garden

For all its soft, pink blossom, a cherry tree can be a brute in a small garden, hogging space and light. Neither is it the most characterful of trees, often having an uninteresting trunk and straight, spreading branches. Little will survive under its heavy canopy of tightly packed leaves. Unless you net the tree to protect the fruit, the birds will get more cherries than you.

A popular choice for a smaller garden is those cultivars that can be grown against a wall. If there was a single spare length of bricks in my garden, it would be home to an espaliered cherry, its branches tied to long cables so that they are encouraged to grow horizontally rather than upwards. A long, low tree would be easier to net and the warmth from the wall would offer slight protection against frost and wind damage. Add to that the blossom and autumn leaf colour and I would have a fine addition to the garden.

There are only a few specialist growers in the UK, but their stock lists are fascinating, featuring varieties you are unlikely to find in any garden centre. They are the home of Napoleon and Montmorency, Guigne d'Annonay and Old Black Heart, varieties more unusual than the ubiquitous, though juicy, Stella. Nurseries such as Keepers in Kent specialise in traditional varieties and will grow an exceptionally rare one especially for you if you have the patience.

If you are thinking of buying a cherry tree for your garden, it is worth checking if it is self fertile. Many, particularly the older varieties, need a mate if they are to produce fruit. Check with your nursery. The compact, almost dwarfing trees from the new rootstocks are a possibility for the smaller garden.

A sour cherry such as a Morello will be happy grown in a little shade but a sweet cherry is best planted in full sun. Shelter is essential: the blossom arrives early and is often hit by frost. Vigilant gardeners will drape a piece of horticultural fleece over the branches on cold nights to protect the buds. What with frost and marauding birds, it is a wonder any cherries survive.

Varieties

The sour cherries
Morello Ancient and revered 'cooking' cherry that is ready for harvest in late summer and early autumn. The one to use in classic duck recipes. Self fertile, though the crop may be improved by having a pollinator.
Nabella Slightly earlier and more recently introduced than the Morello, but with similar acidic qualities.
Kentish Bush Late, red cooking cherry.
Montmorency Mid-season, acidic cherry that makes superb jam.
May Duke Red, mid-season fruit for cooking.

The sweet red and black cherries
Lapins Occasionally known as Cherokee, this late Canadian variety offers particularly sweet, dark red fruits. Self fertile.
Sunburst Early July fruiting. Large and almost black when ripe. This tree is often used as a pollinator for others.
Summer Sun Purple-fleshed, exceptionally sweet fruit. This late variety, which originates from Norfolk, has good frost tolerance.
Stella Sweet, prolific Canadian cherry that appears mid-season. The most popular variety, often found in supermarkets. Self fertile.
Noir de Guben Medium-sized, dull, dark-skinned fruit of moderately interesting flavour.
Burcombe A Cornish cherry with much sweetness and freshness of flavour.

The 'white' cherries
A more complex flavour.
Rainier Exceptionally sweet (for a pale cherry), yellow flesh with a pink flush. A much sought-after modern cross between Bing and Van. Capricious and likes a mild climate.
Summit Heart shaped, with sweet white flesh.
Merton Glory Early, yellow fruits with a pink tinge.
Napoleon Often known as Naps, a Kentish red-on-yellow variety, with plenty of sweetness and a fresh but complex flavour.
Whiteheart Sweet, late fruit. Needs a pollinator.

Also look out for:
Early Celeste, Early Rivers
Mid season Bradbourne Black, Hertford, Old Black Heart
Late Black Eagle, Tartarian, Florence, Noble, Sweetheart,
Turkish Black, Van

Cherries in the kitchen

Cherry jam can be glorious: the colour of Beaujolais, glistening on the
spoon, its texture barely firm enough to hold a shape. Good for breakfast
with brown wheaty toast; on warm, diminutive scones; trapped between
the layers of a Victoria sponge. A cherry pie can be worth the trouble too,
especially with soft, sugar-dusted pastry and a river of unpasteurised cream
running slowly over its warm crust. Even a duck leg, its skin roasted to a
crisp, served with a sauce made from its roasting juices, sharp Morellos and
redcurrant jelly is worth a thought. But there are few other reasons to cook
with a cherry.

That duck needs cinnamon and nutmeg added to a stock made from
its bones and giblets, a dash of port and a knob of butter whisked in at the
end to give it body and a bit of gloss. Elizabeth David describes a dish of
duck with cherries, where the pot-roasted duck has its cooking juices set in
a terrine with stewed cherries, which is then served in squares with the duck.
A terrible faff of a dish, which she describes as a simple version of the classic
canard à la Montmorency.

Then there is the showy dessert, cherries Jubilee, invented by Escoffier
in honour of Queen Victoria's jubilee, where the fruits are flambéed with
kirsch and spooned over ice cream. A recipe now on the culinary scrap pile.
Cherry clafoutis, the sweet batter pudding so beloved of French country
restaurants (and even more so of French country cookbooks) often seems to
look better than it tastes, and I feel is somehow one of those formulas that
only succeed in French hands. Yet none of these classical recipes grabs me
the way a bag of cherries on their stems does.

Cherries dull with age, keeping their lip-gloss looks for only a few days
after picking. A glossy cherry is a fresh cherry. It is difficult to prolong the
look, but they can be kept at their best by storing them in the fridge and
spraying them with a fine mist sprayer every day. Once they have lost their
shine, their crispness is next to go, but they will still be fit for jam.

The joy of cherries is their juice, but it can also be their downfall. Once
they burst, or are split to remove their stones, the juice seeps out like blood
from a cut. The purple juices can sabotage the crispest pie crust and turn a
cake's crumbs to mush. I get round the pastry problem by giving my pie
a top crust only, rather than one underneath as well. If you insist on a
two-crust version, then scatter cornmeal over the base to protect it before

you tip in the fruit. Even then, there will be some sogginess, as anyone knows who has been tempted by a cherry strudel in one of Vienna's swirls'n'drapes cafés.

A handful of cherries can be a startling find in a salad. Halved and stoned, a few sweetly tart Sunburst or Lapins introduce a sharp contrast to the tarry notes of smoked ham or mackerel. Even better, I think, is a salad where they meet crisp lettuce and duck skin, the fruit slicing neatly through the rich, dark fibres of the duck.

Pie aside, the most famous recipe is probably cherry soup. I know that someone, somewhere makes a bowl worth supping but I have yet to bump into them. Most recipes are little more than cherry yoghurt. The real thing – *meggyleves* – is Hungarian, made with sour rather than sweet cherries (a popular mistake) and soured cream, sweetly seasoned with cloves and cinnamon. I have always thought it sounded glorious. Curiously, in all my trips to Budapest I have yet to see it anywhere.

Cherries and...

Cinnamon Sweet, warm and musky, the notes of finely ground cinnamon will add depth to a chocolate and cherry cake. Whole cinnamon sticks add a particularly subtle note when tucked into the syrup of a cherry compote.

Chocolate Something of a perfect marriage. Cherries have an affinity with chocolate like no other fruit. The arrangement can be as spare as the fruit being dipped into molten dark chocolate and left to set into a crisp shell or as sophisticated as an almost-liquid filling for a rich cake. Dried cherries go surprisingly well with white chocolate, their acidity slicing neatly through the intense sweetness of the candy.

Game Woodsy, dense meats contrast successfully with raw, bright-tasting cherries. I find they work best in a salad, though you could add the fruit to the roasting juices if the idea appealed. Pigeon, duck and quail work well.

Ham Smoked meats can be cheered up by a few well-placed cherries. I bring them together in a salad, scattering the stoned fruits in amongst layers of thinly sliced smoked ham and salad leaves.

Tongue Of all meats, tongue has the most natural affinity with cherries. The sharp fruits lift the mild, almost creamy flavour of the meat and prevent it from cloying. A sauce or pickle made from the fruit, seasoned with cinnamon or juniper, is the most usual way to bring these two ingredients together, though a handful of the stoned fruits tucked amongst the leaves of tongue salad is a more straightforward approach.

Goat's cheeses The raw fruit forms an exciting partnership with clean, chalk-white cheeses with a smack of acidity. A plate of chèvre and cherries is a beautifully understated way to bring a summer lunch to a close.

Almonds Most famously paired in a classic cherry and almond tart, the nut can also be toasted and scattered over a plate of poached cherries or ground and included in the crust of a crumble.

* When shopping for cherries, look for green stalks rather than brown ones. They are a sign of a young, recently picked crop.
* Pick the fruit by the stalks rather than risk bruising the flesh.
* Where strawberries and raspberries are best served at room temperature, or even slightly warm from the sun, cherries seem more interesting when chilled, or even served on a plate of crushed ice. The cold tightens their skins and makes them all the more crisp and refreshing.
* Cherries keep longer with their stalks intact.
* The fruit's skin dulls as it becomes overripe.
* Cherries cooked with their stones in often appear to have more flavour. The stones have subtle almond notes, which are particularly noticeable when the fruit is are poached.
* The stones tend to polarise people. Some have no qualms about spitting a few out at the table, others can't be doing with it. I tend to stone them only as a last resort, and rather enjoy lining up the pips around the rim of my plate and playing 'tinker, tailor, soldier, sailor' with them. My feeling is that the stones are acceptable in a pie, less so in an almond tart. A pie where someone has take the time to stone the cherries is a great luxury and, despite the extra time involved, I always think, 'I am so glad I did that.'

A salad of summer leaves, cured pork and cherries

The sweet-sharp notes of the cherries lift the smoky, herbal notes of cured ham in the same way small tomatoes will. Air-dried hams such as Parma, mildly cured ones like speck and coppa or the paprika-spiced lomo or something exceptionally dark and woodsy will benefit from the uplifting quality of a handful of cherries. And yes, I think you must stone them for this.

enough for 2 as a light lunch
salad leaves – 4 generous handfuls
thinly sliced cured ham such as lomo, speck or coppa – 75–100g
cherries – 4 handfuls

for the dressing
Dijon mustard – a teaspoon
red wine vinegar – 2 teaspoons
olive oil – 50ml
double cream – 3 tablespoons
parsley – a little

Make the dressing: put the mustard in a small bowl with a pinch of salt, the red wine vinegar, olive oil and a grinding of black pepper. Mix with a fork or small whisk, then introduce the cream. Finely chop the parsley leaves and add to the dressing.

Toss the salad leaves with the cured ham. Halve and stone the cherries and add them to the leaves. Trickle over the dressing and serve.

Boiled smoked gammon with a sharp cherry sauce

There is a common theme in my cooking of a large ham joint served with a fruit-based sauce. Sweet ham, sharp sauce, it works on several levels: something easy to cook and carve for a group; a dish as enjoyable cold as it is hot; a good-natured dish that will keep till you need it. The cherry version is one for early summer, the meat cooked in apple juice, the cherries only lightly sweetened. Creamed spinach is good with this.

enough for 6
smoked gammon joint, rolled and tied – 2.5–3kg (boned weight)
apple juice – 500ml
water – 500ml
black peppercorns – 12
an onion, halved but not peeled
bay leaves –2
cloves – 3

for the sauce
Morello cherries – 500g
sugar – 50g
juniper berries – 8
a bay leaf

Put the gammon joint in a large pan, pour over enough water to cover and bring to the boil. Carefully tip away the water. Pour the apple juice and water over the meat, then add the peppercorns, the halved onion, the bay leaves and cloves and bring to the boil. Turn down the heat so that the liquid simmers gently and cover with a lid. Leave until the meat is cooked – it will need about two and a half hours. The ham can remain in the cooking liquid until you need it.

To make the sauce, halve the cherries and remove their stones. Put them in a stainless steel or enamelled pan with the sugar, the lightly squashed juniper berries, bay leaf and 2 tablespoons of water. Bring to the boil, then lower the heat to a simmer. Leave for ten minutes or so, with the occasional stir. Turn off the heat and leave till needed.

To serve, slice the ham thinly and place on warm plates. Spoon the cherry sauce to the side.

A top-crust cherry pie

I have always had a soft spot for commercial cherry pie filling. Curiously, I prefer it to any pie made with fresh fruit, something I can only put down to nostalgia getting the better of good taste.

Fresh cherries need a little lemon juice if they are to shine under the crust of a pie. It also helps prevent them browning as you stone them. Sometimes I pit the cherries, sometimes I don't. It adds fifteen minutes or so to the preparation time and it makes a refreshing change to have a mouthful of cherries unaccompanied by their stones. That said, if you take the stoning route, be very thorough – there is no shock greater than hitting a rock-hard pip you weren't expecting.

enough for 4

for the pastry
230g plain flour
140g butter
50g icing sugar
1 large egg yolk

for the filling
1kg plump cherries
a squeeze of lemon juice
3 heaped tablespoons caster sugar, plus extra for sprinkling
2 tablespoons cornflour

Put the flour into a bowl, rub in the butter with your fingertips, then mix in the icing sugar and egg yolk. Bring the dough together and squeeze it into a round before putting it in the fridge for half an hour to chill. I find this pastry works well in the food processor too: first blitz the flour and butter, then mix briefly with the sugar and egg yolk.

Set the oven at 180°C/Gas 4. Pull the stalks from the cherries, dropping the fruit into a mixing bowl and squeezing over the lemon. Scatter the caster sugar and cornflour over the cherries and toss gently. Tip into a baking dish.

Roll or press out the pastry into a round. Lift it on the rolling pin and place it gently on top of the fruit. Cut two or three air holes in it, then bake for thirty minutes or so, until the pie is pale gold (start checking after twenty-five minutes). Remove from the oven, sprinkle with caster sugar and return to the oven for five or six minutes.

Leave the pie to cool a little before serving with a jug of double cream.

A cherry cheesecake

I am no stranger to the *Kaffee und Kuchen* tradition of Germany and Vienna.
As much as I like the claggy cheesecake in *The Kitchen Diaries* and the soft,
almost ice-cream-like quality of the damson one in this collection, I have
an interest, too, in the drier-textured cheesecakes you find in German cafés.
The lightness appeals to me, as do the lack of sweetness and the clean, fresh
note it leaves in the mouth. I take pleasure in pushing the open-textured
crumbs together with the tines of my fork. This is that cake.

You could make a moist cherry topping by warming the stoned and halved
fruit with a little sugar and water and thickening the resulting syrup with
cornflour or, for a less cloudy finish, arrowroot. I prefer to contrast the mild,
milky quality of the cake with fresh, tart and totally naked cherries.

enough for 8
ricotta – 500g
cream cheese or mascarpone – 200g
double cream – 150ml
caster sugar – 150g
lemons – 2
vanilla extract – a drop
eggs – 4
an egg yolk
cornflour – a heaped tablespoon
cherries – 450g

for the crumb crust
shortbread biscuits – 350g
butter – 90g

Preheat the oven to 180°C/Gas 4. Lightly butter a 20cm square cake tin.
Crush the biscuits to crumbs. I use the food processor for this, but it can
be done in a plastic bag with a well-aimed rolling pin. Melt the butter, add
the crushed biscuits and mix well. Tip the buttered crumbs into the cake tin
and pat down lightly. Refrigerate for half an hour, till the butter sets.

Put the ricotta, cream cheese or mascarpone, cream and sugar in a food
mixer and blend briefly. Add the finely grated zest and juice of the lemons,
the merest drop of vanilla extract, then the eggs and egg yolk. Lastly, blend
in the cornflour. Pour the mixture into the cake tin and slide into the oven.
Bake for fifty minutes to an hour, covering the top with foil if it is colouring
even slightly. Turn the heat off and leave the cake in the oven to cool.
Refrigerate overnight.

Halve the cherries and remove their stones. Scatter them over the top of
the cake and serve in small squares.

A clafoutis of cherries

Truth be told, I have never found this classic French dessert quite lives up
to its lofty reputation. It is nice enough – in a bohemian, slightly-too-much-
wine-at-lunch kind of a way – but the tart cherries in their overcoat of
warm, soft batter always feel something of a letdown.

As a result I have spent a long time working on the recipe that follows.
Straying only very slightly from the classic versions, it approaches what I
have always wanted this pudding to be.

enough for 4
cherries – 400g
butter – 70g
caster sugar – 80g
eggs – 2
plain flour – 90g
milk – 150ml
vanilla extract – a little
icing sugar for dusting

Set the oven at 180°C/Gas 4. Stone the cherries. It's a drag, but worth it.
Lightly butter a 20cm-diameter baking dish with a little of the butter, then
dust with a couple of tablespoons of the sugar. Tip in the cherries.

Put the rest of the sugar in a mixing bowl and beat in the eggs, flour,
milk and a drop or two of vanilla extract with a large balloon whisk. Melt
the rest of the butter in a small pan, then beat into the mixture.

Pour the batter over the cherries and bake for thirty-five minutes, till
puffed and golden. Test by inserting a skewer into the centre. If it comes out
damp but clean, then the pudding is done. Remove from the oven and dust
with icing sugar.

Chestnuts

Just look at the chestnuts. Plump shells, flat on one side and as shiny as a mahogany banister, tucked up like sleeping dormice in the chestnut's prickly burr. No other food protects itself quite as effectively as the sweet chestnut, with spikes so long and piercingly sharp you need a leather glove to lift them into your basket.

Late afternoon in November, almost dusk, you suddenly catch the far-off smell of smoke. As you get closer to its source, it is joined by the warm scent of roasting nuts. But you pass by, hurrying home or to the shops. The charcoal brazier, once a popular sight in city streets, is now rare, a quaint remainder of Dickensian times. The habit of eating warm roasted chestnuts from the bag has all but vanished here.

There are four species of chestnut, including the Japanese, the Chinese and the American. The only one that concerns us at the table is the European or 'sweet' chestnut, sometimes known as the Spanish chestnut. It is part of the beech family and its timber is as valuable as its fruits. The ancient name is castanea, a word that crops up in all manner of connections with chestnuts – in the Welsh name *Castan-wydden*, the Dutch *kastanje* and the French *châtaigne* – and in recipes too, including the flat Tuscan cake known as *castagnaccio*.

The tree is rather beautiful, with its saw-edged leaves and grey bark. The honey-coloured male catkins and the spiny green female ones are a familiar sight to anyone walking through the woods in late spring. The sweet odour is heavy and not to everyone's taste – indeed, the chestnut has fewer takers than our other native nuts, the walnut and hazel. I like them roasted, toasted and puréed, but the honey made from its blossom is a flavour too strong for me, with what I detect as distinct notes of cough linctus.

The fruits themselves are hidden inside a spiky shell similar to that of a conker or horse chestnut but with longer, thinner spines that genuinely hurt those who attempt to gather them. As the fruits inside mature, the burrs split open to reveal up to three polished nuts.

Free from their cases, the chestnuts are pleasing to roll over in your hand, like a particularly smooth pebble or the golden coin in a box of Quality Street. I like the fact that each end has a name: the pointed tuft is known as the 'flame', the dark, rectangular patch at the other end as the 'hilum'. (As a student, I remember being just as amused that even the sides of a house brick have their own names.)

The fruit has two skins, three if you count the green exterior. The first, called the 'peel', is polished and dark, the second – the pellicle – directly underneath, is a thin, slightly furry coating that clings tightly to the grooves in the fruit. Easy to remove in the fresh fruit, it gets more fiddly with age and often needs the application of water or heat before it can be peeled off. I have less of a problem with its presence than most and in some cases leave it be, unless I am eating my chestnuts raw.

The sweet chestnut originates from Asia Minor and has at one point or another been a staple food in Italy, Spain and Turkey. Even as late as the 1870s, it was almost the sole carbohydrate for short patches of the year in Tuscany. Pasta, polenta and bread were made from its flour, particularly in mountainous areas where cereals could not be grown. Those grown around the Mugello region are considered by some to be the sweetest. The main production area in France is situated in the Ardèche, with its famous appellation contrôlée, Châtaigne d'Ardèche. Many of the exquisitely wrapped French marrons glacés are in fact made with Italian-grown fruits. Our own chestnut groves are due to the Romans, who planted them wherever they went.

The green cases first appear in early summer and start to ripen from September onwards. As the nut ripens, the starch turns to sugar and the delicate notes of hazelnut and vanilla come into play. We eat them fresh and whole, either raw, steamed or roasted, but most are bought ready prepared and either vacuum packed or frozen. More often than not, the nut creeps softly into our kitchen in the form of a ready-made purée. This comes in cans or tubes and is sometimes ready sweetened.

A chestnut in the garden

Planning for a small town garden can leave you frustrated. There are always trees (and indeed bushes, vines and plants) that you simply don't have room for. The sweet chestnut was one that got 'red pencilled' at the planning stage. Despite the fact that you can keep the trees to a manageable size by coppicing, there just wasn't room. I include it here for those lucky enough to have a tree in their garden or nearby woodland.

Doubtless, my tree would never have reached the size of the famous 'Great Chestnut of Tortworth' in Gloucestershire, which by 1720 measured over 50 feet in circumference. Wild chestnut trees can be spotted in warm lowland areas, particularly in the south of the country. There are extensive sweet chestnut coppices in Kent and the surrounding counties, many protected by preservation orders. Several are temptingly for sale. The trees often go hand in hand with bluebells, the piercing green of the unfurling, saw-edged leaves and the joyous singing blue of the wild hyacinth being a heart-lifting sight in May.

The trees fruit best where they are in good light, so they tend to produce a more prolific crop on a single open tree than in a crowded coppice. Perhaps this is why the Italian nuts, though no less sweet, are far larger than our own.

The mature nuts begin to fall in October, the spiky shells being picked up from the grass beneath the tree canopy rather than pulled from the tree – tricky even with gardening gloves on. Each case will contain up to three nuts, with their distinctive one flat side where they have been nestling up against one another.

Chestnuts in the kitchen

I sometimes toast a few chestnuts on a cold winter's day just for the smell that fills the kitchen. I don't have a chestnut roaster – the flat iron pan with holes and a long handle to keep you away from the heat that is traditionally used for chestnut toasting. I cook mine in a frying pan, their skins pierced with a sharp knife to prevent them exploding and ricocheting round the kitchen, constantly shaking the pan to stop them scorching. They are ready when their shells crisp up, maybe a little scorched here and there – it's inevitable – and they have filled the kitchen with a deep, warm smell of roasted nuts.

Easy though it is to slit the skins with the point of a small, strong knife, you can soak them instead. Boil the kettle, pour the water into a heatproof bowl and leave the chestnuts to soak for a good thirty minutes. By that time, their skins will have softened enough to be easily peeled by hand.

Chestnut flour has a distinctive and rather strong flavour. I have never taken to it, detecting an almost medicinal quality to everything I have baked with it. Bread made with this particularly soft flour (it is like putting your hand into talcum powder) will keep for a good couple of weeks, but it is a heavy flour and does not allow the bread to rise. The Tuscan chestnut cake, *castagnaccio*, is one of the few cakes that I never found a soft spot for, despite the traditional inclusion of pine nuts, raisins and rosemary. Maybe I will learn to appreciate its many charms with age. Anyone with an air-drier may like to know that it is possible to dry the nuts, then grind them to flour in a food mill. The tawny flour is also used for pancakes and pasta (probably very good with a game stew) and was the original flour to use in polenta. The

Corsicans make it into little doughnut-style fritters called *fritelli*.

Chocolate cakes aside, the *raison d'être* of the chestnut is, for me, the plump, foil-wrapped marron glacé. To eat one after lunch on Christmas day, its tissue-paper-thin sugar crust sparkling in the candlelight, is to truly understand the meaning of the word 'sweetmeat'. I have seen them being made in France – where they have been produced since the sixteenth century – and watched with awe as they were packed into boxes, each pleated wrapping being folded by the packer's nimble fingers in what appeared to be one long, poetic movement. You can make them yourself if you fancy simmering the peeled fruits in sugar syrup and letting them dry a little before dipping them in gossamer-thin icing. They are popular in Turkey too, where they are known as *kestane sekeri*.

The most famous chestnut-related recipe is Mont Blanc, the luxurious confection of meringue, sweetened chestnut purée and whipped cream. I can't remember the last time I saw one on a menu. I have never understood how anyone could finish a meal with such a rich dessert, but it used to go down well with cups of dark, treacly coffee at the long-departed Swiss Centre in London's Leicester Square.

In the UK our only significant chestnut dish is that of stuffing for the Christmas bird. Usually a stir-up of day-old breadcrumbs, celery, chestnuts, bacon and butter, it is seasoned with rosemary and sage. Sometimes it contains sausage meat, other times eggs, and it can be cooked in a flat pan or inside the bird. Traditionalists are likely to put sausage meat at one end and chestnut stuffing at the other. I tend to blow hot and cold about the idea of Brussels sprouts and chestnuts. Sometimes I like it, other times I find it an odd match of textures.

Chestnuts and...

Mushrooms Nicely golden, a plump mushroom works well with this nut. Match them in a leafy salad or add a few chestnuts to a pan of sautéed fungi.
Bacon Sizzling rashers or cubes of pancetta have an affinity with the chestnut, as does thinly sliced air-cured ham with the roasted nuts.
Game and poultry The gamier meats such as pheasant, pigeon and partridge appreciate a chestnut or two included in their stuffing or in a sauce in which they are presented. Turkey and strongly flavoured free-range chicken, too.
Venison A stew of this lean, richly flavoured meat is often the home for a few roasted chestnuts.
Grapes Just as they love a walnut, so sweet grapes of any sort are partial to a chestnut. In a salad perhaps, with bacon or smoked ham, or simply sharing a plate at the end of a meal.
Greens Sprouts and the darker members of the cabbage family such as cavolo nero can work splendidly with toasted chestnuts.
Chocolate The darkest chocolate, at least 80 per cent cocoa solids, seems to work particularly well with a sweetened chestnut purée. Anything less becomes a little sickly.
Vanilla A heaven-sent combination, especially when the sweetened purée is lightly flavoured with a few drops of the best extract.

* A kilogram of chestnuts in their shells will yield approximately 700g shelled nuts.
* This nut contains virtually no fat and its flour is free of gluten.
* A roasting chestnut whose skin has not been slashed will inevitably explode as the fruit inside expands, resulting in a hot nut ricocheting around the kitchen, sending little bits of shrapnel flying round the room.
* The Portuguese have a chestnut liqueur that I have never tried.

To roast chestnuts

Score the fruits with a sharp knife, piercing through the skin but stopping before you reach the kernel. One shallow incision on the flat side is usually easiest. The skin is less tight here than on the other side. Drop them into a dry frying pan, and leave till the shells have darkened, shaking occasionally. The nuts are ready when they are soft and fudgy inside.

To peel chestnuts

Use a short, sharp knife (or better still a Stanley knife) to cut a small slit in the flat side of the shell of each chestnut. Put them into a heatproof bowl. Pour over a kettleful of boiling water and leave for thirty minutes. Remove the chestnuts from the water and peel away the outer shell and as much of the brown skin as you can. The chestnuts are now ready to add to a casserole.

Chestnut purée

You may feel that life is too short to purée your own chestnuts, a task that involves piercing the shells, roasting, peeling, then poaching the nuts in sugar syrup before pushing them through a fine vegetable mill or potato ricer. I have to say I would agree with those whose think this is a lot of work for even the most committed of cooks, compared with unscrewing the top of a tube of the ready-made stuff.

> chestnuts – 1kg
> golden caster sugar – 100g
> water – 250ml
> a vanilla pod, split in half

Make a small slit in each chestnut with the point of a sharp knife. Roast them at about 200°C/Gas 6 for fifteen minutes, then cool slightly before peeling.

Make a light syrup by dissolving the sugar in the water over heat, adding the vanilla, then using it to poach the chestnuts for thirty minutes till tender. Drain the chestnuts and pass them through a food mill. The endlessly useful mouli-légumes is the one, or if not, a potato ricer. A food processor is likely to turn them to glue. Cool and sweeten to taste.

A casserole of parsnips, chestnuts and mushrooms

Some good stock is called for here. If it is close to Christmas, the turkey bones simmered with bay and onion will give a suitably rich liquor. If you want to keep meat out of it altogether, then a vegetable stock will work admirably as long as it has plenty of flavour. This is also the recipe in which to use up your ends of Christmas marsala, Madeira or sherry when you add the stock.

Some brown basmati rice, steamed with a cinnamon stick, a clove or two and some black peppercorns, would be good here to soak up the juices. Couscous is another possibility.

enough for 4, with rice
onions – 2
butter – a thick slice
rosemary needles – 2 teaspoons, finely chopped
juniper berries – a teaspoon, lightly bashed
small carrots – 4
large parsnips – 4
celery ribs – 2
small cup mushrooms – 125g
peeled chestnuts – 150g
plain flour – 2 tablespoons
good hot stock (vegetable, chicken or turkey) – 750ml
bay leaves – 2
redcurrant jelly – 2 tablespoons

Peel the onions, then cut them in half from root to tip and slice each half into six segments. Put them in a deep, heavy-based saucepan with the butter, rosemary and juniper berries and leave over a moderate heat till the onions are deep gold and soft enough to crush between finger and thumb. It is important to let them become golden and sticky; much flavour will come from this. They will need an occasional stir.

Scrub the carrots and parsnips and chop into pieces roughly the size of a wine cork, then add them to the pan. Thinly slice the celery and halve the mushrooms. Stir them into the other vegetables together with the chestnuts and leave to colour very lightly. You may need to add a little more butter or some oil at this point. When the parsnips' edges are starting to turn a deep gold, scatter the flour over and continue cooking for a few minutes, then pour in the hot stock. Season with salt and black pepper, add the bay leaves and bring to the boil. Lower the heat and leave to simmer for twenty minutes.

Stir in the redcurrant jelly and taste for seasoning. Simmer briefly till the jelly has melted, then serve with brown rice.

Chestnut, sausage and marsala stuffing

There is a moment, usually on Boxing Day, when I stand and eat a doorstop sandwich. It is often the best sandwich of the year. Made with white bread, layers of thinly sliced, generously salted roast turkey, crisp bacon and thinly sliced stuffing. Coarse-textured and thoroughly seasoned stuffing is essential to what I regard as one of the glories of Christmas.

onions – 2
butter – a thick slice
thyme – a large sprig or two
rosemary – a large sprig
sausage meat – 400g
fresh breadcrumbs – 3 handfuls
cooked peeled chestnuts (boiled or roasted) – 50g, roughly chopped
Madeira or dry marsala – a wine glass

Peel and cut up the onions just short of finely chopped (this is a rough-textured stuffing, but you don't want the pieces so big that the mixture falls apart). Melt the butter in a saucepan, add the onions and let them soften and colour lightly, stirring from time to time. Whilst they are cooking, strip the leaves from the thyme and stir them in. Remove the needles from the rosemary twig and chop them finely. Stir them into the onions.

When the onions are soft enough to crush between finger and thumb, add the sausage meat, breadcrumbs, chestnuts and the Madeira or marsala. Season generously with salt and black pepper. Shape the stuffing into balls slightly larger than a golf ball and set them in a buttered or foil-lined baking dish (they can remain here for a day or so, refrigerated, until you need them). Bake for about thirty minutes at 180°C/Gas 4, till sizzling.

Mushrooms, chestnuts and bacon

A light, late-autumn salad of hot bacon, mushrooms and chestnuts. I have made this with curly frisé and young spinach and both worked well. The spinach leaves tend to soften deliciously under the heat of the mushrooms, the frisé stays crisp. The choice is ours.

enough for 4
streaky bacon – 8 rashers
groundnut or vegetable oil – 4 tablespoons
butter – a thin slice
medium-sized mushrooms – 350g
garlic – a juicy clove, peeled and crushed
peeled chestnuts – 250g
salad leaves – 4 handfuls

Cut the bacon into pieces about the size of a large postage stamp. Warm the oil in a large frying pan, add the butter and then the bacon. Once the bacon fat is golden, lift out and set aside on kitchen paper. Cut the mushrooms in half and add to the pan together with the garlic and chestnuts. Let them cook over a moderate heat, soaking up the bacon-flavoured fat, until pale gold.

Divide the salad leaves between four plates and tip the bacon, chestnuts and mushrooms over them, together with any cooking juices from the pan.

Brussels sprouts and chestnuts

You either feel this classic use for the chestnut is an abomination or consider it an essential and unmissable part of the Christmas feast. Whichever way you lean, here is a really good version with bacon fat and masses of butter.

enough for 4
peeled chestnuts – 100g
milk – 200ml
butter – 75g
bacon – 2 rashers, or even a little bacon rind
Brussels sprouts – 500g

Put the peeled chestnuts into a pan with the milk, simmer for fifteen to twenty minutes, until tender, then drain. Melt the butter in a shallow pan, add the bacon or bacon rind and the drained chestnuts and leave to cook over a low heat. The butter must not colour.

Cook the sprouts in deep, very lightly salted, ferociously boiling water till just tender – a matter of three or four minutes, depending on the size of your sprouts. Drain them thoroughly, then toss gently in the bacon-flavoured butter. I like to add a little black pepper at this point, coarsely milled.

Red cabbage with chestnuts and sherry

The list of vegetables appropriate for Christmas lunch is not long. Red cabbage is one of them and I usually make a dish of it, often cooked with apple and cider, to pass round with the goose. Chestnuts have an affinity with any of the brassica family and especially, I think, with red cabbage.

> *enough for 4–6 as a side dish*
> half a good-sized red cabbage – about 750g
> a little groundnut oil
> pancetta or bacon in the piece – 200g
> peeled chestnuts – 150g
> medium sherry – a glass

Shred the cabbage finely, then rinse and drain. Heat a couple of tablespoons of oil in a large saucepan, roughly dice the pancetta and add to the pan, letting it colour lightly. Add the chestnuts, continue cooking for a few minutes, then add the drained red cabbage. Expect it to hiss and pop. Turn the cabbage in the fat and cover with a lid. Continue cooking over a moderate heat for seven or eight minutes, until the cabbage has wilted slightly. Add the sherry, a little salt (depending on how salty the bacon is) and leave until almost evaporated. Serve immediately.

A chocolate and chestnut terrine

A seriously rich recipe to be enjoyed in thin slices. You will get a good eight or even ten portions from this cake.

enough for 8–10

for the cake
butter – 250g
golden caster sugar – 225g
self-raising flour – 225g
baking powder – 2 teaspoons
cocoa powder – 30g
eggs – 4
milk – 80ml
hot espresso coffee – 3 tablespoons

for the chestnut and chocolate filling
dark chocolate (79 per cent cocoa solids) – 250g
butter – 125g
chestnut purée – 400g
caster sugar – 2 tablespoons

to finish
10–12 cooked or candied chestnuts
dark chocolate – 250g

You will need a 20cm square cake tin lined with baking parchment and a 20cm x 9cm loaf tin or similar for shaping the cake (measurements are taken across the bottom of the tins).

Set the oven at 160°C/Gas 3. Cut the butter into small dice and put into a food mixer with the caster sugar. Beat till light and fluffy. Sift together the flour, baking powder and cocoa powder (don't miss this step; it is really important that the dry ingredients are well mixed). Crack the eggs into a small bowl, beat them briefly to mix, then stir in the milk.

Introduce the flour mixture and the eggs and milk to the butter and sugar, adding a little of each at a time, with the mixer going constantly till you have a smooth mixture. Finally mix in the coffee.

Spoon the mixture into the lined square cake tin and smooth the top, then bake for forty-five to fifty minutes, till risen and firm to the touch. Test with a metal skewer. If it comes out moist but clean, without any raw cake mixture stuck to it, then it is ready. Remove from the oven, leave to settle for fifteen minutes, then run a palette knife around the edges and gently turn out on to a cooling rack. Peel off the baking parchment.

Make the chestnut and chocolate filling. Break the chocolate into small pieces and melt it in a glass or china bowl set over a pan of simmering water. Do not stir, other than to push any unmelted chocolate down into the liquid chocolate. Turn the heat off as soon as the chocolate is melted. Cut the butter into small pieces and stir it gently into the chocolate until it has melted.

Beat the chestnut purée with the sugar until well mixed, then fold gently into the melted chocolate and butter. Try not to over mix. Set aside.

Cut the cake in half to make two long pieces. Slice each half in two horizontally and trim to fit the loaf tin. Place a piece of cake in the base of the tin, add half the chocolate chestnut cream and smooth the top. Place a second piece of sponge on top, followed by the rest of the chestnut cream. Place a third and final piece of cake on top. (You will be left with one remaining piece, which I suggest you freeze for later or nibble at will.)

Wrap the entire loaf tin in cling film, pressing down firmly to encourage the layers to stick together. Refrigerate for at least two hours.

Remove the cling film, loosen the cake from the sides of the tin with a palette knife and turn it out on to a wire rack. Place the chestnuts along the top if you are using them. Melt the chocolate as before, then pour it over the top of the cake, smoothing it over the sides. Leave to set before serving.

Chestnut meringue

Monté Bianco, Mont Blanc, call it what you will. Named after the mountain that stands over the Aosta Valley in Italy and the Haute-Savoie region of France, this is a sweet mountain of meringue, chestnut purée and cream, and is still the signature dish of the Angelina café in Paris where it was, reputedly, invented (some prefer the location as Jiyugaoka in Japan). I cannot think of a more long-winded ending to a meal – meringue shells to be baked, chestnuts to be roasted and then laboriously puréed, cream to be whipped and finally the whole thing assembled to resemble the eponymous mountain. Shortcuts have been known to involve store-bought meringue shells, tins of sweetened chestnut purée and squirty cream.

I would sit on the fence, insisting on homemade meringue, but using ready puréed chestnuts. At the risk of getting my wrists well and truly slapped by traditionalists, I coat mine with a crisp web of melted chocolate. A snowfall of icing sugar, to represent the mountain peaks, is *de rigueur*.

enough for 6–8

for the meringue
egg whites – 4
a pinch of salt
caster sugar – 250g

for the filling
double cream – 250ml
sweetened chestnut purée (or the chestnut purée on page 818) – 500g
icing sugar
dark, bitter chocolate – 150g

Set the oven at 140°C/Gas 1. Put the egg whites and salt into a bowl and whisk till soft peaks form. Beat in half the sugar, in short stages, until glossy and thick. Fold in the remaining sugar with a large metal spoon (a wooden one tends to knock the air out). Spoon the mixture on to a baking sheet lined with non-stick baking paper, making rounds approximately 2cm high and 10cm in diameter. Flatten the tops slightly. Bake in the preheated oven for roughly an hour, until they are crisp but still chewy within.

To assemble, whisk the cream till thick. It should just form soft, rolling peaks. Spoon it on to the meringues. Place the chestnut purée in a bowl with a tablespoon of icing sugar and beat till smooth (it will inevitably be a little grainy; that is the nature of the beast). Mound the purée on top of the cream, or more correctly push it through a mouli-légumes to achieve a lighter, open mass. Melt the chocolate in a basin over simmering water, then trickle in thin stripes over the chestnut and meringue. Dust with icing sugar.

Damsons

Few trees offer such delicate blossom or as charming a fruit, dangling from the tree's fine twigs in early autumn like dusty, violet-black bonbons. In late September, as their short season draws to a close, you may still find a handful of bloom-covered damsons amongst the turning yellow leaves – a particularly poetic moment for any gardener or cook. The trees are self fertile, so you can stick one in a far corner of the garden and in a year or two it will give you enough fruit for a crumble. I planted one almost as soon as I had signed the deeds.

Damsons are ripe in early September, at a time when the garden paths are festooned with spiders' webs and the leaves start their slow journey towards gold and bronze. A time of faint melancholy and mellow scents, of early marrows, fat pears and late, spiky dahlias. At no point in the calendar am I happier. Damsons mark the point in the year when I start to relax, my shoulders unhunch, I can begin to feel the safety of dark nights and damp mornings, the supreme comfort of a favourite, holey jumper. Just as so many are saddened at the end of the summer, I feel curiously rejuvenated, my sap rising as others' does in the spring. Different strokes for different folks.

I value the damson principally for its glorious, inky juice. The sort that seeps into the crust of a crumble or leaves swirls of darkest indigo in custard or cream. The trees that you come across in old gardens and hedgerows are laden with nostalgia for me, their crop – in pies, jam and tender-crusted tarts – being the single best thing about my country adolescence. To run my fingers through a box of tiny, dusty damsons, the occasional stray leaf amongst them, is as much a marker of the year's passing as the summer solstice or the Midnight Mass on Christmas Eve.

The damson is named after Damascus in Syria, where it is suspected to have originated. In Britain it has been in decline since the Second World War. The lack of sugar available during rationing wreaked havoc on the damson industry – one the few fruits almost useless without the addition of sugar – and many ancient orchards were grubbed up. But there is still a white froth of blossom to be seen in April, covering the hedges of what used to be known as Westmorland, now part of Cumbria.

The Westmorland damson is probably the best known of all these marble-sized plums (the fruit has been grown there commercially since at least the 1700s), though it grows well in Shropshire too, where its presence is said to be a legacy of the nearby wool and cotton mills. The royal purple pigment in its skins had been used for dye since Roman times. Often planted as windbreaks for other crops, the 'wild' trees that survive can be found in hedgerows or tucked at the corners of fields. The crop is still sold at farm gates and roadside stalls during September.

Much effort has been spent on reviving the damson's fortunes. There are once again Damson Days in the Lyth Valley, complete with Morris dancers and wandering fiddlers, when the blossom is toasted by its many fans. When people tell me they don't like this fruit I find they generally mean they are bothered by its stones, or aren't prepared to look for it. More often than not, they are suspicious of any fruit you cannot eat without cooking.

There is no cooking fruit I hold in greater regard, none whose arrival in the markets I wait for more impatiently. The arrival of the little violet-black Damascene plum is without question the high point of my fruit-cooking year.

A damson tree in the garden

Wild damson trees can still be found in old hedgerows, their sweet rot a characteristic smell of the countryside in late autumn. Many turn out to be the smaller, shudderingly sour bullace or even the sloe, the ancestor of the damson and the fruit you can use for a glistening crimson gin.

The damson tree shares many of the characteristics of the plum family with the exception of, perhaps, a smoother trunk. A slightly damp clay soil will keep it happy, but it is less than fussy about altitude. Only very sandy or waterlogged soil or serious amounts of shade will cause problems. It can remain productive for at least fifty years.

If you are choosing a tree from scratch, then I suggest going for one with the more modest-sized fruits, such as Farleigh. Their flavour is richer and truer than the large, more maroon-skinned fruits, which are apt to have a prune-like note about them. If I appear to be urging you to plant a tree, it is simply that I want this fruit more than any other to survive the march of time.

Commercial orchards are few, but to witness the tree's rare beauty you might like to take a trip through Shropshire in late March or the Lyth Valley a couple of weeks later, when sudden gusts of wind take the tissue-paper blossom off the trees like snowflakes against a clear grey sky. Or join the small but loyal band of customers waiting patiently each September, jam jars in hand (and none more loyal than this one).

The earliness of the damson's blossom, appearing while there is still a risk of hard frosts, is a constant worry to anyone who has a tree in their garden. There is little we can do other than plant in a sheltered position that gets as much sun as possible. A covering of fleece for short trees on cold nights might help more than just crossing your fingers, but larger trees are pretty much at the mercy of the elements.

One rarely considers feeding an established tree but it can be of sustenance to one that has previously fruited heavily. Some manure in spring will be welcomed, especially for its moisture-retaining properties. Younger trees will benefit from a scattering of potash in winter.

My damson tree fruited from its third year. Hidden in the farthest west corner of the garden, it shelters the compost heaps and provides enough fruit for a couple of crumbles. I live for the day it produces enough for a decent batch of jam.

Young damson trees are available from specialist nurseries. They will arrive probably on the coldest day of the year when you least feel like getting the spade out. Their roots will probably be bound in hessian and your hoped-for tree will look distinctly unpromising. Worry not. Plant as per your nursery's instructions and, come spring, the odd leaf opening here and there along its spindly branches, it will look more hopeful. Within a couple of years you should have a lovely little garden tree, with enough fruit on it for at least one good pie.

Varieties

By mid September the path between the vegetable beds is almost overgrown. Dahlias so dark red as to be nearly black; sagging, tobacco-brown stems of Jerusalem artichokes; a wild lemon verbena and tangled clouds of Mutabilis roses block your route to the little damson tree at the back of the garden. Every few feet means doing battle with a spider's web. I'm willing to bet few know the variety of their own damson tree, so it is worth recording the name somewhere if you put a new one in, so that future generations may know.

Farleigh Damson Introduced in about 1820, large leafed and something of a copious cropper, the Farleigh has small, rich, bloomy purple fruit that appear in September. Makes superb crumbles.
Merryweather Large, late fruits from a variety found in 1907.
Shropshire Prune Regarded by growers such as Keepers Nursery as the classic damson. Around in early September.
Blue Violet A true Westmorland variety, small and early. You may even see it around in early August.
Bradley's King You will find this particularly sweet Nottinghamshire variety from the middle of September. To my knowledge, I have never tasted this one.

Damsons in the kitchen

Damsons are a cook's fruit. None has a deeper, more powerful flavour or such penetrating juice. They will need sugar, probably more than you might wish in these days of healthy eating, and patience with the stones – only a masochist would attempt to remove them before cooking. The intense flavour is unmistakable, and embellished with sugar and a very little water they will produce copious amounts of highly flavoured syrup. Their strident flavour needs tempering with a soft pastry crust or a trickle of cream. Crumbles or fools are the most acceptable but a soft suet dough such as that of a roly-poly pudding would work too.

The simplest way to treat them is to bring them to a simmer with sugar and a little water. I use about 4 tablespoons of sugar for each 500g fruit. As the fruit bursts, its skin colours the juices and the flesh turns from a dull greeny yellow to deep apricot amber. The juice will usually curdle when added to custard or to cream or yoghurt, but no matter. The ensuing flavour, poised somewhere between plums and blackcurrants, will generally win the squeamish eater over.

They will need a good sorting through before cooking, to remove any twigs, leaves and the odd mushy or shrivelled specimen. Stalks should be removed but stones can be left in, adding a faint almond note and providing the necessary details for a game of tinker, tailor, soldier, sailor.

Damsons make the most gorgeous jam. I am not fond of the commercial versions I have tried (too firmly set and too sweet by far) and tend either to make it myself or to seek out homemade versions at village fêtes, farm shops and charity events. The artisan variety found in delicatessens is often worth picking up. It is an easy preserve to make, less of a diva than, say, strawberry, and often sets softly like a good jam should. The stones will sometimes rise to the surface during cooking and can be scooped off with a draining spoon.

The savoury applications are few but outstanding. A few damsons allowed to soften in the gravy of a game bird can produce rewards, as can a pickle made with the whole fruit, vinegar and spices. I like them as a surprising addition to the Christmas ham, using some of my precious store from the freezer.

Damsons and...

Red wine vinegar A good way to brighten up a damson compote that you wish to serve with cold roast meats.
Ginger Both the dried and fresh versions are appropriate.
Almonds Ground almonds are particularly good with stone fruits of any sort. A spot-on addition to a damson cake.
Duck The perfect fruit for slicing through a quacker's copious fat.
Pork and ham A nice change from apple sauce.
Cream cheeses Soft, sweet cheeses such as mascarpone and curd or cream cheese will effectively soften the fruit's sharpness. An excellent topping for a cheesecake.
Aniseed and star anise Use the spice in pickles and savoury sauces.
Cinnamon The plum spice. The earthy sweetness seems very much at home with the knife-sharp, fruity quality of this little plum.
Allspice So says Mrs Beeton.

* The blossom is amongst the earliest and the most fragile. A sheltered spot will help reduce frost damage.
* Damson Sunday was the point in April when tourists thronged the country lanes of Westmorland admiring the damson blossom.
* Damson Saturday was the day in September when many tons were taken to the market in Kendal and then off to be jammed.
* Damson Day is the new celebration of all things Damascene, from blossom and beer to jam and gin. Set up by the Westmorland Damson Association in 1996, it has become the fruit's answer to Apple Day.
* Damson cheese is a preserve similar to membrillo, the Spanish quince paste.

Twice-cooked gammon with damson gin sauce

Damsons are one of the few fruits I freeze. Their season is so fleeting that I pack them into plastic boxes to ensure there is enough for winter crumbles and the occasional sauce for a piece of ham or gammon. Damson is often my preferred sauce at Christmas too, made with frozen fruit and a spiking of damson gin. The sweetness seems entirely in tune with the festivities, but this works for a large autumnal gathering too.

enough for 12
smoked gammon joint, rolled and tied – 2.5–3kg (boned weight)
perry or cider – two 500ml bottles
black peppercorns – 12
an onion, halved but not peeled
bay leaves – 3
cloves – 3

for the damson gin sauce
damsons – 350g
sugar – 2 tablespoons
redcurrant jelly – 400g
sloe or damson gin – 150ml
cloves – 6

for the quince glaze
quince jelly – 400g
Dijon mustard – 2 heaped tablespoons
fresh white breadcrumbs – a handful

Put the gammon joint in a very large pan. Pour over enough water to cover and bring to the boil. Carefully tip away the water. Pour the perry or cider over the meat and top up with water to cover if necessary. Add the peppercorns, the halved onion, the bay leaves and cloves and bring to the boil. Lower the heat so that the liquid is simmering gently and cover with a lid or a dome of foil. Leave to cook until the meat is cooked right through – about two and a half hours. You can leave the ham in the cooking liquid until you need it.

To make the sauce, put the damsons in a stainless steel saucepan with the sugar and 2 tablespoons of water. Bring to the boil and simmer for ten minutes or so, until the fruit starts to burst its skins. Stir in the redcurrant jelly, pour in the gin, then add the cloves and let it return to the boil. Simmer for five minutes, then turn off the heat and leave to cool. The jelly will thicken or maybe even set very softly.

Remove the ham carefully from the liquid and put it in a roasting tin. Peel off and discard the thick dark skin and the string without removing the fat from the joint. (The liquor has served its purpose, but it is worth using as a stock for soup. Just check that it isn't too salty first.)

To make the glaze, put the quince jelly into a mixing bowl and stir in the mustard and breadcrumbs. Spread the glaze over the outside of the gammon and bake at 180°C/Gas 4 for twenty to twenty-five minutes, until the joint is glossy and just starting to colour. Leave for a few minutes before carving into thin slices and serving with the sauce. If there is any sauce left over, pour it into clean jars, cover tightly and store in the fridge.

Roast duck with damson ginger sauce

The damson's sharp kick is a useful contrast to rich meats such as duck (which is why duck is so often teamed with Seville oranges). The spicing works well with the sauce that accompanies the Chinese-style pork roast in the Plum chapter (see page 1040) but is too good not to repeat here with damsons.

enough for 2, with leftovers

a duck, weighing about 2–3kg
Szechwan peppercorns – 2 tablespoons
sea salt flakes – 3 tablespoons
ground anise – a teaspoon

for the sauce
damsons or sharp plums – 900g
sugar – 3 tablespoons
water – 120ml
fresh ginger –a large knob, about the size of a walnut,
   peeled and cut into matchsticks
star anise – 4
salt – ½ teaspoon
smooth red wine vinegar – 2 tablespoons

Wipe the duck with kitchen towel and sit it in a plate or shallow dish. Warm the Szechwan peppercorns in a non-stick saucepan till they smell aromatic and start to crackle a bit, then remove them from the heat. Grind together the salt, toasted peppercorns and the ground anise. Easiest with a pestle and mortar, but you can also do it with a plastic bag and a rolling pin. You want a fine beige powder. Rub the seasoned salt over the duck, taking care to get into the tight corners under and around the legs and all over the breasts. Cover with greaseproof paper and set aside for at least eight hours, preferably overnight in the fridge.

To make the sauce, put the damsons or plums into a colander and give them a good rinse under cold running water, pulling off any stalks and leaves as you go. Tip the fruit into a stainless steel saucepan (aluminium will taint sour fruits such as plums), then add the sugar, water, ginger, star anise and salt and bring to the boil. Leave to simmer for about ten to fifteen minutes, until the fruit has burst and the sauce has thickened to a deep purple-red. Stir in the vinegar and simmer for five minutes more. Watch that it doesn't get too thick or catch on the bottom; it is inclined to become a bit jammy at this stage.

Now, depending on whether you can cope with the stones or not, either put the sauce somewhere to cool or, if spitting out stones at the table really isn't your thing, sieve it. Tip it into a large sieve set over a bowl and push the fruit through the sieve with a wooden spoon. Keep going until all you have left is a few stones. Set aside; you can warm it up just before you serve the duck.

To roast the duck, set the oven at 200°C/Gas 6. Prick the skin lightly all over with a fork. The idea is to go through the skin but not the flesh. You want the fat to escape, not the meat juices. Roast for one to one and a half hours, basting occasionally (if your duck is very fatty, then pour off the excess during cooking). Leave to rest for ten minutes before carving.

A hot compote

Remove the little stalks from the damsons, discarding any squashed fruit. Put the fruit in a stainless steel saucepan and add a small amount of water to come no further than a third of the way up the fruit. Sweeten generously to taste, then bring to the boil, turn the heat down and simmer gently till the fruits have burst their skins and the juices have worked with the sugar to produce a rich purple sauce. Serve warm, with cream or ice cream.

Creamy cheesecake, sharp sauce

Of the several cheesecakes in this book, this is the one for lovers of those with a deeply creamy texture, the sort that sticks to your knife. This is not the cheesecake to partner strawberries or even raspberries; it needs the knife-edge sharpness of damsons or passion fruit.

enough for 10

for the biscuit base
butter – 90g
shortbread-type biscuits – 200g
oatcakes – 150g

for the filling
double cream – 350ml
caster sugar – 150g
cream cheese – 650g
grated zest of a lemon
a drop of vanilla extract

for the damson sauce
damsons – 500g
caster sugar – 150g
water – 4 tablespoons

Line the base of a 20cm springform cake tin with baking parchment or strong greaseproof paper. Melt the butter in a small pan. Crush the biscuits and oatcakes to fine crumbs and stir them into the melted butter. Tip them into the cake tin and smooth them flat. Refrigerate for half an hour or so, until firm. You can speed the process by putting it in the freezer, if you wish.

Put the cream and sugar in a food mixer and whisk until thick. Keep an eye on the mixture all the time, stopping once it starts to thicken. Stir in the cream cheese, grated lemon zest and vanilla. Tip the mixture into the crumb-lined cake tin, cover with cling film and put in the fridge for at least four hours.

To make the damson sauce, remove the stalks, tip the fruit into a stainless steel pan with the sugar and water and bring to the boil. Leave to simmer gently for ten to fifteen minutes, until the skins have split and the fruits have softened. Leave to cool, then transfer to a dish, cover and refrigerate for a couple of hours.

Run a palette knife around the sides of the cheesecake, then release it from its tin. Slide it carefully on to a serving plate. Serve in thick slices, spooning over the damson sauce as you go.

A soft-textured crumble for stone fruits

Should plum crumble be on my lips when I die, then I will go a happy man (damson or gooseberry would be appreciated even more, but let's not push it). Plums suit a crumble crust not because of their juice alone but because of their inherent acidity, which contrasts neatly with the sugary crust.

I offer a crumble recipe without apology. Each tweak to the ratio of flour and butter, every additional ingredient (in this case almonds) produces a slightly different result. My signature crusts tend to be of the soft, buttery, melting kind rather than the fine, tightly packed sand variety that one comes across when people have been parsimonious with the butter.

enough for 6
damsons or plums – 700–800g
caster sugar – 4 tablespoons, or more to taste
a thick slice of butter

for the crumble
butter – 100g
plain flour – 150g
ground almonds – 50g
caster or light brown sugar – 75g

Set the oven at 200°C/Gas 6. Put whichever fruit you are using in a shallow pan with the sugar, butter and a tablespoon or two of water. Cook over a moderate heat until the juices start to flow – a matter of five minutes, depending on the ripeness of your fruit. Tip the fruit and its juice into a deep pie dish.

Rub the butter, which should ideally be cold from the fridge, into the flour with your fingertips. When the mixture resembles coarse fresh breadcrumbs, stir in the ground almonds and sugar. Sprinkle a tablespoon or two of water over the mixture and stir lightly with a fork. Some of the crumbs should stick together in small lumps – this gives a more interesting crumble.

Scatter the crumble over the fruit, then bake for about thirty-five minutes. The crumble is done when the crust is pale gold, smudged with juices. Serve with thick, golden cream.

An ice cream for early autumn

Flavour is numbed by cold. An ice-cream mixture must have a clear and strident flavour before it goes in the freezer, otherwise it will lack any character when it is served. Damsons, whose flavour rings out like a bell, produce the most flavourful of all ices (save possibly blackcurrant), instantly recognisable and barely diminished by a night in the icebox.

That said, my first damson ice was a little too creamy and lacked the clarity I was after. So I cut the custard-to-fruit ratio and swapped half the custard for sheep's yoghurt in order to bring the fruit to the fore. The result is an ice that tastes of autumn.

enough for 4
damsons – 500g
water – 4 tablespoons
egg yolks – 4
caster sugar – 200g
double cream – 250ml
natural yoghurt – 250g

Rinse the damsons, then bring them to the boil with the water in a stainless steel pan. It won't seem like enough water but trust me. Lower the heat so the fruit simmers gently and cook for ten minutes, until their skins have burst and you have a good quantity of deep purple juice. Push the fruit through a fine sieve with a wooden spoon, pressing and stirring till you have nothing left but the stones. Leave the resulting purée, including that rescued from the underside of the sieve, to cool.

Beat the egg yolks and caster sugar till pale and creamy. Bring the cream almost to boiling point in a medium-sized saucepan, then pour it over the egg and sugar, stirring. Rinse the pan, then return the custard to it, putting it over a gentle heat and stirring till you have custard the thickness of double cream. It is essential that the mixture doesn't get too hot. I stir continuously with a wooden spoon, right into the corners of the pan, until it is just thick enough, then immediately transfer it to a cool bowl set in a sink of shallow, cold water. The sudden cooling helps stop the custard curdling, as does a damn good whisking. Let the custard cool.

Mix the damson purée with the custard and the yoghurt. Pour into an ice-cream machine and churn till almost frozen. Remove to a plastic freezer box and freeze till needed.

If you don't have a machine, you can still make the ice cream. Just pour the mixture into a freezer box and place in the freezer, removing it every hour and giving it a good beating with a small whisk, bringing the frozen outer edges into the middle. The result will be less light and creamy than if made in a machine. It will need a good four hours or so to freeze.

A quick damson ice cream

Of all the commercial food products available, I regard ready-made custard – the sort made with cream and eggs and available in the chilled cabinet – as possibly the most useful of all. I love making custard but I can't pretend I always have time for it, especially when I have to cool it to make ice cream. You could make your own for this recipe, warily stirring the mixture of cream and eggs until it thickens. But I have to tell you that once it meets the intense flavour of the cooked damsons, you might as well have used ready-made. This, incidentally, is the one in the photograph.

enough for 6
damsons – 450g
caster sugar – 4 tablespoons
ready-made custard – 250ml

Wash the damsons, tip them into a stainless steel or enamelled pan, then pour over the sugar and 3 tablespoons of water. Bring to the boil and turn the heat down to a simmer. Continue cooking until the fruit starts to soften, its skin splits and deep purple juice has formed in the pan – about ten minutes.

Pour the juice into a mixing bowl, suspend a sieve over the top and push the fruit through the sieve until only the stones are left. Scrape any purée from the bottom of the sieve (it tends to collect there in large amounts) and stir it into the juice. Leave it to cool.

Slowly stir the custard into the damson purée. Pour into your ice-cream machine and churn till frozen – or freeze by hand as in the recipe above.

A damson trifle

Damsons are one of the few fruits I think it is worth freezing, because their season is exceptionally short. I deliberately keep the sugar on the low side for this recipe so that some of the fruit's characteristic sharpness shines through the billowing cream.

Note: it is not worth doing this if you can't be bothered to remove the stones. If you are feeling lazy, then make something else.

enough for 6
sponge fingers – 200g
large eggs – 2, separated
caster sugar – 4 tablespoons
mascarpone cheese – 500g
whipping or double cream – 300ml
a little vanilla extract
a few crystallised violets and chopped pistachio nuts, to decorate

for the fruit layer
damsons – 750g
water – 400ml
caster sugar – 4 tablespoons

Put the damsons, water and sugar into a stainless steel saucepan and bring to the boil. Turn the heat down to a simmer and leave for fifteen to twenty minutes, till the fruit is starting to burst. Remove from the heat and set aside. Some of the stones will come to the surface. Use a draining spoon to remove as many stones as you can (the fewer that end up in the trifle, the better), then extract the rest by squishing the fruit between thumb and fingers. It won't take long (about ten minutes) and is pleasant enough if the fruit is still warm and you are not in a hurry.

Put the sponge fingers in a shallow dish. Spoon the damsons and all their juice over and set aside to cool.

Put the egg yolks and sugar in a bowl and mix well, then stir in the mascarpone. Whip the cream with a few drops of vanilla extract till soft and thick – it should lie in soft, undulating folds rather than stiff peaks – then fold into the mixture. In a clean bowl, and with a clean whisk, beat the egg whites till stiff and frothy. Fold them into the mascarpone mixture.

Spread the mixture over the sponge fingers and damsons, cover with cling film and refrigerate for at least two or three hours, adding any decoration such as violets and nuts before serving.

A moist cake of damsons and spelt

A shallow cake, almost pudding-like at the bottom, with flashes of purple-pink through its soft crumbs. Spelt flour, made from an ancient form of wheat, has a gentle wholemeal note that gives a pleasingly tender and open crumb to the cake. It is not essential. Plain, soft flour will do, but the texture will be firmer. The wetness at the base, where the damsons lie, is entirely deliberate.

I have made plum cakes before, usually incorporating ground almonds or occasionally pine kernels, and eaten them both as dessert and as a cake for tea. Cream seems unnecessary – they carry enough moisture in the fruit. Damson, with its rich flavour and sudden sour note, seems a perfect contrast to the sweet cake crumbs. I just spit the stones out as I go.

> *enough for 6–8*
> butter – 150g
> golden caster sugar – 150g, plus an extra tablespoon
> large eggs – 3
> spelt flour – 110g
> baking powder – 1½ teaspoons
> ground almonds – 75g
> damsons, stalks removed – 400g
> icing sugar, to finish

You will need a square cake tin measuring 20–22cm across the base. Line the bottom of the tin with a piece of baking parchment. Set the oven at 180°C/Gas 4.

Cream the butter and 150g sugar till light and fluffy. It is so much easier to do this with an electric mixer, but I have met others who prefer the wooden-spoon method. Whatever, don't stop until the mixture is almost white in colour. Crack the eggs and beat them gently, then add to the mixture a little at a time, beating thoroughly between each lot.

Mix the flour and baking powder and add to the ground almonds. Fold into the cake mixture gently but firmly. If you over mix, the cake will be heavy. Transfer the mixture to the lined cake tin with a rubber spatula, then lay the damsons on top and shake over the tablespoon of sugar (the damsons will sink during cooking, leaving only one or two peeping through the surface).

Bake for forty-five minutes, covering with foil for the last ten minutes if it looks to be browning too quickly. Remove from the oven, leave to settle, then, when almost cool, remove from its tin. Dust lightly with icing sugar and serve.

A glorious, lightly set jam

In autumn I haunt the farmers' markets and village fêtes looking for jam people. One could say 'stalk'. From time to time I find a jar of damson, a wondrous jam when the fruit's sharpness is allowed to shine through the sugar. I make my own too, leaving it slightly less firmly set than most cottage-garden jam makers, so that it drips off my morning toast and down the sleeves of my dressing gown. More to the point, it makes a good sauce for vanilla ice cream or almond sponge.

> *enough for about four 400g jars*
> damsons – 1kg
> water – 250ml
> granulated or caster sugar – 1kg

Rinse the damsons, removing any stray leaves, stalks and twigs as you go. Tip them into a deep stainless steel saucepan with the water and bring to the boil. Turn the heat down so that the fruit simmers to tenderness. You can expect this to take about twenty-five minutes or so, depending on its ripeness. Stir in the sugar, then bring to the boil and continue to let the fruit and dissolved sugar bubble away for about twenty minutes, until it has thickened a little. To test whether the jam is set enough, dip a wooden spoon into it and lift it clear. Hold it level over the jam. It is ready when the jam that runs down forms a large droplet that falls slowly from the spoon. If it pours off in a steady stream, you need to boil it a little longer. If you have a sugar thermometer, it is ready when the temperature reaches 105°C.

Remove from the heat and leave for ten minutes to let the skins settle throughout the jam, during which time you can scoop off any froth and remove some of the floating skins and stones. It will still have more stones than you may like but removing them all would be an endless task. Ladle the jam into warm, sterilised jars and seal.

A damson fool

The fool came to us as a use for the gooseberry but it makes a pretty good end for a bag of damsons, too. Care is needed here if your cream and fruit are not to curdle. Introduce the softly whipped cream into the fruit a little at a time and stop either when the flavour is as you like it or at the first sign of a grainy quality appearing. I like to keep back a little of the fruit juice to trickle over the fool as I bring it to the table.

enough for 4
damsons – 500g
caster sugar – 4–5 tablespoons
double cream – 300ml

Rinse the damsons, removing any stems or leaves as you go. Put the fruit in a stainless steel pan with the sugar and 3 tablespoons of water. Bring to the boil, lower the heat and leave to bubble gently till the fruit has split and you have a copious amount of juice.

Push the fruit through a sieve suspended over a bowl. Keep going till all you are left with is dry stones (wash the sieve before the fruit dries or you will never get it off). Leave to cool.

When the fruit is entirely cool, pour the cream into a cold bowl and whip gently until soft and thick (I put the cream, bowl and whisk into the fridge first; it makes for better whipping, with less fear of curdling). You want the whipped cream to barely hold its own shape rather than stand in stiff peaks. Slowly, gently, fold some of the cold fruit purée into the cream and keep going until you have a deep purple cream. It should be soft and sweet-sharp. If the consistency has become sloppy, you can give it a brief whisking until it thickens again. Spoon into glasses or little pots and leave in the fridge for an hour to settle before serving.

A sharp damson pickle for cold meats

The effect of pickles on cold meats, pâtés and the like is extraordinary.
Even the most mild-mannered of terrines or workaday slice of cold roast
beef comes alive the second it rubs shoulders with a sharp and spicy pickle.
Think pork pie with a pickled onion; coarse pâté with tiny, comma-shaped
cornichons; cold roast pork with a dark and sinister pickled walnut or two.
Damsons, sour cherries and plums pickle well, offering a fruity sharpness
that cuts through a plate of cold meat like a warm knife through mozzarella.
This is the sort of preserve I plan to dress neatly with a hessian mobcap
and a ribbon and hand out to friends, Martha Stewart style, at Christmas.
I never do.

> damsons – 1kg
> caster or granulated sugar – 650g
> a cinnamon stick
> black peppercorns – 18
> bay leaves – 6
> white wine vinegar – 500ml
> green cardamom pods – 8
> cloves – 6

Check the damsons over thoroughly. Put the sugar, cinnamon stick,
peppercorns, bay leaves, vinegar, whole cardamom pods and cloves into
a stainless steel or enamelled pan and bring to the boil. Tip in the whole
damsons and bring back to the boil. Simmer for five minutes, then remove
from the heat, ladle into sterilised preserving jars and seal. Leave for a couple
of months before eating.

Elderflowers
and elderberries

Early June, the seventh to be precise, and next door's elder tree is a vast cloud of creamy-white blossom, as delicate as Honiton lace. It is not a handsome tree, they rarely are, but I feel honoured that the branches have chosen to hang over my garden, the froth of flowers dancing in the breeze with the same delicate movement as cow parsley or sweet cicely. Those I fail to pick are followed, in early autumn, by clusters of dark and glossy edible berries.

The smell of the blossom is, like that of spreading lavender honey on hot toast, the essence of the English summer Miss Marple might have known. Of cricket matches and policemen on bikes, village greens and shady, leafy lanes. On a less romantic note, I detect a hint of fresh yeast and tomcats.

Last year I cut most of the flowers – flat and open like lace parasols – dipped them into a light batter of egg white, flour and sparkling mineral water and fried them till golden. We dipped each one into a saucer of caster sugar and ate the fritters still crackling from the pan. This year the blossoms made their way into bottles of thick, sweet cordial. And all this from a tree I had no intention of having in the garden. Better still, a tree that appears wild in cities and countryside alike – pudding for the asking.

The berries, purple-black and the size of the lead shot you find in your pigeon casserole, appear in early September. I try to get to them before the fat birds, who will otherwise leave their bright purple calling cards splattered over the garden furniture. These are the tartest of all edible berries, and their copious juice will stain everything in its path. Pick them in your oldest clothes.

It has to be said that *Sambucus nigra*, the common elder, does not produce the most versatile of fruits. A crumble or pie made purely of elderberries is often too potent to be enjoyable (and it will send your guests' teeth a fetching shade of violet). Mixed with apple, however, the flavour is altogether softer and more palatable. The quandary in our house is whether to eat the clotted-cream-coloured flowers or the glossy black fruit. Sadly, you cannot have both, unless the tree is a particularly large one, or you limit yourselves to just a handful of crisp, sugar-dusted fritters each June.

An elder tree in the garden

Most streets, commons and wasteland support a *Sambucus nigra* or two. Untended gardens are often good hunting grounds. At last, something for the urban forager.

They are easily recognised by their flat-topped umbrellas of cream flowers in June and their pointed, somewhat saw-edged leaves. Beware that you identify them correctly. Other trees, such as the rowan, are not dissimilar from a distance but lack the distinctive tom-cat smell of the elder.

As a tree, the elder is a bit of a brute – unattractive, untidily formed and generally considered something of a weed. I have never known anyone actually choose to plant one. I spend too much time in spring pulling up the young 'treelets' that have seeded themselves in my garden.

When I first made this garden, I used to prune the tree drastically, usually in a temper. Then I found a use for its blossoms, and then its berries. Now I welcome it, even though it shades my hollyhocks and phlox, making them bend forward in an attempt to see the sun. For all its uses, I really cannot recommend you plant an elder. There are too many better things to put in its place.

Elder blossoms and berries in the kitchen

Make the fritters; they are light, crisp and have an ethereal Muscat whiff to them. But should you have a glut of elderflowers, then perhaps you might like to make a bottle or two of cordial or a jelly, or dip the heads into a pan of simmering gooseberries. I have read, too, of their use in custard, though have yet to try it.

The elderflower has been popular since Victorian times, though its use as an ingredient for cordial goes back much further. The Romans are said to have made it. The aromatic flavour of the fruit is held by the sugar syrup, which is then diluted with spring water. The large quantity of sugar is balanced by a heavy dose of citric acid or lemons to give a truly refreshing drink.

The cordial can be added in place of the flowers to gooseberry fool or poached fruit, and is often used as the base for a sorbet. I like it as a sticky syrup with which to soak an almond cake.

The berries are not widely used in the kitchen. I have added them to a casserole of pheasant with reasonable success and once, memorably, to a crumble, whose extraordinary purple colour didn't confine itself to the pudding. A small handful will give an inky colour and flavour to a gravy, and I have mashed them into the pan juices of a roast game bird before now.

Both the flowers and berries are a favourite of home winemakers. The flowers produce a straw-coloured drink with soft Muscat notes, the berries a rich and majestically coloured drink of which the makers invariably seem rather proud.

Elderflowers and berries and...

Gooseberries Elderflowers and gooseberries are one of those perfect culinary marriages that feel right in so many ways. Not only do they look beautiful together but both are at their peak at the same time. Use the two together in fools, compotes, crumbles, ices and drinks.
Lemon Citrus flavours bring out the sweetness of the flowers.
Vinegar A softly spoken vinegar such as white wine or cider can be used with the flower heads to make a slightly sweet dressing. Very good with young green lettuces.
Cinnamon A light dusting of sugar and the ground spice on the finished fritters can be pleasing.
Game birds Lean flesh with deep flavours, such as pheasant, pigeon and wild duck, goes well with the tartness of the berries. Add the berries to game casseroles.
Venison The rich, dark meat of venison is flattered by any berry sauce. Elderberries add tart richness to the pan juices.

* Pick the flowers in the morning when the air is cool and the blossoms are at their most fragrant. The sun makes them weary.
* The flowers should not be eaten raw in any quantity, as they are mildly poisonous. Berries, too, must be fully ripe before eating.
* Steer clear of the leaves, bark and twigs. They are poisonous if consumed.
* Tests consistently show that patients who are given elderberry juice recover more quickly from flu than those who are not.
* Make an elderberry vinegar by steeping 400g fruit in 500ml white wine vinegar for two or three days before straining, sweetening with 350g sugar and bringing to the boil, straining again and bottling.
* A few flowers tied in a muslin bag can be pushed into a pan of stewed apple, where they will discreetly flavour it.

Elderflower fritters

You need a really light batter for these to flatter the delicate nature of the blossoms. My batter barely covers the flowers and cooks particularly quickly, leaving the fritters frail and crisp. For a more robust batter, you should add a little more flour to the mixture. When the flowers emerge from the oil, I usually dip them into caster sugar, but sometimes a very faint dusting of cinnamon can be pleasing.

enough for 4
large elderflower heads – 16
oil for deep-frying
a plate thickly dusted with caster sugar

for the batter
plain flour – 100g
sunflower oil – 2 tablespoons
sparkling mineral water – 175ml
caster sugar – a tablespoon
an egg white

Sift the flour into a large basin, then add the oil and water, beating slowly to make a thick paste. Stir in the sugar and set aside for thirty minutes. Don't be tempted to skip the resting time; this is essential for a light batter. Just before you plan to fry the elderflowers, beat the egg white until almost stiff and fold it gently into the batter.

Wash the elderflowers with great tenderness in a bowl of water. Just dipping them briefly in and out of the water should do it. This will not affect their flavour and they are easy to shake dry. Make certain that there are no little aphids hiding amongst the flowers. When you are sure that they are clean, get the oil on to heat up. Snip the flower heads into small stems.

Test the oil to make sure it is hot enough – it should send a cube of bread golden in a few seconds – then dip the elderflowers into the batter and lower them into the hot oil. Push them down, holding them under the oil by pushing down on the stem. The batter will bubble up around the flowers like little pearls. Fry till the batter is pale gold and crisp, then lift out of the oil and dip straight into the caster sugar. Eat the fritters whilst they are hot and crisp.

Gooseberry and elderflower fool

There is another gooseberry fool in the chapter dedicated to that fruit, but this one relies more on the essence of the flower, so I feel it belongs here.

enough for 6
gooseberries – 450g
caster sugar to taste
double cream – 300ml
elderflower cordial

Top and tail the gooseberries, put them into a stainless steel pan with a very little water and cook over a low heat until they are soft and squashy – a matter of ten minutes. Drain off any extra liquid and crush the berries with a fork. I never do this very thoroughly, believing that the texture is more interesting with a bit of fruit in it, but go as far as you want. Stir in the sugar; the amount you will need depends on how sharp the gooseberries are, but take care not to take the sharpness out. I like a tart fool, so I add no more than 2 or 3 tablespoons. Leave to cool, then refrigerate.

Whip the cream to soft folds. You really should do this slowly towards the end so that you can stop at the exact moment the cream starts to feel heavy on the whisk. Gently fold the gooseberries into the cream, taking care not to 'whip' the cream further. Spoon the fool into chilled glasses or pretty cups and leave to settle a while in the fridge. Trickle a teaspoon of elderflower cordial over each as you serve.

Gooseberry elderflower trifle

In summer there is often a bottle of elderflower cordial in my fridge. The Muscat scent as you drop in the ice cubes and pour in the mineral water is one of summer's most potent aromas, like that of honeysuckle, mown grass or sliced cucumber. It adds a note of summer to all it touches, including the sponge for a gooseberry trifle.

enough for 6
gooseberries – 500g
golden caster sugar – 2 tablespoons
a couple of elderflower heads, if you have them
Italian sponge fingers – 200g
elderflower cordial
custard – 500ml
double cream – 300ml
a handful of shelled pistachio nuts

Top and tail the gooseberries and rinse them thoroughly. Tip them into a stainless steel pan with the sugar, 2 tablespoons of water and, if you have them, a couple of heads of elderflowers. Bring to the boil, then cover with a lid and turn the heat down so that the gooseberries bubble very gently. You don't want the liquid to evaporate. Shake the pan every few minutes to stop the fruit sticking. It should be soft after seven minutes or so. Check for sweetness; the gooseberries should be tart but not sour. Remove the elderflowers, leave the fruit to cool, then cover and chill thoroughly.

Line the base of a shallow china or glass dish, about 30cm x 20cm, with the sponge fingers, breaking them to fit where you need to. Drain the juice from the gooseberries and mix it with a little elderflower cordial to make it up to 100ml. Pour the liquid over the sponge fingers, then spoon the gooseberries on top.

Cover the gooseberries with the cold custard, smoothing it flat with the back of a spoon. Pour the cream into a chilled bowl and whip it till it starts to thicken. The cream should be firm enough for the whisk to leave a trail but not stiff enough to stand in peaks. Smooth the whipped cream over the custard, cover tightly with cling film and place in the fridge. It should stay there for a good two hours for all the flavours to marry.

Chop the pistachios roughly and scatter them over the top of the trifle.

Elderflower cordial

My version is only slightly different from most classic versions of this
ancient drink in that I include a lime or two. I find they make it even
more refreshing.

makes 2 medium-sized bottles
elderflower heads – 20 (about 225g)
caster sugar – 1kg
water – 1.25 litres
lemons – 2, cut into quarters
limes – 2, cut into quarters
citric acid – 50g

Inspect the flowers for insects and dust. Shake or quickly rinse, but don't
wash them. Remove the toughest stalks with scissors; they are likely to
be bitter.

Warm the sugar and water together in a large saucepan till the sugar has
dissolved, then remove from the heat. Dunk the flowers and the quartered
fruit into the syrup, stir in the citric acid and set aside to cool. When the
liquid is cold, cover and refrigerate for at least twenty-four hours. Strain
through muslin or a fine sieve and decant into sterilised bottles.

Raspberries in elderflower jelly

A summer delight. Use strawberries and redcurrants too, if you fancy.
It is probably best to stick to one or two fruits, otherwise the effect can
become cluttered.

enough for 4
leaf gelatine – 12g
elderflower cordial – 70ml
caster sugar – 1 heaped tablespoon
sparkling mineral water – 250ml
white wine – 250ml
raspberries – 400g

Soak the leaves of gelatine in cold water. They will start to soften after five
minutes or so. Pour the elderflower cordial into a small saucepan and add
the sugar, mineral water and half the white wine. Lift the softened gelatine
out of the water and drop it into the cordial and wine. Place over a low heat
and stir till the gelatine and sugar have dissolved. Remove from the heat and
add the remaining white wine.

Divide the raspberries between four large glasses. Pour the jelly over the raspberries and leave to cool before refrigerating. The jellies should be set within an hour or two.

An elderflower and gooseberry syrup

This is the syrup to dilute with mineral water on a hot summer's day. A glass with ice, approximately six parts water to cordial, will make you think you have walked into a Merchant Ivory film. The recipe is my version of Constance Spry's, from her charming, long out of print book, *Come into the Garden, Cook.*

makes 2 medium-sized bottles
gooseberries – 1kg
water – 300ml
granulated sugar – 650g
elderflowers – 8 large heads

Put the gooseberries in a large, deep pan with the water and sugar and bring to the boil. Simmer until the fruit is ready to pop, but stop before it does. While the gooseberries are simmering, check the elderflowers, snipped from their stems, for dust and insects. Lay them on a piece of muslin and tie them up in it. When the gooseberries are done, turn the heat off and lower the bag of flowers into the pan. Leave it to steep in the syrup for ten minutes or so (taste it; you may want a stronger flavour, in which case leave the flowers in a while longer), then remove and discard them.

Pour the syrup through a piece of clean muslin or a fine sieve into a large jug and then into a sterilised glass bottle. Store in the fridge.

Roast venison with elderberry sauce

enough for 4
black peppercorns – 10
juniper berries – 12
sea salt flakes – half a teaspoon
thyme – 2 or 3 sprigs
olive oil – 2 tablespoons
venison fillet or boned and rolled leg – 800g
white wine – 200ml
rowan or redcurrant jelly – 3 heaped tablespoons
elderberries – 6 tablespoons

Set the oven at 200°C/Gas 6. Coarsely crush the black peppercorns, juniper berries, sea salt flakes and thyme leaves, using a pestle and mortar. Rub the oil over the venison, then massage in the crushed aromatics.

Warm a roasting tin or shallow, non-stick pan over a moderate heat and add the venison. Brown lightly on both sides, then transfer to the oven and roast for twenty minutes, till rose pink inside. Remove the meat from the roasting tin and set aside in a warm place. Add the wine to the tin and bring to the boil over a high heat. As soon as it starts to bubble, add the rowan or redcurrant jelly and the elderberries, then crush the berries lightly with the back of a spoon. Let the pan juices and seasonings bubble till you have a rich, purple-red sauce.

Slice the venison into thick rounds and serve with the sauce.

Elderberry jelly-jam

I hadn't thought to make a jam with elderberries until I met Linden Monck, whose beautiful allotment with its comfortable shed and lovely old pear tree has a prolific elder bush. Her gorgeous gift of homemade jam, glowing darkly in its pot, inspired me to make my own. Linden's was better than mine.

A jam choc-full of elderberries is almost too much of a good thing (though very good for stuffing a roly-poly pudding – see over), so I now make a soft elderberry and apple jelly instead, and stir in a few of the reserved, cooked berries. The result is a jelly but with some of the berries' texture, so it sits nicely between jelly and jam. Because elderberries have a low pectin content, they generally need to be mixed with crab apples or tart green apples in order to set. On their own, they will produce a jam that may refuse to set.

> ripe elderberries – 1kg
> sharp apples or crab apples – 500g
> water – 800ml
> granulated sugar – 1kg

Pull the elderberries from their stems and place in a deep, stainless steel pan. Halve the apples, but don't peel them, then add to the elderberries with the water. Bring to the boil. Turn the heat down and simmer gently for twenty minutes or until the apples are soft. Remove from the heat, allow to cool slightly, then pour through a clean jelly bag. Leave overnight to drip through slowly. Don't push the fruit pulp through, otherwise the jelly will go cloudy. Retain some of the berries if you want to put them in your jelly.

The next day, add the sugar to the juice (with the reserved berries if you are using them) and bring back to the boil, then boil hard for a full ten minutes or so, until the jelly tests positively for setting (a spoonful on a fridge-cold saucer should quickly form a skin and barely move when the saucer is tipped on its side). Pour into sterilised jars, seal and leave to set.

Black jam roly-poly pudding

It is the sumptuously dark jams – damson, blackcurrant and loganberry – that are best in a suet crust. Their deep hue stands out in a richly coloured spiral; their intense flavour acts as a perfect balance for the bland laundry-coloured dough. The one I made last autumn with elderberry jam was perhaps the jolliest of all.

You can steam a roly-poly, but I much prefer them baked. Yes, the jam leaks a little, but to a certain extent you can prevent it by pushing the roll to one edge of the baking sheet and tipping it at a slight angle in the oven to stop it spreading. I don't really mind if it flattens a bit as it bakes – it is what it is. Enough jam generally stays inside the pudding to keep it interesting.

What we put with such a rib-sticking pudding is up to us. Custard sounds a bit Billy Bunter, but it works superbly here, surrounding the golden dough in a vanilla-scented pool. Cream is another thought, served by the generous jugful.

enough for 4
self-raising flour – 175g
shredded suet – 85g
caster sugar – a tablespoon
cold water – 160–175ml
jam, elderberry for instance – 250g

Set the oven at 220°C/Gas 7. Sift the flour into a mixing bowl, tip in the shredded suet and the sugar, then mix to a sticky but workable dough with the water. At this point you can add a little more flour or water as necessary in order to achieve a rollable dough that doesn't stick to your rolling pin.

Roll the dough out on a well-floured board into a rectangle approximately 30cm x 20cm. Spread the jam over it, then wet one long edge and roll up into a thick sausage. Press the wet edge firmly to seal.

Lift on to a non-stick or paper-lined baking sheet and bake for thirty-five minutes or so, until golden. Serve in thick slices.

Figs

Tender as bruised flesh, a ripe fig is at its most seductive eaten warm from the sun. Jade, amber, purple or almost black, figs need the utmost care to get them from branch to plate in perfect condition. Small wonder, then, that so many are sold underripe. Even then, they need a safe pair of hands to carry them home from the shops without piercing their delicate skin (for once there is an excuse for supermarket-style over-packaging).

Like an apricot, the fig loses all point if it is not perfectly ripe. You might as well eat cardboard. Firm specimens can be ushered into a state of ripeness in a warm room, the fruit set well apart on a plate. They have a tendency to mould when they are stored touching one another. I take pleasure in 'bringing on' fruits like this, fondling them respectfully every day – a sniff, a caress, a watchful eye – to check on their progress.

The fragility of the fruit is also part of its attraction. Stroke the ripest fig and it is as if you are touching flesh. Sniff it and not only is it summer but the hottest day, the air heavy and still, the earth beneath your bare feet cracked and dry. Sink your teeth in and you meet no resistance. Just soft, sumptuous flesh and tiny pearlescent seeds, little crimson beads that dissolve on your tongue.

The skin of most figs is edible, though some insist on its removal. The perfect fruit should probably be eaten in a quiet, respectful moment, but they tend to come in a glut (mine often ripen within the space of a fortnight) and it is then that their potential as the filling for a tart or as a syrupy preserve can be exploited.

Botanically, the fig is not a fruit as such but an 'inflorescence', where flowers and seeds have grown together to form one mass. Tear one apart and it feels like a flower opening in spring.

There is something ancient, almost biblical about the fig, in much the same way as there is about the olive (it is one of the oldest plants in civilisation). It would be difficult to overestimate its importance as a food. Remains have been discovered that pre-date wheat or barley by a thousand years, making it possibly the earliest crop in cultivation. Ancient Egyptians regarded it as the tree of life. To the Greeks it was a symbol of fertility (what wasn't? I hear you ask), and it is even now the National Tree of India. The Romans planted them too: Cato the Elder lists five varieties, including the Mariscan and the black Tellanian.

Mentioned in both the Bible and the Quran, the fig tree is often a sign of prosperity. 'Each man under his own vine and fig tree' (1 Kings 4:25) still conjures up a certain sense of peace, fortune and wellbeing. It is a favourite fruit of artists and has been painted throughout history. Prudish collectors often added a fig leaf to nude portraits long after the original painting was completed.

This fruit almost defines the Mediterranean. Match it to the warmth of thyme or mint and there is no doubting the provenance of your recipe. The fig's friends, anchovy, pomegranate, almonds, prosciutto, honey, goat's cheeses and lavender, tell us much about where it feels at home. This is an ingredient that will also take being baked or simmered in red wine or squashed into jam or chutney and will happily end its days in a simple almond tart. But any attempt to get it into contrived 'haute cuisine' and its magic will generally desert you.

The fig's laxative properties are well known but it also carries favourable levels of calcium, potassium and trace minerals. Add this to its high fibre content and the picture of the historical importance of the fig becomes even clearer. Nowadays a fresh or dried fig is a treat, but for a long time it verged on being a staple food, and was particularly important to early travellers as it could be dried with ease, was light to carry and could be used as sustenance along the way. Now, the principal producers are Turkey – particularly the Aydin and Izmir regions, which send out over a million tons each year – and Egypt.

My own fig trees give me untold pleasure. Their naked, ashen branches, pointed and witchy against a Nordic winter sky, are as beautiful as when they are in full summer flush. The first green shoots unfold in earliest spring like tiny, waving hands. The excitement of spotting the first hard fruits and then, at last, the honey-sweet scent of the tree laden with ripening riches. Most of all, it is the lush shade that I appreciate, the heavy leaf growth protecting the garden table as successfully as any parasol.

Given a long, baking summer, the fig tree will reward us with two crops. 2009 would have been a bumper crop for me, the weight of the fruit pulling the brittle branches almost to the floor, only for the tree to fall prey to a fierce and unprecedented hailstorm (honestly, as big as ice cubes) that snapped its heaviest branches and dashed many of its ripe fruits to jam on the stone terrace.

I should mention that I knew the dried fig long before I had ever seen the fresh. First as the brown crystallised fig, a sweetmeat passed around after Christmas lunch in its black and gold box, oval brown jellies glistening with a hoar frost of sugar. Then came the faintly sinister mahogany rectangles of squashed figs at the early health-food shops, sticky and almost impossible to prise apart. Lastly, the wicker caskets of dried fruit covered in chocolate that appeared in the local Italian grocer's for a few weeks in early winter. The delectably chewy, parchment-coloured dried figs I now munch in lieu of sweets came much, much later.

A fig tree in the garden

When I moved into this house, there was a thriving young Ficus in the lawn that bore as many fruits as we could eat. Tragically, it didn't survive the redesign of the garden (it was in the wrong place and had a root system too sprawling to move). It was quite clearly a happy tree and I have felt uncomfortable about its demise ever since. I have attempted to assuage my guilt by replacing it with two more.

The two new trees, a Rouge de Bordeaux (which should ideally be in a greenhouse) and a Brown Turkey, were joined four years ago by a third, a fan-trained Petite Negri from Reads Nursery in Norfolk (a garden can never have too many figs). This latest addition now spans much of the north-facing wall of the 'courtyard' area outside the kitchen and is exceedingly generous with its small, dark fruit.

Ficus carica is not even remotely fussy about the soil in which it finds itself but the trees do like to be in a sunny spot. It reminds them of home. Mine get very little water and even after a rainstorm the soil around their feet is rarely damp, but the general rule is to give them plenty. I put their generous fruiting down to the fact that their root growth is contained. This is simple enough to do. We dug a deep pit, barely 70cm square, which was then lined with a sheet of zinc. Broken crockpots were placed in the bottom for drainage (we could have used coarse gravel), then the young tree was lowered into the hole and backfilled with ordinary garden soil. Equally we could have used paving slabs or planted the tree in a large pot. The point is simply to contain the roots. This single act of restriction encourages prolific fruiting.

Fig trees can become very large. My red fig has grown to four metres in seven years, its slender, brittle branches snapping off during bad weather. You can train them to cover a wall, as I have done with the Petite Negri. The young, whippy branches are supple for the first year of growth and can be tied along wires to form a dense covering for a wall or even the side of the house. As each new branch appears, you need to tie it to wires or a strong trellis. Smaller varieties will survive in good-sized pots too, but you will need to be generous with the water.

A happy tree will often reward you with two crops a year. The first, called breba, appears on last year's growth. The second, generally a smaller crop, appears mostly, though not exclusively, on new growth. With their smooth grey bark and dinner-plate leaves, the trees love a long, hot summer and without it, the second crop is unlikely to have the chance to ripen.

Varieties

It is the self-pollinating figs that do best in Britain, notably the Black Mission, Brown Turkey and Brunswick, but with a greenhouse or sheltered spot the possibilities get a little more interesting. Most have two crops in a long summer, though if the second fails to ripen, the hard, green infants should be picked off at the end of the season. A jam can be made with the unripe figs but I am honestly not sure it is worth it. Yes, it's jam, but where is the heart and soul of the fruit?

Purple or black figs
Violette Solleis A greenhouse variety with flattish, dark purple fruits on a rose-coloured stalk. A pink-fleshed fruit with dark violet skin.
Violette de Bordeaux Small, dark purple fig with strawberry-coloured flesh.
Rouge de Bordeaux Sweet, dark-skinned fruit that needs a warm, sheltered spot. Revered for the flavour of its raspberry-red flesh.
Petite Negri (sometimes Negra) A neat bush with rich-tasting fruits that are almost black in colour. Good for pots or for training up a wall. Mine has done well on a north-facing wall, the fruit ripening in late September and October.
Fig Grise de St Jean One for a conservatory or large greenhouse. First recorded in 1702, this is a very beautiful violet fig with a dusty, grey bloom and pale pink, fragrant flesh.

Green, yellow and brown figs
Panachee Striped green and yellow fruit from a vigorous tree that I have seen yet sadly never tasted.
White Marseilles Also known as Figue Blanche, an early to mid-season variety with pale, translucent flesh that is particularly sweet. Grows well in British gardens and in pots.
White Ischia Heavy crops of small, pale-skinned fruit with a faint brown blush and sweet pink, honey-scented flesh. Best indoors.
Italian Honey Also known as Peter's Honey, a favourite of Reads Nursery. Sweet, crimson flesh under a beautiful golden skin. Much prefers a greenhouse.

Angelique These charming yellow figs with a distinctive perfume turn red where they face the sun. Available exclusively from Reads Nursery in Norfolk. White flesh with a slightly pink tinge to it.

Brunswick Yellowish-bronze, pear-shaped fruit with a distinct brown blush. This is the one that is meant when people refer to the Madonna fig. Survives our climate well but dislikes rain. Pale red flesh and enormous leaves.

Drap d'Or A late, pale, almost golden fruit with a reddish blush and very fine flavour. The tree needs a warm site, preferably a glasshouse.

Brown Turkey The most popular fig in British gardens. Plump and of fairly good flavour, the Brown Turkey produces green, pear-shaped fruits with a good purple-brown blush and deep red, seedy flesh. One of the most reliably prolific and good natured.

A fig in the kitchen

A fig is ready when it has a bead of nectar at its eye and the skin is bulging. It may even show a little crack, as if the pressure of the ripe flesh within is too much for the skin. Most of the velvet-skinned figs that come my way during the summer and autumn are eaten at the table and almost always with a certain hushed reverence. These are fruits that deserve more than to be chomped from the hand like an apple.

Often there will be a piece of cheese involved in my 'fig-fests' too, and for that I can recommend the blues – Cashel, Gorgonzola, Stilton and Stichelton – and almost any soft goat's cheese, especially if you mix a little chopped fresh thyme in too.

None of this means I am not also prepared to bake a fig or two. Though the heat will give a fulsome silkiness to the texture, the real blisspoint is when you reach the seeds within. Together, the warm flesh and crunchy seeds are as sensuous a mouthful of fruit as you could ever wish for. Even more so when the juices mix with fudge-coloured brown sugar, marsala or a glass of Beaujolais. Eaten warm, the flesh, seeds and juice present a whole package of gorgeousness.

Whilst they don't take well to a pie, a crumble, a crisp or a cobbler, figs can work in place of apples in a tarte Tatin or as thin slices in a puff pastry tarte fine. They bake beautifully in red wine and honey, taking on the colour of deepest claret, and I like them sunk into the frangipane filling of an almond tart. Just spoon a classic almond filling (butter, sugar, flour, eggs and ground almonds) into the tart case, then push the quartered fruits down so they are almost, but not quite, submerged, and bake.

Raw, the ripe fig is a masterful partner to smoked and air-dried meats. The classic Italian plate of figs with Parma ham is just a start. Speck, San Daniele, heavily marbled coppa and any coarse-grained salumi are all possibilities, as are rashers of bacon draped around the fruits and grilled or baked.

The fig delights in hiding beneath the leaves of a salad just as the fruit likes to snuggle under the leaves on the tree. I use it with crisp greens as a contrast to its soft flesh – so chicory, perky spinach, frisé and florets of lamb's lettuce. Often there will be nuts in my salad too, such as walnuts and chopped Kent cobs, and occasionally a few shards of crisp streaky bacon.

As one expects from its provenance, the fig enjoys the company of olive oil, but you may also appreciate it with a cream-based dressing of blue cheese. A mixture of olive oil, egg yolks and finely grated Parmesan given a little spark with lemon juice is a perennial favourite dressing of mine. As is a spoonful of moist ricotta eaten with each fat, ripe fruit.

Fig preserves are amongst some of the most luscious to be had, especially as the fig is less inclined to set firmly than many other fruits. Fig jams and conserves are often the sort that fall lazily from the spoon, making them too soft for the average British jam maker with their love of jams that bounce. Turkish fig jam is often sublime and can be used as an impromptu sauce with vanilla ice cream or, my own choice, a sauce of pale and milky fromage frais scattered with toasted walnuts.

Dried figs

Dried figs are not in any way meant to replace the fresh variety. They are an entity in themselves, sharing little in terms of texture, flavour or sensuality with the fresh. I eat them from the packet as others eat sweets. The crunch of their myriad seeds between the teeth is as much one of the sounds of my day as the ping of the oven timer or the low Zen gong of my mobile ring tone. The ancient, parchment-coloured fruit is my favourite form. I find pleasure in its chewy quality, but the soft so-called 'ready to eat' variety is more user-friendly in the kitchen and can be used straight from the packet in cakes and other bits of baking. The downside is its initial slimy texture and its depressing dun colour. Never mind, it's a pleasure to have in the kitchen and I include it here only for those moments when it is more suitable than the fresh article – never as an attempt at a substitute.

Figs and...

Ham Any sort of ham has an affinity for the fig, from pink, soft-textured York ham on the bone to the firmer-textured air-dried treatments such as Parma and coppa.

Bacon Whether they meet up in a salad or as one wrapped around the other, bacon and the fig are a delectable combination.

Venison One of the best fruits for partnering this lean and surprisingly mild meat. A few halved figs added to the pan when sautéing a venison steak will provide glorious pan juices.

Duck Roast duck likes to be joined by a few figs towards the end of roasting, and they are welcome in a duck casserole too.

Blue cheeses Rarely can fruit and cheese form such a perfect combination.

Mozzarella The cool, milky quality of buffalo mozzarella and the sweetness of the fig make a gentle lunch dish; the texture of the quivery cheese and crunchy seeds is a quiet joy.

Spinach Whether as a textural or flavour combination, the partnership works brilliantly.

Brown sugars Demerara and soft light muscovado are an excellent way to sweeten a fig. They beef up the flavour without intruding.

Marsala and Madeira Rich, sweet alcohols that add much to the fruit. The mellow flavours work in perfect harmony.

Nuts Almonds and walnuts work well with the fruit in recipes but also raw to form a simple dessert. A few cracked walnuts and almonds scattered over a platter of figs has to be one of the most superbly understated ways to end a meal. Ground almonds are pleasing as the base for an open tart of figs.

Chocolate Although fresh figs and chocolate work well enough as a pairing, I prefer chocolate with dried figs.

Orange Elizabeth David used oranges to lift the sweetness of a plate of fresh figs.

Thyme With the exception of basil, there are few herbs that add anything much to the pleasure of eating a fig. However, the resinous flavour of thyme is a different matter entirely. Used together, figs and thyme conjure up scorched hillsides in the baking sun. Try adding a sprig or two to baked figs, then eat them with the goat's cheese below.

Goat's cheeses Fresh, slightly acidic goat's cheeses form the happiest of all fig and cheese marriages. A gentler pairing than the blue cheeses with which figs are more usually married, the effect of the fig's crunchy seeds with the soft, slightly sharp notes of the cheese is a delight.

Honey Especially that sourced from clover and wild flowers, often feels a more appropriate sweetener for fig dishes than sugar. Try it trickled over torn figs and a sharp, young goat's cheese.

* The sap from the tree and leaves is an irritant to the skin. Something I found out the hard way.

* The term 'I don't care a fig' is generally thought to originate from the fig's abundance. Personally I tend to use 'I couldn't give a fig' as a polite alternative to what I really wanted to say.

Figs and Cashel Blue

On a late summer's evening, I will occasionally put a plate of purple figs on the zinc table in the garden together with a lump of blue cheese from Ireland or Italy. We help ourselves, cutting the fruits in half and placing a piece of Cashel Blue or Gorgonzola on their deep maroon flesh.

Figs with creamed Gorgonzola

Gorgonzola is often the softest of the blue cheeses. Mixed with cream or oil, it will form a less grainy dressing than the firmer varieties such as Stilton. Ideally, the cheese should be excessively ripe, almost to the point of liquidity.

enough for 4
figs – 8
spicy leaves such as rocket, watercress and mizuna – 4 handfuls

for the Gorgonzola cream
ripe Gorgonzola – 250g
double cream – 100–150ml
a teaspoon of white wine vinegar

Put the cheese in a mixing bowl and stir in enough of the cream to give a creamy, slightly lumpy sauce. It should be thick enough to spread. Add the vinegar.

Cut the figs in halves or quarters, depending on their size. Divide the salad leaves between four plates, then add the figs and a spoonful or two of the Gorgonzola cream.

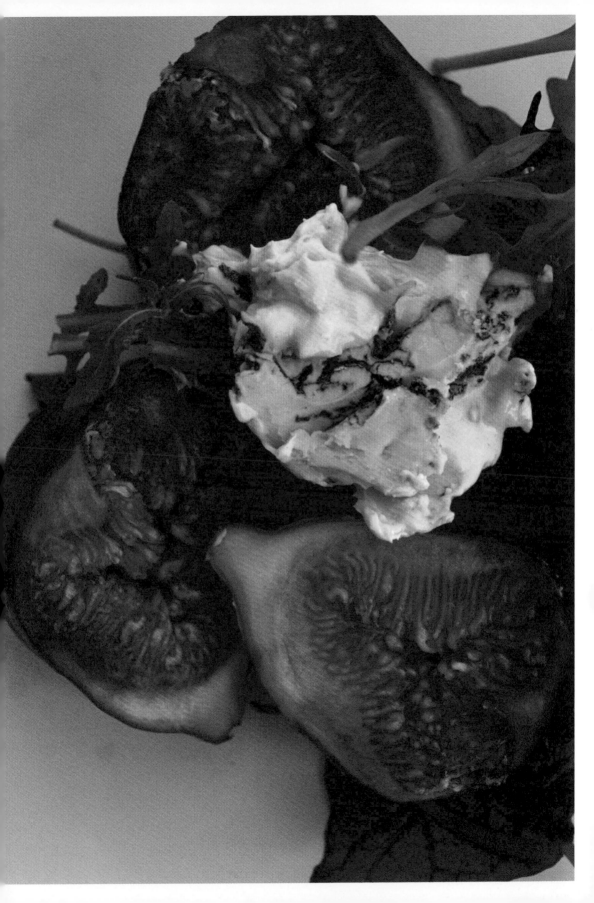

Baked feta, figs and flatbread

Warm feta, salty, herbal and nicely sharp, is something I eat in high summer, baking it in the oven or warming it wrapped in foil on the grill. Its appearance with figs was an accident, but one that has been repeated several times. The warm, slightly salty cheese and its notes of thyme and rosemary work very well with the lusciousness of the figs.

Middle Eastern flatbreads, soft and warm as a baby's skin, are well known for scooping up dips of aubergine and cod's roe, but you can use them for so much more. I have been known to eat an entire stew with them, and often serve them with roast vegetables. Whether you have pitta, lavash or even Italian focaccia doesn't really matter, they all perform the same task. Unwrap the hot cheese at the table so that everyone gets to smell its lactic, deeply herbal scent. Some cold beers would be good here, too.

enough for 2 as part of a mezze
olive oil – 3–4 tablespoons
thyme – several sprigs
rosemary – a few short sprigs
bottled green peppercorns – a tablespoon
a clove of garlic
a small red chilli
feta – 200g

to serve
warm flatbread, such as Iranian lavash or Turkish pitta
6 ripe figs

Heat the oven to 200°C/Gas 6. Pour the olive oil into a mixing bowl. Hold the herbs over the bowl and strip off the leaves, letting them fall into the oil. Stir in the green peppercorns and a coarse grinding of black pepper. Peel the garlic and crush it so that it resembles a thick paste, then stir that in too.

Cut the chilli in half, scrape out the seeds and chop the flesh finely. Stir it into the oil and herbs. Place a piece of foil on a baking tray, lay the cheese on top, then spoon over the oil and herbs. Fold into a loose parcel and bake for fifteen minutes.

Warm the breads, then serve them with the figs, halved, and the hot feta.

Marinated goat's cheese for a fig and cheese lunch

The fruit and cheese lunch takes many forms in my house: a Russet apple and a lump of orange-fleshed Cheshire; a pear with a mild goat's cheese; melon with snow-white feta. Figs can take the strongest of cheeses, from the saltiest of blues to the most strident of washed-rind varieties. I like them with goat's cheeses that have been marinated in oil and aromatics so that they take on a more pungent note. They are often brought to the table with slices of coppa or speck, too.

enough for 3
small goat's cheeses – 6
thyme – 6 small sprigs
bay leaves – 3
small dried chillies – 2
black peppercorns – 8
olive oil to cover
figs – 6 or 8 ripe

Cut the goat's cheeses in half horizontally. Put into a large bowl and tuck the herbs and chillies around them. Crack the peppercorns with a heavy object such as a pestle or even a can of something – you just want to split each one into two or three rather than crush them – and add them to the bowl.

Pour enough olive oil over the cheeses to just cover them, then cover the bowl tightly with cling film and set aside somewhere cool overnight. The refrigerator will do, but you should bring them out and back to room temperature for a good hour before serving with ripe figs.

Duck with figs and Barolo

The rich flesh of a roasted duck – sumptuous, fatty, glorious – needs
something in the way of contrast if it is not to cloy. A single piece of fruit,
orange say, or plum, generally fits the bill. For a midweek supper, I often
roast a leg or two (more interesting meat than the breast), then make a
thin, simple gravy with a glass of wine. The addition of figs, cut in half and
allowed to soften in the wine, works very well as a contrast of texture. Any
fruity red wine will do.

enough for 2
duck legs – 2
a few sprigs of thyme
figs – 4
a wine glass of red wine such as Barolo

Season the duck legs with salt and black pepper, tuck in the thyme sprigs,
then roast in an oven preheated to 200°C/Gas 6 till golden and crisp –
skinned – a matter of twenty-five to thirty minutes or so. Holding the duck
in place with a spatula, pour off the fat and reserve for another day. It will be
wonderful for potatoes. Cut the figs in half and tuck them, cut-side down,
around the duck. Pour in the red wine and place over a moderate heat till
the wine has evaporated by half and the figs have softened, scraping any
crusty bits from the pan into the wine.

Pot-roast guinea fowl with figs

A simple pot-roast bird takes five or ten minutes to prepare, followed by an hour or so of unattended cooking. The result is meat that is both tender and flavoursome, cooking juices instilled with the essence of the meat and only one pan to wash up. The figs here offer a certain harmony to an autumn dish of gentle flavours.

> *enough to serve 2 generously*
> a guinea fowl
> an onion
> rosemary – a small sprig
> white vermouth such as Noilly Prat – a wine glass
> half a lemon
> figs – 4

Set the oven at 200°C/Gas 6. Season the guinea fowl with salt and pepper. Peel and roughly chop the onion and put it into a large, deep casserole. Add the rosemary, vermouth, guinea fowl and the lemon half, cut in two. Cover with a lid and roast in the oven for an hour, until tender. Half way through cooking, add the figs cut in half. Check for doneness by inserting a skewer in the thickest part of the thigh. If the juices run clear, then the bird is cooked. Serve in thick slices with the onion, figs and cooking juices.

Baked figs, red wine and vanilla

enough for 4
fruity red wine – 500ml
golden caster sugar – 3 tablespoons
thick honey – a tablespoon (or more to taste)
a short length of orange peel
a vanilla pod
cloves – 2
figs – 12

Set the oven at 200°C/Gas 6. Place the wine, sugar, honey, orange peel, split
vanilla pod and cloves in a stainless steel saucepan and bring almost to the
boil. Gently wipe the figs and place them snugly in a shallow ovenproof
serving dish (they look wonderful in earthenware). Pour the hot wine
over the figs, then bake them till they are soft and full of juice – this
will take thirty to forty-five minutes. Turn the figs over and baste them
during cooking.

Pour the juice through a sieve back into the original saucepan, bring
to the boil, turn down the heat and simmer till the liquid starts to thicken.
It should end up the consistency of thin syrup. Pour the syrup over the figs
and chill thoroughly before serving.

Roast figs with marsala and muscovado

Dark-skinned figs, warm from the oven with a drizzle of cream, are one of the most sensuous of late summer desserts. Effortless to make and to eat, they are best served straight from the oven. Lucky those with their own fig tree. I have used both sweet and dry marsala for this before now. If you have the latter, add a further tablespoon of sugar.

enough for 4
figs – 8 (maybe more if they are small)
sweet marsala – a small wine glass
light muscovado sugar
cream, to serve

Set the oven at 200°C/Gas 6. Cut the stalks from the figs and slice a deep cross into each fruit, going about half way down. Press each fruit around its middle so that it opens up like a flower (or a baby bird in its nest yelling for food). You can cut them in half, if you prefer. Place the figs in a baking dish, then sprinkle over the wine and a couple of tablespoons of sugar. Bake for about twenty to twenty-five minutes, till the fruit is meltingly tender and the edges have started to caramelise. If they haven't browned nicely, then pop them under a hot grill for a minute.

Serve the fruit, pouring over a little of the pan juices (there won't be many) as you go and a drizzle of cream.

Fig, orange and polenta cake

This cake, scented with cardamom and sweetened with honey, works both as something to eat with glasses of mint tea and as a dessert, in which case you might like to serve it with yoghurt.

enough for 8
butter – 220g
golden caster sugar – 220g
almonds – 150g
ground almonds – 150g
large eggs – 3
polenta – 150g
baking powder – a level teaspoon
finely grated zest and juice of a large orange
green cardamom pods – 12
figs – 6

for the syrup
the juice of 2 oranges
the juice of 2 lemons
honey – 4 tablespoons

Line the base of a loose-bottomed non-stick 20cm cake tin with a piece of baking parchment. Set the oven at 180°C/Gas 4.

Beat the butter and sugar in a food mixer till light and fluffy. Put the almonds in a heatproof bowl and pour boiling water over them. Remove them a few at a time with a draining spoon and pop them from their skins. Blitz the almonds in a food processor till they are finely chopped (or chop them by hand if you prefer), then add them, together with the ground almonds to the cake mixture.

Break the eggs into a small bowl, beat them lightly with a fork and stir them into the mixture. Mix the polenta and baking powder together, then fold them into the mixture together with the grated orange zest and juice. Crush the cardamom pods and extract the little black seeds, then grind them to a fine powder. I use a pestle and mortar for this, but you can do it in a coffee grinder if you want. Add the spice to the cake mixture.

Cut the figs in half. Transfer half the cake mixture to the lined tin, add the figs, then add the remaining cake mixture and smooth the top level. The figs will appear as a moist layer at the bottom of the cake. Bake for thirty minutes, then turn the heat down to 160°C/Gas 3 and bake for a further twenty-five to thirty minutes or until the cake is firm to the touch. Test it for doneness with a metal skewer – it should come out clean, without wet cake mixture sticking to it.

To make the syrup, squeeze the orange and lemon juice into a stainless steel saucepan, bring to the boil and dissolve the honey in it. Keep the liquid boiling for four or five minutes, until it has formed a thin syrup.

Spike holes into the top of the cake (still warm and in its tin) with a skewer, then spoon over the hot citrus syrup. Leave until almost cool, then lift out of the tin. Serve in thick slices, with thinly sliced fresh oranges and, if you wish for something more decadent, a little natural yoghurt.

A crumbly, upside-down tart of figs

I like my tarts to be warm, crumbly, messy and sweet. To this end, I use a very short pastry with a high proportion of butter and treat the raw pastry very gently, patching it where it crumbles. To deliver perfection, I add a tart cream such as crème fraîche or a ball of ice-cold vanilla or cinammon ice cream.

enough for 8

for the pastry
cold butter – 175g
plain flour – 225g
large egg yolks – 2
golden caster sugar – 2 level tablespoons

for the filling
butter – 75g
golden caster sugar – 75g
figs – 10, halved and tough stems removed

vanilla or cinnamon ice cream or crème fraîche, to serve

You will need a tarte Tatin mould or a metal-handled frying pan or sauté pan about 20–23cm in diameter.

To make the pastry, cut the butter into cubes, then rub it into the flour until the mixture resembles fine fresh breadcrumbs. Sometimes I do it by hand, other times the speed of the food processor beckons. Mix in the egg yolks and sugar, then bring the mixture together into a ball with your hands. Wrap in greaseproof paper and refrigerate for twenty minutes.

Set the oven at 220°C/Gas 7. Melt the butter and sugar in the Tatin mould or frying pan over a moderate heat, stirring from time to time. When the mixture looks syrupy and is starting to colour, add the figs, cut-side down. Let them cook for three to five minutes, until they are soft and starting to darken. Remove the pan from the heat.

Roll out the pastry to make a circle a couple of centimetres larger than the frying pan. Fold the extra pastry over to make a double 'rim' around the edge. Place the pastry rim-side down on top of the figs (the best way to move this very short and crumbly pastry is to wrap it lightly around the rolling pin, then carefully lift it on to the pan). Place in the oven and bake for about forty minutes, until the pastry is a deep biscuit colour. Take it out of the oven and leave it to calm down a bit. Cut into slices and serve straight from the pan (the slices will crumble a bit), with ice cream or crème fraîche.

Baked figs, red wine, fruit jelly

The fruit jelly I suggest here gives body to the cooking liquor.

enough for 4
small, plump figs – 12
red wine or port – 250ml
a vanilla pod
runny honey – 2 tablespoons
redcurrant jelly – 2 heaped tablespoons

Put the fruit into a stainless steel pan. Pour the red wine over the fruit together with 125ml of water, then tuck the vanilla pod underneath and drizzle over the honey and redcurrant jelly. Simmer gently for thirty minutes or so, until the fruit is tender.

Lift the figs into a serving dish, then bring the juices to the boil and keep an eye on them until about half has evaporated. They will have thickened into a dark red, glossy syrup that will thicken even further, almost to the consistency of liquid honey, as it cools. Strain the syrup over the figs and put them aside to cool. I serve these at room temperature.

Slow-baked figs with orange and Vin Santo

I much prefer the old-fashioned, hard and intensely chewy lumps of beige fruit to the new squidgy, soft-dried version. The pale, fudge-coloured dried figs from Turkey have a deep flavour and a moreish crunchiness and are better suited to long, slow cooking than the soft variety.

enough for 4
whole dried figs – 450g
Vin Santo – 250ml
water – 250ml
an orange
cloves – 2
redcurrant jelly – a heaped tablespoon

Set the oven at 190°C/Gas 5. Tip the figs into a casserole dish with a lid and pour over the wine and water. Remove three wide strips of zest from the orange with a vegetable peeler, then add it to the figs, along with the cloves and the redcurrant jelly.

Cover with a lid and bake for one hour, by which time the figs will have plumped up into fat, wine-laden bundles. Eat warm or chilled.

Baked figs with red wine and blackcurrant jelly

I used a glass or two of Madiran for this because that is what happened
to be open, but any heavy red wine would have done. This is an occasion,
perhaps, to use one of those oak and vanilla red wines from California.
A very light wine will give a correspondingly thinner syrup.

enough for 4
small, whole dried figs – 200g
red wine – 250ml
a vanilla pod
runny honey – 2 tablespoons
blackcurrant jelly – 1 heaped tablespoon

Find a baking dish into which the figs will fit comfortably, then pour in
enough warm water to barely conceal them. Set them aside for several hours
so that the fruit softens; if you can leave them overnight they will be even
better, the water thickening to a light amber syrup.

Set the oven at 180°C/Gas 4. Pour the red wine over the fruit and its
soaking liquid, then tuck the vanilla pod underneath and drizzle over the
honey and blackcurrant jelly. Bake for a good hour, until some of the syrup
has evaporated and the figs are plump.

Lift the figs into a serving dish, then pour the baking juices into a
stainless steel pan. Bring the syrup to the boil and keep an eye on it until
about half has evaporated. It will have thickened into a claret-coloured,
glossy syrup that will thicken even further, almost to the consistency of
liquid honey, as it cools. Strain the syrup over the figs and put them aside
to cool. I serve these at room temperature, with a somewhat unnecessary
jug of pouring cream for those who wish.

Steamed fig pudding

An old-fashioned steamed pudding, a recipe that I am continually asked for, so here it is again.

enough for 4
dried figs – 450g
port – 150ml
a cinnamon stick
a bay leaf
runny honey – 2 tablespoons

for the sponge
butter – 100g
golden caster sugar – 100g
large eggs – 2
fresh breadcrumbs – 50g
self-raising flour – 100g
ground ginger and cinnamon – ½ teaspoon each

Cut all but six of the figs into quarters, then place them all in a small, heavy pan with the port, cinnamon stick, bay leaf and honey. Bring to the boil, then turn down the heat and simmer for about ten minutes. Lift the figs out with a draining spoon and then reduce the syrup to about 5 tablespoons by boiling rapidly. Butter a 900ml pudding basin. Place the whole figs (only) and syrup in the bottom.

Beat the butter and sugar with an electric beater till pale and fluffy. Add the eggs one at a time and beat in. If the mixture curdles, and it probably will, it will come to no harm. Just fold in the breadcrumbs, chopped figs and the sifted flour and spices.

Spoon the mixture into the basin, on top of the whole figs and syrup, and smooth the surface flat. Place a piece of greaseproof paper over the top of the basin, folding a pleat down the centre as you do so, and secure with string. Cover with a muslin cloth or foil and secure that also. Place the basin on a trivet in a large saucepan with enough water to come two-thirds up the sides of the basin. Steam, covered with a lid, for an hour, topping up the water from time to time.

Carefully remove the pudding from the water, leave for a few minutes, then remove the covers and turn out. Serve with cold cream or hot custard.

Dried fig and pumpkin seed bars

Chewy, oaty, buttery biscuits. Like a luxurious flapjack.

makes 12
walnut halves – 60g
soft dried figs – 70g
sour cherries – 40g
pumpkin seeds – 30g
porridge oats or rolled oats – 200g
ground almonds – 35g
butter – 100g
maple syrup – 100ml
caster sugar – 90g

Set the oven at 160°C/Gas 3. Roughly chop the walnuts, figs, cherries and pumpkin seeds. This is done in seconds in a food processor but will take a bit longer by hand. The rougher your mix, the more crumbly the biscuits will be. The biscuits will hold together better the finer the mixture.

Tip in the oats and ground almonds. Melt the butter in a large saucepan, pour in the maple syrup and add the caster sugar. When it all comes to a rolling boil, add the dry ingredients, stir thoroughly and tip into a non-stick baking tin, about 24cm square. Press the mixture down firmly again and bake for twenty to twenty-five minutes.

Press the mixture down firmly as it cools. Cut into 12 small bars while warm and leave to cool completely.

Gooseberries

This garden fizzes in spring. The infant leaves of the hornbeam, fig, crocosmia and redcurrants sparkle in shades of lime and gold against the sombre black-green of the yew hedges. In particular, I like the way the light shines through the tiny leaves of the three Hinnomaki gooseberry bushes. Amongst the very first to burst in March, they smack of freshness and change, of the excitement of a new gardening year.

I like the way you can see through a gooseberry on the bush, the transparency of it. Despite the angry thorns that have so regularly drawn my blood, I have a soft spot for this small and splendidly sour fruit. Especially its part in the dreamy, creamy gooseberry fool that so perfectly sums up our careless, buttercup-meadow summers.

The gooseberry's short season and lack of friends (it is rarely exploited commercially like the strawberry or blueberry) means that this is not the easiest ingredient to track down in mainstream shops. But come June and July, farmers' markets, farm shops, greengrocer's shops and street markets have a few in cardboard punnets, usually amongst the sea of strawberries. They are one of the few fruits I buy in quantity and freeze (the other being the damson). Not normally a fan of the freezer, I challenge anyone to tell frozen gooseberries from fresh once they are hidden in the sweet rubble of a crumble.

British cooks are amongst the most prolific users of *Ribes uva-crispa*, yet the genus is indigenous throughout Europe and Western Asia. No cuisine seems to have quite as many gooseberry recipes devoted to it as we have. Wild bushes are rare, I have certainly never seen one, and any surviving ones may well be those that have made a bid for freedom near allotments and vegetable patches.

As with redcurrants and blackberries, cool weather is more favourable for the gooseberry's cultivation. They are found right up to the Arctic Circle.

The bushes do particularly well in Lancashire and Yorkshire (the flavour is said to improve the further north you go), where there are societies and clubs devoted to growing, showing and celebrating the fruit. The oldest, dating from 1800, is at Egton Bridge near Whitby, and has an annual show on the first Tuesday in August. Plenty of time for the fruit to plump up to a size suitable for winning prizes – like vegetable shows, flavour barely comes into it.

In the south, the gooseberry needs a bit of shade. My bushes live on the cool side of the garden, under the spreading arms of the medlar tree. It is not just shady here but cool, and the soil rarely dries out. My previous bushes often produced barely enough for a single fool or crumble, yet somehow that was enough to justify their existence. That is all I asked of them.

I rank the green gooseberry, with its piercing sharpness, as one of the finest kitchen fruits we have. In my book it comes only just behind the damson and the blackcurrant as a bringer of fresh, piquant flavours to our puddings. The fruit's astringency is bracing, and is why it is one of the few fruits that work in place of lemon in a meringue pie. It is also surely in the running for a pavlova.

Victorian cookery books offer more possibilities than contemporary ones, and their recipes for ice cream, fools, jellies and compotes are still in use by fans. Yes, the fruit is a celebration of nostalgia, but also one for fresh thinking: in my kitchen it is included not only in its well-known forms of fool and compote but also in cakes for tea and sauces for fish and roast pork.

I still rate the soft-crusted gooseberry pie made by the cooks at my Worcestershire school as one of the most memorable puddings of my life. To this day I can taste the softly-softly pastry with its fine sugar crust and the grey-green filling, slightly sweet and bracingly sharp. This is not the fruit of instant appeal to the masses like the strawberry, but a fruit of quiet pleasure, something for the few who understand and appreciate its charms.

A gooseberry in the garden

Three Careless gooseberry bushes were amongst the first plants to go into this garden. Within a fortnight of the lawn being uprooted and the ground being turned I had dug them in, and within a year they were fruiting well enough for an early-summer crumble and a pie. As the years went on, and despite careful pruning and generous feeding, they bore fewer and fewer fruits and sadly had to go (you can normally expect a decade or more out of a healthy bush).

A vegetable patch needs a gooseberry bush like it needs a crown of rhubarb, so it wasn't long before three replacements went in. I chose Hinnomaki, a variety known for its flavour and disease resistance; one of each colour, green, yellow and red. They now live in light shade in the medlar bed, a few feet away from the rhubarb crowns.

Gooseberries are not the fussiest of bushes and are one of the few fruits to tolerate shade or soil that is less than perfect. Hardy bushes, they will cope with cold and even frosts, despite their early flowering. Rhubarb aside, they are amongst the first fruits to ripen in the garden, with some varieties giving tart fruit suitable for cooking as early as late May. Be ready with the sugar bowl.

New plants may arrive in pots at any time of year, or from November to April as bare root plants. They can be grown as low bushes or as standards, if you have a feel for the pruning knife, and the latter's long stem will give better air circulation. Dig plenty of manure into the soil before planting your young bushes. Ideally put them in during late autumn to give them a chance to get their feet down before the sap starts rising in spring. If you can't plant till spring, no worries, they will almost certainly forgive you. At least, mine have.

Whatever the variety, the plants need at least a metre between one another. They love good air circulation. Very little upkeep is required other than keeping the base of the plant free of weeds (a prickly, skin-tearing task) and giving the odd early-winter feed of well-rotted manure. Large quantities of manure can increase the size of the fruit, if that is something that interests you.

Pruning is straightforward. In winter, cut the previous year's growth back to two buds. In summer, trim new growth back to five or six leaves along each branch. Snip out any crossing branches in the centre of the bush to allow the air to get in there.

There are two harvesting possibilities. The first is to remove the acid green fruit in early summer and use it in cooking, while the second is to leave it on the stem to ripen fully. Even the sharpest of varieties can often sweeten up enough to eat raw if given plenty of sun and patience.

Varieties

Green 'white' gooseberries
White Eagle An old variety that has recently been reintroduced. Long, pale fruits that are almost transparent.
White Lion Large, sweet, white fruits from large bushes. This old variety is a late but vigorous cropper.
Whitesmith Large, white berries of good flavour that appear early in the season.
Invicta A prolific modern cultivar from East Malling that is particularly resistant to mildew. Pick in July. Very thorny.
Careless This is the variety I grew for ten years. A good, sharp berry that

is perfect for pies, although I sometimes let it ripen on the bush for dessert eating. Less hairy than most, it appears in mid season.

Greenfinch Very resistant to disease, this new compact variety is a prolific cropper.

Yellow gooseberries

Leveller Oval, yellowish, mid-season fruit of excellent flavour. Not as generous a cropper as some, but it did well enough in my garden.

Early Sulphur Early, medium-sized fruit with a good golden colour. The plants are vigorous and spreading, the fruit long rather than round.

Hinnomaki Large, green to gold fruit with good disease resistance. The plants can grow to quite a size, so allow a good metre between them.

Howard's Lancer A middle-to-late-season, medium-sized berry. Round and gold, with a thin skin, this spreading variety is one of our oldest. Wonderful for jam.

Golden Drop A much-liked mid-season berry with a deep gold colour. An upright bush, suitable for a small garden.

Red gooseberries

May Duke Possibly the earliest fruiting berry I have come across, this is the one for that first, lip-puckering crumble of early summer.

Whinham's Industry One of the dark red varieties well suited to eating as a dessert fruit as well as in a crumble. Large, oval berries appear mid-season.

Lancashire Lad A long-established red variety, found on many an allotment.

Hedgehog Great name for a favourite old dessert variety. The fruits are large and crop well on an upstanding bush.

Achilles A large, red berry good for both cooking and eating as a dessert fruit. Left on the bush, its flavour will soften.

Hinnomaki Red Large berries, good flavour and a strong resistance to disease.

Gooseberries in the kitchen

Considering this little green fruit is far from the country's favourite, it has managed to secure everlasting fame in both a classic dessert and a hot pudding. Gooseberry crumble is one of Britain's most celebrated hot puds, as well known as treacle tart or roly-poly pudding. Its enduring popularity is in part due to the contrast between the sharp, soft fruit and sweet, crisp crust. The fruit is also known for its role in the quintessential summer dessert, gooseberry fool.

Once it meets the heat, the gooseberry loses its translucency and turns opaque. Its skin collapses and the fruit slides towards a delicious mush.

While this quality excludes it from open tarts, it means it can be used in fools and creams with little more than a mild crushing from a fork. On the down side, it is almost impossible to make a jam where the whole fruits are visible.

Some form of sweetening is almost always necessary. The butterscotch notes of the unrefined sugars work particularly well, especially golden caster. Honey too, has something of an affinity. The herb sweet cicely can be used to sweeten if you want to cut down on the amount of sugar (first find your sweet cicely). The amount of sugar or honey you need will obviously depend on the variety of your fruit, but more importantly on its ripeness. Early in the season, even red gooseberries can be extremely tart. A June crumble will generally need more sugar than one baked in late July. I often mix sugar and honey.

Savoury applications are few and far between. The best known is that of serving gooseberry purée with mackerel, but I also like a slithering dollop on the side with a pork chop. It works in the same way as apple sauce or poached rhubarb, slicing through the fat with its inherent acidity. Be parsimonious with the sugar if you use this fruit in a savoury way.

Gooseberries and...

Elderflowers The white flowers appear at the same time as the first of the gooseberries and have an extraordinary affinity with them. Simmer whole flower heads with the fruit and a generous amount of sugar.

Honey A small amount will lend warmth to poached gooseberries.

Pork The fruit has the effect of removing the fatty quality from roast pork or pork chops, slicing through it like a sharp knife. I sometimes throw a few berries in with the pan juices when making gravy for a roast.

Mackerel Although gooseberry sauce can be served with cold salmon, I find it most successful with mackerel, especially when the fish has been grilled and its edges lightly charred.

Cream Few fruits have quite the same affinity with cream as this one. It is as if they are inseparable. Gooseberry pie or pudding without cream seems almost pointless. Where the flavour of most fruits is diminished slightly once cream comes into the picture, in this instance its presence is of great value in bringing out the fruit's best qualities.

Ginger One of the few spices that have a rapport. Added to a gooseberry jam or a sauce, the sweet heat of ginger works well.

* The sawfly is the bush's main attacker. It can be kept at bay – to a certain extent – by opening the bush to get good air circulation. Cutting out any crossing branches in the centre of the bush will help, as will opening up the middle to create a goblet shape.
* 'Topping and tailing' means removing both the dead flower head and the gooseberry's tiny stalk. It is not a difficult job, though mildly irritating if you are in a hurry. I try to choose a day when I am not too busy and, if possible, do it outside, sitting on the back step, when the peaceful repetition can be strangely relaxing.
* This fruit is high in pectin, making for a firm jam set. A few gooseberries added to a strawberry or other low-pectin fruit jam can help the setting.
* Carol Klein recommends removing half the crop in early summer and using it in the kitchen, then leaving the rest in place to ripen enough for eating raw. Best of both worlds, I would have thought.
* The quantity of sugar needed will depend on the variety; less sugar is needed as the season progresses.

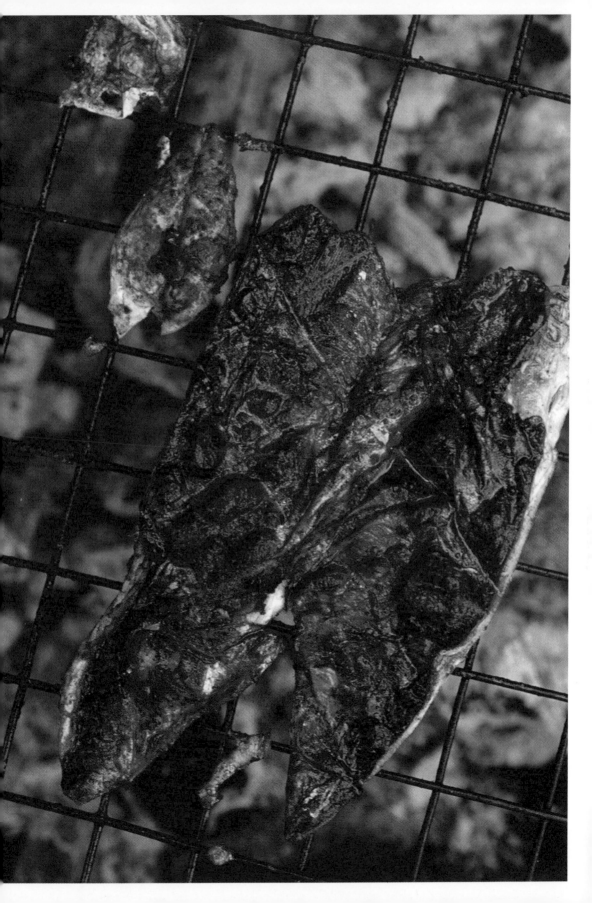

A gooseberry sauce for grilled mackerel or roast pork

Makes enough to accompany grilled mackerel or roast pork for six.

gooseberries – 500g
sugar – 50g
water – 3–4 tablespoons

Top and tail the gooseberries, tip them into a stainless steel pan, then add the sugar and water. Bring to the boil, lower the heat and simmer for ten minutes. Use warm or at room temperature.

A hot gooseberry and ginger sauce

The pairing of the berries with elderflower is used primarily in sweet treatments, such as compotes and jams, but rarely have I seen the two brought together in a savoury context. The idea is that of Yotam Ottolenghi, whose food I find exciting, original and extraordinary.

enough for 6
gooseberries – 400g
caster sugar – 100g
elderflower cordial – 4 tablespoons
fresh ginger – a large lump about the size of your thumb

Top and tail the gooseberries and tip them into a pan with the sugar and cordial. Peel and coarsely grate the ginger and add to the pot. Bring to the boil, turn down the heat and simmer for ten minutes. Serve with pork or oily fish.

Gooseberry, apple and elderflower pie

Slightly different from the one over the page, this pie has the age-old pairing of elderflowers and a marginally crisper crust.

enough for 8

for the pastry
butter – 150g
golden caster sugar – 150g, plus extra for sprinkling
a large egg yolk (reserve the white)

plain flour – 250g
baking powder – a level teaspoon

for the filling
gooseberries – 500g
cooking apples – 800g
golden caster sugar – 125g
elderflower cordial – 3 tablespoons

You will need a 24cm (18cm across the base) metal tart tin with a shallow rim.

Cream the butter and sugar together till soft and pale, in a food mixer or with a wooden spoon. Mix in the egg yolk. Mix the flour and baking powder, then add to the creamed butter and sugar. Bring the dough together and squeeze into a ball. Cut the pastry in two, putting half in the fridge, wrapped loosely in greaseproof paper. Flour the work surface and roll out the first piece of pastry to fit the tart tin, smoothing it up the sides and over the rim – I tend to roll this particular pastry a little thicker than usual. Leave any overhang in place for the time being. Refrigerate for thirty minutes.

Set the oven at 180°C/Gas 4. Top and tail the gooseberries. Peel the apples, quarter them and remove their cores, then slice them thickly (I usually cut each quarter into about three pieces). Put the apples, gooseberries, sugar and elderflower cordial into a stainless steel pan (aluminium will taint the gooseberries) and cook over a low to moderate heat for about ten to fifteen minutes, until the apples are showing some signs of tenderness and the gooseberries are starting to soften. Remove the fruit from the pan with a draining spoon and set aside in a bowl, leaving the juice behind.

Turn up the heat under the juice and let it boil for five to ten minutes, until it has started to turn a little jammy, stopping before it turns brown and caramelises. Let it cool (it may set, no matter).

Put a baking sheet into the oven. Roll out the second piece of pastry. Put the fruit into the pastry-lined tart tin, again using a draining spoon. Spoon over the concentrated fruit syrup. Brush the rim of the pastry with egg white, then place the second piece of pastry over the top, pressing it down on to the rim to seal the edges. Trim any overhanging pastry with a sharp knife. Cut three small slits in the centre of the pastry to let out the steam, then, if you wish, decorate the pastry with leaves made from the trimmings. Bake the pie on the hot baking sheet for thirty-five minutes. Gently beat the egg white until bubbles appear on the surface, then remove the pie from the oven, brush with egg white, scatter a thin layer of sugar over the surface and return to the oven for five minutes. Leave for twenty to thirty minutes to settle down before serving with double cream.

Gooseberry pie

A soft, fragile pastry crust the colour of old linen is sometimes more appropriate than something crisp and honey coloured. I have worked at such a crust for some time now, and feel that this is the one for a gooseberry pie. Tender and pale, this is pastry that collapses beneath the fork, as gentle as a whisper.

enough for 6

for the pastry
butter – 140g
plain flour – 230g
icing sugar – 50g
a large egg yolk

for the filling
gooseberries – 850g
sugar – 160g
water – 4 tablespoons

Rub the butter into the flour with your fingertips, then mix in the icing sugar and egg yolk. Bring the dough together and squeeze it into a round, then put it in the fridge for half an hour to chill. I find this pastry works well in the food processor too; first blitz the flour and butter, then mix briefly with the sugar and egg yolk.

Top and tail the gooseberries, then put them into a non-reactive saucepan with the sugar and water and simmer until the fruit has softened slightly – it will go paler in colour too. But stop before the gooseberries collapse. Lift the fruit into a bowl with a draining spoon, then turn up the heat and boil the liquor down to a thick syrup, stopping before it caramelises.

Set the oven at 200°C/Gas 6. Roll out half the pastry and use to line a 20cm tart tin, pushing it up the sides. I use a crinkle-edged tart ring on a loose base or an old-fashioned metal tart tin. Chill thoroughly, or freeze for fifteen minutes, then bake for fifteen minutes, baking blind if you wish, until the pastry is dry and pale-biscuit coloured. Transfer the drained berries to the pie shell, pour over the thickened syrup and leave to cool a little.

Roll or press out the remaining pastry into a round. Lift it on the rolling pin and place it gently on top of the pie, pressing the edges down to meet the bottom crust. Cut two air holes in the top crust, then bake for twenty minutes until the pie is pale gold. Remove from the oven, sprinkle with caster sugar and return for a further five or six minutes.

Leave the pie to cool a little before serving with a jug of double cream.

Gooseberry pudding

A twist on the usual summer pudding made with raspberries and redcurrants. Whether it will stand up when you turn it out is up to the fruit itself. I feel the pudding is inclined to be more delicious if it doesn't, when the fruit and bread are too soft and silky to stand up. A jug of cream is not an embellishment here, it is essential. Preferably thick, yellow and unpasteurised.

enough for 3
gooseberries – 750g
caster sugar – 3–4 tablespoons
water – 250ml
brioche or bread – 8 or 9 thickish slices
double cream, to serve

Top and tail the gooseberries, then drop them into a stainless steel pan with the sugar and water. Bring to the boil, reduce the heat and simmer gently for seven to ten minutes, until the sugar has dissolved and the berries are soft enough to crush. Remove the crusts from the brioche or bread and use these to line the bottom and sides of a medium-sized pudding basin. Spoon the filling into the basin, then pour over the juice, pressing down gently so that the bread is thoroughly soaked in juice. This is really quite important if the pudding is to be truly luscious and juicy.

Put a small plate and a heavy weight on top and set aside in the fridge overnight. Serve from the dish, or turn it out if you are feeling confident (it may well collapse), and accompany with cream.

Gooseberry fool

I like my fools to have a slightly rough texture, with crushed fruit in amongst the cream. This is easy to do if you crush the berries with a fork rather than sieving them. The seeds add important contrast to the general creaminess, and the streaks of greeny-gold are pleasing to see through the glass. Add a tablespoon of elderflower cordial to the berries as they cook, if you wish.

enough for 6
gooseberries – 450g
sugar
double or whipping cream – 300ml

Top and tail the gooseberries, put them in a stainless steel pan and sprinkle over a little sugar. How much you use will depend on the sourness of your fruit. I use about 3 tablespoons for this quantity of gooseberries, but you can always add more after the fruit has softened.

Put the fruit over a gentle heat and leave to soften. Take care that the berries do not catch on the bottom – you can add a tablespoon of water if you wish, but I don't find it necessary if you keep the temperature low. When the fruit is pale and swollen, squash it gently with a fork, leaving a rough mash rather than a smooth purée, and set aside to cool.

Whip the cream softly, so that it rests in folds rather than stiff peaks. Fold the fruit into the cream, leaving trails of unblended fruit throughout. Spoon into glasses and rest for a while in the fridge before serving.

Honey polenta cake with elderflower and gooseberries

A moist, honey-scented cake with a slightly crunchy texture, which works both as a cake for tea and as a dessert to serve with poached gooseberries and thick yoghurt. Incidentally, it is gluten-free.

enough for 8
butter – 220g
golden caster sugar – 220g
unblanched almonds – 50g
ground almonds – 150g
large eggs – 3
polenta – 200g
baking powder – a lightly heaped teaspoon
finely grated zest and juice of a large lemon
thick, cold yoghurt, to serve

for the syrup
the juice of 2 lemons
elderflower cordial – 150ml
honey – 4 tablespoons

for the gooseberries
gooseberries – 450g
caster sugar – 4 tablespoons

You will need a loose-bottomed non-stick cake tin about 20cm in diameter, the base lined with a piece of baking parchment.

Set the oven at 180°C/Gas 4. Beat the butter and sugar in a food mixer till light and fluffy. Put the almonds in a heatproof bowl and pour boiling water over them. Remove them a few at a time with a draining spoon and pop them from their skins. This will seem an endless task at first but in practice it actually takes about ten to fifteen minutes. Discard the skins. Blitz the almonds in a food processor till they are finely chopped (or chop them by hand, if you prefer), then add them, together with the ground almonds, to the butter and sugar mixture.

Break the eggs into a small bowl and beat them lightly with a fork, then stir them into the mixture. Mix the polenta and baking powder and fold them into the mixture together with the grated lemon zest and juice.

Transfer the cake mixture to the lined tin and smooth the top level. Bake for thirty minutes, then turn the heat down to 160°C/Gas 3 and bake for a further twenty-five to thirty minutes, until the cake is firm to the touch. Test it for doneness with a metal skewer – it should come out clean and without wet cake mixture sticking to it.

To make the syrup, squeeze the lemon juice into a stainless steel saucepan, add the elderflower cordial and bring to the boil. Dissolve the honey in it and keep boiling until it has formed a thin syrup (about four or five minutes).

Spike holes into the top of the cake (still warm and in its tin) with a skewer and spoon over the hot syrup. Leave until almost cool, then remove it from the tin.

Top and tail the gooseberries, put them into a baking dish or small roasting tin and scatter with the sugar. Bake at 200°C/Gas 6 till the fruit has burst and the juices are starting to caramelise in the tin. Serve with the cake and some thick yoghurt.

Gooseberries with honey and elderflower

My first bushes were of the Careless variety, whose name makes me wonder if it wasn't exactly these fruits that inspired Elizabeth David to refer to a fruit fool as 'untroubled'. Gooseberries need sugar – its popularity was at its height in the late 1800s with the abolition of the sugar tax – but honey works well too, as in this recipe for baked gooseberries with elderflower. If the flowers have finished but you still have gooseberries, then stir in two or three tablespoons of elderflower cordial and cut down a bit on the honey.

enough for 4
gooseberries – 400g
mild honey or sugar – 2–3 tablespoons
water – 4 tablespoons
a single head of elderflowers or 2 tablespoons of elderflower cordial

Top and tail the gooseberries, put them in a heavy-based non-reactive pan with the honey or sugar, water and the sprig of elderflowers, then bring to the boil. Turn the heat down so that they simmer gently. They will take about ten to fifteen minutes to soften. When they have started to burst and have produced much sticky syrup, turn off the heat. Remove the elderflowers. If you are using cordial instead, add it now.

Serve warm or cold, as they are or with a jug of cream.

Grapes

Climbing the wall either side of the kitchen doors is a vine, planted about six years ago in the hope of the occasional grape to pick at as I cook. That is all I asked of it. A few grapes for a mellow autumn afternoon, to be picked when the garden is damp with autumn mist and there is a pall of woodsmoke in the air. But it has given me so much more. Eighty small bunches last year, fifty or so this, of quite the most handsome clusters of fruit this side of Fauchon. I'm surprised, amused and a wee bit proud.

The ripening grapes are a part of this garden's slow descent into winter sleep. A time which, if I am honest, I look forward to as much as the first buds of spring. Those grapes that live in direct sunlight, perhaps where I have purposefully snipped off a leaf or two, are sweet enough to attract the blackbirds by late October. Weather permitting, they will stay on the vine in good condition for a further month. As the leaves fall on to the gravel paths and the garden starts its annual collapse, the bunches continue to swell till the hoar frost. I eat some of the last few frozen, when they taste like a glass of chilled Beaumes de Venise. Those that remain are my gift for the blackbirds, who swallow them whole, like a pelican wolfing a fish.

I have always delighted in the juicy pop of a grape in my mouth. With their tight skin and spurt of cold, sweet juice, they are refreshing fruits to eat, especially if you have remembered to put them in the freezer for a few minutes beforehand. You can sugar them too, dipping hand-snipped bunches first into fork-beaten egg white, then into caster sugar. The effect under candlelight is like sugar-snow on the rosehips in the garden on a winter's evening.

There are a few home-grown bunches about in the markets, smaller, sharper and often more interesting than the characterless grapes of commerce. There are good grapes elsewhere, too, with some shops stocking the pale, wine-like Muscats with their heavy juice and almost alcoholic sweetness. The major supermarkets often have these, sold as speciality grapes. There is more than a hint of the golden pleasures of Beaumes de Venise to them, and I can barely sleep knowing there is a bunch in the fridge.

My own vines arrived, bare rooted, as two bent and sorry-looking sticks, and I had little hope for their survival. They did fairly well those first few years, annually sending out a few leafy shoots and the odd grapes that barely ripened; until the autumn they suffered a ruthless pruning at the hands of the painters who needed to get at the wall behind them. From then on they have produced more grapes than I can handle – festoons of bloomy, deep purple fruits literally dripping from the vines.

I will occasionally take a bunch of grapes of some sort into the kitchen, either to bake alongside a partridge or pheasant once the price has come down a bit or perhaps to fold into the undulating yeast dough of a foccacia or schiacciata. I have put them into a batch of muffins but wouldn't do it again, and I rather like the plump black ones in a white cabbage salad, especially when I have included toasted walnuts, apples and a dark cured meat such as speck or bresaola.

The leaves come in useful when they are young and pliable and can be roped in to wrap bundles of long grain rice flecked with sweet raisins, softened onions, dill and pine kernels. I have used them to wrap a partridge for roasting. A romantic use – the leaves turn gold, then tobacco-coloured in the oven's heat – but a useful one too, keeping the breasts moist during the early part of cooking just like a few rashers of bacon. Very young leaves, if you can bear to pick them, can apparently be shredded and used in a sauce for fish, though I have never tried it.

The prunings have their use too, the twigs making aromatic kindling for a barbecued fish. They add nothing in terms of flavour, but the act has an aesthetic significance and a certain French country charm.

Of course, there is another application of the grape, or rather its juice, in the kitchen, the nectar that is sweet-sour verjuice. It is not easy to find here, and is far from cheap when you do. I pick it up occasionally as a treat, and use its mellow sourness to work a certain magic with rabbit or chicken. A dish to celebrate the return of sparkling, frosty mornings.

Grapes in the garden

Grapevines often seem to do best where they have to struggle, growing in stony ground in direct, baking heat. I see them surviving in otherwise inhospitable places, often scrambling up greenhouses and lean-tos, seemingly happy with their feet in thin soil. My own are never fed and only occasionally watered. Generally, they are not fond of particularly fertile soil that is inclined to encourage leaf growth at the expense of fruit.

Many dessert grapes need a greenhouse if they are to ripen fully, unlike wine grapes (with which we are not concerned here) that will happily grow outside in our climate. Those varieties that will grow outside need a warm wall and plenty of sunshine, especially in late summer and autumn when the fruit is ripening.

You will need some way of keeping the birds at bay. I use plastic netting, pulling it over the vines as the fruits start to ripen. The down side is that the grapes and netting can get in a bit of a tangle.

Prune your vines in late winter. Any later than the end of February and they will bleed sap. I do mine round about St Valentine's Day, trimming each stem right back to the first or second visible bud with the secateurs. I have found that the more severely I prune my vines, the better they fruit.

Varieties

The varieties here are sweet dessert grapes that will work in the garden or in a greenhouse.

Boskoop Glory A well-flavoured black grape for mid to late autumn.
Black Hamburg You will need a greenhouse for this one, but it can be excellent given the right conditions, cropping in October.
Buckland Sweetwater Sweet and easy to grow. Not the most prolific of vines, so suitable for the smaller greenhouse.
New York Muscat Given a warm wall, this white grape will provide sweet fruit in mid autumn.
Muscat of Alexandria Usually known simply as Muscat, this golden-pink grape prefers a warm wall and, given the right conditions, should produce fruit of an excellent flavour. Rich and spicy.
Fragola Small, thick-skinned grapes with flavours of hazelnut and strawberry. The flesh is particularly soft and juicy. This grape literally pops in the mouth. I can pick eighty or more bunches from one vine.

Grapes in the kitchen

Rarely do grapes make it to the cooker, the majority being eaten straight from the vine. Yet they are really rather good when tossed into a salad of pointed spinach leaves and crisp bacon, providing a sweet freshness to contrast the salty meat. They are also good with game, duck and thick shards of smoked ham.

Grapes can be cooked, too, though they tend to lose any subtlety of flavour. When the skin of a black grape bursts, the juices delightfully stain whatever sauce or crust they come into contact with. Grapes added to a foccacia dough will send purple streaks throughout it. A few added to the pan juices of a roast game bird will add a sweet-sharpness to the gravy. Small dark grapes can be used in a baked puff pastry tart in the style of a *tarte fine*.

The leaves of the grapevine have been used for centuries to wrap food, whether it is a ripening cheese such as Oregon's Rogue River Blue or the little parcels of seasoned rice we know as dolmades.

A word about verjuice

Verjuice is a rare and fascinating ingredient – the juice of unripe green grapes (they are picked about half way through ripening) that was at one time used in lieu of lemon juice. Verjuice has a complexity far greater than lemon juice or vinegar and is at once both sour and sweet, mellow and warm. It is produced by only one or two artisan companies and is easier to buy in southwest France and Australia than here in the UK. Were it not so difficult to track down, I would use it more than I do. I appreciate it in salad dressings and for sharpening cream sauces, but this is a deeply intriguing ingredient that is currently underexploited and deserves to be better known.

* The tiny Corinth grape is the variety most often used for the dried 'currants' we put in Christmas cakes and mincemeat. The word currant is a corruption of Corinth.
* When shopping for green grapes, those with a slight hint of amber to them will be sweeter than those of an acid green.
* Could I also take this opportunity to remind you of the pork with grapes recipe in *The Kitchen Diaries*.

Chicken with verjuice, celery and cream

This is a rich dish, but stops short of cloying thanks to the grapey-apple sharpness of the verjuice. Greens of some sort are essential here, and spinach would be my choice. I used the tiniest black grapes I could find for this, tart and deeply flavoured at the same time.

enough for 6
olive oil
chicken thighs – 8 large
celery – 4 thinnish ribs
verjuice – 200ml
bay leaves – 3
double cream – 150ml
capers, rinsed – 2 heaped teaspoons (more if you wish)
black grapes – a handful, seeded if large

to serve
large floury potatoes
greens

Turn the oven to 200°C/Gas 6. Warm a casserole – a heavy one, perhaps of enamelled cast iron or stainless steel – over a medium heat with enough olive oil to cover the bottom. Rub the chicken pieces generously with oil and salt and pepper, then lay them skin-side down in the hot oil and let the skin colour appetisingly.

In the five or so minutes it takes the chicken to colour, wash and chop the celery. You need it to be in short pieces the length of a cork. Turn the chicken over and, as you do so, add the celery to the pan. Leave for a couple of minutes, tucking the celery in around the meat, then add the verjuice and bay leaves. As the steam rises, cover tightly with a lid, then put the whole thing in the oven. Bake for forty minutes.

At this point you can peel and cut the potatoes and get a pot of water boiling for them. Get the greens ready, too, washing them thoroughly and removing any tatty bits of leaf or tough-looking stems. Drop the potatoes into the boiling water and salt them.

Put the greens on. I just put a steamer pan over the boiling potatoes, but you could cook the (still wet) greens in a pan with a lid, if you prefer. Remove the chicken from the oven and switch it off. Lift the meat out on to a serving dish and return it to the oven, then pour off the fat from the pan, leaving any interesting-looking juices in place. Put the pan over a moderate heat. Once the juices start bubbling and reducing a little, pour in the cream, stirring at the bottom of the pan to dislodge any tasty bits. Season with salt and black pepper, then let the liquid bubble until it starts to thicken a wee bit and turns deep ivory in colour. Add the capers and grapes and correct the seasoning.

Spoon the creamy juices over the chicken and serve with the greens and potatoes.

Celeriac and grape salad

An ice-white salad for a crisp day. Perhaps when there is a roast loin of pork with crackling singing in the oven, or some fatty chops in the pan, their flesh freckled here and there with crushed juniper berries.

enough for 4
red cabbage – a quarter
celeriac – a medium-sized root
half a bulb of fennel
a Russet apple
a little lemon juice
grapes – 2 large handfuls
walnuts – a handful

for the dressing
parsley leaves – a large handful
crème fraiche – 250ml
the juice of half a lemon
smooth Dijon or grain mustard – 2 tablespoons

Shred the cabbage, celeriac and fennel finely. Cut the apple into quarters, discard the core, then slice very finely. Toss the apple slices immediately in a little lemon juice to stop them discolouring. Cut each grape in half and remove and discard the pips. Toast the walnuts in a non-stick pan till they smell warm and nutty.

Make the dressing. Roughly chop the parsley. Mix the parsley, crème fraiche, lemon juice and mustard together and stir in a little salt and black pepper. Toss with all the salad ingredients and serve.

Black grape focaccia

I have previously added blackberries to my sweet focaccia, but black grapes are more traditional. This is excellent with a fresh, mild cheese.

enough for 8
strong white flour – 450g
easy-bake yeast – 1 sachet (7g, or 2 teaspoons)
sea salt – 1 teaspoon
caster sugar – 1 tablespoon
warm water – 350ml

for the topping
sweet black grapes – 400g
olive oil – 2 tablespoons
caster sugar – 2 tablespoons
a little icing sugar

Put the flour in a large bowl, add the yeast, the sea salt (if you are using coarse salt, crush it finely first), then the sugar and warm water. Mix with a wooden spoon, then turn the dough out on to a generously floured board and knead lightly for five minutes or so. You need not be too enthusiastic. A gentle pummelling will suffice.

Once the dough feels elastic and 'alive', put it into a floured bowl, cover with a clean cloth or cling film and leave it somewhere warm to rise. It will take approximately an hour to double in size. Once it has, punch it down again, knocking some of the air out. Tip it into a shallow baking tin about 30cm in diameter. Gently knead half of the grapes into the dough, scattering the remaining ones on top. Cover the dough once more and return it to a warm place to rise.

Set the oven at 220°C/Gas 7. Once the dough has expanded to almost twice its size, drizzle over the olive oil, scatter with the caster sugar and bake for thirty-five to forty minutes, till well risen, golden brown and crisp on top. It should feel springy when pressed. Leave to cool slightly before dusting with icing sugar. Cut into thick wedges and eat whilst it is still warm. It will not keep for more than a few hours.

Roasted grapes

Snip bunches of dark grapes into small sprigs, place them in a baking dish or roasting tin and cover them lightly with olive oil. Roast in a hot oven for fifteen minutes or so, until the skins have started to wrinkle and the fruits are bleeding juice. Serve with roast pork, steak or game birds.

A salad of game, grapes and verjuice

At the butcher's counter I often pause, wallet in hand, to double up on what I am buying (a chicken or a pair of duck breasts, partridge or quail) for eating cold. They will be roasted at the same time as those intended for supper, saving time and cash, but then they will be removed, left to cool and wrapped in cling film for the following day. Nine times out of ten, the cold roast birds have their flesh stripped from the bones in large pieces, which is then tossed with salad leaves, a simple dressing and perhaps some fruit. Duck with pomegranates is good, as are quail with spinach leaves and slices of blood orange.

enough for 2
cold roast game or chicken – 400g boned weight
grapes – 2 handfuls
celery – a large rib
walnut halves – 2 tablespoons
trevise, radicchio or other slightly bitter leaves – a couple of handfuls

for the dressing
verjuice – 70ml
lemon thyme – 3 or 4 little sprigs
smooth, mild mustard – 1 teaspoon
olive oil – 70ml

To make the dressing, pour the verjuice into a small mixing bowl. Pull the thyme leaves from their stalks and chop them finely, then add them to the verjuice, together with a good pinch of salt, a little black pepper and the mustard. Pour in the olive oil, beating with a fork or tiny whisk.

Keeping the meat in large strips and chunks, stir it into the dressing. Halve the grapes and flick out their pips with the point of a knife. Finely slice the celery. Add the grapes and celery to the meat and dressing.

Toast the walnut halves for a couple of minutes in a shallow pan. Rinse the salad leaves. Toss gently with the rest of the ingredients and divide between two plates.

Hazelnuts

I catch my breath and stand quite motionless;
a moment of quiet excitement. I feel as if there
is a butterfly in my chest. There, two feet away,
is the first catkin of spring, already heavy with
yellow pollen and dangling like a lamb's tail from
a bare, brittle twig. Then another, and as I crane
my neck to get a closer look I spot the first tuft of
female flowers on the same tree, like tiny crimson
stars. The ground is still icy, dry leaves crackle
underfoot, but slowly I start to notice everything
else that is happening: the leaf buds already on
the gooseberries; the snowdrops suddenly visible
through the trailing ivy; the crocuses waking up beneath my feet.

The hazelnuts were among the first trees to go into this garden, taking
their place close, too close as it turned out, to the mulberry, the medlar,
the mirabelle and the quince. The nut trees grew faster than the others,
unfettered by my timid attempts at pruning. They grew to almost five
metres, their whippy branches swaying each autumn under the weight of
the local grey squirrels.

In early spring the hazel family, including the cultivated cob and filbert,
produces a canopy of piercingly green leaves bright enough to lift even the
darkest of winter spirits. Mine were, till I dug them out in a desperate quest
for more space, a refreshing dapple of brightest lime against the black-green
of the ivy walls behind. The one a Cosford Cob, the other a slightly shorter
and more delicate Purple Filbert, fruited well enough, but trying to catch
the nuts before the squirrels got to them became increasingly frustrating.
As much as I valued their charming catkins, their flash of verdant green
and the coolness under their canopy on a summer's day, they had to go.
One late-spring day, I took a saw to them, then wrenched up their
eight-year-old roots.

The young cobnut marks the change of season as clearly as turning the
page of a calendar. The last week of August and the first two of September
are our only chance to catch sight of the new-season's nuts, pale, sweet,

almost milky. Easily spotted at the greengrocer's by their frilly-edged husks, their freshness is astonishing, almost spring-like, and shakes you by its immaturity when all else seems to be crisping to gold and bronze.

The protective husk of a little cobnut seems too big for the sweet nut within, like a child's blazer at the start of a new school term. You can peel away the husks and rub your thumb over the downy covering of the shell, which is soft enough to crack with your back teeth. Inside, a plump kernel of mild-flavoured nut.

At this point in the year there is a milky quality to the nuts, a gentle sweetness and a faint hint of fresh coconut about them. Those that aren't munched from the hand could end up in a salad. As September wears on, their pale green husks crisp up and turn a dusty brown. The bumfluff on their chins disappears and their shells harden. This was the moment when children, impatient for autumn, would use them as makeshift conkers.

The cultivated hazel is generally separated into cobnuts and filberts, though the difference is minimal in terms of flavour and appearance. The filbert has the longer husk, the papery frill almost completely covering the little nut within. The cobnut husk is shorter, leaving a clearly peeping nut. Since the nineteenth century the most cultivated has been the Kentish Cob, a particularly plump and juicy variety of hazelnut. But others are planted too. Kent is the cobnut's commercial home. Yes, new orchards, known as plats, are being planted, but we are still far from the 7,000 acres that the Victorians had. And if they seem a little expensive when they first appear, then it is simply because they are handpicked.

As September starts to curl in on itself, the nuts ripen. By the end of the month, most of those for sale will have the rich brown shell we know from Christmas stockings and Beatrix Potter watercolours. Throughout the autumn, the nuts continue to ripen, the husks crisp up and the starches in the kernel turn to sugar. The golden brown nuts are sweeter than when in the green, but their flavour is richer. Toast them a little in a dry, shallow pan and you will have the deepest flavour of all.

A hazelnut in the garden

A hazelnut grown on richly fertile soil is likely to produce leaves at the expense of nuts. I know mine did. Ideally they like a light topsoil with a well-drained subsoil. Most are not fussy about the acid levels and will grow happily in partial shade and woodland, but they are not keen on wet feet. The trees will grow from one end of the country to the other, but seem happiest in the warm orchards of Kent.

It is the female flower, like a tiny red star on the bare stems, that produces the nut and only if it is fertilised by the pollen from a male flower. The male flowers are the long yellow catkin and cannot pollinate the female flowers of the same variety. Most of their pollen is distributed by the wind, though I have probably done enough pollinating myself, walking through the woods with streaks of yellow pollen on my fleece. The male and female flowers are out at different times on different varieties, hence the need for each tree to grow near a pollinator of an alternative variety.

I failed to prune my trees, which resulted in them reaching a good five metres in height. An act of sloth for which the squirrels were doubtless exceedingly grateful. Anyone who intends to pick their nuts green rather than waiting for the ripe ones to fall will need to keep their trees at two metres. Cut them back in late winter (a wonderfully bracing job on an icy day that leaves you curiously satisfied and ready for toasted muffins); this will encourage flower production. This is also the time to snip away any thin, whippy shoots from the base.

If you are mulching the garden and have a little to spare, then chuck a spade or two in the direction of your nut tree. It will thank you for your generosity.

Varieties

Kentish Cob So many qualities. The trees will stand up to any amount of cold, they crop abundantly and produce fat, juicy nuts possessing a good flavour. The trees are sometimes known as Longue d'Espagne. They will need to be pollinated by a nearby Gunslebert, Cosford or Merveille de Bollwiller.

Cosford Cob A little less prolific than some, Cosford is not as widely grown as it could be. But this is a deeply flavoured nut with a thin, easily crackable shell. You will need a neighbouring Gunslebert or Kentish Cob to serve as pollinator. Unpruned, they can get to a great height. Mine did.

Purple Filbert The deep-maroon-leaved filbert, Purpurea, brought a wave of melancholy to the top end of the garden but I managed barely a handful of nuts, which is not unusual for what is essentially an ornamental variety. The sight of a cluster of nuts with their purple-edged husks is quite poetic.

Gunslebert You will need Cosford or a Kentish Cob to pollinate this prolific bush.

Merveille de Bollwiller Sometimes known as Hall's Giant, this producer of particularly large nuts needs another such as Cosford or Butler to pollinate it.

Butler This large and vigorous nut is a classic filbert. You will need Ennis, Cosford or Merveille de Bollwiller as a pollinator.

Ennis There are claims that the flavour of this one is better than the rest, but it is hardly prolific and is rarely grown commercially. A nearby Butler will be necessary.

Hazelnuts in the kitchen

We shouldn't let ourselves get bogged down with the differences between wild nuts, cobs and filberts. They are all hazelnuts and once they have lost the greenness of youth they are interchangeable for cooking with. It seems only polite to bring some green nuts into the kitchen on 20th August, the feast of St Philibert of Jumièges (*c.* 608–684), for whom the filbert was named. In a good summer, the nuts should be just about ready to pick by then.

Once the green nuts have been celebrated (for themselves; in a salad with early apples and young spinach; or toasted, chopped and rolled around goat's cheese), then you can use them in any number of baking recipes, in both chopped and ground form. Whether you are using them ground to moisten the crumb of a cake, as you might ground almonds, or as nuggets in a chocolate chip biscuit, the flavour will be richer if the nuts are toasted first. They will be less moist but their flavour will be deeper. To toast them, I usually scatter the shelled whole nuts in a frying pan, let them toast over a moderate heat, then tip them into a tea towel. Rub the nuts in the towel to loosen their skins, then pick the naked nuts out and return them to the pan. Inevitably there will be some skins that refuse to peel away, no matter. Toast the skinned nuts till pale gold, watching them carefully, as they burn in the blink of an eye. Grind them in a food processor.

Ready-ground nuts are a temptation but in my experience they have a mealy quality to them, and toasting them when already ground has a tendency to dry them out.

A pastry to which the ground nuts have been added makes a flattering crust for a blackberry or fig tart. One of the classic uses for hazelnuts in the kitchen is for a meringue that is to be filled with peaches or apricots. A recipe that screeches Cordon Bleu Cookery School as loudly as Constance Spry screams Coronation Chicken. The effect is sublime, but I like it even better when used with a coffee butter cream instead of fruit.

We shouldn't forget the beauty of a dish of whole cobnuts, complete with their parchment-crisp hulls. Nutcrackers and a glass of something rich and deliberately out of fashion, like an amber Madeira or a glass of bone-dry sherry, turn a handful of nuts into something rather special.

Hazelnuts and...

Chocolate In many ways a perfect marriage, this well-known partnership seems to work best with chocolate that is on the creamy side.

Cinnamon The most appropriate spice with these nuts. Add a dusting to hazelnut cookies or use it in the butter cream for a hazelnut cake.

Oranges Really juicy, sweet-sharp oranges appreciate the warm, crisp qualities of a scattering of toasted nuts. There are few finer ways to end a January lunch than slices of meticulously peeled blood oranges with a dressing of coarsely broken hazels and a flick of ground cinnamon.

Pork One of the few meats that work with this nut (pheasant and pigeon are other possible candidates). Use the nut in a stuffing to accompany a roast loin or added to a pan of pork steaks sizzling in butter and sage.

Coffee Try filling a hazelnut cake with coffee butter cream or trickling coffee icing over it.

Raspberry Austrian Linzertorte is at its best with warm hazelnut pastry filled with raspberry jam.

Pear Include young nuts in a salad of pear and spinach or scatter toasted nuts over slices of ripe pear.

* You can buy fat, juicy cobnuts by mail order. It is hardly the cheapest way to do it but the nuts are carefully sorted and you tend to get the pick of the crop.
* Hazelnuts are about 17 per cent protein.
* Pick the nuts as soon as the green leaves show signs of turning gold, in an attempt to beat the squirrels.
* You can store cobnuts in their shells and husks till Christmas if you put them in an airtight tin.
* Don't worry if the cobnuts you store in a tin take on a slight musty smell. They are fine inside. However, once husked and shelled, they should be stored somewhere dark, airtight and cool.
* Someone who tends a nut orchard is known as a 'nutter'.

Hazelnut and breadcrumb ice cream

A rather wonderful little recipe, this. It has an innate simplicity that appeals to me but it would be very good with the merest trickle of melted bitter chocolate.

enough for 4
soft, fresh breadcrumbs – 60g
light muscovado sugar – 80g
golden caster sugar – 80g
skinned hazelnuts – 100g
double cream – 250ml
pouring yoghurt – 250ml

Put the breadcrumbs on a baking sheet and scatter over the sugars. Blitz the hazelnuts to coarse gravel in a food processor or chop by hand, then add to the baking sheet. Place under a hot grill and leave until the sugar, nuts and crumbs are deep golden. You will need to keep your eye on the job, as the sugar can burn very easily. Leave to cool, then break up into small pieces.

Add the sugared crumbs to the cream and yoghurt, pour into an ice-cream machine and churn till frozen. Put into a freezer box and store in the freezer till needed. If you have no ice-cream machine, you can freeze the mixture once you have mixed the cream and crumbs, stirring every hour or so till frozen.

Toasted hazelnut biscuits

A chunky, rather crumbly cookie, best eaten warm.

> *makes 8–10*
> butter – 170g
> golden caster sugar – 100g
> skinned hazelnuts – 60g
> ground almonds – 40g
> plain flour – 200g
> icing sugar

Set the oven at 160°C/Gas 3. Cream the butter and sugar together till light and fluffy (I recommend a food mixer with a beater attachment). Toast the hazelnuts in a dry pan until golden, then reduce them to a coarse powder in a food processor and mix them with the ground almonds. Add the nuts and flour to the butter and sugar mixture and stir until thoroughly mixed. I sometimes knead the mixture a little to mix it fully.

Take generously heaped tablespoons of the mixture and shape them into large, unruly balls. Place them on a non-stick baking sheet and bake for twenty-five minutes, till the biscuits are barely coloured. The insides should be slightly soft. Remove from the oven and leave to cool for five minutes before attempting to lift them from the tray with a palette knife. Roll them in icing sugar. Eat the biscuits slightly warm, or certainly within twenty-four hours.

Hazelnut cookies

Sweet, soft and tender, these fragile biscuits are made with both hazelnuts and nut butter, which is available from health-food shops, near the peanut butter. Although they are very much meant to be eaten the day they are made, they will keep for a few days in an airtight tin. They are extraordinary with vanilla ice cream. Serve them on the side, or maybe crumble them over the top.

makes about 12
butter, at room temperature – 100g
light muscovado sugar – 50g
golden caster sugar – 50g
toasted hazelnuts – 60g
hazelnut butter – 100g
plain flour – 100g
bicarbonate of soda – ½ teaspoon
baking powder – ½ teaspoon

Set the oven at 190°C/Gas 5. Cut the butter into chunks and put it in the bowl of a food mixer. Add the sugars and beat for several minutes at moderate speed until very pale and smooth. Roughly chop the toasted hazelnuts. Mix in the nut butter and most of the nuts.

Mix the flour, bicarbonate of soda and baking powder and stir gently into the butter and sugar mixture to form a soft dough. Spoon heaped tablespoons of the dough on to a non-stick baking sheet lined with baking parchment (you can push them down a bit with a fork if you like, but the chunkier they are the more moist they will be). Scatter over the remaining hazelnuts and bake for twelve to fourteen minutes, until the biscuits are pale gold and just dry on top. Inside, they should be slightly moist. Remove them from the oven and let them cool slightly before transferring them to a cooling rack (you won't be able to move them when they are warm).

Soft hazelnut chocolate cookies

Softly textured, fragile cookies. Lightly crisp outside, soft inside.

makes 9 large biscuits
dark chocolate, at least 70 per cent cocoa solids – 200g
butter – 75g
light muscovado sugar – 225g
eggs – 2
vanilla extract
skinned hazelnuts – 50g
self-raising flour – 150g

Set the oven at 180°C/Gas 4. Snap the chocolate into pieces and put them in a small heatproof china or glass bowl. Place the bowl over a small pan of simmering water, with the base of the bowl not quite touching the water. Allow the chocolate to melt. Don't be tempted to stir other than to occasionally push any unmelted chocolate down into the liquid chocolate to encourage it to melt. Turn off the heat as soon as the chocolate has melted.

Beat the butter and sugar together in a food mixer till smooth and creamy. Break the eggs into a small bowl or jug with a drop or two of vanilla extract, whisk them just enough to break them up, then add gradually to the butter and sugar, beating constantly. It is worth scraping down the sides of the bowl with a rubber spatula from time to time to ensure a thorough mixing. Add the melted chocolate.

Toast the hazelnuts in a shallow pan till golden, shaking regularly so they colour evenly. Grind the nuts coarsely to the texture of gravel, then remove half and continue grinding the other half until it resembles fine breadcrumbs. Add the flour and both textures of nut to the mixture. Stop beating as soon as everything is combined.

Place large heaped tablespoons of the mixture on a baking sheet lined with baking parchment. You should get nine large biscuits. The mixture is fine to wait for a few minutes if you are doing them in two batches. Don't be tempted to flatten the cookies, they will do so in the oven anyway.

Bake for ten minutes. The cookies will have spread and be very soft to the touch. Remove them from the oven and set aside to cool a little. As soon as they are cool enough to move without breaking, slide a palette knife underneath and carefully lift them to a cooling rack. They will keep in good condition in a biscuit tin for a few days.

A cake of roasted hazelnuts, muscovado and coffee

The point of introducing hazelnuts into a cake is often twofold: the oil in the ground nuts will help to keep the cake moist, while the toasted nuts will add much in terms of flavour. A nutty cake is something for an autumn afternoon, and even more so once the leaves have fallen. Eat it to the scent of wood smoke.

enough for 8–10
butter – 250g
golden caster sugar – 125g
light muscovado sugar – 125g
shelled hazelnuts – 200g
eggs – 3
self-raising flour – 65g

for the coffee icing (optional)
icing sugar – 250g
espresso – 1–2 tablespoons

Cut the butter into small pieces and beat together with the caster and muscovado sugars till light and fluffy. Even with a food mixer, this will take quite a time – you want to end up with a mixture that is smooth and latte-coloured.

Whilst the sugar and butter are creaming, set the oven at 160°C/Gas 3 and line the base of a deep 22–23cm cake tin with baking parchment. Tip the nuts into a dry frying pan and toast over a moderate heat till golden and lightly flecked with brown on all sides. Grind half of them to a fine powder and the other half rather less so, so they retain a certain knubbly quality, like very fine gravel.

Break the eggs into a small bowl and beat them lightly with a fork, then introduce them a little at a time to the creamed butter and sugar, beating thoroughly between each addition. Tip in both lots of ground hazelnuts and mix lightly.

Gently add the flour to the creamed mixture, incorporating it thoroughly but carefully, then scrape into the lined cake tin using a rubber spatula. Smooth the top gently so that it doesn't peak during cooking. Bake for forty-five to fifty minutes, covering the top lightly with foil for the last ten. Remove from the oven and leave to settle for fifteen minutes or so before turning out on to a cooling rack. Gently peel away the paper from the base and leave the cake to cool. Mix the icing sugar and coffee together till smooth, then trickle over the cake and leave for an hour or so to set.

Praline tiramisu

One Sunday in late autumn, the day after a serious storm that had wrecked my television aerial and blown all the ripe medlars off the tree, I felt the need to drown my sorrows in pudding. A classic tiramisu, like trifle, with its layers of soft, damp sponge and alcoholic creaminess, is something I tend to think of as the food of angels. The hazelnut liqueur is only a suggestion. The idea of incorporating a hazelnut praline came out of the blue.

enough for 6

for the praline
skinned hazelnuts – 200g
caster sugar – 100g

for the sponge layer
trifle sponges or sponge fingers – 200g
hot espresso coffee – 150ml
Frangelico hazelnut liqueur – 4 tablespoons

for the mascarpone cream layer
large eggs – 3, separated
caster sugar – 50g
mascarpone cheese – 500g
Frangelico hazelnut liqueur – 3 tablespoons

Put the skinned hazelnuts in a non-stick frying pan and let them toast gently over a moderate heat till they are pale gold. Toss the pan occasionally and keep a close eye on them. Lightly oil a non-stick baking sheet.

Scatter the sugar over the nuts, lower the heat and let it melt. Do not stir. Just watch the sugar melt and become pale gold in colour. Gently move the hazelnuts occasionally with a spoon to check the progress of the sugar, but avoid too much movement in the pan. When the caramel is deep golden (and well before it starts to smoke), stir the nuts gently and tip them on to the oiled tray. Leave to cool.

Put the sponges in a large serving dish, preferably in one tight layer, squeezing them in to fill the gaps wherever you can. Pour over the coffee and, if you are using it, the hazelnut liqueur.

Make the mascarpone layer by creaming the egg yolks and sugar together until they are pale, then mixing in the mascarpone and, if you are using it, the hazelnut liqueur. Beat the egg whites till stiff and fluffy, then fold them into the mixture.

Remove slightly less than half of the sugared hazelnuts from the tray and blitz them in a food processor till they look like coarse crumbs. Fold them into the mascarpone mixture, then tip it on top of the coffee-soaked sponges. Smooth the top, cover with cling film and refrigerate for a good five hours, preferably overnight.

Set the remaining sugared hazelnuts aside. About an hour before you want to eat the dessert, roughly crush the nuts – a texture akin to coarse gravel is about right – and scatter them over the top.

Chocolate praline truffle cake

A cake for serious chocolate fans only – I serve this in extremely thin slices. It needs something to offset its extraordinary richness. Raspberries work beautifully, as do poached pears.

enough for 10–12

for the praline
skinned hazelnuts – 100g
caster sugar – 80g

for the truffle
dark chocolate, about 70 per cent cocoa solids – 350g
double cream – 170ml
butter – 85g
a little cognac, rum or Frangelico hazelnut liqueur

Line a 20cm x 10cm loaf tin with baking parchment or cling film.

Make the praline. Put the nuts in a shallow pan and toast over a moderate heat till they are fragrant and a deep, golden brown (if your hazelnuts still have their brown skins on, rub them vigorously in a tea towel until the skins flake off, then toast the nuts once more).

Put the sugar in a small, heavy-based saucepan (it will burn in a thin one), place over a low to moderate heat and allow it to melt and slowly turn toffee coloured. This is not the time to be distracted. An occasional stir or shake is useful, but too much will prevent it from melting and cause the caramel to crystallise. Stir in the toasted nuts, leaving them to cook in the caramel for one minute. Lightly oil a baking tray. You can use groundnut oil but I prefer hazelnut oil if there is some around. Tip the praline mixture on to the tray and leave to cool. Should any of the caramel have stuck stubbornly to the pan, it can be removed with a little boiling water.

To make the truffle mixture, snap the chocolate into pieces and melt in a bowl resting on top of a pan of simmering water. The base of the bowl should not be low enough to touch the water. Stir just once or twice, no more. As soon as the chocolate has melted, switch off the heat. Gently stir in 2 tablespoons of hot water and leave be.

Scrape the cold praline off the tray, put it in a plastic bag and bash with a rolling pin. You could use a food processor if you prefer, but take care not to crush it too finely. It should be the size of coarse gravel rather than fine grit. Uneven-sized lumps add to the interest.

Whip the cream till it will stand in soft folds rather than stiff peaks. Beat the butter with a wooden spoon till soft and light, then stir into the melted chocolate until the butter is melted. Fold in the crushed praline and the cream. Now is the time to add the cognac, rum or Frangelico if you are using it. Spoon the mixture into the lined tin and smooth flat. Leave overnight in the fridge to set (if you are impatient, you can probably get away with three or four hours).

When the cake has set, slide a warm knife down the sides of the tin and unmould on to a serving dish. Serve in thin slices, with raspberries or, even better, a dish of poached pears.

Chocolate chip hazelnut cake with chocolate cinnamon butter cream

I like birthday cake. I love making them and, if truth be told, I rather enjoy receiving them too. This is my first choice for such an occasion, a nutty sponge cake rich with chocolate nibs and a dark chocolate and cinnamon frosting. I serve it in appropriately thin slices.

> *enough for 10–12*
> butter – 250g
> golden caster sugar – 250g
> shelled hazelnuts – 75g
> dark chocolate – 120g
> large eggs – 4
> self-raising flour – 125g
> ground cinnamon – ½ teaspoon
> strong espresso – 4 teaspoons
>
> **for the spiced chocolate butter cream**
> dark chocolate (70 per cent cocoa solids) – 250g
> butter – 125g
> ground cinnamon – a knifepoint

Set the oven at 180°C/Gas 4. Line the base of a 20–21cm loose-bottomed, deep cake tin with baking parchment. Cut the butter into small chunks and put it with the sugar into the bowl of an electric mixer, then beat till white and fluffy. Toast the hazelnuts in a dry pan over a moderate heat, then rub them in a tea towel until most of the skins have flaked off. There is really no need to be too pernickety about this, you just want most of the skins removed. Grind the nuts to a coarse powder, less fine than ground almonds but finer than they would be if you chopped them by hand. Chop the chocolate into what looks like coarse gravel.

Break the eggs into a small bowl and beat them gently. Slowly add them to the butter and sugar mixture, beating all the time – it may curdle slightly but it doesn't matter. Stop the machine. Tip in half the ground nuts and half the flour, beat briefly and at a slow speed, stop the machine again, then add the rest, together with the chopped chocolate and cinnamon, and mix briefly. Gently fold in the espresso, taking care not to knock the air from the mixture, then scoop into the lined cake tin. Smooth the top and bake for thirty-five to forty-five minutes, covering the cake with foil for the last ten minutes if it is colouring too quickly. Remove the cake from the oven and test with a skewer – you want it to come out moist but clean, without any uncooked cake mixture clinging to it. Leave the cake to cool a little in its tin before turning out on to a cooling rack and peeling off the paper from its bottom.

To make the chocolate butter cream, snap the chocolate into small pieces and let it melt in a small bowl balanced over a pan of simmering water (the water should not touch the bottom of the bowl). Leave to melt, with little or no stirring, then add the butter, cut into small pieces, and the spice. Stir till the butter has melted. Leave to cool until the mixture is thick enough to spread. (I sometimes impatiently put mine in the fridge for about fifteen minutes.) Spread the chocolate cream over the top of the cake, decorate as the whim takes you and leave for an hour or so before cutting.

Peaches
and nectarines

There is a solitary peach on my desk, picked up at the local farmers' market. Diminutive compared to the Italian- and French-grown varieties, a little flat on one side where it has snuggled against a sibling on the twig. Grown on a tree older than its owner, its skin is covered in fine grey down. And that for me is the point of the peach and why I hold its qualities above those of the nectarine – the feel of the peach's soft fuzz on first my upper and then my lower lip, the way the skin puckers as I bite, a teasing prelude to the sweet flesh that will follow. And all this before the juice – sweet, cool, sensuous – even touches my tongue.

When a peach is at its most sublime, it needs a plate to catch the juice, though I invariably forget. Or is it that I can never quite believe I will need one? Either way, it is usually followed by that embarrassing little noise that comes from the corner of your mouth as you try to catch the escaping trickle of juice.

For all its intimate pleasure, the skin that covers those blood-red cheeks is usually removed after cooking, when it is easy to slide off with your thumb, revealing the golden flesh beneath. Removing it before cooking is an almost impossible task.

The peach and the bald, bright nectarine are available in our shops all year, imported from Spain, Italy and France in summer and Egypt, the United States or South Africa during winter. The further they travel, the more disappointing they generally are. There is something depressing about these fruits in winter, pointless even. I usually wait till early summer for my first taste.

Thousands of trees fruit regularly in this country too, but the crop rarely makes it to market. Most ripen in private gardens and allotments in too small a quantity to be offered for sale. Local farmers' markets have them sometimes, in varying stages of quality, in July, August and early September. We grew them in our Worcestershire garden when I was a child, at the top of the little orchard, the long, grey branches trained along the wall that separated us from the damp buttercup meadow beyond. The tree got the dreaded leaf curl, of course – they always did in those days, before new, disease-resistant varieties were developed and everyone learned to protect the vulnerable early buds with fleece.

The single factor that deems a peach or nectarine worth eating is not so much its variety or colour or even where it is grown, but its ripeness. An unripe peach is crunchy, dry and flavourless. An unripe nectarine is barely distinguishable from munching a rubber ball. Few fruits are quite so reliant on 'the moment' as these two. We must catch them where and when we can.

It is rare to find a perfectly ripe peach in the shops, with good reason. A peach that is truly ready to eat is too fragile to get home without bruising. The supermarket 'ripe and ready to eat' sticker is only partly true (some things we must learn the hard way). What it means is that the fruit within is indeed edible, but far from being at the moment of perfection. To reach that point, the fruit will need some tender, loving care from us. Take your nectarines and peaches home, remove the wrapper so they don't sweat, but leave them in the soft, protective cradle the supermarkets have so sensibly provided us with. Keep the fruits in a warm room, turning them each morning until they are ready (I do it while I am waiting for my first espresso of the day to drip through, as I do with Indian mangoes in June or pears at Christmas).

Check their progress daily. Poking them with your thumb will almost certainly lead to disaster. There are few more easily damaged fruits. Picking them up, cradling them in the palm of your cupped hand and sniffing them is a more reliable and respectful test. Peaches tend to announce their ripeness with a scent that is almost rose-like. The white varieties often seem even more fragrant, their perfume a Jean-Baptiste Grenouille-like blend of raspberries, rose and honey. Though of course, that could just be my imagination.

Prunus persica is native to China. The flowers are pink or occasionally pink and white and appear in early spring, before the frosts are over. (Stay in a Japanese hotel, or *ryokan*, in February and March and you may find sprigs of tight peach blossom on display.) This goes some way towards explaining how precious a ripe peach is when grown in this climate. They need to be in the hands of someone who will rush out at the first hint of frost and wrap the tree in protective fleece. In France, I have seen farmers light fires at the end of the rows to stop entire orchards being decimated by a late and sudden frost. None of which should put us off planting a tree – they survive well enough.

The name peach may come from the belief that the fruit originally came from Persia, now Iran (it was the Persians who brought the peach to the attention of the Romans and from them to us). Yellow peaches, depending on their variety, can have a stone that is either loose or impossible to extricate without mashing the flesh. Neatly halving a ripe clingstone peach is one of those kitchen tasks that defeats me. These latter 'clingstones' are generally used for canning, although a few have ended up, usually as a squashed mess, on my chopping boards. Use in a salsa.

The peach promises much. Cradled in tissue paper or packed into cartons, it tempts as few other fruits can. But the peach can disappoint, so much so that for a while I stopped buying them, burned one time too many by those that failed to ripen.

A single fruit was to change everything. I bought my first white peach out of curiosity, intrigued by its floral scent and gentle colour and mesmerised by its beauty on a simple jade-green plate. It was that first white-fleshed peach that I held against my face, felt its down brush against my lips, breathed in its rosewater scent. This was the fruit that made me fall in love with the peach again. This is the variety so beloved of Japan and China, and which, on a good day, stands second only to the Alphonso mango as the fruit I hold in the highest esteem.

The nectarine has become more popular of late. It has a smooth 'plum skin', removing much of the peach's quality even before we are through the threshold. The nectarine's appearance is not due to any cross-breeding with a variety of plum but to a 'recessive gene', and can sometimes appear unexpectedly as a 'sport' of a fuzzy peach. So, your peach tree may suddenly send out seedlings that produce fruit as bald as a coot. The skin of a nectarine, though its sunset hues appear stronger than those of the peach, is in fact no different. It is the fine grey down that gives the peach a more sophisticated appearance.

The nectarine is a newer fruit altogether, and where the peach is mentioned in Chinese literature from 10 BC, its smooth mate is first noted around the early seventeenth century. The two fruits share a flavour. You would be hard pushed to tell the difference between them once they are cooked.

In China the peach has long been held as a symbol for immortality. The Jade Emperor and his mother fed them to the gods to ensure their eternal presence. I eat them all summer, sometimes with a piece of torn mozzarella or even a wedge of Roquefort – the salty character of the latter bringing out the sweetness of the juice.

I like the fact that the stone of the peach contains a little cyanide, though not as much as its sister, the bitter almond. The far-off hint of danger seems only to add to the peach's exotic and sensual qualities.

A peach in the garden

I have known three or four peach trees over the years. Only one suffered with the dreaded leaf curl that tends to put off even the most enthusiastic gardeners. All were trained against walls, their branches bound to wires or strings nailed into the wall, rather than grown as an orchard tree. Every one of them fruited, albeit intermittently, causing much excitement. Perfectly edible as they were, none quite reached the rich, juice-soaked heights of those grown in France and Italy.

Last year I picked up quite a few grown here. Not quite the perfect-looking specimens I buy from the supermarket, but their flavour was impressive. The rash of pockmarks on their skin was the only telltale sign that they had not come from a warmer place. The juice and flesh were everything you expect of a peach.

There is no doubt that the trees enjoy our warming climate, but they still need to be watched carefully at blossom time and covered with horticultural fleece if necessary. Most of my peach-growing friends say they often forget about this, and regularly lose a few buds to the frost.

If I ever find myself with a larger garden, then a peach will be planted, maybe even two. I will dig them in somewhere where they have as much protection as possible, a south- or southwest-facing wall, perhaps close to the house. The *Prunus* family loves rich soil. I recently saw a stunning tree on an estate where they feed the soil annually with organic matter. The tree was in hog heaven.

In many ways the peach tree is perfect for the smaller urban garden. They can be bought ready trained into a fan shape so you are spared the intimidating task of early pruning; rarely grow very large (the rootstock on to which they are grafted prevents this) and they are self-fertile too, so don't need a mate to produce fruit. You can even grow them successfully in pots, though I have only seen those growing in conservatories, not outside. Get your new tree in the ground in the autumn, preferably in deep, rich soil, and water it copiously in its early growing stages.

Peach blossom appears early, often in March, long before the insects necessary for pollination are around. My father used a paintbrush to transfer pollen from one piece of blossom to the next. Others swear by a rabbit's tail. He very gently took pollen from the stamens of one pink blossom on his brush, then gently brushed them on to another. It was something he looked forward to enormously, one of the more intimate moments of an old gardener's life.

However tempting it is to leave all the young fruit in place, a bit of careful thinning, removing any small, crowded fruits, will encourage larger peaches. The generally accepted rule is a final thinning to leave 18cm or so between fruits, but none of the proud growers I have spoken to can bring themselves to be quite that ruthless. It's not like thinning radishes, where you still eat the unlucky ones whose lives are cut short. Try to keep the birds off. Towards the day of harvest, increase the supply of water.

Ideally, we should let our fruit ripen on the tree, but with that comes the risk of something pinching the prized fruit at its peak. It happens with my strawberries and apples, so it is an idea to harvest just before the fruits ripen and bring them on using a warm indoor windowsill.

Varieties

Peaches

Avalon A new variety with a high resistance to leaf curl. I have only eaten commercially grown fruits of this yellow-fleshed variety, but was impressed with their flavour and juice.

Blood Peach I would dearly like to grow this dark-fleshed peach with its streaks of ruby, like a blood orange. Unfortunately, you need a greenhouse for this one. Reads Nursery, from where I have bought several fruit trees over the years, say that this is 'collector's' fruit.

Dixired Deep-coloured skin with rich, yellow flesh. The stones do cling to the flesh.

Duke of York Well-known, heavy-cropping variety that ripens a little earlier than most. Give it a warm, south-facing wall and by all accounts it should do well.

Dymond An old variety from the 1800s. Rarely colours well, being on the green side, but with a fine flavour and soft, white flesh.

Early Alexander Small to medium fruit. One from the Rivers Nursery that brought us so many excellent plums. Known for its juice.

Kestrel A long-established cross between the Early Rivers nectarine and Hales Early Peach. Dark skinned and as sweet as they come.

Peregrine Reliable white-fleshed peach of great repute. In the north of the country it will need a greenhouse, though it does well outside in the south.

Red Wing Named for its red skin without the usual yellow or white flashes, the fruits are almost completely dark red. Suits a cooler climate.

Rochester A dependable, late-flowering variety. Needs protection from heavy rains during winter.

Saturn Fashionable, flat-topped fruit that can disappoint when purchased commercially. Its pale flesh is sweeter and more interesting when allowed to ripen on the tree.

Nectarines

Lord Napier A popular old variety of deep colour and dependable white-fleshed fruit.

Early Gem Likes a warm wall, but can produce deep-coloured fruits with well-flavoured yellow flesh.

Firegold Orange skin, yellow flesh. I have yet to taste this one.
Fantasia Larger fruits than is usual, with yellow flesh. Should be ripe by mid August.
Snow Queen A late, white-fleshed variety that is considered to be the best flavoured of the nectarines.

A peach in the kitchen

I rarely cook a peach. They are seen in my kitchen nestling next to the crisp skin of a roast chicken salad or perhaps cold gammon or hot roast guinea fowl; stuffed with mascarpone or ricotta or amaretti; or simply nudging a few slices of Parma ham and a fistful of spiky-leaved rocket. I will grill them, stuffed with cream cheese and glazed with molten sugar, bake them with almonds and honey and poach them with honey and a drop of rosewater. Occasionally (very occasionally), I will tuck them into the cream filling of a meringue with passion fruit or raspberries or add them to a salad of wine-dark cherries.

The idea of cooking a peach under a pastry crust can work, though its sweetness can cloy. Better, to my mind at least, eaten cold with a jug of unpasteurised cream. Hot, it can tempt with a slowly melting ball of vanilla ice cream, mostly because of the contrast of temperatures between the sugary crust and the freezer-cold ice.

Lacking the acidity present in even the ripest apricot, peaches and nectarines are difficult to marry with savoury ingredients. As a knife-sharp salsa with roast duck; in a coriander-speckled couscous; layered in a salad of white crab meat maybe. But generally, I keep my peaches and nectarines as they are, fragile globes of sweet flesh and sticky juice.

Peaches and...

Pork and bacon Roast pork, particularly when spices are involved, and salty smoked bacon bring out the sweetness of the peaches.
Cream Despite the roll-off-the-tongue term 'peaches 'n' cream', I have never felt the two do each other many favours. Two sweet, mild things stirred together do not make for interesting eating. A fool or an ice cream made with the fruit is always bland. Warm, a peach pie can be good with ice cream or very softly whipped cream.
Lemon juice Even the smallest squeeze of citrus will lift the flavour of a peach to great heights. I tend to use lemon rather than vinegar in salads where peaches make an appearance.
Honey A little in a dressing for a fresh peach and Little Gem lettuce salad can be a good thing, as can a trickle of liquid honey over baked peaches.

Mozzarella Soft, milky cheeses make nice bedfellows for a ripe peach.

Almonds Use a frangipane base for an open peach tart; a few ground almonds in the pastry for a peach shortcake; scatter chopped almonds over a dish of peaches and honey before baking.

Duck Crisply roasted duck and a gravy made from the pan juices, sliced peaches and a drop of Grand Marnier can certainly be worth the trouble.

Blue cheese All the blue cheeses such as Roquefort, Beenleigh Blue, Gorgonzola and Fourme d'Ambert go well with excessively ripe peaches.

Fresh soft cheeses Ones such as *caprini freschi*, the sort that come in a shallow paper case, are heavenly with nectarines that are heavy with juice.

Basil The slight peppery heat of sun-baked basil leaves is extraordinary with a fridge-cold, juicy peach.

Mint Chopped mint added to a lemon juice dressing will make a ripe peach really sing.

* When ripening peaches at home, make sure they don't touch one another. They will mould where they butt up against each other.
* Peaches are particularly low in pectin. They make an extraordinarily beautiful preserve, soft and difficult to keep on your toast. A good shot of lemon juice is essential if the jam is to thicken even slightly.
* Few will ripen before August in our climate, though on a good warm wall in a clement season, an established tree should give us something in late July.
* Early peaches tend to be of the clingstone variety and the flesh can be the very devil to get off the stone in one piece. Later in the season you can easily halve a peach with a knife and cleanly twist one half away from the other.
* Adding a peach stone or two to a dish of poached peaches may enhance the flavour.
* Nectarines can be substituted for peaches in all the recipes that follow.

A salad of peaches, mozzarella and basil

enough for 4
splendidly ripe peaches – 4
Parma ham – 16 thin slices
mozzarella – 2 large balls
salad leaves – 4 handfuls

for the dressing
white or tarragon wine vinegar – a tablespoon
olive oil – 4 tablespoons
crème fraîche – 2 tablespoons
basil – a small bunch (about 20 medium-sized leaves)

Slice the peaches in half, pull out the stones and slice each half into three.
Divide the Parma ham between four plates, tear the balls of mozzarella in
half and place a half on each plate.

Make the dressing by putting the vinegar in a small bowl and stirring
in a pinch of sea salt. Gently beat in the olive oil and crème fraîche to give
a creamy dressing. Tear the basil leaves and stir them in, then season with
coarsely ground black pepper. Toss the salad leaves in the dressing and add
to the plates, tuck in the peaches and serve.

A mint and peach tabbouleh

enough for 4
cracked wheat – 150g
slim spring onions – 6
ripe peaches – 4
a hot red chilli
mint – 6 bushy sprigs
coriander – 2 large handfuls of leaves
parsley – 2 large handful of leaves
juice of a lemon
olive oil – 2 tablespoons

Pour the cracked wheat into a bowl and just cover with boiling water, then
set aside.

Cut the spring onions into small pieces and put them in a mixing bowl.
Slice the peaches in half, remove their stones and cut the flesh into small
dice, then add to the onions. Seed and finely chop the chilli, then roughly
chop the mint, coriander and parsley and add to the onions. Add the juice
of the lemon, the olive oil and a good grinding of salt and black pepper.

Fluff the cracked wheat up with a fork. Crumble into the peaches and onions, then serve.

A salad of chicken, mint and peaches

Warm roast chicken and its golden skin, ripe peaches, the sting of watercress, chillies and basil. A light lunch, crisp, bright, invigorating. And one of the very few times I use peppers raw.

enough for 4, as a light main course
chicken breasts – 600g, bone in, skin on
a little olive oil
mint leaves – a large handful
basil leaves – about 30
watercress – 4 handfuls
red or orange peppers – 2
peaches – 4

for the dressing
lime juice – 3 tablespoons
fish sauce – 3 tablespoons
palm or caster sugar – 2 teaspoons
small, hot red chillies – 2
spring onions – 4

Set the oven at 200°C/Gas 6. Put the chicken breasts in a small roasting tin, rub with olive oil and season generously with salt and ground black pepper. Roast for twenty minutes, or until golden and lightly cooked right through. Remove from the oven and leave to rest for ten minutes.

Make the dressing: put the lime juice and fish sauce in a small bowl and stir in the sugar. Finely chop the chillies and add to the bowl. Trim and finely chop the spring onions, add them to the dressing and set aside.

Keep the mint and basil leaves whole. Put them in a bowl with the watercress, minus its toughest stems. Halve the peppers, remove and discard the seeds, then slice the flesh into long, very fine strips. Slice the peaches in half, remove the stones and slice the peaches into thick pieces. Add to the herbs with the peppers.

Shred the chicken and its crisp skin finely. Toss all the ingredients together with the dressing, leave for five minutes, then serve.

Crisp pork belly, sweet peach salsa

Ask your butcher to score the skin finely for this, as the crackling is essential.
The first brief roasting at the higher temperature sets the crackling on
the route to crispness. These ribs are not sweet and sticky like the ones
in *The Kitchen Diaries*, but lightly crisp and lip tingling.

enough for 4
pork belly – 1–1.5kg, boned, skin intact and finely scored

for the rub
garlic – 3 cloves
light soy sauce – 2 tablespoons
groundnut oil – a tablespoon
salt – 2 teaspoons
dried chilli flakes – half a teaspoon
Chinese five-spice powder – a lightly heaped teaspoon

for the peach salsa
spring onions – 2
a small red chilli
peaches – 3
cherry tomatoes – 8
coriander – a small bunch
juice of 2 limes
olive oil – 3 tablespoons

Put the pork in a china or glass dish. Peel and crush the garlic to a paste,
stirring in the soy, oil, salt, chilli flakes and five-spice powder. Spread this
paste over the skin and underside of the pork and leave it to marinate for a
good four hours, if not overnight.

Set the oven at 220°C/Gas 7. Place the pork in a roasting tin, then cook,
skin-side up, for about twenty minutes. Lower the heat to 200°C/Gas 6 and
continue cooking for a further forty to fifty minutes, till the skin is dark and
crisp. Leave to rest for ten minutes before carving.

Make the salsa. Trim and finely chop the spring onions. Finely chop the
chilli. Peel, stone and finely chop the peaches and tomatoes and chop the
coriander. Toss gently, then dress with the lime juice and olive oil. Serve the
ribs with the salsa.

Peaches with lemon verbena

Something to serve alongside cups of green tea in the afternoon. You can use dried verbena leaves too, but they lack a little of the magic of the fresh herb.

serves 3
small peaches – 6
water – 250ml
lemon verbena – 10 large leaves
sugar – 3 tablespoons

Put the peaches in a small saucepan with the water, verbena leaves and sugar and bring to the boil. Turn the heat down and leave to simmer for seven to ten minutes, till the peaches are soft. Leave to cool, then chill thoroughly before serving.

Peaches with lime leaves and lemongrass

A refreshing recipe for the dog days of summer.

enough for 4
sugar – 300g
water – 600ml
lime leaves – 6
a stalk of lemongrass
peaches – 4

Put the sugar and water in a saucepan and bring to the boil. Once the sugar has dissolved, turn down the heat so that the syrup is quietly simmering and add the lime leaves, crushing them slightly as you go. Bash the lemongrass so that the stalk splits into fibres, then add it to the syrup.

Lower the peaches, their skins intact, into the syrup. Let them poach to total tenderness – the point of a small knife or skewer should glide effortlessly into the flesh. Turn off the heat and let the fruit cool in the syrup.

Slide the skin off the peaches with your thumbs, halve and stone the fruit carefully and place in a shallow dish. Strain the liquor through a sieve and pour over the fruit, then chill until ready to serve.

Baked peaches with maple syrup and vanilla

Like honey, maple syrup is a more interesting way to sweeten a peach than sugar, adding subtle notes of walnuts and caramel.

enough for 4
ripe peaches – 4
maple syrup – 4 tablespoons
vanilla seeds – a pinch (the contents of a single pod)
juice of a lime

Set the oven at 200°C/Gas 6. Wipe the peaches and slice them in half. Discard the stones and place the fruit, cut-side up, in a shallow baking dish.

Put the maple syrup in a bowl with the vanilla seeds and the lime juice. Mix well, then pour over the peaches. Bake for approximately thirty-five minutes, till the peaches are thoroughly tender. It is a good idea to baste the fruit from time to time as it cooks.

Baked peaches with an almond crust

This rough, buttery almond crust works with nectarines and apricots too. Just scatter it over the halved and stoned fruit before baking. Good though this is on its own, I can see every reason for cream here.

enough for 4
ripe peaches or nectarines – 4
almonds – 50g
golden caster sugar – 50g
butter – 45g

Set the oven at 180°C/Gas 4. Wipe the peaches or nectarines and cut them in half. Tug out the stones, then place the halved fruits cut-side up in a shallow baking dish.

Put the almonds in a food processor – there is no need to skin them first – and blitz them to a coarse texture. They should be somewhere between gravel and traditional ground almonds (you just want them to lend a crunch to the soft fruit). Add the sugar and butter and briefly continue to mix.

Spoon the almond mixture on top of the peaches and bake for forty-five to fifty minutes or until the fruit is meltingly soft and the top is crisp. An occasional basting with the buttery juices in the dish can only help.

Grilled peaches, mascarpone vanilla cream

Stone fruits grill well. Whether you use peaches or nectarines – or, later in the year, plums – the fruit needs to be really ripe in order to soften. Unripe fruit will simply dry out. It is probably worth making sure the bars of the grill have no savoury residue on them.

enough for 4
peaches – 4
lemon juice

for the cream
eggs – 2, separated
caster sugar – 2 lightly heaped tablespoons
mascarpone – 250g
a knifepoint of vanilla seeds or a few drops of vanilla extract
a little grated orange zest

Whisk the egg yolks and sugar until they are pale and creamy in colour. Add the mascarpone and beat till mixed, but take care not to over-mix. Beat the egg whites till stiff and fold in gently, together with the vanilla and orange zest. Leave to firm up a little in the fridge.

Cut the peaches in half and twist gently to separate the halves, then tug out the stones. Rub them with lemon juice and put them cut-side down on the bars of a preheated grill. Leave to soften, turning them once. They will take a good ten minutes or so – a bit longer than you might expect. When they are hot and thoroughly tender, serve them with the mascarpone cream.

Peaches with rose petals

Zucchini frites and elderflower jelly aside, I have barely begun to explore the virtues of flowers in cooking. Scatter a fistful of dill flowers on cooked sea bass; fold dandelions into the egg and milk batter for pancakes; toss vermilion nasturtium petals into a spinach salad, and you begin to get their visual worth. Let a handful of rose petals fall on to a peach salad and your heart will melt.

A fragrant and very gentle dessert here – one to follow a salmon and cucumber salad on a calm summer day.

enough for 4
large, ripe peaches – 4
water – a litre
elderflower cordial – 3 tablespoons
sugar, to taste
rose petals

Wipe the peaches and put them in a stainless steel pan. Pour in the water, then stir in the elderflower cordial and at least 2 tablespoons of sugar. Bring to the boil, turn down the heat and leave to simmer gently until the peaches are completely tender. Turn off the heat and leave the peaches in their syrup to cool. When they are cold, chill thoroughly.

Serve a peach per person, skinned if you wish, with some of the chilled syrup and a few scattered rose petals.

Warm peaches and blueberries

enough for 2
peaches – 2
blueberries – 200g
caster sugar – 2 tablespoons
water – 3 tablespoons
cream, crème fraîche or vanilla ice cream, to serve

Cut the peaches in half and discard the stones. Rinse the blueberries and tip them into a medium saucepan together with the sugar and water. Nestle the halved peaches amongst the berries and place over a low to moderate heat. Leave to simmer gently for ten to fifteen minutes, spooning the sauce over the peaches as you go, until the berries have started to burst and the juice has mixed with the sugar and water to make a thick sauce.

Transfer to warm bowls and serve with cream or ice cream.

Peach and blueberry cobbler

A further thought on the marriage of peaches and blueberries, but this time with a scone crust. Something for when the late September evenings start to get a bit nippy.

enough for 6

for the cobbler crust
plain flour – 150g
baking powder – 2 teaspoons
caster sugar – 1 tablespoon
butter – 80g
soured cream – a small pot (142 ml)

for the filling
large, ripe peaches – 3
blueberries – 350g
juice of a lemon
caster sugar – a tablespoon, plus extra for dusting
plain flour – a tablespoon

Set the oven at 200°C/Gas 6. Put the flour, a pinch of salt, the baking powder, sugar and butter in a food processor and blitz for a few seconds, until the mixture resembles soft, fresh breadcrumbs. Tip into a bowl. Slice the peaches, pulling the stones out as you go and dropping the fruit into an ovenproof dish. Toss the sliced peaches with the blueberries, lemon juice, sugar and flour. At this point it will look less than inviting, but worry not.

Mix the soured cream into the crumb mixture; you will have a soft dough. Break off walnut-sized pieces, flatten them lightly and lay them on top of the fruit. Dust the rounds of dough with sugar, then bake in the preheated oven for twenty-five minutes, till the cobbler is golden and the fruit is bubbling.

Pears

Like a snowflake, the perfectly ripe pear is
a fleeting thing. Something to be caught, held
tenderly, briefly marvelled at, before it is
gone forever.

Ripeness is all. Pears have a tendency to turn
gritty in texture if left to ripen on the tree (that is
the sugar crystals turning to starch). The dessert
varieties are generally picked when approaching
softness and brought to perfection indoors.
Summer and autumn pears are gathered before
they are fully ripe, while they are still green, but
snap from their branches easily when twisted.

This is a fruit whose progress you must watch if you are not to miss it
at its peak. I ripen mine on a plate, taking care their skins do not touch,
and check them each morning, usually whilst waiting for the coffee to drip
through. The window of perfection is indeed brief, a day or two at most,
then a slow descent towards soft shapelessness.

The pear was domesticated long after dates, the fig and the
pomegranate, around 1000 BC. Though wild trees have been recorded
here since Anglo-Saxon times, it appears most likely that the domestic pear
was introduced by the Romans. From the genus *Rosaceae*, which includes
meadowsweet, brambles, hawthorn and quince, members of the *Pyrus*
family possess a sophistication that can only be dreamed of by the apple,
with hints of wine, rose, honey and nuts of extraordinary subtlety.
Occasionally you might detect a note of musk or a distant breath of aniseed.
The apple has these too, but more obvious and upfront.

Unless we are very lucky, there are few varieties of pear available to us.
I get my first taste as late as October, with perhaps a Beurre Hardy, a crisp,
lightly flavoured fruit with a distinct grain to it. I like it. But there are many
earlier varieties that can be found from late July onwards, such as Beth and
the tiny Doyenne d'Eté with its fresh, lemony notes.

We talk of apples and pears in the same breath, as we might salt and
pepper, yet they are as different as you can imagine. An apple is about a loud

crunch, a quick hit, a fruit to be enjoyed on the run. The pear is of a more gentle nature, something to take our time over. At its point of perfection, an apple shouts, a pear whispers.

If a pear does speak in a quieter voice, it is partly because of its texture: melting, luscious, sensual. The flesh of a ripe pear is giving and its effect on the eater calming. It is the most serene of fruits and often brings about a certain thoughtfulness.

We have eaten this fruit since prehistoric times and the word appears in all Celtic languages. It probably comes from the Germanic *pera*, a variation of the Latin, *pira*. Anything pyriform indicates that something is pear-shaped.

It is a long way from the Tian Shan mountains to Birmingham, but the genus is thought to have originated in the Central Asian mountain range, whilst Perry Barr, a neat suburb of the West Midlands, is one of the few places named after the fruit. It is mentioned in the Domesday book as Pirio and, curiously, is where I spent much of my childhood, at my aunt's house in Perry Avenue. No sign of the ancient tree for which the area was named now, of course. Even the greengrocer's closed down a while ago.

Like roses, many varieties of this fruit carry a French name. Christopher Stocks, in his book *Forgotten Fruits* (Random House, 2008), points out that this is because it was French breeders who 'took the initiative in pear breeding from the seventeenth century on'. But then, they have the climate for it, this fruit liking just that bit more warmth than the apple.

As I write, there is a thrush on the Winter Nelis pear outside the window, pecking at a small, overripe fruit almost hidden by the reddening leaves. Each sharp peck is preceded by a long, bright-eyed look around, then in he goes again.

A pear in the garden

If you went to the top of our sloping Worcestershire garden, past the bent and lichen-encrusted plum tree, the tallest golden gages and the rhubarb patch, there were two aged and rather splendid pear trees. Pear trees tend to grow taller and more upright than apples, their branches less spreading. My father balanced a long, wooden ladder against the trunk to collect the lowest hanging fruit, whilst I watched from below, giddy with the vertigo that dogs me to this day. Too high to reach, the remaining fruits were left to ripen till they dropped, in sweet, canary-yellow splashes, on the ground below.

I have two pear trees in my garden now. A weeping Winter Nelis, whose blossom is used as a pollinator and whose hard, bauble-sized fruits are good for poaching with vanilla and honey. The second, of which I am rather proud, is an espaliered Doyenne du Comice that I have trained along a south-facing wall outside the kitchen. The blossom is large and less fine than the Nelis, and its fruit generous in size and prolific in quantity. I feel honoured.

The foliage of both trees is distinct and glorious. The leaves of the Winter Nelis become crimson in November, the Doyenne basks in shades of shiny green, tangerine and ochre. A metre away from one another, they got off to a good start ten years ago and have become excellent and happy roommates. I recommend them to anyone with a small garden like mine.

The blossom, almost snow-white, occasionally blushed with the softest pink, is less fragrant than the sweet apple. You could almost say fetid. Not that that stops me inhaling it in March, when it is amongst the first to appear. Along with blackcurrant, it is a scent I appreciate and others shun. A good show in spring is less reliant on a cold snap than the apple.

The dense wood of the pear tree has long been used for the manufacture of high-end woodwind instruments and is often employed for pipes now that briarwood has become expensive. In the United States it is much used as a smoking wood for barbecues, supplied in chips or short logs. As a wood for furniture making, it is particularly revered. Hard and flesh pink, it requires sharp tools to work it and is considered to be a joy to handle. Furniture maker David Savage describes it as a 'well-mannered wood. Pleasant to be with. One of the most pleasant things about it is the way it works. The way fine silky shavings will come off with a well-sharpened bench plane. The way new hues and colours are exposed with each shaving. Working with pear wood is a genuine sensuous experience, and one that should be cherished.'

Plant a pear tree in a warm corner and it will be happier than one left to fierce winter winds. An alternative is to train them low, to make a thick fence to edge a path or even a vegetable bed. Care and a little expertise are needed to train the branches along low wires or hurdles, but it is certainly an option. Trees trained in this way can often bear heavy crops because all the plant's strength is put into the fruit rather than the tree.

Varieties

There are something like 460-odd varieties of dessert pear and many cider varieties, too. Although commerce tends to concentrate on just a handful, farm shops and farmers' markets are a sensible hunting ground for more unusual types. The names are as much a joy to read as the fruit is to eat. Who could resist the short, fat Bishop's Thumb or a Christmas-ripening variety called Santa Claus?

Early pears (ripening August–September)

Chalk A Scottish pear that dates from the 1790s, now quite rare, this is often the first dessert pear to ripen in August. Straightforward, simple flavour.

Beth A small, pale-green Kentish fruit from the 1930s, this little pear has much charm and a surprising amount of flavour for an early-ripening fruit. Ripens in September.

Moonglow I have never seen, let alone tasted, this small, yellow-skinned variety but who could resist such a beautiful fruit with its flash of crimson?

Doyenne d'Eté Also known as Doyenne de Juillet or Roi Jolimont, the summer Doyenne is small and sweet with yellowish flesh that offers a hint of lemon. It has been around since the 1700s, for which some say we must thank Capuchin monks. Look for it in late August.

Beurre Hardy A sweet, well-flavoured pear, yellow-green, with a coppery russet. The trees have glorious scarlet autumn foliage. The fruit is large, its creamy, perfumed flesh often melting. I detect a hint of rosewater.

Merton Pride An English pear from the 1940s. Large, green and with pale flesh and plenty of juice. Many unnamed garden pears are actually this variety.

Marguerite de Marillat An exceptionally large dessert variety, dating from 1872 and still around in many French gardens. Look for it in mid September.

Triomphe de Vienne Of French origin, this large fruit has green-bronze skin and juicy flesh. Around until October.

Williams Bon Chrétien Often simply called Williams or Bartlett and the world's most planted pear, this is a very beautiful fruit, with pale, clear yellow skin and scarlet streaks from where it has been in the sun. Originally found in a schoolmaster's garden in Aldermaston in the late 1700s, it has very white and buttery flesh, with little of the grainy quality that one either likes or not. With its heavy, musky aroma, this is a pear you can smell the minute you walk into the room. Its name comes from the Williams fruit nursery in Turnham Green, which bred and distributed it. It is called Bartlett in the US, after Enoch Bartlett who imported it there. This is the universal canning pear. Although it is revered by many (some even say it is the finest pear), I have to say I find it rather sweet and sickly.

Mid-season pears (ripening September–October)

Bergamotte d'Automne Dating from the time of Julius Caesar, this rough-skinned variety is one of the oldest pears in existence. The Bergamotte family – Heimbourg, Marbré, d'Eté, Précoce, d'Hiver, etc. – are French in origin. The Autumn Bergamot is small, roundish and perhaps a little dull, but it can be heavily perfumed with exceptionally juicy, tender flesh.

Beurre d'Amanlis A warm corner is needed for this old variety. I have yet to try this pear, whose skin starts green, then slowly forms patches of russet and reddish brown as it ripens. The flesh of this long and slender French pear can apparently become exceptionally sugary and perfumed.

Beurre Superfin A new variety of utmost beauty. At the RHS autumn shows, it takes everyone by surprise with a scarlet-blushed cinnamon and russet skin that seems to glow from within. The flavour is of the best, and the tree is a useful size for a small garden. September cropping.

Concorde A recent variety from East Malling, a cross between Conference and Doyenne du Comice, with large pale fruit and melting, sweet flesh. I am not fond of this rather sweet fruit.

Robin Some consider this Norfolk pear to be one of the finest of all. Needless to say, the fruits are small and have a scarlet blush.

Swan's Egg Who could resist a fine old pear called Swan's Egg? A roundish fruit, yellow-green on the shaded side, slightly red on the other and with a handsome russeting.

Durondeau A large, cinnamon-coloured fruit, its skin shiny and slightly russeted and streaked here and there with crimson. A very fine pear of which the original tree is said still to exist at the home of the late M. Durondeau, at the village of Tongre-Notre-Dame in Belgium. Ripens at the end of October.

Conference With its elongated fruit, green, freckled skin and grainy texture, this is one of our most popular and easily recognisable pears. It keeps well under refrigeration. It is a variety I am not fond of when ripe, and I prefer to eat it as a crisp, ice-cold pear with cheese, ideally on a chilly October or November day.

Doyenne du Comice Exquisitely perfumed, this large, lemony-yellow fruit has patches of russet speckling. With its very fine flavour and juicy, almost buttery flesh, there is something voluptuous about this fruit. In perfect condition, when you may need a cloth to cope with the juice, it can be memorable. Ripening in October, it can keep through to April. Pears don't come sexier than this one. France, 1849.

Pitmaston Duchesse An excellent old English fruit as good for cooking as it is for dessert. I have seen enormous examples of this beautifully russeted pear, the size of a clenched fist. Originally recorded in 1841 in Worcestershire, where it was raised in the same nursery as the Worcester Pearmain apple. Look for it in October and November.

Fertility (Improved) A late-nineteenth-century variety, and a heavy cropper, but a slightly underwhelming dessert fruit.

Beurre Hardy One of the finest dessert pears, this is tender, juicy and sweet with a hint of rosewater. It was first named in 1820, in France.

Glou Morceau A pea-green Belgian dessert fruit from the 1750s, with a melting texture and good flavour – I would say excellent, on occasions. Best planted in a warm place.

Late-season pears (ripening November onwards)

Forelle Charming, scarlet-orange fruit with freckled skin, like the trout after which it is named. A German variety from the 1670s, it is eye-catching in the garden but needs a sheltered position.

Black Worcester An ancient variety from the 1570s that is generally used for cooking. I knew it as the pear on my school badge and from the wild trees dotted through the local hedgerows. Like most wardens, it makes a very fine winter compote. A good keeper, around till March.

Double de Guerre A handsome, red-skinned fruit that is at its best when poached. Appearing late and with its nutmeg and crimson skin, it makes a good pear to have around at Christmas.

Easter Beurre One of the latest fruits of all, the Easter Beurre – good until the early spring – is a Belgian pear with a distinctive musk flavour.

Joséphine de Malines A very rich, almost buttery modern pear (1993) to have around at Christmas. Grown in a warm location, it will be a reliable cropper, but the fruit is delicate and easily bruised.

Uvedale's St Germain A large, very old English cooking pear. It can be around till March.

Winter Nelis A small and rather hard Belgian variety, best for cooking. The tree itself is untidy, the branches thin and tending to weep like a willow, but it has profuse and delicate spring blossom. The autumn foliage is simply gorgeous, showing maroon, crimson and tangerine leaves throughout October and early November. The fruits, heavily russeted, will stay on the tree till November.

Jargonelle The old pear whose name was used for the pear-shaped boiled sweets known as Jargonelle pears. The fruits are generally left on the tree and picked as you need them. The autumn Jargonelle is small, with pale green skin that ripens to pale yellow, dotted and streaked with dark crimson on the side next to the sun. Sugary, a little perfumed, it doesn't keep for long once off the tree. Leave it be till you need it.

A pear in the kitchen

The pear is often the first fruit we eat. Its mild flavour and soft texture appeal to a baby's palate, but more importantly, it is rare that it produces an allergic reaction. The pear is perhaps the gentlest of fruits. At the other end of our lives, it can help lower blood pressure and cholesterol and is one of the few fruits allowed on exclusion diets. The large amount of insoluble fibre gifts the fruit with gentle laxative effects.

My first pear was from a can, sitting in a pool of thin, sweet syrup (always wonderful when generously chilled), the violin-shaped hollows of the fruit filled with evaporated milk, which would float off into the syrup like oil paint poured into water. If I am honest, I still rather like canned pears in syrup, the agony being whether to eat them with or without cream. Sometimes I add it just to watch the cream following the hollows of the halved pear.

The pear behaves differently from the apple in the heat. As ripe as a Comice may be, it doesn't always translate as such once under the crust of a crumble or a pie. The flesh seems to dry out in the oven rather than forming juice, as might an apple (I get round this with the addition of that liquid amber of the kitchen, maple syrup). But for the most part, the pear is cooked less often than the apple because it tends to lose its subtlety when heat is applied. The flavour can appear elusive.

That said, I like a baked pear, perhaps with a stream of honey to caramelise on the dish, or hollowed out and stuffed with mincemeat, when it is a thoroughly good thing. Poaching in a light sugar syrup is often the most successful way to enjoy them. The flesh keeps its flavour, stays juicy and takes on a glowing transparency. As a breakfast dish, it is pure and clean; as a dessert, its hollows can be stuffed with whipped cream, crushed florentines or ginger biscuits and trickled, Jackson Pollock style, with dark and piercingly bitter chocolate.

In a savoury sense, the old cream cheese and herb option, stuffed into the hollows left when the core is removed, is still relevant. The thick, fresh cheese and chopped herbs work in more than a tongue-in-cheek retro way.

Pears can be cooked around a roast in much the same way as a parsnip. Their edges catch in the roasting juices and take on appetising flecks of gold and bronze. Pork is without doubt the best choice here, but a guinea fowl or a pheasant might appreciate their company too. A spoonful of rowan jelly, shimmering like an uncut ruby, might be good when dissolved in the roasting juices.

Sautéing a pear, cut into thick segments, produces something mellow and buttery to go with a jagged lump of Cheshire cheese, or perhaps a coleslaw salad with toasted cobnuts or salted almonds. They can be slipped on to a slice of toast and covered with a modest amount of grated cheese, or served alongside a thick slice of warm ham.

I find you need a good squeeze of lemon when peeling a pear to stop the exposed flesh browning. Rub the cut side of the lemon over the pared pear. Even so, they still discolour more quickly than apples. Stewed pear, which can be wonderful for breakfast with sheep's or goat's yoghurt, or even cream, can be difficult to accomplish without it turning the colour of old tights. I tuck half a lemon into the peeled and sliced fruit and sugar as it simmers.

There are some varieties that are exclusively for the kitchen. I include the Winter Nelis and Beth in this. A cooking pear is one that refuses to soften without the application of heat, or whose flavour has little interest until warm. A cooking pear used to be known as a warden – (warden pies are mentioned in Shakespeare's *A Winter's Tale*). Their name comes from Warden Abbey in Bedfordshire, one of the senior Cistercian monasteries in the country, founded about 1135. It is now leased by the Landmark Trust and can be hired for holidays. I would imagine there's a waiting list in autumn. Some varieties are simply stubborn and never come to ripeness. I see these fruits hanging forlornly in gardens all over the country. But then I see uncollected fruit all over the place. They would make a good pickle or a chutney but may well be glorious when brought to tenderness in sugar syrup.

Pears and...

Ham and bacon The more herbal or salty, the better the marriage. Air-dried hams, such as Parma, excel at bringing out the sweetness of the fruit and its juice. The two probably work most successfully in a salad with spinach or pale winter leaves such as frisé or chicory. I often add a pear to the pan when I am cooking a gammon steak. But it needs to be very ripe.

Pork A few pears tucked around a roasting loin is a great autumn and winter favourite in this house, as are a few slices sautéed in the same pan as a pork chop. I sometimes include slices of crisp, grainy pear with a plate of cold pork and home-made pickles.

Game Pheasant, duck, partridge and pigeon enjoy a pear or two, particularly when the pears are pushed around the birds as they roast.

Chocolate Whilst a raw pear and a sliver of chocolate is a simple enough way to end a supper, the marriage takes on a more luxurious note once the pear is cooked and the chocolate melted. The poached fruit served with a thick, dark chocolate sauce is the classic interpretation, but it can be extended to a chocolate mousse served alongside poached pears; a chocolate cake filled with pears and cream; a pear and chocolate trifle; and nuggets of chocolate tucked into a pear crumble or betty. Even milk chocolate, not normally associated with the kitchen, can work here.

Caramel Toffee-style sauces such as butterscotch and caramel send shivers of joy down this writer's spine. The ice-cold juice of the pear neatly contrasts the smooth and buttery notes of the sauce.

Cinnamon Sticks of this sweet, musky spice can be added to the syrup used for poaching pears or in a sauce to accompany them.

Almonds An almond frangipane mixture is the classic support for pears in a French-style tarte aux poires or a more homely pear Bakewell. A careless scattering of toasted flaked nuts provides a crisp contrast to a cooked pear. Pistachios and walnuts are natural bedfellows too.

Aniseed flavours Star anise, aniseed, tarragon, chervil and fennel all work with the pear in different ways (Conference and fennel being a crisp, refreshing autumn salad). I assume liquorice would work too, though I can't say I have ever tried it.

Vanilla While it is difficult to think of a fruit that vanilla does not complement (only melon and oranges spring to mind), it is particularly welcome here.

Greens Watercress, spinach and the bitter salad leaves are a masterful addition to a salad that contains pears. Throw in some air-dried ham or crisp snippets of fried bacon.

Wine Both red and white wine can be used as the cooking liquid for pears. A fair bit of sugar is needed too, plus orange peel, cloves, a cinnamon stick and maybe a spoonful of honey. The sweet wines such as a Muscat or a treacly Sauternes are more suitable than the drier whites. A good, fruity red such as a Beaujolais or Zinfandel gets my vote for the red. I tend to serve the latter on cold winter nights. A drop of medium-sweet sherry is no bad thing in a pear trifle.

Blackcurrants A tart, purple-black purée of the sieved and sweetened fruit is a gorgeous sauce to trickle over a melting poached pear.

Raspberries Not so much as partners in a salad, more as a sauce for the cooked fruit or as a purée to serve with a pear sorbet.

Honey A spoonful or two added to the simmering water in which you are bringing the fruits to tenderness is worth trying, as is using it to baste pears you are baking in the oven.

Ginger Either as a ground spice to season a pear cake or in its fresh form as coins dropped into a sugar syrup for cooking the pears.

Cheese A jagged lump of Parmesan and a ripe pear have been lunch for me on many a winter's day. The cold juice and salty cheese form a tantalising partnership. Cheeses with a salty note, such as Parmesan, pecorino and many of the blues, will tease out the sweetness of the pear's juice in much the same way that Parma ham does for a ripe melon.

The punchy blues, such as Picos, Roquefort and Stichelton, seem particularly at home with the melting flesh of a bulging Comice but crisp pears, the sort that makes your gums ache, their flesh hard and white as snow, can be strangely addictive too – a heavily blued Roquefort and a slender, underripe Conference being a particular favourite.

In a salad, the two ingredients will benefit from some toasted hazelnuts or almonds, or fresh, pale walnuts. White winter salad leaves, with their blush of maroon and scarlet freckles, work better with a pear than soft leaves, though a crisp pear and spinach salad is an exception worth trying.

The softer, milder cheeses are pleasing, too, for when I want something altogether gentler. Perfectly fine but less interesting than those that have a pungency to contrast the pear's sweet juice.

* Perry is fermented pear juice.
* Pears will ripen faster if placed next to bananas in a fruit bowl. They stay fresh longer if kept in the fridge.

A pork pot-roast

Perry is an astonishing drink – refreshing, dry and fruity. A small bottle upended into a pot-roast will ensure a moist result and leave you with a decent amount of fruity pot juices to spoon over.

enough for 4, with some left for cold
olive or groundnut oil – 2 tablespoons
a lump of pork on the bone, about 1.5kg in weight
a large onion
large pears – 4
bay leaves – a couple
perry (or cider) – 400ml
mild honey or maple syrup – 3 tablespoons

Set the oven at 200°C/Gas 6. In a deep, heavy pan, warm the oil over a lively heat and add the pork, generously salted and peppered. Let the meat colour a little – it should be pale gold here and there – then turn it so the other sides take on a little colour too.

Peel the onion, slice it fairly thinly, then add it to the pot. While it softens, slice the pears thickly, removing the cores as you go. I see no reason to peel them. Add the pears, bay leaves, perry or cider and honey or maple syrup to the pot with a little salt and black pepper. Cover with a lid and bake for fifty minutes to an hour.

Serve in thin slices, with the pears and the thin, delicious juices, some mashed potato and perhaps a little braised red cabbage.

A weekday supper of pork and pears

enough for 2
pork chops – 2
groundnut oil – 2 tablespoons
garlic – 2 large cloves, crushed flat
pears – 2
dry white wine or vermouth – a wineglass
stock – 75ml

Season the chops with salt and pepper. Heat the groundnut oil in a shallow pan with the crushed garlic cloves. When the oil is hot, slide in the pork chops – take care, they will spit at you. Seal on both sides. Meanwhile, cut the pears into eighths and core them.

Turn down the heat, add the pears to the pan and cook for about ten minutes, until tender and browned lightly. Remove the chops and pears to warm plates. Pour most of the fat from the pan and return to the heat. Pour in the wine or vermouth and scrape away the bits of pork and pear stuck to the pan. Add the stock and simmer until reduced by half. Pour over the chops and pears.

Eat with
* A salad of bitter leaves such as rocket or frisé.
* Chicory leaves dressed with lemon and chopped walnuts.
* Spinach leaves, cooked for a few seconds with some drops of water till they wilt, black pepper, no butter.

A Sunday roast of pork, perry and pears

Slow-maturing, hardy varieties of pig, particularly Tamworth and Gloucester Old Spot, make an extraordinarily succulent roast. I like to rub their skin with a salt and rosemary paste to encourage it to turn into good crackling. Perry, the cider made from pears, has been made in the south of the country for 200 years and is undergoing a renaissance. I use dry apple cider – and apples instead of pears – when perry proves evasive.

Pork will produce more reliable crackling if the meat is dry before roasting. Leaving it unwrapped and in open air for an hour will help.

enough to serve 4–6
rosemary leaves – 2 tablespoons
sea salt – 1 tablespoon
black peppercorns – 1 teaspoon
olive oil – 5 tablespoons
a rolled leg or loin of pork, about 1.5kg, scored
onions – 2
pears – 4
perry – 250ml

Set the oven at 220°C/Gas 7. Finely chop the rosemary leaves and crush them with the sea salt and peppercorns, using a pestle and mortar. When you have a sand-like mixture, pour in 3 tablespoons of the olive oil to make a paste.

Put the meat in a roasting tin and massage the rosemary paste into its skin and cut edges. Roast for twenty minutes, then reduce the temperature to 200°C/Gas 6 and continue to roast for twenty-five minutes per 500g.

Whilst the pork is roasting, peel the onions and chop them roughly. Let them cook with the remaining oil in a shallow pan over a moderate heat till soft and palest gold. Peel and quarter the pears (I keep them from browning with a little lemon juice). Add the onions and pears to the roasting tin after the pork has been cooking at the lower temperature for twenty-five minutes, basting the pears with any available pan juices.

When the pork is ready, remove it from the oven and let it rest in a warm place with the pears, lightly covered with foil (a tight covering will make the crackling soften).

Put the roasting tin over a moderate heat, add the perry and boil the juices until reduced to about 200ml or so. They won't thicken, but you just want to concentrate the flavour a little. Adjust the seasoning.

Serve the pork in thin slices, together with chunks of its crackling, pears and oniony pan juices.

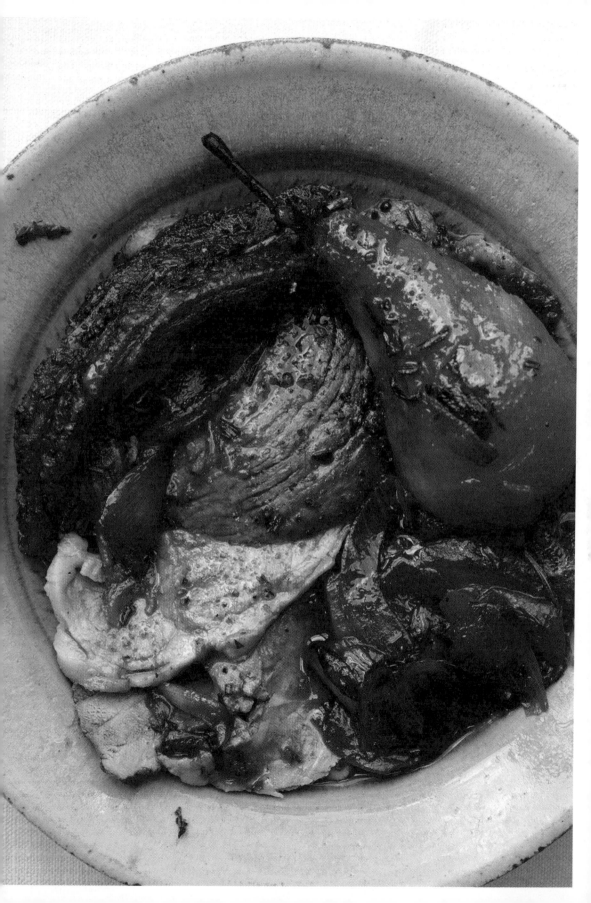

Roast partridge, juniper and pears

enough for 4
young, plump partridges – 4
thyme – 6 bushy little sprigs
juniper berries – 12
butter – 100g
green bacon – 8 thin rashers
pears – 2
a squeeze of lemon juice
white bread – 4 small, thick slices
redcurrant, rowan or quince jelly – 2 tablespoons
vermouth or white wine – a glass

Before I start, I always check the birds all over for any stray feathers or bits of shattered bone. Set the oven at 220°C/Gas 7.

Pull the leaves from the thyme branches and mash them with the juniper berries, butter and a hefty pinch of sea salt and black pepper, using a pestle and mortar. Reserve a tablespoon for cooking the pears, then spread the butter all over the birds, but particularly on their breasts.

Lay each rasher of bacon flat on a chopping board, then stretch with the flat of a knife blade to give a longer, thinner rasher. Wrap the rashers round the birds and place in a roasting tin.

Cut the pears into thick slices, core them, toss them in a little lemon juice and cook briefly in the reserved herb butter in a shallow, non-stick pan. When both sides are pale gold, transfer them to the roasting tin.

Roast for twenty minutes, then peel off the bacon, setting it aside if it is crisp enough or leaving it in the roasting tin if not. Return the birds to the oven for a further ten minutes' roasting.

If you want to make croûtes, warm a little butter or oil in a shallow pan (I use the same one I used for the pears), then fry the bread till crisp. Drain on kitchen paper.

Remove the tin from the oven, set the birds on the fried bread, with the bacon and pear beside them, then leave to rest (I use a warm plate for this with an upturned bowl on top). Put the roasting tin over a moderate flame, drop in the jelly and let it melt into the pan juices. Add a small glass of vermouth or wine and stir to dissolve the pan-stickings. Bring to the boil, put the birds and their bits and pieces on to warm plates, then spoon over the 'gravy'.

Pears with maple syrup and vanilla

The double cooking of these pears, first in a light syrup and then baked, ensures that they are truly soft and tender. You could use honey if maple syrup proves elusive.

enough for 4
large pears – 4
sugar – 4 tablespoons
water – 750ml
maple syrup – 4 tablespoons
vanilla extract – 2–3 drops
cream, to serve

Peel the pears, cut them in half and scoop out their cores. Bring the sugar and water to the boil, slip in the pears and let them simmer for ten to fifteen minutes, till approaching tenderness. Drain and discard the syrup; it has done its work. Set the oven at 180°C/Gas 4.

Place the pears in a shallow baking dish. Drizzle with the maple syrup and the vanilla extract. Bake for about an hour, till the pears are meltingly soft and pale gold here and there. Serve with a jug of cream, though they are quite pleasing as they come.

A crisp salad of red cabbage and pears

The variations on cheese and pears are almost endless. The one I exploit the most is that of blue cheese with ripe pears – here, in a salad of crisp cabbage, soft and powerful blue cheese and pears. I suggest Picos, but Cashel Blue would work well here, as would Roquefort.

enough for 4
red cabbage – 400g
crisp white cabbage – 200g
pears – 2 (crisp rather than ripe)
Picos or other blue cheese – 150–200g
poppy seeds – a tablespoon

for the dressing
tarragon vinegar – 1 tablespoon
crème fraîche – 300ml
grain mustard – 1 tablespoon

Discard any less than crisp outer leaves from the cabbages and shred the heart leaves finely. I use a large knife for this, though others may prefer to find a suitable disc in their food processor's box of gadgets. Soak briefly in cold water and drain. Cut the pears into thin slices, removing the core as you go. Mix the pears and cabbage together. Cut the cheese into thick slices, break each slice into large, flat crumbs, then add to the cabbage and pears. Make the dressing by dissolving a large pinch of salt in the tarragon vinegar, then stirring in the crème fraîche and grain mustard, together with a little black pepper. Taste for sharpness, adding more mustard or vinegar as you wish. Scrape the dressing into the salad and toss gently, taking care to coat all the cabbage and pears. Pile into a serving dish or divide between four plates, then sprinkle over the poppy seeds.

A winter salad of pears and blue cheese

Slightly underripe pears with a little crispness to them are better for this than truly ripe ones – the contrast works well with the cheese. Salad leaves such as frisé and maybe some red-leaved chard would be good here. You might like to continue the pomegranate theme or use golden sultanas or raisins instead.

enough for 2
a plump pear, ripe but still slightly crisp
lemon juice
small, crisp salad leaves – a couple of handfuls
Stilton, Stichelton or other firm blue cheese – 4 thick slices
walnut halves – a handful
half a pomegranate

for the dressing
cider vinegar or white wine vinegar – a tablespoon
groundnut oil – a tablespoon
walnut or hazelnut oil – 2 tablespoons
double cream – a tablespoon

Slice the pear into quarters, remove the core, then cut the fruit into thin slices. Brush each piece with lemon juice.

Make the dressing. Pour the vinegar into a small mixing bowl and dissolve a pinch of sea salt in it. Stir in the oils, then the cream, and whisk well. Divide the salad leaves, pear and cheese between two plates and pour over the dressing. Toast the walnuts, break the pomegranate into separate seeds, then scatter both nuts and seeds over the salad.

Pear, pecan and maple syrup betty

enough for 4
pears – 850g
a little butter
golden caster sugar – 2 tablespoons
a pinch of ground cinnamon
a handful of pecans or shelled walnut pieces

for the crumb layer
butter – 75g
maple syrup – 3 tablespoons
soft white breadcrumbs – 65g
rolled oats – 65g
light muscovado sugar – 90g

Set the oven at 180°C/Gas 4. Peel the pears, remove and discard their cores
and chop the flesh into large chunks. Melt the butter in a small casserole
over a moderate heat and add the pears. Let the fruit cook till it starts to
colour appetisingly around the edges. It should be tender but not soft.
Add the sugar, cinnamon and nuts and turn off the heat.

To make the topping, put the butter and maple syrup into a saucepan
and let it melt slowly over a moderate heat. Mix the breadcrumbs, oats and
muscovado sugar together and tip them over the pears. Spoon the melted
butter and maple syrup over the top, then bake in the preheated oven for
thirty-five minutes, till the crust is lightly crisp and the fruit is fully tender.
There will be crisp crust, juicy pears and a layer of delicious syrup at
the base.

Baked pears with cranberries and orange

There is something about an ice-white winter sky that makes me abandon my usual breakfast of yoghurt and fruit for a chilled fruit compote. Most times it's stewed apple but occasionally there are pears to use up.

enough for 4 as breakfast or dessert
pears – 1kg
a pinch of ground cinnamon
the juice of half a lemon
cloves – 4

for the compote
dates – 200g
dried cranberries (or cherries) – 50g
a stick of cinnamon
honey – 3 tablespoons
the finely grated zest and juice of a large orange

Set the oven at 200°C/Gas 6. Peel, quarter and core the pears and roughly chop them. Put them in a baking dish, then toss with the cinnamon and lemon juice and tuck in the cloves. Bake the pears till they are soft. Depending on your choice of pear, this will take anything from thirty to forty-five minutes.

While the fruit is cooking, remove the stones from the dates and toss them in a small saucepan with the dried cranberries, cinnamon, honey and the orange zest and juice. Bring to the boil, turn the heat down to a gentle simmer and leave to bubble very gently for about ten minutes, till the fruit has plumped and softened.

To serve, spoon the pears and their juice into dishes, then top with the hot dried fruit. Both will keep well in the fridge for several days.

A dish of baked pears with marsala

When the oven has been on for a roast, I sometimes sneak in a dish of baked fruit.

> *enough for 4*
> large pears – 4
> a lemon
> sweet marsala – 4 tablespoons
> caster sugar – 3 tablespoons
> butter – 50g

Set the oven at 200°C/Gas 6. Peel the pears but leave them whole, dropping them into cold water with a squeeze of lemon juice in it as you go to stop them browning.

Put the marsala, caster sugar and butter into a baking dish, then add the whole pears. Bake for about an hour, till the pears are butter soft. It is essential to baste them once or twice, turning them over in the juices. Serve them warm, spooning over the sweet, buttery juices.

Pears with a brandy-snap cream

Simmered in juice or water and sugar, pears can end up as soft as butter. A crisp element such as a biscuit or wafer offers a welcome contrast. Little chocolate florentine biscuits or brandy snaps are an alternative. Brandy snaps are available in boxes from good supermarkets, delicatessens and grocer's. You will probably find them with the posh biscuits.

enough for 4
caster sugar – 100g
water – a litre
a lemon
a vanilla pod
small pears – 8
whipping cream – 200ml
a little vanilla extract
small brandy snaps – 100g
dark chocolate – 100g

Dissolve the sugar in the water over a low heat with a good squeeze of lemon juice and the vanilla pod. You are making a light, mildly flavoured syrup. Peel the pears, rubbing with the lemon as you go, then cut them in half and remove their cores. Slide the fruit into the syrup. With the pan covered, bring the syrup to the boil, then turn the heat down immediately. Let the pears simmer very gently until translucent and tender to the point of a knife. Depending on the ripeness of the fruit, this will take about fifteen minutes, maybe longer. They really must be butter soft if they are to be good.

Let the pears cool in the syrup for a good hour, then lift them out and put them in a shallow dish in the fridge. Whip the cream softly – it should not be too stiff – then fold in a couple of drops of vanilla extract and the roughly crushed brandy snaps.

Break the chocolate into small squares and melt it in a small bowl set over a pan of simmering water. Just let it melt – don't stir it. As soon as the chocolate has melted, turn off the heat, then fill the pears with the brandy–snap cream. Drizzle over the chocolate in thin zigzag lines, then leave in the fridge for a few minutes to crisp.

Poached pears with pomegranate sorbet

I adore a feast as much as anyone, but I do find those at Christmas can be just too rich. I constantly look round for something light and refreshing with which to end my meal. A dish of cool, luscious pears full of mildly spicy juice slithers down easily after a rich meal. The accompanying ice, rose pink and as refreshing as a waterfall, is a deeply fruity accompaniment to the softness of the pear.

It is essential to use unsweetened pomegranate juice here. That means either using fresh fruit and squeezing it yourself or checking the labels of your juice carefully. Pom brand is the one I use.

enough for 4
caster sugar – 100g
water – a litre
a lemon
a cinnamon stick
star anise – 4
a vanilla pod
a small orange
large pears – 4

for the pomegranate sorbet
caster sugar – 120g
pomegranate juice – 900ml

Dissolve the sugar in the water over a low heat. Add a good squeeze of lemon juice, the cinnamon stick, star anise and vanilla pod. Remove 2 or 3 long strips of peel from the orange with a vegetable peeler and add them to the pan. You are making a light, mildly flavoured syrup.

Peel the pears, rubbing with the lemon as you go. If you wish, you can cut them in half and remove their cores. But I tend to cook mine whole. Slide the fruit into the syrup. With the pan covered, bring the syrup to the boil, then turn the heat down immediately. Let the pears simmer very gently until translucent and tender to the point of a knife. Depending on the ripeness of the fruit, this will take about thirty minutes, maybe longer. Continue cooking till they are butter-soft.

Let the pears cool in the syrup for a good hour, then lift them out and put them in a shallow dish in the fridge. Chill till you need them.

For the sorbet, stir the sugar into the pomegranate juice till dissolved. If it isn't disappearing, then warm the mixture slightly till it does. Don't let it boil though, as this will affect the flavour and colour. Pour the mixture into an ice-cream machine and churn till almost frozen. Remove and transfer to a plastic freezer box.

No machine? Then you are probably better off making a granita. Pour the mixture into a shallow plastic freezer tray and freeze for about an hour. Stir with a fork, bringing the ice crystals that have formed around the edge into the middle. Return to the freezer. Leave for a further hour or so, then repeat. Do this till the mixture is almost frozen solid. It will freeze quite hard, but when shattered with a fork or knife will break into a quite granular ice. If it is frozen solid, allow a good twenty minutes to come to room temperature, then break up with a fork into deep pink snow.

A water ice of pear and lemon

There is much elegance in this delicately flavoured, ivory-coloured sorbet. Depending on the time of year, I sometimes eat it with apricots that have been poached in a little light sugar syrup, or perhaps with a handful of velvet raspberries. The texture is smoother if the sorbet is made in a machine. If you are making it by hand, then it is probably best to treat it as a crystalline granita instead.

enough for 4–6
water – 500ml
caster sugar – 250g
pears – 6
a lemon

Bring the water and caster sugar to the boil in a stainless steel saucepan. Peel the pears, cut them in half and scoop out the pips and tough core with a teaspoon. Rub each piece of pear with a cut half of the lemon. Slide the pears and the lemon halves into the hot syrup and let them cook at a low simmer until the pears are truly tender. They should take the point of a sharp knife without you having to exert any pressure. Switch off the heat and leave them in the syrup until completely cool.

Put the pears and their cooking syrup – but not the lemons – into a blender and blitz till smooth and white. Now either pour into an electric ice-cream maker and churn till almost frozen or pour the mixture into a shallow plastic freezer box and place in the freezer. If you are making it without a machine, leave the sorbet for a couple of hours until ice crystals are forming around the edge. Stir them into the centre with a whisk, then return to the freezer for another couple of hours. Remove and whisk again, continually bringing the frozen edges into the middle, then freeze once more. Just as the sorbet is almost frozen, give it one final beating with the whisk and leave it to freeze. Once frozen, it is a good idea to take it out of the freezer twenty minutes or so before serving, leaving it in the fridge.

Pears in sweet wine

Sweet wines – Sauternes, Tokay, Beaumes de Venise and the occasional orange Muscat – tend to accumulate in the cupboard. Often received as gifts, they are wines I have to be in the mood for and, frankly, rarely drink. This recipe is a good end for those you might be wondering what to do with.

enough for 4
hard pears – 4
juice of half a lemon
sugar – 250g
a vanilla pod
half a bottle of sweet white wine, Sauternes or orange Muscat

Wipe the pears and cut each one in half lengthways. Put into a deep saucepan with the juice of the half lemon, the sugar, vanilla, wine and 400ml water. Bring to the boil, then turn the heat down to a simmer. Let the pears cook gently until they are completely tender to the point of a knife. This will take a good forty-five minutes, maybe longer. Don't even think of undercooking them.

Lift the tender fruit out with a draining spoon and remove the vanilla pod. Now remove any bits of froth with a draining spoon, put the liquor over a high heat and let it reduce to a thin syrup, taking care not to let it boil to jam. Pour it over the pears and leave it to cool, then refrigerate. Serve cold.

Pears with praline ice cream and chocolate sauce

Another example of the marriage of pears and chocolate, but this time with
a nutty ice cream. It is a seductive contrast of texture. Silky pears, heavy with
syrup, cold, nubbly ice cream and warm, velvety chocolate sauce.

enough for 4
golden caster sugar – 2 tablespoons
a vanilla pod
juice of half a lemon
pears – 4
praline ice cream
fine dark chocolate – 200g

Pour a good litre of water into a deep, wide pan, then add the sugar, vanilla
pod and lemon juice and bring to the boil. Peel the pears and tug out their
stalks, then halve the fruit and scoop out the cores with a teaspoon. Drop
the fruit into the sugar syrup and let them simmer for about fifteen minutes,
till translucent and tender. Leave them in the syrup to cool. During this
time they will become silkily soft and soaked through with syrup.

Get the ice cream out of the freezer. Chop the chocolate. Bring 200ml
water to the boil, then whisk in the chocolate, removing the pan from the
heat as soon as it has melted – a matter of seconds. Place two pear halves on
each of four dishes, add the praline ice cream, one ball per person should be
ample, then pour over the warm chocolate sauce.

Poached pears with warm chocolate sauce

The marriage of pears and chocolate is extraordinary. It is as if they were made for each other (curiously, apples and chocolate have little affinity with one another). The effect is possibly at its most sumptuous when the pears are poached in a light sugar syrup till almost translucent and the chocolate comes in the form of a warm, flowing sauce.

enough for 4
golden caster sugar – 100g
water – a litre
a vanilla pod
a little lemon juice
plump pears – 4

for the chocolate sauce
fine plain chocolate – 200g
strong black coffee – 2 tablespoons
whipping cream – 180ml
butter – a small knob

Bring the sugar, water, vanilla and lemon juice to the boil, then turn down the heat and leave to simmer gently. Meanwhile, peel the pears, cut them in half lengthways and remove the cores with a sharp knife and a teaspoon. Slide them into the syrup and let them simmer gently till they are tender to the point of a knife. You can expect this to take anything up to thirty-five minutes, depending on the ripeness of the pears. I think they should be really tender and full of juice. Leave them to cool in the syrup.

Break the chocolate into small pieces and put it into a heavy-bottomed saucepan with the coffee and cream. Heat slowly, stirring from time to time, until the chocolate has melted. It is essential that the heat is kept low. Once the chocolate has softened, stir until smooth, then stir in the butter and pour the sauce into a warm jug.

Drain the pears and put them on a dish. Pour over the warm chocolate sauce.

A cake of pears, muscovado and maple syrup

Cakes like these, where the sugar and butter are creamed first before the other ingredients are added, are so much easier to make when the butter is at room temperature rather than straight from the fridge. It's a small and perhaps obvious point but one that I continually forget. It will make life much easier.

enough for 8
butter – 100g, softened
golden caster sugar – 50g
light muscovado sugar – 50g
plain flour – 150g
baking powder – a teaspoon
ground almonds – 50g
large eggs – 3
milk – 2 tablespoons
vanilla extract – a couple of drops

for the pears
ripe pears – 450g
butter – 20g
ground cinnamon – a couple of pinches
maple syrup – 3 tablespoons, plus a little more to serve

Line the base of a deep 20cm baking tin with baking paper. Peel, core and chop the pears. The pieces should be quite small, about 1cm square. Put them into a shallow pan with the butter and cinnamon and let them soften for ten to twelve minutes over a moderate heat, stirring from time to time so they do not burn. Pour in the maple syrup, let the mixture bubble up briefly, then remove from the heat. The pears should be sticky and deep golden.

Set the oven at 180°C/Gas 4. Put the butter and sugars into a food mixer and beat till pale and thick. They should be the colour of milky coffee. Sift the flour and baking powder together (I don't normally suggest sifting flour but it is essential when you are incorporating baking powder to ensure it is evenly distributed). Add the almonds to the flour. Beat the eggs and milk in a small bowl with a fork, then add to the butter and sugar mixture a little at a time, alternating with the flour and almonds. Stir in the vanilla extract.

Tip the mixture into the cake tin and smooth the top. Spoon the pears and any remaining syrup over the mixture. They will gradually sink on cooking to make a sticky layer further down.

Bake for forty minutes, or till golden and lightly firm. Serve warm, in thick slices, with cream and a little more maple syrup.

Mulled perry with pears and spices

Soft pears, crisp biscuits. Every year I make a trip, you could call it a pilgrimage, to one of Europe's Christmas markets: Berlin, Brussels and Vienna all get a visit. Whilst there is an element of tat about some of the stalls, there are good things too: old-fashioned decorations for the tree, gingerbread cookies with sugar frosting and glasses of mulled cider. There is something quite magical about these frosty evenings, holding mugs of hot cider in mittened hands.

Back home, with a grey Christmas rather than a frosty white one, the magic somewhat disappears, but the warm, fruity drink is still more interesting than our own mulled wine. I use perry or cider, which glows in the glass, spiked with cloves and pieces of pear that soften in the heat. A wonderfully refreshing drink, even when warmed with sugar and spice. The smell as it fizzes on the stove is pure Christmas. I serve it with crisp spiced biscuits, their ginger notes just right for the pear.

> *enough for 6–8 glasses*
> large pears – 2
> butter – a thick slice
> pear cider – a litre
> soft brown sugar – 2 tablespoons
> cloves – 12
> cinnamon sticks – 3
> a nutmeg
> the juice of a small orange

Peel and core the pears and cut them into large dice. Melt the butter in a shallow pan, add the pears and leave them to soften for ten minutes or so. They should be tender but still retain some shape.

Pour the pear cider into a stainless steel saucepan, tip in the sugar, then add the cloves, cinnamon sticks and a fine grating of nutmeg. Squeeze the orange into the cider and let the mixture warm slowly, allowing it to come almost to the boil. Lower the heat to keep it warm.

Divide the softened pears between the glasses, then pour in the spiced cider. Have some spoons around for the pears.

For the brown sugar spice biscuits

The simplest of biscuits for Christmas. Dark, mildly spiced and the sort of crisp cookies you find hanging from Christmas trees all over Europe. If by any chance you are ever looking for the ideal mixture to make gingerbread men, this is it.

butter – 70g
light muscovado sugar – 80g
black treacle or molasses – 2 heaped tablespoons
cardamom pods – 8
plain flour – 250g
bicarbonate of soda – half a teaspoon
ground cinnamon – 2 teaspoons
ground ginger – a teaspoon
an egg yolk
milk – 3–4 tablespoons
icing sugar

Set the oven at 180°C/Gas 4. Cream the butter and sugar together in a food mixer till light and fluffy, then add the treacle or molasses. Break the cardamom pods open and crush the seeds finely. Add them to the mixture with the flour, bicarbonate of soda, cinnamon, ginger and egg yolk. Beat in a couple of tablespoons of milk, then slowly add more until you reach a point where the dough is soft enough to roll. Bring the ingredients together, then roll out on a floured board like pastry. Cut out into rounds, moons and stars. I sometimes do a few Christmas trees too. Lay them on a lightly buttered baking sheet and bake for twelve to fourteen minutes. Remove and cool on a wire rack, then toss in icing sugar.

Pear and pecan tart

I am honestly not sure if this is a tart or a cake, I only know that it is delicious when served warm, with cream.

enough for 6
butter – 180g
golden caster sugar – 180g
large pears – 2
a little lemon juice
large eggs – 3
plain flour – 120g
baking powder – 1 teaspoon
ground almonds – 70g
milk – 80ml
vanilla extract – a few drops
halved pecan nuts – 60g
pouring cream, to serve

Set the oven at 180°C/Gas 4. Line a shallow baking tin, approximately 22cm square, with baking paper.

Cut the butter into small chunks and put it into a food mixer with the sugar. Beat till pale and creamy. Meanwhile, cut the pears into thick slices, coring and tossing them in lemon juice as you go. You can peel them or not as you wish, but I rather like the contrasting texture of the unpeeled ones.

Beat the eggs into the butter and sugar one at a time. Fold in the flour, baking powder and almonds, then the milk and vanilla. Scrape into the lined baking tin, press the pecans and pear slices lightly on top and bake for an hour, till pale gold and risen.

Leave to cool slightly, then cut into thick slices and serve warm, with cream.

Cinnamon pear cake with vanilla fudge sauce

This is the most gorgeous fudge sauce imaginable, tasting like melted, creamy vanilla toffee. The pear cake isn't bad either.

enough for 8–10
butter – 200g
golden caster sugar – 200g
large eggs – 3, lightly beaten
self-raising flour – 200g
baking powder – half a teaspoon
vanilla ice cream, to serve

for the pears
ripe pears – 750g
half a lemon
butter – 40g
light muscovado sugar – 3 tablespoons
ground cinnamon – a heaped half teaspoon

for the fudge sauce
unrefined light muscovado sugar – 100g
golden syrup – 100g
butter – 50g
double cream – 150ml
vanilla extract

You will need a 24cm loose-bottomed, non-stick cake tin, very lightly buttered. Set the oven to 160°C/Gas 3.

Peel the pears, then halve, core and roughly chop them, dropping them into cold water acidulated with a good few squeezes of the lemon. It will stop them turning brown. Melt the butter and muscovado sugar in a shallow pan over a moderate heat, stirring occasionally. Drain the pears and add them to the pan, taking care that they don't spit at you. Let them cook in the melted butter and sugar until they are tender and the sauce is thick and coats the pears. Stop before the sugar turns dark and bitter. Set aside to cool.

To make the cake, put the butter and sugar in a food mixer and beat till light and creamy. It should be almost white. Add the eggs and a little of the flour alternately, so that the mixture doesn't curdle. Fold in the remaining flour and the baking powder, followed by the cooked pears and their syrup. Scoop the mixture into the buttered baking tin and smooth the top lightly. Bake for forty-five minutes, till risen and golden, then check for doneness with a metal skewer; it should come out clean. Remove the cake from the oven and leave to cool before taking it out of the tin.

To make the sauce, put the sugar, golden syrup and butter in a small, heavy-based saucepan and bring to the boil, stirring only enough to stop it sticking. Stir in the cream and the vanilla and leave to cool. The sauce will thicken as the temperature drops.

To serve, put a slice of cake on each plate with two balls of ice cream, then pour over the fudge sauce.

And to go with the perfect pear

Sometimes you want to eat your perfect pear alone; its flesh and juice may demand a plate all to itself. But there are several good things to consider eating alongside your pear: a slice of melting Reblochon; a moussy-fresh goat's cheese; something more mature and fudge-like; or perhaps a herb-speckled scone straight from the oven or a slice of fruit-flecked wholemeal loaf.

Goat's cheese and thyme scones to eat with pears

enough for 4–8, as a snack or part of a light lunch
plain flour – 450g
baking powder – 6 teaspoons
cold butter – 85g
strong Cheddar cheese – 100g
strong, firm goat's cheese – 250g
chopped thyme leaves – 2 teaspoons
buttermilk – 350ml
a little more grated cheese and a few sprigs of thyme, to finish

Set the oven at 200°C/Gas 6. Sift the flour into a large mixing bowl with the baking powder. Cut the butter into small cubes and rub it into the flour using your fingertips or a food processor. You are after fine crumbs. Grate the Cheddar into the flour, crumble or cut the goat's cheese into small cubes and add to the mixture with the thyme leaves.

Pour in the buttermilk and bring the ingredients together to form a firmish dough. Turn on to a well-floured work surface and pat gently into a large round, about 20cm in diameter. Lift on to a lightly floured baking sheet. Score deeply (though not through to the baking sheet) with a large knife to divide the scone into eight wedges. Grate a little more cheese on the surface and scatter with a few remaining herbs.

Bake in the preheated oven for forty to forty-five minutes, till golden and firm to the touch. Allow to cool for a few minutes, then slide carefully on to a wire cooling rack. Serve warm (rather than hot from the oven).

Plums

When I find the perfect plum, jelly-fleshed and incandescently ripe, its golden skin flashed with crimson freckles, I make a great fuss of it. I have even been known to get out a small plate and a napkin. I eat slowly, imagining time stopped. More usually, I come across such a fruit without warning, having little alternative but to scrump it from the hand, spitting the stone into the long grass below.

The British plum season runs for about six weeks, from the Pershore Yellow Egg and Early Rivers in late July to the sultry Marjorie's Seedling that I have found in good condition as late as mid October. August and early September is greengage time, when we also see some of our 350 varieties, though only the luckiest of us will ever taste more than a handful. From the small, round wild plum of the country hedgerow to the rare Kea plum of Cornwall, they vary in shape, sweetness and colour, but all have one thing in common – luscious, honeyed flesh that tastes of the very essence of summer turning to autumn.

It breaks my heart to think of the plum orchards we have lost in the last two decades, but what else can a farmer do when the crop is no longer profitable, consumers have more interest in peaches and nectarines, and the stores continue to sell imports even during our own brief season? I salute the British plum grower.

The flavour of a plum is somewhat reliant on the amount of sugar it contains – the higher the percentage, the richer the flavour. But more importantly, as with any fruit, much also depends on the soil and climate in which it finds itself. Old Transparent has long been revered for its flavour. It is the plum I grew up with, and I cannot help measuring everything else by the memory of its honeyed notes and golden, almost liquid flesh. Early and Late Transparent, Denniston's Superb and the Jefferson are consistently discussed as the finest of the bunch and I would certainly agree.

The single most important point in finding the perfect plum is to catch it at its ripest – that brief moment just before it starts to soften that little bit too much. When its flesh has almost, but not quite, turned to jelly and the fruit appears to be glowing from within. It is a moment worth waiting for.

The gages

There is no real difference between plums and gages, though we use the latter name to describe the smaller and more prized members of *Prunus domestica*. They are named for Sir William Gage, who first imported the tiny, chartreuse-coloured Reine Claude variety from France. The name stuck, and now any small, green plum is called a gage. They are interchangeable in cooking with our own larger Pershore varieties, but when left to ripen can excel in terms of flavour.

I grow Oullins Gage, an early cropper with green-gold flesh that needs a good summer to show itself at its subtle best. If I were to choose again, it would be an Early Transparent, a fruit so sweet and honeyed the word nectar springs to mind as you eat. This is the plum, along with perhaps an Old Greengage and a few Mirabelles, that I regard as some the finest fruit on earth.

A plum tree in the garden

I like to think everyone has a special tree. A tree they may be lucky enough to see every day, or pass on a regular journey. Perhaps it is one they remember from their childhood. A tree whose trunk is memorably gnarled or whose exposed, twisting roots run like serpents through the grass. Perhaps the memory is of a particular branch they used to sit on in more carefree days. A tree can welcome you as one might an old friend.

My 'special' tree was an ancient plum, its trunk covered with dusky grey lichen. Barely taller than a man, its bent and craggy trunk had to be held up by a pile of old bricks. And once the fruit had fallen, its shape became almost sinister, its brittle twigs pointing like witches' fingers against a cold winter sky. I knew it through most of my childhood and can recall almost every branch.

The plums, typically as it turns out, could be few and far between or so prolific we thought the branches would snap under their weight. The variety, like many of the best fruit trees, had been lost in time; the fruits were almost translucent, a deep saffron yellow flashed with rusty crimson. Large too, at least that is how I remember them.

On a brief trip back to my childhood cottage, a little saddened by the state of the once-immaculate garden, I dared not look at the top end of the paddock, the bit we referred to as the orchard, in case my tree had vanished. What worried me more, I suspect, was finding that my tree never existed.

Those plums are now tainted with the rose-pink glow of nostalgia, but I like to think they were as sweet and luscious as I remember them. My guess is that they were some form of the much-maligned Victoria that the late Alan Davidson sniffily dismissed as 'good marketing rather than inherent distinction'. Perhaps he didn't know it as I did, when left to ripen properly, until each fruit looks as if there is a candle burning inside it and you have to shoo the wasps away.

There are now five plum trees in my tiny garden, all of which I have planted in the last decade (I must admit to a slight obsession with this fruit). A golden Mirabelle, whose marble-sized fruits as sweet as maple syrup come in their hundreds; a Crimson Drop that has only recently started to show its hand; an Oullins Gage, whose fruits glow deep gold though their dusky skin; a damson for crumbles; and a wild plum, whose stone may have come from a careless bird or maybe from my habit of hurling plum stones and apple cores out of the window. Either way it is welcome. I recommend a semi-dwarfing St Julian 'A' rootstock for a smallish garden. Otherwise it will take over the entire space, like a carelessly purchased greengage once did here.

The plum tree is a member of the same family as the apricot and the cherry but has a slightly mistier history. What is clear is its presence in monastery gardens. I sometimes think if I had to limit myself to just one tree it would be some sort of plum.

Planted and staked they require little in the way of pruning, although I do cut out crossing branches at the start of the growing season. The blossom is some of the earliest and can be lost to frost but, God willing, there will be fruit turning gold by early July and truly ripe by mid August or September.

Varieties

We will never know the names of many of the old trees in our gardens. We just eat their fruits and say thank you. Anyone planting a tree now would be lucky to come across the Cox's Emperor, with its majestic growth and dark red, yellow-spotted fruits, or the apricot-fleshed Manaccan, so prized for its jam. Specialist nurseries still have many time-honoured varieties suitable for a small garden, such as the purple Angelina Burdett, the sugary Reine Claude de Bavay and the yellow- and red-mottled Golden Bullace. Many are self-fertile. Some, such as Opal, require a friend.

Pershore Yellow Egg One for the pot. Not the juiciest or most flavoursome when eaten raw but makes jolly good jam. It was discovered in the wild, at Tiddesley Wood near Pershore, some time between 1827 and 1833 (accounts vary). As a kid, I saw more of this canary-coloured plum in my local Worcestershire farm shops than any other. They were even sold in the post office.

Early Laxton A yellow fruit with flashes of pink and a faint, lavender bloom, introduced in 1916. The trees are long leaved, with graceful, drooping branches. An early variety for kitchen or table.

Old Greengage Known in France as Reine Claude and named after the wife of François I, who died in 1547, so we are talking about a variety of great antiquity. Rich, sugary fruits of a deep yellow green. Superb flavour. Perfect for the larger garden. Mine shades most of my vegetable patch.

Czar A dark purple and green plum, often rather large, named after the Russian Emperor, Tsar Alexander II. Grown since 1874, with large, primrose-flecked blossom, its yellowish flesh is probably at its best in a crumble. I see a lot of these at farmers' markets.

Blue Tit Small, sweet, bright blue plum. A good flavour and useful both in the kitchen and for eating from the tree.

Kirke's Blue A large, heavy plum with plenty of juice when truly ripe. Likes a warm spot.

Warwickshire Drooper Orange-yellow flesh, often used for jam but can be good at the table if left long enough. A plums-and-custard plum.

Kea A rare variety from a chance seedling grown only near the Fal estuary in Cornwall. Sweet, with a deliciously acid note, this highly sought-after plum has been grown since about 1635. Available locally from mid August to late September. This small, round, blue-red fruit is my favourite kitchen plum. Usefully, you can buy them frozen via the internet. But it makes a very costly crumble.

Victoria Variable, ubiquitous crimson and gold all-rounder, found in July and August.

Excalibur Burgundy-red flesh, a little russeting.

Marjorie's Seedling A vigorous grower with bloomy, purple-maroon fruit that can be found in late September and October. I get less than excited about this one, but others disagree.

Oullins Gage Often the first of the gages to ripen; needs a good, hot summer to be at its best.

The plum season

Blink and you risk missing your favourite member of the plum family. I include a list of their approximate seasons, purely as an *aide-mémoire*.

July Pershore Yellow Egg, Victoria, Opal
August Jubilee, Avalon, Excalibur, Kea (late), Victoria, Oullins Gage, Cambridge Gage, Transparent Gage
September Marjorie's Seedling (late), Warwickshire Drooper, Kea, Kirke's Blue, Reine Claude de Bavay (late)

Plums in the kitchen

There has been a plum of one hue or another in my kitchen every day of July, August and September for as long as I can remember (save 2008, when there was a national shortage due to bad weather at blossom time). Any plum is suitable for cooking but some more so than others, often because they need a little heat and sugar to tease out their character. The most widely used in the kitchen are the Laxtons, Rivers, Pershore Yellow Egg and Czar, with Marjorie's Seedling and all members of the damson family calling time in late September and early October. Victorias are fine too, but prone to collapse and with a tendency to produce a surfeit of rather pale juice. Leave the skins on to retain the fruit's characteristic sharpness. The Cornish Kea is my number-one kitchen plum but, rarely available outside its manor, it is not exactly the easiest for those of us north of the Tamar to get our hands on.

Most varieties will need sweetening, for which you can use sugar or a subtle honey such as clover (avoid the strongly flavoured chestnut). Vanilla is a wise seasoning, though probably not if you used honey as the sweetener. Together they can be overpowering. Ground ginger has an affinity with all plums, as do the warm bun-spices, particularly cinnamon. For savoury use, juniper berries, coriander seeds and fresh ginger all bring something worthwhile to the party.

I cannot join in with Enid Blyton or even Jane Grigson's disdain for stewed plums. In our house, finding a crock-pot of soft, silk-textured stewed fruit in the fridge, with juice the colour of a semi-precious jewel, is one of the delights of early-autumn mornings. When the fruits and their stones have been cooked with sugar, the juice is sweet-sharp, almost cough-syrup thick, and will glisten in the early morning light. It is difficult to think of a more uplifting start to the day. Though I probably could if pushed. Sometimes I stir in a spoonful of sheep's yoghurt. It always curdles, but no worse than custard, stewed plums' knee-jerk accompaniment. Baked, the plums' flavour is possibly even richer.

The plum family is perhaps the perfect crumble fruit, having the correct amount of juice and tartness to balance the dry, butter-sugar-flour crust. The inherent sharpness comes from the mouth-puckering hedgerow blackthorn, or sloe, that is part of the ancestry of our modern plum. The 'undercrust', my word for that damp, almost magical place where crumble meets fruit, can be particularly blissful when plums are involved. It is a question of balancing the sweet layer with the slightly sour fruit. Which is why most of us hold the plum, damson or gooseberry in higher esteem than the apple or peach as a crumble contender. A handful of rolled oats, sesame seeds or flaked almonds added to the crumble topping can be a pleasing note that shouldn't offend the purist. Walnuts have a tendency to burn.

As a pie fruit, the plum can produce too much juice for a double crust. More successful, I find, is to have only an upper crust – the downside being that you never get a neat slice the way you do with the fruit trapped between the two pieces of pastry. I make up for this by using a chunky, almost shortcake-like pastry as the top crust (you can never have too much pastry as far as I'm concerned).

Jam seems like a cop-out to a writer who tries to offer at least a modicum of fresh thinking, but is there a more wonderful jam than plum? (Blackcurrant, possibly.) It is the one jam we make that most resembles the sumptuous, soft preserves of the Middle East. I pick mine up from market stalls. Despite plums having high levels of pectin, the natural gelling agent found in ripe fruits, plum jam is often to be found gently set rather than in true bouncy British style (you might like to see my note about the British obsession with heavily set jams in *Eating for England*).

Plum pudding, incidentally, was made with raisins, the word plum meaning any old dried fruit, so we can quickly dispense with that one. It was often known as Sussex plum duff and was very comforting on a December night. But true plum recipes abound, particularly those from the Victorian era, which was probably the golden age for the kitchen plum. Look out for traditional crumble and recipes such as the lighter American 'crisp', made with breadcrumbs (there's a good one in my book *The Kitchen Diaries*); plums and custard; plum pie; and preserves such as plum and ginger jam. I also offer here a seriously crumbly tart, a single-crust pie, a sweet-hot chutney and a sharp, ginger-spiked sauce for a crisp pork roast.

This fruit will take a savoury treatment too. I am not big on fruit with meat, other than gooseberries or apples with pork and bitter oranges with duck, but game birds, especially wild duck, pigeon and partridge, have the sort of smoky, woodsy flesh that works well with a plum sauce. As does roast pork, especially the fatter breeds such as Gloucester Old Spot and Tamworth. I keep the sharper, less ripe fruit for this. There's usually plenty around. A sticky pulp of stewed Victorias, sugar and a splash of red wine vinegar will make a piece of smoked pork and shredded cabbage happy. Cinnamon is the spice you want.

I have tried using greengages and larger varieties in a stuffing, but the result was too wet, even when mixed with blotter-like breadcrumbs. It is worth making a salad with them though. Stone them, then chop and toss with soaked bulghur wheat, lemon juice and masses of chopped parsley and coriander. The result is sensational. We ate it one autumn with cold roast duck, another with grilled pigeon. As pigeons are so fond of picnicking on my Mirabelles, I find the marriage particularly apt.

Plums and...

Almonds A few ground almonds introduced into a sponge or crumble mixture or a tart filling is appropriate with any member of the plum family. A scattering of flaked almonds on an open plum tart or the surface of a crumble can be good too.

Hazelnuts Stir ground hazelnuts into the flour, butter and sugar crust of a crumble. Throw a few toasted and chopped hazelnuts over a dish of poached plums.

Game birds Most richly fleshed game birds appreciate a few poached plums on the side, seasoned with ginger and perhaps juniper. A plum chutney or relish is a sound partner for cold roast game birds.

Pork and duck The fattier the meat, the more appropriate a side relish of plums.

Ginger Ground, fresh, preserved. It all works.

Honey Often works better than sugar when you are looking for something with which to sweeten your fruits.

Spices Almost any spice, from cinnamon to cardamom and chilli to coriander seeds, works with the plum family. Use them in cakes, puddings and pickles.

A Chinese-style pork roast with plum ginger sauce

The rule is that a sharp sauce is needed with pork to cut its fattiness. More important, I think, is the fact that the sauce should flatter the gamey notes of the meat. Apples do this well enough but gooseberries do it better, having more natural sharpness than any 'cooking' apple. Plums and damsons flatter the flesh of the pork as well as the fat, and their fruity notes blend harmoniously with the pan juices.

The Chinese flavours here demand something other than potatoes as an accompaniment, so I go for some dark green cabbage, coarsely shredded the width of pappardelle and cooked in a very little water till bright emerald green. No butter, just vital, earthy greens to contrast with the richness of the meat and its sauce.

enough for 4–6
a piece of pork belly, about 1.5kg
Szechwan peppercorns – 2 tablespoons
sea salt flakes – 3 tablespoons
ground anise – 1 teaspoon

for the sauce
sharp plums or damsons – 900g
sugar – 3 tablespoons
water – 120ml
fresh ginger – a large knob about the size of a walnut, peeled
  and cut into matchsticks
star anise – 4
salt – ½ teaspoon
smooth red wine vinegar – 2 tablespoons

Put the pork in a shallow dish. Warm the Szechwan peppercorns in a non-stick pan till they start to crackle a bit, then remove from the heat. Grind together the salt, toasted peppercorns and the ground anise. Easiest with a pestle and mortar, but you can also do it with a plastic bag and a rolling pin. You want a fine, beige powder. Rub the spice mixture over the pork and its skin, cover lightly with greaseproof paper and set aside for at least 8 hours, preferably overnight in the fridge. This is for the dry marinade to work its magic.

To make the sauce, put the plums or damsons into a colander and give them a good rinse under cold running water, pulling off any stalks and leaves as you go. Tip the fruit into a stainless steel saucepan (aluminium will taint sour fruits such as plums), add the sugar, water, ginger, anise and salt and bring to the boil. Leave to simmer for about ten to fifteen minutes, until the fruit has burst and the sauce has thickened to a deep purple-red. Stir in the vinegar and simmer for five minutes more. Watch that it doesn't become too thick or catch on the bottom; it is inclined to get a bit jammy at this stage.

Put the sauce somewhere to cool or, if spitting out stones at the table really isn't your thing, sieve it first: tip it into a large sieve set over a bowl and push the fruit through with a wooden spoon. Keep going till all you have left is a few stones. Set aside; you can warm it up just before you serve the pork.

Roast the pork in an oven set at 200°C/Gas 6 for about an hour, basting occasionally. Leave to rest for ten, or even fifteen, minutes before carving, and pass the sauce around at the table.

A plum tabbouleh

Ripe fruits live happily with the nutty texture and flavour of bulghur, the cracked, steamed and crushed wheat grains used in many versions of tabbouleh. They need soaking in hot water rather than cooking, making them a quickly assembled base for a starchy salad. I have tossed bulghur with everything from redcurrants to mangoes as an accompaniment to grilled or cold meats.

enough for 4 as a side dish
bulghur wheat – 150g
slim spring onions – 6
large, juicy plums – 6
a small, hot red chilli
mint – 8 bushy sprigs
flat-leaf parsley – 8 bushy sprigs
juice of a lemon
olive oil

Put the cracked wheat into a bowl and just cover with boiling water, then set aside.

Finely slice the spring onions, discarding the toughest of their leaves, then put into a mixing bowl. Halve, stone and roughly chop the plums. Seed and finely chop the chilli, then roughly chop the mint and parsley leaves and add everything to the onions. Pour in the lemon juice, a couple of tablespoons of olive oil and a generous seasoning of salt and black pepper.

Rough the bulghur wheat up with a fork, making sure it has absorbed all the water. Crumble it into the plum and onion mixture, stir in another glug or two of olive oil – the grain should not be wet – then serve.

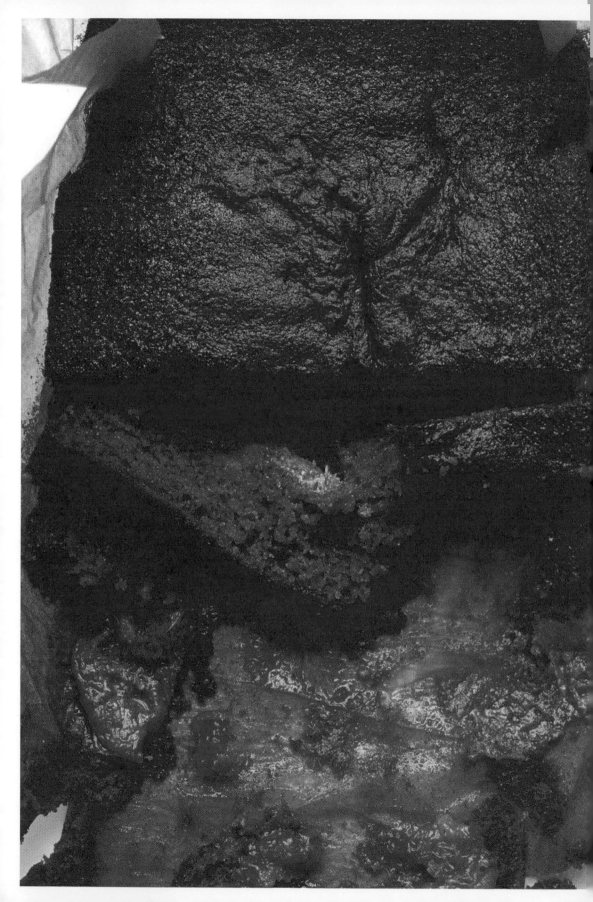

A 'pudding-cake' of honey, cinnamon and plums

The plum harvest of 2009 was legendary for its quality. I probably ate the most luscious fruits I had had since childhood. I brought them back from the market by the bagful. Avalon and Jubilee from Witney market near Oxford, Excalibur and Old Greengage from my local farmers' stalls, Black Kea from Tregothnan in Cornwall.

Plums were poached for breakfast, pickled for Christmas ham and simmered for jam. They also found their way into cakes, such as the almond-based teacake in *The Kitchen Diaries*. One Sunday afternoon, late – swathes of golden light had already hit the back garden – I started work on a plum cake that had the faintest stickiness of a gingerbread but the mellow qualities of a spice cake. Sponge-like on top, moist (almost soggy) with warm Victorias underneath, it was the sort of cake you could serve as a dessert with a jug of cream or cut into squares to tuck into the week's lunchboxes.

enough for 8
plain flour – 250g
baking powder – a lightly heaped teaspoon
bicarbonate of soda – a level teaspoon
ground cinnamon – a lightly heaped teaspoon
golden syrup – 200g
thick honey – 2 heaped tablespoons
butter – 125g
light muscovado sugar – 125g
plums – 350g
large eggs – 2
milk – 240ml

Set the oven at 180°C/Gas 4. Use baking parchment to line a cake tin or baking dish about 24cm square. Sift the flour, baking powder, bicarbonate of soda and cinnamon into a bowl.

Warm the golden syrup, honey and butter in a pan until the butter melts. Stir in the muscovado sugar. Halve the plums, or cut them into quarters if they are very large, then pull out their stones.

Break the eggs into a bowl, pour in the milk and whisk lightly to mix. Pour the golden syrup mixture into the flour and mix with a large, metal spoon. Pour in the egg and milk and continue stirring till you have a loose, almost sloppy batter without any traces of flour.

Tip the mixture into the lined cake tin, drop in the plums and bake for thirty-five minutes. Place a piece of foil loosely over the top of the cake and leave to cook for ten to fifteen minutes longer. Switch off the oven, but leave the cake in for a further fifteen minutes, then remove and leave to cool.

Plum crumble tart

Is this a tart or a cake? I'm not sure it really matters what you call something as moist and tender as this.

> *enough for 6–8*
> plain flour – 260g
> soft brown sugar – 125g
> ground almonds – 100g
> fridge-cold butter – 220g
> plums, greengages or damsons – 600g
> pine kernels – 50g

Set the oven at 180°C/Gas 4. Line the base of a 22–24cm square baking tin with a single piece of baking parchment, bringing it up two opposite sides of the tin so you can use it to lift the tart out easily.

Put the flour, sugar and almonds into a mixing bowl, cut the butter into small chunks and rub it into the flour mixture with your fingertips. Stop when what you have resembles coarse fresh breadcrumbs. Tip two-thirds of the crumb mixture into the baking tin and gently flatten it to form a thin base, pushing it well into the corners. Firm it gently, but don't compact it.

Cut the plums in half, unless they are huge, in which case quarter them. Remove the stones and lay the pieces of fruit on the crumb base. Mix the pine kernels into the remaining crumbs and scatter them loosely over the plums. Let some of the fruit show through.

Bake for forty-five to fifty minutes, when the fruit should be gently bubbling, the crust golden. Leave to settle before lifting out of the baking tin and on to a cooling rack.

Poached plums, spices and ginger

The British have long had a love of ginger: gingerbread, gingernuts, ginger beer and ginger wine are all part of our culinary history. I sometimes include its sweet, sticky heat in the syrup for poaching fruit such as pears (wonderful) and large plums, especially on a cold day. The syrup from a jar of preserved ginger is worth using too, and the glistening orbs themselves can make comfortable bedfellows for any of the plum family.

enough for 4
plums – 12 large ones, or more if small
caster sugar – 90g
water – 250ml
star anise – 2 whole flowers
cloves – 6
lumps of preserved ginger in syrup – 3, chopped
syrup from the ginger jar – 4 tablespoons

Wipe the plums and remove their stalks. Stir the sugar and water together in a heavy-based saucepan. Bring to the boil, then add the star anise, cloves, chopped ginger and the ginger syrup. Lower in the plums and turn down to a gentle simmer, then partially cover with a lid. Let the fruit poach in the scented syrup for twenty minutes or so, until it is truly soft and melting.

Serve warm, three fruits per person, in little dishes or glasses, with some of the glowing syrup spooned over.

Note: Poached fruits such as these can also be served with roast pork. Add a little of the sweet cooking liquor to the pan juices of the roast, then serve the fruit on the side. Plums work well with pork and duck and with baked ham.

A hot, sweet plum chutney

Just as curry, stew or trifle left for a day or two in the fridge will often taste more interesting (rounded, deeper) than when freshly made, the character of a chutney can change over time. My first taste of a homemade plum preserve appeared to have a jam-like sweetness. Two weeks later, the same chutney had taken on a mellowness, the underlying heat from the chillies coming forward, the initial hit of sugar taking a step back.

It is into this recipe I dip for something to go with a few slices of cold roast pork, beef or the remains of a roasted game bird. Its autumnal sweetness flatters a lump of cheese too – an orange-fleshed Cheshire or a Wensleydale.

Plums

1052

makes a couple of jam jars' worth
plums – 750g
onions – 350g
raisins – 125g
light muscovado sugar – 250g
crushed dried chilli – ½ teaspoon
salt – a teaspoon
yellow mustard seeds – 2 teaspoons
cider vinegar – 150ml
malt vinegar – 150ml
a cinnamon stick

Halve the plums and discard the stones. Peel and roughly chop the onions. Put the fruit and onions into a large stainless steel or enamelled pan with the raisins, sugar, chilli, salt, mustard seeds, vinegars and cinnamon stick. Bring to the boil, turn down the heat and leave to simmer for an hour, giving the occasional stir to reduce the risk of the chutney sticking.

Spoon into sterilised jars and seal.

Cinnamon and anise plums

Wipe the fruit, remove its stalks and bring to the boil with 4 tablespoons of water and 2 tablespoons of sugar per 500g fruit. Tuck a cinnamon stick and 2 stars of anise amongst the plums and turn the heat down to a gentle simmer. Leave the fruit to bubble slowly to tenderness – a matter of ten to twenty minutes, depending on its ripeness. Eat warm or cool, for breakfast.

Plums for breakfast

A pot with a sturdy bottom, 500g plums, or damsons, maybe greengages, 100g golden caster sugar, a vanilla pod split down its length, its seeds exposed, and just enough water to leave a wet film on the bottom of the pan. Place over a gentle heat, let the sugar melt, the plums burst, their juices mingle with the sugar. Keep the heat low, your eyes on the job. After ten minutes, maybe fifteen, the plums will have collapsed, their juices taken up some of the warm vanilla notes, and you will have a dish of plums to cool, then thoroughly chill, and eat for breakfast.

A single-crust pie for particularly juicy plums

Asked to define the 'bliss point' in a culinary sense, I would venture to suggest the underside of a pastry crust where it meets the fruit. Still crisp and sugary on top, it is moist, almost sodden underneath with sweet-sharp, scarlet juice. But some fruits can produce so much juice that the bottom crust collapses. Plums are particular culprits. The answer, a single crust on top of the pie. Fine in dispensing with a soggy bottom, but as a pastry lover I feel robbed. My version uses a top crust of shortcake thickness. Intensely crumbly, this solves the riddle of how to get enough crust when using a particularly juice-producing fruit. The pastry crust here is thick but very tender, and will crumble as you serve it.

Occasionally cream is called for with a pie, and this is just one of those occasions.

enough for 4

for the pastry
butter – 100g
golden caster sugar – 100g
an egg, lightly beaten
plain flour – 175g
baking powder – ½ teaspoon
a little milk for brushing

for the filling
ripe plums or greengages – 800g–1kg
caster sugar – 2–3 tablespoons
ground cinnamon – a knifepoint

Cream the butter and sugar in a food mixer till light and fluffy. Mix in the lightly beaten egg, then gently add the flour and baking powder. Remove from the bowl and roll into a ball on a heavily floured work surface. Knead the dough for a minute or two until smooth and soft. Wrap in greaseproof or waxed paper and refrigerate for about twenty minutes.

Set the oven at 180°C/Gas 4. Cut the plums in half and remove their stones. Cut the fruit into large pieces, toss with the sugar and cinnamon and put into a lightly buttered 20–22cm baking dish. Roll out the pastry on a floured board, then lift carefully on to the pie. There will be a little left over. The crust is very short and it really doesn't matter if it tears as you lower it over the fruit. Some of the juice will probably erupt through it as it cooks anyway. At least I hope so.

Brush lightly with milk and bake for forty minutes. The pastry should be pale-biscuit coloured. Dust with caster sugar and serve warm.

A plum feast

2nd July, 2007, a wet summer's evening and we had finished our steaks, the smokers amongst us had lit up, and the rain poured torrentially against the glass roof. Suddenly, my hosts put a vast branch on the table, its end apparently ripped from the tree, still in leaf and covered with wild red plums.

A memorable way to end a meal, but somehow brutal too; it was the tree's last stand. The branch had been rescued from an elderly plum tree in a century-old East End allotment near the River Lea in Hackney. A much-loved site that was to be bulldozed for an Olympic walkway and its tenants evicted. Grown almost certainly from a wild seedling, its small, bright-red Myrobalan fruit had been as much a part of the allotment as the beds, sheds and broad beans. We pulled at the tiny crimson fruits, breaking off laden twigs and passing them round the table, sucking at the sweet-tart fruits while my hosts told the story of the community of allotment holders, their fig trees and fertile land and their futile fight to stop the march of the bulldozers.

I now kick myself for not planting one of the many stones that lay sucked on my plate. But their house is not far from mine, and I often wonder about the ancestry of the wild cherry plum that has appeared in my vegetable patch.

Quince

There is a quince on the kitchen table. Plump, golden, curvaceous. A fat cherub of a fruit, with waxy skin and, here and there, patches of soft, pubescent down. Leaf attached, it has an extraordinary scent that you catch in occasional wafts like blossom on a breeze, part floral, yet a little sickly too.

I sometimes buy a paper bag of quinces simply for their presence in the house. Their arrival marks the start of winter as surely as a tomcat marks his territory. They live in a shallow Chinese dish in the hall, welcoming me home. I cook them eventually, just as the odd blemish appears on their deep, imperial-yellow skin. A fruit that, once cooked, has an incomparable subtlety, whispering in low notes of honey and rose.

The spreading, deciduous tree has the most elegant blossom in late April, each loose bud opening to reveal a milk-white flower of moth-like fragility, its edges brushed a pale and watery pink. A flower so gentle it could be shattered by a shower of rain or blown apart by a sharp gust of wind. It is hard to believe that a bloom so soft will eventually produce a fruit impenetrable to all but the sharpest of cook's knives.

Native to Iran and Armenia, the quince – *Cydonia oblonga* – was introduced to Europe via Serbia, Albania, Greece and Turkey, the latter of which now produces almost a quarter of the world's output. The quince is the most ancient of fruits, pre-dating the apple and the pear, and is considered in many cultures to be a symbol of love, fertility and happiness. Sacred to Aphrodite, the fruit was offered by the Greeks at their weddings, where, it is said, the bride would nibble a quince to sweeten her breath before 'entering the bridal chamber'. It is the fruit of Edward Lear's poem, 'The Owl and the Pussycat', where they 'dined on mince and slices of quince, which they ate with a runcible spoon'. Runcible being one of the poet's favourite nonsense words.

There is a certain abandon in a bowl of large quinces, like the women in a Beryl Cook painting. But for all its gorgeous looks, most varieties of quince are virtually inedible raw. Like damsons, rhubarb and the gooseberry, this is one for the kitchen rather than the fruit bowl. A cook's fruit, if you like. It can be baked or simmered in syrup or used to fill a shallow puff pastry tart. After a long, slow cooking with sugar, the flesh of the quince often turns a majestic crimson. I sometimes pot-roast them with sugar and a little water, leaving them to putter away till they are glowing red and almost transparent.

The quince is most often seen in the form of a jam or paste such as the Spanish membrillo. The fruits are peeled and cored, chopped, then boiled with the pectin-rich trimmings tied up in muslin until you have a thick purée, sometimes referred to as a fruit cheese. Sugar is then added and the mixture cooked once again till thick and smooth. On cooling, the paste sets to the point where it can be sliced.

Quince paste is most often served with sharp cheeses such as Manchego, the sheep's milk cheese from La Mancha in Spain. It works well with many of our artisan-made cheeses. I eat it with both Caerphilly and Wensleydale. On winter afternoons I sometimes put a slice of quince paste and a smidgen of crème fraîche on a water biscuit and eat it as the light outside fades to grey.

Despite its Rubenesque quality and heavenly fragrance, the quince will never be the most popular of fruits, as is the case with any fruit you cannot simply bite into. But for this cook it will always hold a certain mystery and intrigue and, with its ample curves and sensual fragrance, a sense of both the exotic and the erotic.

A quince in the garden

It is one of those mellow afternoons in autumn, the garden a scene of peaceful rot. Mauve stars of Michaelmas daisies twinkle through the tangle of brown stems and dew-covered cobwebs that stick to your face as you walk through them. Nature is taking the garden back from me once again. At the far end, past the compost and the yew hedge, is a handful of awkward, misshapen fruit trees: a damson, a young mulberry and a quince that has fruited every year since it was planted.

Amidst the dark green leaves, a single fruit – a downy, golden orb – hangs from a black branch too weak and pliable for any thieving squirrel to climb. The only sign of life in a garden slowly falling asleep, like a pensioner in a much loved but threadbare chair. It is late and time for tea, but tomorrow I will pull the branch down and take a closer look.

Even before this garden was dug, I knew the first trees to plant: damson, medlar, mulberry and quince. Quince is frost hardy and requires a cold period below 7°C to flower properly. It is suited to the small domestic garden, rarely growing larger than 5 metres, although it can become wide unless pruned. Small and deciduous, it is often used as rootstock on which to graft apple trees.

The trees like moisture, particularly during the summer. Like clematis, they prefer their roots to be cool (the most prolific I have ever seen were growing beside a waterfall in a Croatian nature reserve). They need a long growing season and fare best in a warm, secluded spot. It is worth watering them well if the weather has been dry for any length of time.

The immature fruit are charming, covered by a thick, grey down that wears away as they grow and ripen. By late summer they will be the size of a small pear and on the turn from green to canary yellow. The hue darkens as they ripen. Though ripening quinces can be left on the tree, they tend to become heavy as the season develops and have a habit of dropping off. I pick them as their skins turn from green to yellow and bring them on indoors. Unripe and full of pectin, they make a heavier-set preserve.

The fruits will keep for months, but need air around them. Slatted shelves are good, especially if the fruits aren't touching. With luck and a modicum of care, they will stay in fine condition till after Christmas.

Varieties

It is unlikely you will be offered anything but the most popular varieties, though there are many grown elsewhere in Europe, including such romantically named ones as Le Bourgeaut, Lescovacz, Orange, Perfume, Pineapple and Van Deman.

Champion Rather round, perfectly formed fruits, which grow quite prolifically.
Meech's Prolific Pear-shaped fruits of good flavour.
Portugal Works in a warm spot, but keep away from frost. Good flavour, some suggest the best.
Vranja Large, popular, pear-shaped and heavily perfumed variety that I have much success with.

A quince in the kitchen

The quince is the fruit of frosty mornings and blackened leaves, keeping in sound condition through the cold months. I sometimes bake a few in a low oven with a glass of marsala or quince liqueur and a thick trickle of maple syrup or honey. They emerge, a good couple of hours after you put them in, a transluscent, glowing amber. They rarely fluff up like an apple, but take on the texture of melting fudge.

We cannot hurry a cooking quince. They are ready when they feel like it. I have known the most stubborn to take forty minutes or more to poach to tenderness in sugar syrup. The really large ones, the weight of a small pineapple, can take even more of our precious gas. But the scent of them cooking fills the house with a rich, mellow sweetness, especially if I have used a glass or two of wine in the poaching liquid.

The Romans were fond of this fruit, and the cookbook of Apicius gives recipes for them stewed with honey and even combined with leeks. (Rather you than me.)

Quinces love to end their days with a glass or two of something alcoholic and sugary, such as Muscat de Beaumes de Venise or a cheap Tokay. Even so, a little extra sugar is needed, too, and some water, and more than a little patience. Once cooked, they will keep in the syrup for a few days. Eat them in all their purity, or lower one into a dish of baked rice pudding, or eat with thick yoghurt for a hedonistic breakfast.

You cannot eat the skin, so it should be pared before poaching, but you can happily bake them whole or halved in their skins. Once the peel is removed the flesh browns almost instantly – certainly faster than a pear or apple. I brush them with lemon juice and drop them into acidulated water. A little lemon juice on the peeler blade can help too.

The old notion of tucking a few cubes of the fruit into an apple pie works. The small amount of quince flesh is enough to send its mild, floral notes throughout the whole pie. I have used this trick with a crumble, too. Quinces are rarely used in open tarts, which is a shame, but a jelly of them is often used to glaze French-style pastries. The colour is flattering to all manner of fruits and the flavour mild and complementary.

The quince contains a very generous amount of pectin. It is almost impossible to make a quince jelly that doesn't set. The pectin levels are higher in unripe fruit and diminish as it turns yellow. Quince jelly sometimes sets heavily enough to slice. In Malta, a jam – *gamm ta l-isfargal* – is produced, rather like the Lebanese *sfarjel*, Portugal's *marmelada* and Pakistan's glowing, orange-red *muraba*. Thick and fragrant, this conserve is wonderful as a breakfast jam but also, served in elegant spoonfuls, with a soft cheese or crème fraîche. The word marmalade, incidentally, was originally used to describe quince jam rather than the conserve of bitter oranges we know now.

Drinks are made from *Cydonia oblonga*, too: a brandy in the Balkans, a digestive known as *liqueur de coing* in Alsace and in Britain a glowing liqueur by Bramley and Gage, whose fig and date notes make it a smooth and moreish after-dinner drink.

Quinces and...

Honey More than just a sweetener, honey offers a subtle warmth to baked or poached quinces without intruding on their flavour.

Apples A large quince gives an extraordinary perfume to an apple pie. The two fruits manage to co-exist without one cancelling the other out.

Lemon A sharp seasoning that works to enhance the quince's flavour.

Verjuice Somewhat elusive, this mellow juice of unfermented grapes makes a pleasing cooking liquor for the fruit. Whenever I see it, I buy several bottles, as it keeps almost indefinitely.

Lamb A useful stuffing ingredient for the fruit, especially when seasoned with sultanas, cumin, onion and pine kernels.

Vinegar The marriage of sour liquid and fragrant fruit works very well. Hence the inclusion of the pickle recipe on page 1080.

Cinnamon A stick dunked into the sugar syrup for a compote will lend a warmth to the finished dish. Works especially well with honey.

* Quinces are especially high in pectin. It is just unfortunate that they are rarely around in summer, when they would be exceptionally useful for setting strawberry and other low-pectin jams.

* The fruit's lasting properties were particularly useful before the advent of refrigeration, when it was one of the few that would keep the family in pies all winter.

* The strong aroma of a ripe quince will permeate all the other food in the fridge, especially the milk, so best store it in another cool place.

Lamb with quinces

Rather than painstakingly designed, much of my daily cooking is made up on the spot. It was very much the case with this lamb stew. I had planned a slow-cooked casserole of lamb shoulder, adding sweet spices and honey as it cooked to serve with a simple rice pilau (white rice, steamed with a couple of cloves, a few peppercorns and a bay leaf). The addition of quinces was very much a last-minute decision, as was the final flourish of bright-tasting herbs. Later, whilst writing this book, I discovered that my idea was far from original and the combination is well known in parts of the Middle East. This is a rich, slightly sweet dish, fragrant and gently spiced.

enough for 4
olive oil
butter – a thick slice
lamb shoulder – 800g, cut into large cubes
onions – 2
a cinnamon stick
fresh ginger – a thumb-sized lump, peeled and finely shredded
saffron stamens – a good pinch
honey – 2 tablespoons
quinces – 800g
the juice of a lemon
coriander – a small bunch
mint – 4 bushy sprigs

Warm a little olive oil in a deep, heavy-based pan. Add the butter and as soon as it melts add the lamb, seasoned with a little salt and black pepper. Let it colour nicely on all sides, but avoid moving the pieces around the pan too much. While the lamb colours, peel and thickly slice the onions. Lift the meat out with a draining spoon and set aside.

Put the onions in the pan and leave over a moderate heat to soften and colour lightly. Stir from time to time. As the onions cook, they will pick up some of the caramelised pan stickings left by the lamb. Add the cinnamon stick, ginger, saffron stamens and a generous seasoning of salt. Return the lamb to the pan and trickle in the honey.

Pour enough water over the lamb to just cover the surface – about 750ml – then bring to the boil. Lower the heat so the lamb simmers gently. Partially cover with a lid and leave to cook for an hour and ten minutes, checking the liquid level and giving the occasional stir until the meat is tender.

While the lamb is cooking, peel the quinces and remove the cores. Tie the peelings in a muslin bag and put it in the stew as it cooks; this will add flavour to the sauce. Cut the quince flesh into cubes or thick slices and keep in a bowl of water to which you have added the lemon juice until needed.

When the lamb is tender, add the pieces of quince and continue to simmer for twenty minutes, till the fruit is almost soft. Chop the coriander and mint leaves and mix together. Stir into the lamb stew, check the seasoning and serve with a simple rice pilaff.

Slow-roast loin of pork with quinces and marsala

Roasting the pork on the bone will give you more succulent meat. The downside is that meat on the bone is harder to carve. I get round this by asking my butcher to 'chine' the meat for me, a neat little technique that results in leaving the bone intact but cutting it almost through, making it a doddle to carve. Best ask your butcher the day before (ask him for a few bones for stock, too). I find a piece of scored, bone-in loin with eight to ten bones will serve six, plus enough for seconds the next day.

It is worth getting the bottle of dry or semi-dry 'cooking marsala' as soon as you can. The more easily found sweet version isn't really suitable.

enough for 6 with leftovers
an 8–10-bone pork loin (about 3kg), on the bone
olive oil
garlic – 8 cloves
quinces – 6
dry marsala – 125ml
chicken stock – 250ml

Set the oven at 200°C/Gas 6. Unwrap the pork and make sure that the fat is dry to the touch. Wet fat won't crisp. Rub the meat generously all over with olive oil, then season it with salt. Lay the meat in a roasting tin so that the fat is facing upwards. Roast for 30 minutes, then reduce the heat to 180°C/Gas 4 and continue to cook for thirty minutes per 450g.

Put a small pan of water on to boil. Add the garlic cloves and cook for fifteen minutes. Drain and pop the cloves from their skins.

An hour before the meat is due out of the oven, wipe the quinces, then tuck them in around the roast, together with the garlic cloves. Wet them with a little oil and continue roasting.

Test the roast for doneness. The fat should be golden and crisp. Pierce the skin with a metal skewer and check that the juices contain no sign of blood. Lift the meat out on to a warm serving dish. Cover with foil and leave in a warm place to rest. Lift out the quinces and put them in a warm dish. If they are not quite tender and fluffy, then return them to the oven.

Tip the layer of oil from the roasting tin into a heatproof jug; you can use it for roasting potatoes another day. Place the roasting tin over a low heat and pour in the marsala and the chicken stock. Bring to the boil, scraping at the sticky sediment in the pan as you go, stirring it into the gravy. Crush the garlic cloves with the back of a wooden spoon, then leave the gravy to bubble slowly for three or four minutes. It should be thin, glossy and deeply flavoured. Taste for seasoning, adding salt and pepper as you think fit.

To serve, slice the meat thinly, pulling the bones away as you go – though no one should mind if they get one. As your knife reaches the backbone, the meat should come away quite easily. Place a quince on each plate, then drizzle over the marsala gravy.

Buttered quinces – a bowl of glowing, tender fruit

Quinces tend to give up less juice than an apple or pear. I find they also benefit from a little sugar. Their flavour, which can be ethereal and rose-like, is best appreciated when they are lightly cooked with butter and golden caster sugar. This can be in the oven or, if you want to experience them with a little more juice, in a pan on the hob. In the final moments before they are tender, the quinces will be incandescently beautiful, the thick syrup that has formed in the pan the colour of a winter sunset.

> *enough for 4*
> quinces – 1.5kg
> the juice of 2 lemons
> butter – 50g
> golden caster sugar – 90g

Peel and quarter the quinces, then core them and cut into thick slices, dropping them into a bowl of cold water into which you have squeezed half a lemon.

Melt the butter and sugar in a shallow pan, then add the quinces and the remaining lemon juice. Leave the fruit to soften, stirring occasionally, until they are pale gold, translucent and tender enough to require only the merest squeeze to crush them (if they are not thoroughly tender, they won't be worth eating).

Lift the slices carefully into a bowl with a large spoon, leaving the juices behind. Turn up the heat and bring the liquid to the boil, letting it thicken slightly, then pour it over the warm fruit.

Roast quinces

You can cut a quince in half and bake it like an apple but I prefer to poach
them first so that their flesh becomes melting and almost transparent. Maple
syrup offers a deep, almost caramel-like autumnal warmth, but you could
use honey if you prefer. Cream would be no bad thing here.

This is a dessert to me, but I wouldn't mind trying it with some slices
of grilled gammon; a contemporary take on the 1960s gammon and
pineapple idea.

enough for 4
sugar – 4 heaped tablespoons
water – 500ml
cloves – 4
star anise – 2
smallish quinces – 4
half a lemon
maple syrup – 4 tablespoons

Put the sugar and water into a saucepan and bring to the boil. Add the cloves
and star anise. Peel and halve the quinces, scoop out the cores and rub them
with the lemon to stop them browning. Lower the quinces into the sugar
syrup and let them simmer till tender. They may be ready in twenty-five
minutes or perhaps take a little longer, depending on their size and ripeness.

Set the oven at 180°C/Gas 4. When the quinces are tender to the point
of a knife, lift them out and put them in a shallow baking dish or roasting
tin. Measure out 150ml of the cooking liquid, add the maple syrup and,
together with the aromatics, pour them over the quinces. Bake for thirty
minutes or so, till very soft and tender. Serve with the cooking juices.

Soft quinces under a crisp crust

My guess is that this recipe would also work well with pears, which could be useful when quinces elude you. As well as at farmers' markets and the occasional greengrocer's shop, quinces tend to turn up in Turkish and Cypriot stores in autumn. Farm shops are a good hunting ground too. I always buy more than I need, simply because they are rarely around when you want them and they have a good shelf life (I have kept them for weeks in the larder).

enough for 4
lemons – 2
quinces – 1.75kg
butter – 40g
caster sugar – 100g

for the crumble topping
plain flour – 75g
cold butter – 70g, diced
large, soft, fresh breadcrumbs – 40g
light muscovado sugar – 40g
ground almonds – 40g
water – 2 tablespoons

Preheat the oven to 190°C/Gas 5. Fill a bowl with cold water and the juice of one of the lemons. This will help to keep the quinces from browning. Peel, core and thickly slice the quinces, dropping each piece into the bowl of water. They brown quickly, so I try to get them in the water as soon as possible. Heat the butter in a large frying pan over a moderate heat, add the sugar and the juice of the remaining lemon and toss the fruit in gently. Cook for twenty-five to thirty minutes, keeping the heat fairly high, until the fruit is tender, deep gold and juicy. Tip into a shallow baking dish.

To make the crust, put the flour into a bowl, then add the cold diced butter. Rub the butter into the flour with your fingertips (or, of course, use a food processor, if you prefer) until the mixture resembles coarse breadcrumbs. Stir in the fresh breadcrumbs, sugar and ground almonds. Drizzle over the water, then stir it lightly into the crumble with your fingertips. It should make tiny 'pebbles' amongst the crumbs. Tip the mixture over the quinces and bake for twenty-five to thirty minutes, until the top is golden and the fruit is bubbling.

Apples and quinces baked in cream

A soothing, warm dessert for a cool autumn evening.

enough for 4
a large quince
medium-sized sweet apples – 4
a little butter
golden caster sugar – 3 tablespoons
a little plain flour
grated nutmeg
double cream – 400ml

Wipe the quince and rub the fluff from its skin, then put the whole, unpeeled fruit into a small, deep saucepan and cover it with water. Bring the water to the boil, then turn down the heat, so that it simmers gently. Lift the fruit with a draining spoon after twenty minutes or so and squeeze it gently. If you can feel the quince flesh give a little, then lift it out and leave to cool. If the fruit is still firm, let it simmer a little longer. It needs to be really quite soft.

Peel and core the apples, slicing them thickly. Peel the quince too, remove its core and cut into slices a little thinner than the apples. Butter a medium-sized baking dish – it should hold the fruit comfortably in a single layer – then scatter over the sugar. Toss the fruit in a little flour, just a dusting really, and grate over some nutmeg. Pile the floured fruit into the sugared and buttered dish, then pour over the cream. You will find some of the fruit stands proud of the cream, no matter. Bake at 160°C/Gas 3 for forty-five to fifty minutes, until the cream is thick and scented and the fruit is thoroughly tender. Serve warm rather than hot.

Slow-cooked quinces with cassis

The combination sounds a little unlikely, yet it works rather well.
The colour, too, is glorious.

enough for 6
golden caster sugar – 175g
water – a litre
large quinces – 3
a vanilla pod
crème de cassis or blackcurrant liqueur – 250ml

Put the sugar and water in a deep pan and bring to the boil. Meanwhile, peel the quinces, cut them in half and scoop out the cores. I use a large, heavy kitchen knife to halve the fruit, which is sometimes so hard as to be almost impenetrable. The peeled fruits brown quickly too, so I like a halved lemon on hand to rub over the surface as I proceed.

Slide the halved fruits into the sugar syrup and add the vanilla pod and cassis. Bring back to the boil, turn down the heat to a gentle simmer and leave to cook for a good forty to sixty minutes, till the fruit is totally soft and full of juice, like a canned pear. I test mine with a metal skewer, and don't switch off the heat until the skewer will slide effortlessly through the fruit.

Take to one side and leave to cool a little. I tend to serve this dish warm or at warm room temperature, when all the heady blackcurrant scent is at its strongest.

Quince paste

Quince paste is best known for its affinity with sheep's cheeses, but I have also used it as a glaze for the Christmas ham instead of marmalade and stirred it into the pan juices of a roast loin of pork. In most cases I would buy it ready made but, having twice been presented with a box of quinces, I have sometimes ended up making my own. It is a labour of love, stirring the fruit purée and sugar till thick, and can sometimes feel a little extravagant (it needs to be left in a very low oven for several hours or even overnight) and yet there is great satisfaction in making your own. Its production also neatly deals with a glut of quinces in one swoop.

> large quinces, unripe if possible – 8
> the juice of a lemon
> caster sugar

Peel, core and quarter the quinces. Put them in a pan with the lemon juice and just enough water to barely cover them. Bring to the boil, then turn down the heat and leave to simmer, partially covered with a lid, for about twenty minutes, till the fruit is soft.

Blitz the fruit in a food processor, then push through a sieve (lots of washing up, but a finer result). Weigh the purée (more mess) and put it into a heavy-bottomed pan with half its weight in sugar. Cook the mixture over a low heat, stirring almost constantly, until it is dry and thick. The mixture is likely to splutter up like polenta. Take care. Cook until the paste is almost firm and is heavy to stir around the pan.

Scrape out on to a shallow tray with a rubber spatula. Set the oven at its lowest temperature, and leave the paste in for at least three hours, until set. Pack into jars and cover with a lid.

A fragrant winter breakfast

A bowl of pale ivory-pink stewed fruit for those winter mornings when the sky is white and a sugar-frost has caught on the spider's webs in the garden.

enough for 6
quinces – 2
apples – 800g
lemon juice – 2 tablespoons
sugar – 150g

Peel the quinces, remove their cores and roughly chop the flesh. Put the peel and cores into a small pan, pour over just enough water to cover, then simmer for fifteen minutes. Set aside.

Meanwhile, cook the quinces in a very little water over a low heat for about twenty minutes, till soft and pink. Peel and core the apples, roughly chop them and add them to the tender quince with the lemon juice, sugar and the liquid from the simmered cores and peel. Continue to cook until the apple is tender. Mash to a purée with a fork or potato masher, then beat with a wooden spoon and serve.

A quince pickle

A razor-sharp, lip-smarting pickle is a permanent fixture of any meal I throw together involving the remains of Sunday's roast. Quinces, shining amber and gold in their pickling liquor, are unusual, offering a pleasing change from the icy crunch of the more usual pickled onion.

enough for 2 medium-sized storage jars
cider vinegar – 750ml
golden granulated sugar – 400g
juniper berries – 12
black peppercorns – 8
a bay leaf
quinces – 3 medium or 4 smaller ones

Pour the vinegar into a stainless steel pan. Add the sugar, juniper, black peppercorns and bay leaf and bring to the boil. Turn the heat down to a merry simmer.

Peel, halve and core the quinces, cutting them into six lengthways. Lower the fruit into the simmering vinegar and leave to cook for fifteen to twenty-five minutes, till the fruit is soft enough to pierce effortlessly with a skewer. Lift the quince out with a draining spoon and lower into clean storage jars. Pour over the liquor, then seal and leave to cool. They will keep for several weeks.

Raspberries

 I can clearly remember the moment I fell totally,
hopelessly in love with the scarlet berries. It is
seven or maybe eight o'clock one morning in
October, the garden is sombre with mist and
the heavy air is damp and fungal. The raspberry
canes have fallen across the path through want
of a stick. I lift them to pass. Hanging down from
the canes are crisp brown leaves and bunches of
berries, some rotting, others about to collapse,
their beads heavy with arterial red juice. I pick
them and they are so soft they break in my
fingers, sending beads of red juice down my
hand. I eat what I can and lick the rest from my skin. The single leaf by
which I am holding the branch tears and the cane crashes back, its sharp
thorns scratching my arm, leaving a long gash with little blood dots here
and there along its length. I run my tongue along the scratch, then I go
back indoors.

The raspberry family suffers from fragility and purple-red juice that
stains everything in its path. They are not one berry but a collection of
smaller berries – drupelets – fused together. This is why they freeze more
successfully than the strawberry. Overripe to the point of leaching their
juices, they are the most stimulating of fruit to the senses, more so than
a ripe Cantaloupe melon, though less than a dripping honey mango.
Their smell has a wine-like quality, their flavour can be warm and almost
alcoholic, and to look at they are the most alluring of fruits, especially
when they come in a little balsawood punnet lined with their own dark
green leaves. We eat them in our breakfast muesli, as a layer in a moist
sponge cake, but most of all with deep yellow cream and maybe a crisp
meringue whose broken crust glistens with sugar.

It is hard to justify doing anything more complicated to a raspberry
than serving it as it is, warm from the sun and unadorned or adulterated.
Most times that is how I want my berries. If guests are here I will sometimes
pile the berries on to a plate lined with raspberry leaves and pass it round the

table. They can agonise over the jug of cream for themselves. That said, I do love them in a fool, a trifle or an ice cream, particularly when their juices bleed a little.

Raspberries in the garden

I planted my first raspberry patch almost a decade ago. The fruit likes the cool and the damp, which is why it does so well in Scotland and in particular the Vale of Gowrie. I planted it on the shaded side of the garden at the suggestion of Monty Don, the side whose soil rarely dries out, even in high summer. The canes had arrived as a bundle of short sticks, their roots still damp but looking distinctly dead. I planted them in rich soil on a freezing cold January day, the soil claggy as chocolate cake, convinced they would never survive.

Tradition has it that they are happiest on a slightly acidic soil, but they are generally not as fussy as many other fruits. The trick is not to plant them too deeply – 6cm down is enough – and to spread the roots out flat rather than pointing down. I covered mine with topsoil and then a spade or two of manure. The shallowness of the root system, which hates to sit in sodden ground, means you must weed by hand rather than by hoe. The ideal spot is somewhere sheltered but sunny, with moist soil that doesn't become waterlogged in winter. Incredibly, I have such a spot at the rear of the vegetable patch.

The canes need a little care as the year progresses. It is generally accepted that you should cut down new growth to 15cm in height in early spring, once the leaves start to unfurl. As they grow, tie them to wires in early summer, as soon as they are long enough. After summer fruiting, cut out any brown canes, tying in any new green shoots as you go. Autumn fruiting varieties should be cut right down to the ground in mid winter.

For six years, my canes provided almost as many berries as I could eat, and I loved them for that, and the fact that the almost vinous scent of the overripe fruits added a certain sensuality to the garden in autumn, but they had to go. I wanted the bed for other things – beans, tomatoes, parsley, lettuce – so I ripped them out. Save one, that kept coming through the soil each spring. I left it to wind its way up the frame with the beans, its occasional fruits a stinging reminder not to always want more.

Two years ago I realised my mistake in having a fruit patch without the heady pleasure of a row of raspberry canes. This time I planted two varieties, the beloved Autumn Bliss, whose presence in the garden I missed so much, and Fall Gold, the autumn-fruiting yellow variety whose berries are sweet but fragile, with a slight tendency to crumble as you pick them. Never again will my garden be without them.

Varieties

The golden raspberry

Amongst the most rare and exquisite of fruits, the yellow raspberry has possibly the richest, brightest flavour of all. Autumn-fruiting **Fall Gold**, sometimes known as All Gold, is one to grow – a chance seedling found amongst a planting of Autumn Bliss.

Red raspberries

There are two distinct types, known by the season in which they ripen. The first 'summer-fruiting' raspberries appear in mid to late May, the later 'autumn-fruiting' varieties can be picked right up to the first frosts.

Summer fruiting

Malling Jewel Ripens in mid summer and is loved for its old-fashioned raspberry flavour.
Glen Prosen Probably at its best if you leave it till it is almost overripe.
Glen Ample Not the easiest to grow, but a very fine fruit if you are successful.
Tullameen A summer variety that does well on lighter soils. If you leave it on the cane longer than the commercial growers are inclined to, you will be rewarded with a more aromatic flavour.

Autumn fruiting

Autumn Bliss I was very happy with its late-August cropping that lasted till the first frosts, and with its deep flavour.
Lloyd George A classic from a chance seedling found in a wood in Kent.
Autumn Treasure Delights in deep flavour, strong canes and a good resistance to root rot. Generally, the deeper-coloured berries tend to have the richest flavour.
Galante Exceptionally large fruits and prolific cropping. I have yet to taste this one, but reports are good.

Raspberries in the kitchen

There is little to be gained by cooking a raspberry. Gentle warmth will bring its flavours to the fore, teasing out the berry's sweetness, but a thorough cooking will lose all the fruit's subtlety and destroy its texture. Jam aside, and perhaps the odd handful tucked inside a roasting game bird, I prefer to keep this one well away from the stove.

A few of the berries tumbled into a glass of sweet wine is dessert enough for me. Include them in a salad of melon or blueberries, or crush them with sugar syrup to form a glowing sorbet. All will produce something of great beauty that is worth the trouble we have taken. But the raspberry is often at its happiest when in the presence of cream.

Cream, sweet, yellow and thick, has an extraordinary effect on these fruits, heightening rather than subduing their flavour. The lexicon of classic raspberry recipes, from fools to ice creams and syllabubs, gives a pretty clear idea of the esteem in which we have historically held this culinary marriage.

The sharper the fruit, the better it is in the presence of dairy produce. This is why gooseberries, damsons and rhubarb make a better fool than strawberry or peach. The raspberry has a nip of acidity that, in my book, sends it soaring over even the best strawberry. And it is that acidity that makes it the perfect contender for a pavlova or a trifle, working in contrast to the layers of blissfully sweet cream and meringue or sponge.

Eau-de-vie de framboise, the clear liqueur made from the fruit, is a potent reminder of the fruit at its most ripe and heady. Only the smallest amount is needed to bring a raspberry intensity to a syllabub. In Britain we make a raspberry liqueur that is softer and more quaffable. Framboise is a very sexy addition to dark chocolate truffle mixtures.

The raspberry's leaves can be made into a refreshing tea.

Raspberries and...

Cream Ideally yellow and unpasteurised, either to pour over the fruit or to crush them with to make a fool.

Rosewater Either shaken delicately over the fruit or stirred into stewed berries as a more romantic alternative to a fruit liqueur.

Goat's cheese Especially the sharp, chalky kind.

Ground almonds As used in a sponge cake to slice and serve with the fruit.

Pistachios Toasted and scattered on the fruit or in a raspberry ice cream.

Sugar To make a jam or simply to sweeten the fruit before serving with cream.

Mascarpone As a filling for a raspberry tart.

Champagne Drop a couple of drippingly ripe ones into each glass, or put one or two berries on your tongue between each mouthful of wine, as if you were popping pills.

Peaches The berries' best friend. I use them in both a fruit salad and a trifle. The two mashed with a fork and stirred into shattered meringues and cream is a ridiculously indulgent dessert.

Chocolate One of the few fruits to be truly happy in the presence of dark chocolate. Serve them whole or as a purée to freshen up a slice of chocolate truffle cake or mousse.

Game birds A few berries can be mashed into the gravy for grouse or partridge to surprisingly successful effect.

* Raspberries should be picked dry rather than after a rain shower. They keep better than when they are wet.
* Store them in the fridge, but bring them to room temperature before eating. A warm berry has a deeper flavour.
* Raspberries freeze better than most other fruits because of their structure, being made up of lots of tiny drupelets.
* There is no need to thaw a frozen berry before adding it to a smoothie.
* Prue Leith has a neat recipe for making 'instant' raspberry sorbet by simply blitzing frozen berries in a food processor.
* To cook grouse or partridge with raspberries, mash a handful of berries with a little butter and stuff it inside the bird. Roast the bird in a very hot oven, covered with bacon and with a sprig of thyme up its bottom. What emerges is a glistening roast bird with mildly fruit-flavoured pan juices. The smell is as good as the taste.
* The soft white hull inside a raspberry is known as a torus.

A dish of warm, heady berries

Warmth is a good friend to the raspberry. Put a little fire under this fruit and its juices become intense, rich and almost heady. The colour is arterial, glowing like damson gin. This is meant as a simple dessert, but I must admit to having eaten it for breakfast before now, even with its dash of eau-de-vie.

enough for 6
raspberries, loganberries, tayberries – 400g
caster sugar – up to 4 tablespoons
English raspberry liqueur or eau-de-vie de framboise – 2 tablespoons

Put the berries in a thick-based saucepan. Scatter over the sugar, then pour in the framboise or raspberry liqueur and 4 tablespoons of water. Bring slowly to the boil, turn down the heat and leave until the berries appear on the verge of bursting and their juices colour the liquor in the pan.

Serve warm, in glasses or small bowls, or spoon it over ice cream, watching the warm juices trickle down the cold vanilla ice.

A raspberry syllabub

The citrus zest and sweet wine go some way towards balancing the rich effect of the whipped cream, as does the streak of crushed berries at the dessert's heart. Nevertheless I serve this elegant summer cream in very small portions. A dish of berries, perfect, headily ripe and warm from the sun, would be a perfect side offering, as would more of the raspberry purée, crushed and chilled.

enough for 4–6
a lemon
caster sugar – 3 tablespoons
sweet wine (such as a Sauternes or an orange Muscat) – 60ml
double cream – 300ml
raspberries – 150g

Grate the lemon zest into a bowl, squeeze in its juice, then add the sugar and sweet wine. Leave to steep in the fridge (it is important the bowl is kept cold) for a couple of hours or, better still, overnight.

Using a large balloon whisk or electric mixer, slowly beat in the cream, getting right to the bottom of the mixture. Watch the texture carefully; I refuse to take my eyes from it until the mixture will sit in thick, soft, billowing folds. It should still leave a slow, falling trail from the whisk. If you take it too far, it will become grainy and separate.

Crush the raspberries with a fork and fold tenderly into the syllabub. Spoon into chilled glasses and leave for at least half an hour in the fridge before serving.

A lemon posset for raspberries, mulberries and the like

Whenever I am making this classic dessert, I always wonder if there will be enough – it looks such a small amount in the saucepan. Yet once it is poured into glasses and left to set, you realise that it is so rich and lemony that a small amount is all that is required.

Pleasing as it is served in unadorned simplicity, I do think it is the perfect accompaniment for raspberries, mulberries or loganberries. A crisp biscuit such as a brandy snap could be useful here too.

makes 4 small glasses
double cream – 500ml
caster sugar – 150g
lemon juice – 75ml

Put the cream and caster sugar in a saucepan and bring to the boil, stirring occasionally to dissolve the sugar. Reduce the heat so that the mixture doesn't boil over and let it bubble enthusiastically for about three minutes, stirring regularly.

Remove from the heat, stir in the lemon juice and leave to settle. Pour into four small wine glasses or cups and leave to cool. Refrigerate for a couple of hours before serving.

Watermelon and raspberry salad

I am not a great one for using alcohol in cooking, but the faintest hint of raspberry or blackcurrant eau-de-vie is one I can happily live with. This is a dessert for following an exceptionally spicy main course.

enough for 4
a large chunk of watermelon, about 800g
raspberries – 350g
caster sugar – a scant tablespoon
framboise liqueur or crème de cassis – a tablespoon

Cut the melon flesh into fat chunks, removing the skin and pips. Anything too small will just turn to slush. Put them in a bowl with the raspberries. Sprinkle the fruit lightly with sugar and pour over the alcohol. Leave to macerate for an hour or so. Serve chilled.

A frozen ice of raspberries and cream

A simple ice cream made without the need for a sorbetière.

enough for 6
large eggs – 3
caster sugar – 80g
a few drops of vanilla extract or a knifepoint of vanilla seeds
double cream – 300ml
raspberries – 250g

You will need a loaf tin approximately 22cm x 12cm, lined on the base and sides with cling film, greaseproof paper or waxed paper.

Separate the eggs. Add the sugar to the yolks and beat until thick and pale, the colour of vanilla ice cream. I find this easiest with an electric whisk. Stir in the vanilla.

Whisk the cream till it is thick but still soft enough to slide a little when the bowl is moved from side to side. You don't want it to be stiff. Fold the cream into the egg yolk and sugar mixture.

Crush the berries with a fork. I like to keep some of their seedy texture here, so I just mash them with a light pressure – enough to bruise rather than mash.

In a clean bowl, beat the egg whites till stiff. Fold them tenderly into the mixture, followed by the crushed raspberries. Pour into the lined tin. Tap firmly to level the mixture, then cover loosely with cling film and place in the freezer for a good four to six hours, till frozen. I sometimes think it is best frozen overnight.

To serve, leave out of the freezer, at room temperature, for about fifteen to twenty minutes, then slice into thick pieces with a heavy knife.

A meringue with red berries and cream

Crisp meringue, sugar-frosted like the yew hedges on a winter's day, billowing cream and scarlet fruit.

enough for 8
large egg whites – 6
caster sugar – 280g, plus some for dusting
cornflour – a heaped tablespoon
mild white wine vinegar – a teaspoon
a handful of flaked almonds

for the filling
double cream – 300ml
raspberries, loganberries or tayberries – 400g

Set the oven at 220°C/Gas 7. Line a shallow rectangular cake tin or Swiss roll tin, about 33cm x 24cm, with baking parchment. The paper needs to come right up the sides of the tin. Brush lightly with flavourless cooking oil.

Put the egg whites into the bowl of an electric mixer and whisk at high speed till light, fluffy and stiff. Introduce the sugar gradually, continuing to whisk all the time. Fold in the cornflour and vinegar. Spread the mixture lightly into the lined tin, smoothing it level as you go, then scatter the top with flaked almonds. Bake for ten minutes, then lower the heat to 160°C/Gas 3 and cook for a further fifteen minutes or so, till the meringue is golden on top. Place a sheet of greaseproof paper on a work surface, dust it with caster sugar, then remove the meringue from the oven and tip it upside down on to the paper. The meringue should fall out together with the lining paper. Gently peel the paper from the meringue, cover lightly with cling film and leave to cool.

Pour the cream into a basin (it always whips better in a cool bowl) and whip lightly, so that it will almost stand in peaks. Peel off the cling film and spread the cream over the meringue, smoothing it out almost to the edges with a palette knife.

Scatter the berries over the cream. Take the long edge nearest you and roll it up tightly, like a roulade. Transfer to a long dish and leave to settle for half an hour before serving.

Raspberry yoghurt ice cream

The British have a history of making fine dairy produce but our love of yoghurt is more recent. We produce some splendid farmhouse yoghurt, not just from cow's and goat's but from sheep's milk too, and all of it can be made into very good ice cream. The goat's and sheep's versions have a particularly refreshing quality when used with soft fruit, and are my first choice where berries are concerned. Wholefood stores and farm shops are particularly good hunting grounds for locally made natural yoghurt.

> *enough for 4*
> natural yoghurt – 400g
> icing sugar – 4 tablespoons
> raspberries – 300g

Put the yoghurt into a bowl and beat in the sugar with a small whisk or fork. Crush the raspberries with a fork and stir them into the sweetened yoghurt.

Pour into an ice-cream machine and churn till almost frozen. Transfer to a plastic freezer tray and freeze till needed.

Note: You can make this without a machine but it will lose its creamy texture. Simply pour the mixture into a freezer box and freeze for two hours. Stir well with a fork or small beater, bringing the frozen outer edges into the unfrozen middle, then repeat once every hour till frozen.

Purple figs with crushed raspberry cream

Crush a handful of raspberries with a fork. Fold into twice the volume of softly whipped cream, stopping when the fruit has bled into the cream. Cut a cross down each fig from the stalk to the base, then push the sides to open the fruit up. Drop a spoonful of the crushed raspberry cream into the hollows and serve.

A quick peach and raspberry mess

It is worth making certain your peaches are very ripe before using them for this recipe.

enough for 4
whipping cream – 250ml
meringue shells – 4
raspberries – 400g
very ripe peaches – 3

Put a large mixing bowl in the fridge for half an hour to chill. When the bowl is cold, pour in the cream and whisk till it lies in thick, soft folds, before it is stiff enough to stand in peaks.

Crumble the meringues into the cream, making sure to get a mixture of very fine crumbs and large pieces so that the texture is interesting.

Put two-thirds of the berries into a bowl and crush them with a fork – not to make a sauce, but so that they start to give up some of their juices. Cut each peach in half, twist out the stone, then slice the flesh of each half into four or five pieces (you could chop them, if you prefer). Mix the peaches and raspberries together.

Add the raspberry and peach mixture to the cream and meringue, stirring slowly and gently so that the fruit doesn't really colour the cream but leaves a trail of juice and fruit throughout the mixture (rather like an old-fashioned raspberry ripple). Fold in the reserved whole raspberries. Pile into glasses or elegant bowls and serve.

Banana, peach and raspberry brûlée

I struggled with this inclusion. The recipe is something I made virtually every day at a London café for six years. I have always felt the layers of soft fruits smothered in whipped cream and given a thin crust of hot caramel produce something altogether too creamy, too sweet and too rich. Yet for all that, it is an unsurpassed crowd pleaser and I have been asked for the recipe on countless occasions. Take the caramel to deepest coffee colour before pouring it, carefully, over the hills and valleys of whipped cream.

enough for 4–6
caster sugar – 175g
bananas (peeled weight), peaches and raspberries,
   mixed – 700g total weight
chilled double cream – 350ml

Put the sugar in a heavy pan and pour in enough water to cover. Set over a medium to high flame to boil while you prepare the fruit. Slice the bananas, stone and slice the peaches and remove any stems from the raspberries. Put all the fruit in a heatproof serving bowl.

Whip the cream until it forms gentle peaks. Take care not to overwhip it. Spoon in high waves over the fruit. The sugar in the pan will start to turn a pale, golden caramel after ten minutes or less – watch it carefully, as it is prone to burning. The caramel is ready when it turns a rich golden brown. Immediately, taking care not to splash or burn yourself, pour the caramel over the cream and fruit. It will at once set to a crisp and shiny coat. Eat within thirty minutes.

Raspberry cranachan

The magical combination of oats and raspberry is experienced nowhere better than in the classic Scottish dessert, cranachan. There are as many versions as there are tartans. This is mine.

enough for 4
rolled oats – 175g
light muscovado sugar – 80g
double cream – 300ml
raspberries – 150g

Put the rolled oats on a baking sheet and toast under a hot grill till golden. They burn easily, so watch them carefully; it shouldn't take more than a couple of minutes. While the oats are still hot, add the sugar and stir well.

In a cool bowl, whip the cream till it starts to thicken on the whisk. It should loosely hold its shape but not be thick enough to stand in peaks.

Crush the raspberries lightly with a fork. Gently fold the cream, oats and sugar into the raspberries. Don't over mix. Pile into a serving bowl, or four individual glasses or dishes if you prefer, and chill for a good hour before serving.

A quick raspberry tart

As much as simple fruit salads, fools and compotes appeal to me, there are moments when only ripe, scarlet fruit, crisp pastry and whipped cream will do.

The most straightforward interpretation involves laying a sheet of ready-rolled puff pastry on a baking sheet, scoring a rim on all four sides, about 2cm from the edge, pricking it all over with a fork and baking in a very hot oven till crisp. I then pile on whipped cream and perfectly ripe raspberries, loganberries or tayberries. No pâtissier's shining glaze, no dusted sugar crust, in fact no adornment of any kind. Just fruit, pastry and cream. For a pastry sheet of approximately 200g in weight, you will need 250ml double cream and 250g raspberries.

Peach and summer fruit sundae

Oh joy of joys, such greedy bliss!

enough for 4
caster sugar – 90g
water – 500ml
a vanilla pod
large peaches – 4
vanilla ice cream – 8 balls (about 500g)
whipped cream, to serve (optional)

for the summer fruit sauce
raspberries – 150g
redcurrants – 100g, removed from the stalks
icing sugar – 2 heaped tablespoons, or to taste

Make a syrup by putting the sugar, water and vanilla pod in a saucepan
and bringing to the boil. Turn the heat down to a light simmer – the water
should be just bubbling – then add the halved and stoned peaches (if the
stones refuse to budge, leave them in till the peaches are ready; they will
come out more easily then). Let the peaches simmer till tender to the point
of a knife. Switch off the heat and let them cool.

Put the raspberries and redcurrants in a food processor and blitz till
smooth, then stir in the icing sugar. If there are any lumps, whiz once more.
(Alternatively, push the berries and currants through a sieve, then stir in
the sugar.)

Divide the balls of ice cream between four dishes. Add the peaches and
a spoonful of their cooking liquor, then spoon over the fruit sauce. Add
whipped cream if you wish.

Raspberry tiramisu

Okay, this is about as much a tiramisu as I am, but the principle of booze-soaked sponge and mascarpone cream is the same as in the classic Italian dessert. It may make your heart sink to find that it needs to be made the day before, but that is the only way to get the sponge and cream cheese layer to marry successfully. Rush it and you will be disappointed.

enough for 8
white wine, not too dry – 100ml
crème de cassis – 80ml
a packet of sponge finger biscuits
raspberries – 400g
mascarpone – 500g
eggs – 3, separated
caster sugar – 3 tablespoons
double or whipping cream – 200ml
a handful of rose petals, if you wish, to serve

You will need an oval or rectangular dish approximately 35cm long. Mix the wine and cassis. Dip the biscuits in this and lay them snugly in the dish. Pour over half the remaining liquid (you can dump or drink what's left, it has done its job). Scatter half the raspberries over the sponges.

Beat the mascarpone, egg yolks and sugar together with a hand-held electric whisk. Rinse the beaters, dry them thoroughly, then beat the egg whites till they are stiff and hold firm peaks. Carefully fold the egg whites into the mascarpone mixture. Spread this over the infused sponge fingers and set aside.

Whip the cream, but only till it will sit in soft folds. If it will stand in peaks, you have gone too far. Spread it over the mascarpone mixture. Scatter over the remaining raspberries and cover tightly with cling film. Refrigerate overnight. The next day, scatter with rose petals, should you wish, and serve.

Raspberry fool

I think of fruit fools, be they gooseberry, strawberry or raspberry, as the very essence of summer. These soft, lazy-day puddings are nothing more than ripe fruit at the height of its season that has been crushed and stirred through with whipped cream, custard and perhaps a little sugar. I am not certain the sugar is entirely necessary with strawberry or raspberry fools; taste and sweeten as you go. Some crisp almond biscuits or shortbread would be good here.

enough for 6
raspberries – 300g
double cream – 150ml
ready-made custard – 150ml
a little icing sugar, if needed
pistachio nuts – 12

Rinse the berries and crush them roughly with a fork. I think you should stop long before you reach a purée, so that the finished fool will have a more interesting texture. Pour the cream into a chilled bowl and whip it till it stands in soft folds. It shouldn't be stiff. Gently fold in the custard and a good two-thirds of the crushed raspberries.

Should you wish to sweeten the fool, do it now. I suggest a tablespoon of icing sugar, but taste it for sweetness as you go. Stir in the reserved third of raspberries, leaving a trail of red through the pink of the fool. Halve or chop the pistachios and scatter them over the top.

Raspberry ripple yoghurt fool

You can spend a lifetime chasing flavours from your childhood and never quite finding them. It has been this way with ice cream, a quiet, plodding hunt for the milky ices I enjoyed as a boy. One of the flavours I hanker after is that of the raspberry ripple ice lollies I bought from the Midland Counties Dairies with my pocket money. Even if I captured the essence of them, I doubt they would hit the same spot, but it is worth trying. This fool was part of that attempt. The result is a finer, more pure thing than I remember, though with much the same flavour. All I need now is to capture it in frozen form.

enough for 4
double cream – 250ml
goat's milk yoghurt – 125g
raspberries – 250g
shortbread, to serve

Put the cream into a cold bowl and whisk until it starts to thicken. You want it to be thick enough to sit in heaps rather than stand in peaks. Now gently fold the yoghurt into the cream with a large spoon. Don't beat it, which might over-thicken the cream, just firmly, smoothly fold the two together.

Crush the raspberries lightly with a fork. I think you should resist the temptation to mash them too much; you want some texture in amongst all this billowing cream.

Gently fold the cream and yoghurt into the raspberries. I find this easiest with a large metal spoon. Again, I don't think you should mix too thoroughly. You want each spoonful to have some of the sharpened cream and a ripple of crushed, scarlet fruit.

Spoon into bowls or glasses and serve with shortbread.

Victoria sponge with raspberries and custard sauce

enough for 6

for the sponge
butter, at room temperature – 110g
golden caster sugar – 110g, plus a little for dredging
eggs – 2
self-raising flour – 110g

for the custard sauce
whipping cream – 150ml
ready-made custard – 200ml
a vanilla pod

for the raspberry sauce
raspberries – 300g
kirsch, or raspberry liqueur – a tablespoon (optional)
icing sugar – a tablespoon

a few raspberries and fresh rose petals, to finish

Set the oven at 180°C/Gas 4. Butter and line a round 20cm cake tin.

Cream the butter with the sugar in a large bowl till light and fluffy. This is easiest done with an electric beater or in a food mixer. Beat in the eggs one at a time. Sift the flour into the mixture and mix very gently till the flour is no longer visible. Spoon the mixture into the prepared cake tin, smooth the top and bake for twenty to twenty-five minutes, till a skewer inserted in the middle comes out clean. Cool the cake on a wire rack.

To make the custard sauce, put the cream into a chilled mixing bowl and beat till thick. You should aim for a texture that sits in soft folds rather than whipping long enough for it to stand in stiff peaks. Gently fold the custard in. Split the vanilla pod in half, scrape out the seeds with the point of a sharp knife, then stir them into the custard. Set aside in the fridge for an hour or so for the vanilla to work its magic.

Make the raspberry sauce by blitzing the fruit, alcohol and icing sugar in a blender or food processor. If you wish, you can sieve this to remove any pips, but I rather like the crunch amongst the soft sponge and custardy sauce. Set aside.

Dredge the surface of the sponge with caster sugar. Cut into twelve narrow wedges. Place two in each of six shallow bowls. Pour the custard sauce around the slices of cake, then drizzle the raspberry sauce into the custard. Decorate with a few raspberries and even a few rose petals, if you wish.

Raspberry panna cotta

Pure raspberries and cream but made in the style of an Edwardian custard-cup pudding. Something for eating with a teaspoon.

makes 6 small puddings
milk – 100ml
double cream – 400ml
gelatine – 2 leaves
icing sugar – 4 tablespoons
raspberries – 200g, plus more to serve
rosewater – 2 teaspoons
rose petals, to serve

Pour the milk and roughly two-thirds of the cream into a small saucepan. Simmer gently for five or six minutes without letting it boil. The mixture will reduce a little.

Meanwhile, soak the gelatine in a bowl of cold water. After five minutes or so, it will have softened to slithery sheets. Pour the remaining cream into a bowl, add the icing sugar and beat gently till it starts to feel heavy on the whisk, but stop before it stiffens.

Remove the cream and milk from the heat and stir in the sheets of softened gelatine. Stir in the sweetened cream. Pour the mixture through a sieve balanced over a large jug (don't be tempted to skip this, or the panna cotta will lose something of its purity).

Blitz the raspberries in a food processor for a few seconds (you can sieve out the seeds if you wish, but I prefer not to) and add the rosewater. Pour the raspberry purée into the cream mixture and stir gently, then pour into six small cups or white ramekins. Cover each with cling film and chill for three or four hours, until lightly set. Turn them out if you wish by briefly dipping the dishes into hot water, then turning upside down on to a plate and scattering with raspberries and rose petals, or simply eat them from the dish.

Ricotta cake with raspberries

This is about as complicated a dessert as I ever make. There is a sponge
to bake, flecked with dried apricots and ground almonds, a ricotta and
mascarpone filling and a purée of raspberries to serve alongside. But the
finished dessert is worth the trouble for a special occasion. A simpler version
might involve a shop-bought sponge or even simply serving the filling
alongside some slices of the sponge with a little raspberry purée over the top.

enough for 8–10

for the apricot sponge
butter – 250g
golden caster sugar – 250g
large eggs – 4
the grated zest and juice of a lemon
ground almonds – 50g
plain flour – 100g
soft dried apricots – 100g, finely chopped

for the ricotta filling
ricotta – 150g
mascarpone – 250g
icing sugar – 2 lightly heaped tablespoons
the grated zest of an orange
a few drops of finest vanilla extract
whipping or double cream – 280ml

for the raspberry purée
raspberries – 350g
caster sugar – 50g
framboise liqueur or kirsch – a few drops

icing sugar and fresh berries, to serve

Set the oven at 180°C/Gas 4. Line the bottom of a 20–22cm shallow square
cake tin with a sheet of baking parchment. Cream the butter and sugar in
a food mixer till truly light and fluffy. It should be very pale and creamy.

Beat the eggs lightly and add them in three or four goes to the butter
and sugar. They might curdle slightly but don't worry, just keep beating.
Add the lemon zest, reserving the juice, then mix the ground almonds and
flour together. Slowly fold in the flour and almonds, then add the lemon
juice and dried apricots. At this point you should treat the mixture gently.
Smooth the mixture into the lined cake tin and bake for thirty to thirty-five

minutes. Remove and turn upside down on to a cake rack to cool.

Put the ricotta, mascarpone and icing sugar in a food mixer and beat thoroughly to a thick and relatively smooth cream. Beat in the orange zest and vanilla extract. In a separate bowl, softly whip the cream. Stop whilst it is still in soft folds, before it gets thick enough to stand in peaks. Fold it gently into the ricotta mixture.

To assemble the cake, line the base of a long, thin cake tin, about 28cm x 8cm (though you can improvise with other dimensions easily enough; just use what you have). Cut the sponge into three long strips, then cut each half in two horizontally. Line the bottom of the tin with a slice of the sponge, using some from a second one where you need to. Spoon one half of the mascarpone mixture on top of this, smoothing it gently. Cover this with another layer of sponge and a second layer of mascarpone cream. Finish with more sponge, patching any gaps where necessary. Tightly cover in cling film and refrigerate for a good two hours. Overnight will not hurt. You will inevitably have some sponge left over after this, but it will no doubt soon disappear.

Make the raspberry purée by blitzing all the ingredients in a blender or food processor, then pushing everything through a fine sieve. Set aside in a covered bowl till needed.

Run a palette knife around the edges and turn the cake out on to a long, flat plate. Dust with icing sugar and serve with the purée and berries.

Redcurrants

In high summer I often start my day with a handful of redcurrants, snatched from the bush as I walk round the garden before breakfast. If I don't wolf them then and there, I drop the glistening red baubles, pulled from their brittle stalks, into a little bowl and eat them with sheep's yoghurt. No sugar.

The redcurrant is not a fruit that responds well to embellishment or to heat – which is why it gets a separate chapter from the blackcurrant, with which it shares fewer characteristics than is often observed. A little pressure can have worthwhile results: burst the raw or lightly cooked berries and their tart juices will flow. The quintessential summer pudding, where raspberries and redcurrants are pressed between layers of bread to form a juicy but solid mixture, is a case in point. Redcurrant jelly is another.

The acidity of the rich, claret juice is the whole point of the redcurrant. It is pleasingly sour amongst a bowl of sweeter berries, strawberries perhaps, and its sharp pinch is welcome in a fruit salad. Its presence is both charming and useful in a plate of peaches and raspberries. The currant's piercing notes add spice to the sweet peaches and make the berries sing.

Red and white currants, sitting like jewels in their paper caskets, are pleasant enough eaten in small handfuls, like raw peas, but become astringent in quantity. A light dairy product such as fromage frais will temper their bite.

This fruit is celebrated in these pages because of, rather than in spite of, its woefully short season and its limited use at the table. Blink in late July and you will miss them. Most of all I love their exhilarating sharpness and old-fashioned charm. No sweet or bonbon has ever been made with this; no jelly for a children's birthday party. This is the fruit that, if commerce had its way, would be culled, ripped up for more woolly Elsanta strawberries. That the redcurrant has survived in these days of monotone sweet blandness is nothing short of a miracle.

A redcurrant bush in the garden

One of the first bushes to break into leaf, tiny fresh green leaves that appear when all else is still sleeping, and that signal spring is almost here. The fruit comes as something of a wake-up call too. One day the flowers will be hanging down in lacy, green festoons, the next time you look the berries are almost ripe. By July you can be picking the fine stems with their rows of fruit hanging like costume jewellery. But the birds are attracted to the red variety, so you need to move quickly or cover the bushes with nets.

Every garden needs a redcurrant bush, if only for the pleasure of snaffling a currant or two when you are down that end of the garden. Undemanding, and happy to grow on poor soil, they will live quietly in an untended bit of the allotment or near the compost heap. They like sunshine and shelter. They fruit on old and new wood, but need regular pruning to keep the bush in shape. Mine thrive on it. Wielding the pruning knife is a job I enjoy each summer, directly after fruiting, when I shorten new growth back to about five leaves from the beginning of the stem. Then in winter, I shorten the branches by at least a quarter of their length, cutting just in front of a bud. I prune as much wood as possible out of the centre of the bush to keep it ventilated, reducing the chances of mildew.

My bushes arrived in mid January, thin, twiggy sticks in a brown sack. As I dug them into the cold soil with a shovel of manure, I doubted their survival. But currants like the cold, it reminds them of their home further north, and they settled in happily. By late April there were bright leaves, then the first signs of fruit. Not enough for a summer pudding, but just enough to encourage a new gardener.

Varieties

There is not much to choose between varieties other than their fruiting times. I grow Laxton's No. 1 for its reliable, sharply flavoured fruit. If I had the space, I would plant three or four varieties to get as long a season as possible.

Junifer Earliest ripening, a lovely start to summer fruit.
Jonkheer Van Tets Vigorous, upright grower.
Laxton's No. 1 Prolific fruit with a good flavour, ripening early, in mid July.
Rondom Bountiful fruit on a compact Dutch bush, very late (September) ripening.
Stanza A high-yielding fruit from the Netherlands.
Red Lake American variety with long, upright branches.
Red Start Late fruiting, despite its name.

Redcurrants in the kitchen

The extreme acidity of these fruits will help in setting the softer, low-pectin jams such as raspberry or strawberry. Add a good handful or more to the fruits as they simmer.

Redcurrants catch the light and sparkle like frost on a rosehip if you brush them with very lightly beaten egg white – a quick bash with a fork till the white froths – and then dip them into caster sugar. Their acidity makes them a welcome candidate for decorating a vast and undulating pavlova, though they look better kept in sprigs. Slightly annoying to eat when still on the stalk, but better than a meringue dotted with loose currants. The effect looks spotty no matter how many you pile on.

Beware the juice, it stains, though less so than pomegranate or blackcurrant. Check shop-bought specimens for any sign of mildew before you put them in the fridge. Just one bad one will quickly turn the rest. That said, they keep for several days in good condition, though they lose their shine as they age.

Any hue of currant makes an interesting addition to a crème brûlée but dark colours are probably most satisfactory to the eye. There will be an element of curdling around the fruit but no matter. It's the contrast with the smooth, vanilla-scented custard and ice-crisp sugar lid that is the magic here. Their presence will please those who find a plain (and some would say perfect) crème brûlée a little cloying.

I have, once or twice, stirred the little berries into the pan juices of a roast shoulder of lamb, adding a sharp snap to the gravy whilst at the same time playing on the lamb and redcurrant jelly theme. The idea was more interesting than the result. Likewise, adding a handful to the roasting juices of a little game bird from the freezer. In principal the addition works, but in practice it looks a bit too clever for its own good. A spoonful of glistening redcurrant jelly looks far more comfortable.

Redcurrants and...

Raspberries Classically in a summer pudding, but also in fruit salads and jams. You can make a gorgeous purée for sponges and ice cream by mixing the two in equal quantities and pushing them through a sieve.

Bread This bright, tart, strident juice soaks into soft bread to great effect, especially in summer pudding, but I also like to pile the berries on a slice of oven-fresh bread, crisp crusted and warm crumbed, spread generously with cream cheese.

Game Stir the fruit into the pan juices of a roast bird, or serve redcurrant jelly on the side.

Lamb The punch of good redcurrant jelly brings out the sweetness in roast lamb or a grilled chop. The jelly made by small, artisan companies seems to be more interesting than the over-sweet, over-set stuff sold by the more commercial companies.

A dish of warm peaches with summer berries

I sometimes use members of the currant family to lift the flavours of sweeter fruits. A little blackcurrant purée will bring life to a dish of strawberries; raw white currants do the same to a salad of oversweet tropical fruits. Peaches, when served warm – under a crumbling pastry crust, say, or afloat in a simple syrup – have an effect that is both sexy and curiously cloying. Spooning a sharp, vividly flavoured sauce over them can put a spring in their step. I use a rough-textured sauce of currants and berries that works in perfect contrast to the smooth, slippery notes of the warm peaches. A deep-summer dish of ravishing beauty.

enough for 4
large, ripe peaches – 4
water – a litre
sugar – to taste

for the sauce
redcurrants – 225g
blackcurrants – 100g
caster sugar – 4 tablespoons
water – 2 tablespoons
raspberries – 350g

Wipe the peaches and put them in a stainless steel pan. Pour in the water and add at least 2 tablespoons of sugar. Bring to the boil, then turn down the heat and leave to simmer gently until the peaches are completely tender. This is unlikely to take more than twenty minutes or so, but will depend on the ripeness of your fruit. Turn off the heat.

Remove the stalks from the currants and put the fruit into a stainless steel saucepan with the sugar and water. Bring slowly to the boil. When the currants start to burst and flood the pan with colour, tip in the raspberries. Simmer for two minutes, no longer.

Serve the peaches, drained of their poaching liquid and skinned if you wish (I remove the skin to reveal the glowing colour of the poached peaches), with the warm fruit sauce.

A little dish of custard, fruit and sugar

I like my crème brûlée unadulterated. But I also like the sublime partnership of tart currants and rich dairy produce, so a brûlée with a layer of currant compote was an accident waiting to happen. It does curdle slightly where the two meet but I am not especially bothered by this. The flavour and the contrast between fruit, custard and crisp sugar is too good.

It has taken me a while to get crème brûlée right. I was being impatient, and failed because I hadn't yet discovered how much easier success is if you chill the finished custard before you sugar it, and that you also need to be a little brave. The kitchen blowtorch has changed everything too. Crème brûlée is not complicated, but it needs both courage and a tender touch.

I work on the principle of 125ml double cream to each large egg yolk.

enough for 4

for the fruit base
blackcurrants – 150g
redcurrants – 250g
sugar – 4 tablespoons
water – 2 tablespoons

for the custard
double cream – 625ml
a vanilla pod, split along its length
egg yolks – 5
caster sugar – a heaped tablespoon

for the crust
caster sugar – 8 tablespoons

Start with the fruit base (it will make too much, so you will have some for breakfast). Pull the currants from their stalks. Put the fruit into a saucepan with the sugar and water and bring to the boil. As soon as the berries start to burst and the juice turns a dramatic purple, remove from the heat and set aside. Leave to cool slightly. Spoon a couple of tablespoons into each of four small ramekins or cups and leave to chill in the fridge. It is best not to include very much juice. Save the rest for later.

Make the custard: put the cream and vanilla pod into a small saucepan and bring to the boil. Before the cream actually boils, turn the heat off and leave to infuse for a good ten minutes. This is to allow the vanilla seeds to scent the cream.

Beat the egg yolks and caster sugar together lightly, just until they turn pale. Pour the warm cream on to the eggs, removing the vanilla pod as you

go, stirring to mix. Wipe the pan, then pour the custard back in, place over a low to moderate heat and allow to get hot, but on no account to boil. This is the bit where it is worth concentrating. Stir the custard regularly with a wooden spoon, getting right down into the corners of the pan. After a while you will see movement where the custard is getting hot. At this point, stir enthusiastically – the custard is at its most crucial curdling point – and do not let it boil. The custard is ready when it is starting to thicken a little; it should look almost wobbly.

A word about curdling. If there is any hint of graininess or curdling at this point (and there might well be), then pour the custard quickly into a bowl, dunk it in a shallow sink of cold water and beat furiously with a whisk. I have rescued many a dodgy one at this point.

Pour the custard over the chilled fruit and allow to cool. Refrigerate for a good three hours, preferably overnight.

To make the sugar crust, sprinkle the sugar over the cold custard. It should be about as thick as a pound coin. For the best results, blowtorch the sugar till it caramelises. If you don't have such a thing as a kitchen blowtorch, then get the grill really (really) hot and place the dishes underneath for a few minutes, until the sugar is golden and crisp.

Redcurrant jelly with sloe gin

Take your own, or a high-quality, softly set artisan-made jam, and melt it in a small saucepan. Add a few tablespoons of sloe gin, tasting as you go, till you have a bright, sharp, piercingly flavoured sauce. Use with game, pork, lamb or even the Christmas turkey.

Little currant cakes

Ten years old, I would help my aunt make little cakes in her kitchen. The usual fairy cake mixture, some would be transformed into butterfly cakes, others with trickles of coloured icing and pastel sugar strands. I'm not sure whether I was proud or embarrassed. Nowadays they would be decorated with a generous swirl of butter cream and called a cupcake. Occasionally, she would insist we put dried currants into the mixture, which I would later fastidiously pick out one by one.

Cookery books are now awash with recipes for every possible type of cupcake and it is easy to see their charm. What with the instant sugar rush, the warm wave of nostalgia and the ease with which they are produced, it is no wonder they are so popular. I see no need to add to the tidal wave of recipes but a sudden notion to toss a handful of currants – red and black – into the raw cake mix resulted in cakes that had the warm butteriness of the genre but here and there a shot of dazzling, sour fruit. For those for whom butter cream holds no calling.

makes 12
butter – 125g
golden caster sugar – 125g
large eggs – 2
self-raising flour – 125g
milk – 2 or 3 tablespoons
red and blackcurrants (or just black) – 150g, removed from their stalks

Set the oven at 200°C/Gas 6. Line 12 patty tins with paper muffin cases. Put the butter, sugar, eggs and flour into a food processor and blitz till all is well creamed. Introduce enough milk into the mixture (probably a couple of tablespoons) to produce a consistency that will fall lightly from the spoon. Stir in the currants.

Divide the mixture between the muffin cases and bake for about twenty to twenty-five minutes, till risen. They should be light but firm to the touch. They will fall slightly on cooling.

Rhubarb

How could anyone not love something known as the pie plant – or indeed, anything whose stems offer such vibrant colour at a time of the year when so much of our fruit is sleeping? Yet rhubarb has never found the broad audience enjoyed by the raspberry or the apple. Instead, it has a loyal, almost cultish following, happy to indulge in its piercing crimson sharpness. Firmly amongst that number, I hold a crown of rhubarb an essential part of any garden I turn my spade to.

Rhubarb has been used medicinally since 2700 BC, often given to relieve serious constipation. It was the darling of the Victorian kitchen, finding its way into pies, fools, crumbles and tarts quite by chance. Tired of the escalating price being asked by Chinese exporters, British apothecaries decided they could grow their own, and imported plants from Central Asia. Unfortunately (or perhaps fortunately) they got hold of *Rheum rhaponticum* rather than the required *Rheum palmatum*. The imported plants proved less than successful for medicinal use but, as our luck had it, turned out to be more than edible.

It was down to Victorian market gardener Joseph Myatt to bring this relatively recent addition to our kitchens to the cook's attention. Myatt's persistence, persuading sceptical shoppers at London's Borough Market to try the stalks in a pie, had the same impact on our kitchens as when Mr Bramley discovered his famous seedling. Rhubarb crumble is now as well known, if not quite as well loved, as apple pie.

The first 'forced' rhubarb, those gently tart stalks that appear in the market around Christmas time, came to prominence in the 1800s, thanks to an 'accident' at Chelsea Physic Garden. The story goes that it was here in the winter of 1815, when the garden's rhubarb patch was accidentally covered with builder's rubble, that this particularly fine-tasting form was first discovered. The pale pink stalks that were unearthed by the gardeners in early spring were found to be extraordinarily mild and sweet, and a new kitchen ingredient was born.

There are two distinct seasons for rhubarb. First to appear in the shops are the long, pale sticks of forced rhubarb from Christmas to early spring, followed by the stouter, often more astringent, outdoor-grown rhubarb for the rest of the year. The appearance of the forced stalks – pale pink, like sticks of rock, the leaves primrose yellow and tightly furled – is due to the darkness in which they are grown, many in the long, black sheds of Yorkshire's famous rhubarb triangle (actually more of an irregular square), where the precious shoots are kept away from the light. These fine, rather delicate stalks have been grown like this since the 1880s, in an industry set around the Wakefield area.

The tall, lidded terracotta rhubarb forcers that are such a common sight in grand kitchen gardens are useful for creating a warm, dark environment (a mini-shed) in which to bring on – force – the plant to produce tender early shoots. I have one in my little rhubarb patch for Stockbridge Arrow, one of three varieties I grow. It was recommended by Janet Oldroyd Hulme, fifth-generation rhubarb grower and known as the 'high priestess of rhubarb', as 'an excellent all-round performer, a must for every garden'. Mrs Oldroyd Hulme is right, and the glowing sticks with their arrow-shaped leaves provide a good start to the rhubarb year, coming several weeks before my Brandy Carr Scarlet and the late Alan Bloom's Grandad's Favourite.

Late rhubarb, coming shortly after the forced variety has finished, is an easy garden plant to live with. The slugs love their umbrella-like leaves but, asking for little more than a shovel of manure in the winter, the crowns will provide endless spring and summer desserts.

Rhubarb in the garden

Rhubarb revels in rich soil. By rich, I mean moist ground that is well seasoned with rotted manure – preferably somewhere that isn't sodden in winter or bone dry in summer. I dug a trench under my plants and filled it with horse manure. They seemed to appreciate it.

The crowns, as the roots are called, are usually sent out in the autumn, though pot-grown ones can be put in at any time. They like to have their growing tips just peeping above the surface of the soil. I put a copper collar around mine to ward off the slugs, which love a rhubarb supper almost as much as one from my dahlia patch. I put a forcer over one of the plants in January to bring the stalks on. An old bucket would do.

They like a spot of nitrogen, and a top dressing of pelleted poultry manure or well-rotted farmyard manure applied around, not directly on to, the crown. Other than that, there is little to it. Plants can last for years but they tend to get tired after three or four years, when it is best to split them. I do it Carol Klein's way, splitting each root into two or three pieces with the spade, making certain there are two undamaged buds on each.

To harvest, you pull rhubarb rather than cutting it. Tug each stick downwards, then turn to remove. Sometimes it needs quite a tug. Taking no more than half the sticks at a time will allow the crown food with which to rejuvenate itself next year. I stop picking on midsummer's eve.

To force rhubarb, you need to give it extra warmth and protection. Simply put a large flowerpot, terracotta forcer or an upturned bucket over the crown in December or January. A little manure pushed around the outside of the pot will warm things up and encourage the tender young shoots to come up early.

Varieties

The hundred or more varieties of rhubarb include many that now only survive in old allotments and kitchen gardens, such as the rare Appleton's Forcing that I am keen to get my hands on. Names from the past include Riverside Giant, Browns Crimson, Muriel (who could turn away a plant called Muriel?), Early Cherry, Early Devon, Stockbridge Emerald, Cutbush's Seedling and The Streeter. Many of the modern varieties were developed at Stockbridge House near Cawood in Yorkshire. These include all the ones that have Stockbridge or Cawood in their name. Specialist growers such as Brandy Carr Nurseries send crowns out in the spring and autumn and can supply you with rare varieties too if you are patient.

Glaskin's Perpetual Well known since the 1920s, a green and freckled-pink variety famous for its sweetness. It is unusual in that it can be picked in its first year. According to Christopher Stocks, John Jessie Glaskin was a Brighton baker who won prizes for his hot cross buns. I feel the need to honour him with a pudding incorporating both rhubarb and his spice-speckled bakery goods.

Early varieties
Appleton's Forcing Rare variety much revered for its flavour. The early shoots are red, turning green with maturity. One to bring on under an upturned bucket or terracotta forcer.
Timperley Early Red mostly at the base of the stems, this thin-stemmed, heavy-cropping variety is often the first up and can even be forced in time for Christmas. You can pick until early summer, by which time its sticks will have turned almost completely green. The flavour is deliciously sharp, making it ideal for crumbles. Raised by Mr Baldwin of Timperley in Cheshire in the 1920s.
Hawke's Champagne A good red colour, sweet flavour (some say the sweetest of all), beautiful, heart-shaped leaves and, once established, acute reliability make this early-season variety a popular choice.

Early Champagne A strong, reliable cultivar that produces exceptionally sweet and early stalks of a deep red.

Stockbridge Arrow A modern variety with blood-red stems, arrow-shaped leaves and pink rather than the more usual green flesh. Keeps its colour well in the garden and will do well outside from late winter onwards.

Goliath Lives up to its name, with huge leaves and often thick stalks. The flavour gets a good rating from most.

Grandad's Favourite Named by horticulturist Alan Bloom, a variety with cherry-red stems flashed with green near the leaves. Strong and reliable, it is a prolific cropper.

Prince Albert An exceptionally early variety that has no fear of the cold. A single crown will provide a good crop of long, scarlet stalks.

Mid-season (April to early summer)

Cawood Delight Not known for its prolific cropping, this maroon-stemmed variety is exceptional at keeping its shape and colour once cooked. Not suitable for forcing.

Strawberry A fine-tasting rhubarb with good, dark-red skin and pink flesh.

The Sutton Red and green flecks with green, well-flavoured flesh. The thick stems often produce enormous leaves and can take up considerable space in the garden. So not one for me.

Late season (June onwards)

Valentine The brilliant red stems end in a heart-shaped leaf. It is exceptionally sweet and prolific.

Victoria Lovely old variety with rather thick maroon stems and red and green flesh. Often found in traditional kitchen gardens. Apparently easily raised from seed, though I have never tried it.

Rhubarb in the kitchen

Rhubarb is sometimes thought of as purely a pie fruit, or even just something to hide under the tender lid of a crumble. I like to think there is a little more to it than that. The sour quality of the stalks can be as useful in the kitchen as that of cooking varieties of apples, gooseberries and verjuice. As a razor-sharp accompaniment to rich, fatty meats or fish, rhubarb is somewhat underused. It works in the same way as apple sauce with pork, and is appropriate for baked, fried or grilled mackerel.

Whilst it excels in fatty company, nicely balancing a dish that may be a bit too rich, the stalks can also be added to lamb stews or served as an accompaniment to the darker game birds. I also use it with ham in place of a Cumberland or cranberry sauce. Others have found it a safe home in soups with chickpeas, spinach or parsnip. (Adventurous cooks might like to get hold of a copy of Mary Prior's wonderful *Rhubarbaria*, published by Prospect Books.)

Rhubarb is arguably at its most comfortable in puddings and cakes. The sharp qualities of the sticks work in contrast to the rounded, buttery notes used for cake mixtures and pastry crusts. A simple, crisp butter biscuit can be an effective addition to a dish of slithery poached rhubarb. A single-crust pie, pale, sugar frosted and served without the intrusion of cream or custard, can be charming, especially if the fruit is of the palest pink.

The excess juice that comes from the stalks as they cook is both a joy and a heartbreak. The flavour, when diluted with sugar, is uplifting, especially at breakfast. But there is often too much for a supporting pastry crust to stay crisp in its company and it can render a cake crumb a soggy mess. The trick is to make a single-crust pie such as the one in the Plum chapter (see page 1054), or to bake the fruit first, drain it, then use the cooked stalks to fill a tart. Even then you might need a layer of ground almonds or biscuit crumbs (Chez Panisse uses crushed amaretti biscuits) under the fruit. I have yet to make a double-crust rhubarb pie whose bottom crust wasn't the wrong side of moist.

That juice can be put to wonderful use. Nigella Lawson uses it for a shimmering jelly, whilst I have poured it into a glass and filled it up with jagged ice cubes (I like to smash them with an ice pick, *Basic Instinct* style, rather than use ice-cube trays), topping up with sparkling mineral water. There are few more bracing drinks.

Rhubarb and...

Honey Possibly the most appropriate sweetener, introducing a mellowing note to the poached or roasted stalks.

Vanilla A pod and its dislodged seeds can be tucked into a dish of baked rhubarb. A vanilla-scented panna cotta is a pleasing way of introducing a dairy note.

Mackerel and salmon Oily fish like the bite of poached rhubarb to balance their oily qualities.

Cinnamon A sweet, musky note for rhubarb cakes. A stick of the spice can be used in a rhubarb compote.

Ginger Use the dried spice in cakes, the fresh root in compotes.

Pork Contrast the meat's fatty sweetness with a few stalks of roast rhubarb or maybe a purée.

Almonds Use the ground nuts in cakes with the fruit layered in the centre.

Yoghurt Poached rhubarb, drained, then stirred into yoghurt, makes a sharp, kiss-ass fool.

Mackerel with rhubarb and sherry vinegar

A purée of rhubarb brings out the inherent sweetness of mackerel well enough, but I prefer the stalks to have some texture and tend to serve them with the fish whole rather than as a sauce. The colour, alongside the shimmering silver of the mackerel, makes for a beautiful and extraordinary supper.

enough for 2
rhubarb – 200g
caster sugar – 2 tablespoons

for the mackerel
a little plain flour
mackerel – 2, filleted
olive oil
rosemary – a small sprig
sherry vinegar
capers – a tablespoon (optional)

Preheat the oven to 180°C/Gas 4. Trim the rhubarb, and discard the leaves. Cut it into short lengths and put in a roasting tin or baking dish with the sugar. Bake until just soft enough to take the point of a knife, about twenty minutes. Allow to cool, then drain, reserving the cooking juices.

For the mackerel, season the flour with salt and a little black pepper. Lightly coat the skin side of each mackerel fillet with the seasoned flour. Heat a little oil in a large, non-stick frying pan. Gently place the mackerel fillets in the hot pan, skin-side down. Chop the rosemary needles and scatter them over the fish. Press the fish down with a palette knife to stop it curling. As the underside of the fish starts to crisp lightly, carefully turn over and cook the other side. It shouldn't take longer than two or three minutes on each side. Lift the mackerel fillets out on to warm plates.

Pour a couple of tablespoons of sherry vinegar (or less, to taste) into the hot pan. Add the cooked rhubarb, together with the rhubarb juices. Add the capers if you are using them. Let the rhubarb briefly warm through, then spoon it over the mackerel and serve.

Roast leg of pork with spiced rhubarb

Rhubarb makes a change from the more traditional apple sauce in the depths of winter, and shares its ability to balance the richness of the meat. Rather than leave the pieces as a rough purée, as I would with apple, I whiz the rhubarb into a smooth sauce – a nice contrast to the roughness of the crackling.

enough for 2, with seconds
a piece of pork leg, boned, scored and rolled, about 1kg
a tablespoon each of sea salt and black pepper
the leaves from 3 bushy thyme sprigs
white wine – 2 glasses

for the sauce
rhubarb – 400g
sugar – 2 tablespoons
the zest and juice of a small orange
ground cinnamon

Set the oven at 220°C/Gas 7. Put the meat in a roasting tin. Mix together the sea salt, black pepper and thyme leaves to make a rub for the pork. Massage it into the skin, making sure to get it right down in between the score marks.

Roast the meat for twenty minutes, then lower the heat to 180°C/Gas 4 and cook for a further twenty-five minutes per 500g.

Make the rhubarb sauce. Trim the stalks, removing the leaves (which are poisonous in quantity), and cut into short pieces. Put them into a stainless steel or enamelled pan with the sugar and the orange zest and juice. Bring to the boil, then turn the heat down to a slow simmer. Leave until the fruit has virtually collapsed. Whiz in a food processor or blender till smooth. Season to taste with salt and a very little cinnamon.

Remove the pork from the oven and let it rest for fifteen minutes, lightly covered with a dome of foil (too tight and it will soften the crackling). Put the roasting tin on the heat and pour in the white wine, stirring and scraping at the sticky bits in the pan as you go. Bring to the boil, then season carefully and pour into a warm jug.

Carve the roast, serving each plate with some of the gravy and passing round the rhubarb sauce.

Rhubarb custard fool with rhubarb syrup

A new take on a nursery stalwart.

enough for 4–6
rhubarb – 400g
water – 3 tablespoons
sugar – 2 tablespoons
double cream – 220ml
custard – 250ml

Trim the rhubarb, taking care to discard the leaves. Cut the stalks into pieces about the length of a wine cork. Put the rhubarb into a stainless steel or enamelled saucepan (aluminium reacts badly with the acidity of the rhubarb), add the water and sugar, then bring to the boil. Immediately turn down the heat so that the rhubarb simmers gently. You want it to soften but not totally collapse into strings. When the rhubarb is soft, remove it from the syrup with a draining spoon. Pour the syrup into a small dish and let it cool, then refrigerate it.

Whip the cream lightly. It needs to be thick, but not whipped so far that it forms stiff peaks. It should lie in soft folds. Stir the custard in gently.

Put the drained fruit into the cream and custard and fold gently, so that the fruit forms pale pink streaks through the custard and cream. Set aside in the fridge for half an hour or so. Spoon into glasses and serve, pouring a little of the chilled rhubarb syrup over the top of the fool.

Cinnamon panna cotta with spiced roast rhubarb

Panna cotta makes a rich and subtle accompaniment to poached or roast rhubarb. If you want a stronger cinnamon flavour, add half a teaspoon of ground cinnamon to the milk, too.

enough for 4
full cream milk – 200ml
double cream – 200ml
a cinnamon stick
a vanilla pod
crème fraîche – 200ml
leaf gelatine – 6g (that is, 3 small leaves)
icing sugar – 3 tablespoons

for the spiced roast rhubarb
young rhubarb – 400g
honey – 3 heaped tablespoons
a small orange
a cinnamon stick
star anise – 2

Pour the milk and double cream into a small saucepan and add the cinnamon stick. Cut the vanilla pod lengthwise in half, scrape the seeds into the cream with the point of a knife and drop the pod in too. Bring almost to the boil, turning off the heat immediately the liquid is approaching the boil. Stir in the crème fraîche. Cover with a lid and leave for fifteen minutes. This will give the vanilla and cinnamon time to flavour the cream subtly.

Put the gelatine leaves in a bowl of cold water and leave to soften for 5 minutes. Remove from the water and add them, together with the icing sugar, to the cream mixture. Stir till they have dissolved. Pour through a sieve to remove the spices, then divide between four 200ml moulds or ramekins and place in the fridge for four or five hours, till set.

Set the oven at 160°C/Gas 3. Trim the rhubarb, discarding any leaves, and cut it into short lengths. Put the pieces into a baking dish, then trickle over the honey. Grate the orange zest, cut the orange in half, squeeze it over the rhubarb and add the orange shells and zest to the dish. Add the cinnamon stick and the star anise. Cover with a piece of foil or a lid and bake for thirty minutes or until the rhubarb is soft but has kept its shape.

To release the panna cottas from their moulds, carefully lower each one into a bowl of tap-hot water for a few seconds, then upturn on to a small dish or saucer. Serve with the rhubarb.

Baked rhubarb with blueberries

Lovely clear flavours here, a dessert for a day when the sky is grey and you need something sharp and fresh.

> *enough for 2–3*
> rhubarb – 240g
> blueberries – 200g
> caster sugar – 2 tablespoons
> water – 2 tablespoons

Set the oven at 160°C/Gas 3. Trim the rhubarb, taking care to discard the leaves. Cut the stalks into short lengths. Put them into an ovenproof china or glass dish, tip in the blueberries, then add the sugar and water. Bake, uncovered, for forty minutes to an hour, until the fruit is soft and the sugar and water have turned to deep pink juice. Serve warm or thoroughly chilled, without cream or any other embellishment.

Rhubarb with orange

This looks particularly elegant in martini glasses.

enough for 4–6
rhubarb – 750g
blood oranges – 4
golden caster sugar
a vanilla pod

Set the oven at 200°C/Gas 6. Rinse the rhubarb, then cut off and discard any leaves. Chop the stalks into short lengths and tip into an ovenproof dish.

Remove the peel from two of the oranges, carefully cutting away any white pith, then slice the fruit thickly and tuck it in with the rhubarb. Squeeze the juice from the remaining oranges and pour it over the rhubarb. Sweeten with a small amount of sugar – a heaped tablespoon will be enough unless your rhubarb is very sharp. Tuck in the vanilla pod. Cover the dish with foil and bake till the rhubarb is tender enough to crush with a fork.

Let the rhubarb cool. You should have soft fruit and clear ruby-pink juices. Spoon everything into glasses, cover each with cling film and chill for a good hour.

Sloe rhubarb

A surprisingly fine marriage of ingredients here, which leads to a dish of glowing garnet juices. You really don't need cream, and don't even think of making custard. Sloe gin isn't easy to track down, but the website www.bramleyandgage.co.uk will send it by post.

enough for 4
rhubarb – 750g
sugar – 100g
sloe gin – 120ml
water – 2 tablespoons

Set the oven at 160°C/Gas 3. Cut the rhubarb into short lengths, pulling off any strings as you go. Put it into a glass, stainless steel or china dish (not aluminium, as it will taint the rhubarb).

Stir together the sugar, sloe gin and water, then pour it over the fruit. Put the dish into the oven and bake for forty minutes to an hour, depending on the youthfulness of your rhubarb. The toughest will take a good hour. Baste the rhubarb from time to time with the juices.

When the fruit is tender, remove from the oven and leave to cool a little. I think this is best eaten warm rather than hot, though it is very good chilled.

Rhubarb cinnamon polenta cake

You need the coarse polenta meal for this, the one that actually feels a bit gritty. The finer version, with the texture of holiday beach sand, will not do at all. The contrast of the gritty, sugary crust and the slithery fruit is what makes me go back for more. The cake is fragile when warm, so neat cooks will want to serve it cool, together with the reserved juices from the cooked rhubarb.

enough for 8

for the filling
rhubarb – 500g
golden caster sugar – 50g
water – 4 tablespoons

for the crust
coarse polenta – 125g
plain flour – 200g
baking powder – a teaspoon
ground cinnamon – a pinch
golden caster sugar – 150g
grated zest of a small orange
butter – 150g
a large egg
milk – 2–4 tablespoons
Demerara sugar – a tablespoon

Lightly oil or butter a 20cm loose-bottomed cake tin, preferably springform. Set the oven at 180°C/Gas 4 and put a baking sheet in it to get hot. Trim the rhubarb, cut each stem into short pieces and put them in a baking dish. Scatter over the sugar and water and bake for thirty to forty minutes, till the rhubarb is soft but still retains its shape. Remove the pieces of fruit from the dish and put them in a colander or large sieve to drain. Reserve the rhubarb juice to serve with the cake.

Put the polenta, flour, baking powder, cinnamon and caster sugar in a food processor. Add the grated orange zest and the butter, cut into smallish pieces, then blitz for a few seconds till you have something that resembles breadcrumbs. I sometimes prefer to do this by hand, rubbing the butter into the polenta with my fingertips as if I were making pastry. An extraordinarily peaceful thing to do if one has the time. Break the egg into a small bowl and mix with 2 tablespoons of milk, then blend into the crumble mix, either in the food processor or by hand. Take care not to over mix; stop as soon as the dry ingredients and liquid have come together to form a soft, slightly sticky dough. If it isn't a little sticky, then add a touch more milk.

Press about two-thirds of the mixture into the cake tin, pushing it a couple of centimetres up the sides with a floured spoon. Make sure there are no holes or large cracks. Place the drained rhubarb on top, leaving a small rim around the edge. Crumble lumps of the remaining polenta mixture over the fruit with your fingertips, and don't worry if the rhubarb isn't all covered. Scatter over the Demerara sugar.

Place on the hot baking sheet and bake for forty-five to fifty minutes, then cool a little before attempting to remove from the tin. Serve in slices, with the reserved rhubarb juice.

Strawberries

Our family's move to the Worcestershire
countryside brought new responsibilities:
chopping wood for the fireplace, chasing copper-
coloured pheasants off the cabbage patch, taking
the dogs for endless walks through the bracken
and collecting eggs from the farm. The last of
these involved a slow walk along a narrow, shady
path cut through the hillside. In summer, heavily
overgrown with ferns, it was dark and damp, even
on the brightest of afternoons. At one particularly
shaded point, dog-toothed violets, ragged robin
and moss lined the stone walls of the lane, and
here and there snow-white strawberry flowers twinkled in the dark. The
tiny scarlet berries were few and their crunch as intense as their flavour.
As a displaced town dweller, I regarded the idea of strawberries from the
wild as both a curiosity and a treat beyond measure.

As we settled into the rhythm of country life, with its annual village
fête on the banks of the River Theme, the country shows with their Morris
dancers and cake stalls, summer seemed like an endless round of pick-your-
own farms. Wherever we drove, the car would always pull up at poppy fields
and 'pick your owns'. At one point its interior seemed to smell permanently
of slightly squashed strawberries. It is estimated that there are still a good
thousand farms that open their fields to private gatherers. It's a pleasant
enough way to spend an hour or two, the good point being that you can
choose each berry yourself.

The modern strawberry is a tale of disappointment and delight. I have
learned to treat each punnet of really good berries I encounter as a box of
fleeting, precious jewels, a treat to be enjoyed with unalloyed pleasure;
no cream, sugar or splash of Beaujolais, just the warm berry in all its
scarlet glory. That perfect fruit is a rare find, but once you chance upon it
life seems, for an instant, to stand still. Eyes closed, you are briefly lost in
buttercup meadows, with bees buzzing on the heavy afternoon air. You need
to make much of a truly excellent strawberry when you find it, otherwise

most of us would probably have given up on this hit-and-miss fruit long ago.

Even at its ripest, the strawberry is not a connoisseur's fruit, in the way of a melting pear or a fig warm from the sun, but more of a cheeky chappie out to please the masses. Strawberry is still the nation's favourite flavour.

Fragility is both the strawberry's charm and its downfall. So tender is its ripe flesh that big business demands something more resilient, a berry that will travel and hold well on the shelf. This has resulted in richly flavoured yet delicate varieties being lost and replaced by tougher specimens that will stand a few knocks on the journey from field to plate. Compounded by a propensity for viral infection that can weaken and even wipe out a variety in just a few years, *Fragaria* is a difficult fruit to find at its best. But when you do, and that berry is melting on your tongue, it is as if all your summers have come at once.

The robust varieties of berry can be superb if they are left to ripen fully. An Elsanta that is allowed to ripen gradually and develop its true sweetness will be a revelation to those who have written the variety off as the 'supermarket strawberry'. Slow ripening produces a deeper flavour because the sugars are given time to develop. This is why the outdoor-ripened fruit in June and July often tastes more interesting than the early hothouse-ripened varieties in late April and May. They are brought to ripeness too quickly. Whilst an unripe apple will be sour, a pear impregnable and a green orange bitter, an unripe strawberry will simply taste of nothing. Warmth, preferably from the naked sun, is crucial.

By all accounts the berries we enjoy in the twenty-first century are also less red than the dark bloodied Victorian varieties. The green and white tinges so common now are rarely seen in early portraits of the fruit. At the height of the season, 'strawberry girls' were a well-known sight in Regency times, the young women walking around the town balancing a large basket of berries on a cushion on their heads. Buyers would walk away with their fragrant purchase in a pottle, rather like a cornet but made of wicker. Wine-red berries in a cane cornet – a far more romantic prospect than the blue cellophane carton of today.

It can glow all it wishes, and fill the room with its scent of pineapple, balsam and honey, but the strawberry will never be my favourite fruit. It lacks the lusciousness of the mulberry, the sensuality of the fig, the mystery of the pomegranate. But once a year I find myself falling for a cardboard punnet of misshapen, organic fruits the loud scarlet-red of a Ferrari. It is then, breathing in their honey-sweet scent, the prickle of their yellow seeds on my lips, that I wish they could always be like this.

Strawberries in the garden

The exquisite berries that grow in the dark and shady part of my garden now are a larger form from the wild, the 'hautbois', a variety often found wild in Scandinavia and the Low Countries that made its way here in the sixteenth century. Though small, its fruits are less seedy and have an intense flavour. The flowers are acid green. Before I got tough with their rambling manner, I once gathered enough for a plate of tiny sugar-pastry tartlets filled with fromage frais and dusted with a snowfall of icing sugar.

I grow the rest of my plants in rich garden soil in large terracotta pots, a layer of heavily rotted manure in the bottom, the fruit hanging enticingly over the edges. Home-grown fruit for anyone with a few feet of outside space. They do well as long as the soil is moist. In the garden, the ripening fruits were consistently half-inched by the squirrels or nibbled at by slugs that found their way over the straw I laid under each plant to keep the crop from becoming muddy. The Florence variety has done particularly well in pots. The bushes remain little more than a spread hand across and survive frost and the occasional drought, yet still produce prolific quantities of richly flavoured berries.

In their own bed, the plants like to be about 50cm apart in rich, easily draining soil, but I have found them to be tolerant of both wet and cold. They need a sunny site if they are to ripen aromatically. Green netting will keep off the birds. An under-blanket of thick straw will prevent them getting muddy and lift the berries nearer the sunshine. In winter it is a good idea to pull away dead leaves to reduce the chance of infection, but don't expect the plants to live forever; they are naturally short-lived.

Varieties

Strawberry varieties seem to come and go, but with good reason. Their susceptibility to viral infection means that few old varieties survive. Many of the reputed cultivars developed in the first half of the 1820s are now lost forever, including the deep burgundy Black Prince, Keen's Seedling, the reliable British Queen and the corpulent red Waterloo that Edward Bunyard described as 'too carnal in appearance for vegetarians'. Bad luck.

Early varieties such as Elvira, Honeoye, Mae and Gariguette will be ripe from early to mid June if we have enough sun. Mid-season varieties include Darselect, Hapil, which is good for drier soils, and the heavy-cropping Cambridge Favourite. Late-fruiting varieties, often smaller but with a deep colour, include Alice, Florence, the firmer French Daisy and the exceptionally red Chelsea Pensioner that specialist Ken Muir has high claims for and I too have done rather well with.

Royal Sovereign A gorgeous berry that elicits as much praise now as it did when nurseryman Thomas Laxton introduced it in 1892.

Gariguette The French equivalent of the Royal Sovereign. A long, sugar-sweet berry as bright as a tart's lipstick that is the star of the market stalls of Provence. The fruit is too soft and tender for commercial use here, and so is something for the gardener and allotment holder.

Cambridge Favourite A heavy cropper, this old variety fruits during July. Reliable and tolerant of both disease and neglect, the berry is less red than it might be. It has particularly dense leaf growth, which makes it a little more susceptible to botrytis in wet seasons.

Cambridge Late Pine Bred since 1947, the Cambridge Late Pine is considered by some to be the best-flavoured strawberry variety ever. It has a good dark colour and is exceptionally fragrant.

Florence The most flavoursome berries I have ever eaten turned out to be Florence, so I ordered several plants and have grown them ever since. Although they have never reached the intensity of those first berries, this is a very finely flavoured variety that excels in pots and rarely gets too big. I warmly recommend them.

Occasionally you will come across someone selling the seed of cultivated varieties of wood or Alpine berries. These small but well-flavoured berries, with a rich flavour and fragrance, include the exceptionally rare and aromatic heirloom Baron von Solemacher. I have been told you can sometimes eat the fruit just a few weeks after sowing.

Strawberries in the kitchen

The grumbling of cookery writers and consumers, the constant media bashing of the ubiquitous Elsanta variety and the heart-rending disappointment on children's faces must have finally pricked the growers' collective conscience. Of late, the strawberry of commerce seems to have picked up its little feet, and the promise of sweet, summer-scented berries is often fulfilled. Supermarkets, whose demands for extended shelf life and sturdy flesh had led to the debasing of our proud fruit, seem to have got the message. Varieties grown for flavour rather than shelf life are being offered, necessarily at a premium, and smaller berries too, more intensely flavoured and more fragrant. There are still moments of dissatisfaction, but rarer and more forgivable. Disappointment may not be a thing of the past, but I like to think it is getting less usual, and the future for this delicate berry is looking a little more positive.

If ever there was a case of leaving well alone, then this is it. Churn your berries into an ice cream, dip them in dark chocolate, freeze them as a water ice or simmer them into a simple homemade jam. Once you start getting clever in the form of mousses, pies, charlottes, crumbles, cakes and the like, the strawberry's magic will all too often be lost. A fool, where the fork-crushed berries are folded into lightly beaten fridge-cold cream, or a smart tart is about as sophisticated as things should get.

You have chosen your berries, for their looks, for their heavy scent, for their lack of blemish, yet once home their flavour somehow fails to deliver. What do you do? Warmth will help. There is no love in a fridge-cold strawberry. If a few hours on a sunny windowsill doesn't work, then slice your cargo into a bowl and dust them with caster sugar. In an hour, maybe even half that, you will have sweeter berries, slightly softer but of richer colour, and there will be juice too. Cutting them into quarters rather than slices will keep the texture firm. A dribble of balsamic vinegar or a glug from the Beaujolais bottle will introduce a mellowness that may surprise. Grated sweet orange zest works too. Lime juice will tease out the shyest flavour, as will lemon.

Strawberries and...

Cream Much debate about the merits of sweet dairy with this fruit, but on a good day, when the fruit is ripe and the cream is particularly yellow and preferably unpasteurised, a dish of strawberries and cream takes some beating. Sharp creams such as mascarpone, crème fraîche and clotted cream are good here too.

Black pepper I have never really agreed with this, but some find a grinding of pepper, black and very, very fine, brings out the flavour of a shy berry.

Beaujolais The fruity quality of young Beaujolais is good for soaking the fruit in, with a little sugar, before serving. Make sure it is nicely chilled.

Balsamic vinegar The tiniest amount, added to a strawberry ice as it churns, will make the fruit taste richer and sweeter.

Chocolate Generally I can live without this marriage, but dark and almost bitter chocolate can be an effective partner if used crisp and sparingly. (A thin drizzle allowed to set like a fragile spider's web on a fruit tart can be excellent.) Soft chocolate mixtures, such as a mousse or ganache, will give the fruit a sickly edge.

Orange Make up a dry marinade of caster sugar and finely grated orange zest for lacklustre berries. Set aside for an hour. It will save their lives.

* Bring the box of berries close to your face. If you don't get a hit of ripe strawberry, then put them back. A good batch is often detectable by its aroma.

* It is better to wash strawberries before you twist out the green hulls, so the water does not penetrate the fruit and make it soggy.

A strawberry ice for a summer's day

The simplest and best. No other flavouring is needed for this straightforward ice cream, and it is one of the few that is worth making without an ice-cream machine. The ripeness of the berries is essential. I always marinate them in sugar for an hour or so before I make the ice, even though I have never heard of anyone else doing it. I believe it makes the flavour all the more intense.

enough for 4
strawberries – 450g
caster sugar – 100g
double cream – 300ml

Rinse the berries quickly under cold running water and remove their leaves. Cut each berry into three or four slices, then put them in a bowl, sprinkle with the sugar and set aside for an hour.

Lightly whip the cream. You want it to be thick enough to lie in folds rather than stiff enough to stand in peaks. Put the strawberries, sugar and any juice from the bottom of the dish into a food processor and whiz till smooth, then stir gently into the cream. How thoroughly you blend the two together is up to you. I like to leave a few swirls of unmixed cream in the mixture.

Transfer to a freezer box, level the top, cover with a lid or a piece of cling film or greaseproof and freeze for three or four hours. It is worth checking, and occasionally stirring the ice as it freezes, bringing the outside edges into the middle.

Remove the ice from the freezer about fifteen to twenty minutes before serving to bring it up to temperature.

A fromage frais cream with strawberries and passion fruit

A light cream for strawberries. There are several options with this recipe. You can use just double cream, fromage frais (full fat), crème fraîche or a mixture of any two of them. The choice will depend on what sort of piquancy you want. My favourite is a mixture of fromage frais and crème fraîche, a rich but fresh accompaniment to strawberries, and perfect with fraises de bois.

enough for 4
strawberries – 400g
the juice of a large orange
passion fruit – 6

for the cream
fromage frais – 300g
crème fraîche – 150ml
egg whites – 2

Line a stainless steel sieve or colander with clean, new muslin, leaving enough overhanging to fold over the top. In a cold bowl, mix the fromage frais and crème fraîche. Do this thoroughly but gently.

Beat the egg whites in a separate bowl till light and stiff. Fold the whites into the cream mixture, taking care not to knock the air out. A large metal spoon is good for this.

Spoon the mixture into the lined sieve. Fold the muslin over the top, place the sieve over a basin and leave in the fridge overnight (if you have a small fridge, as I do, you may have to take a shelf out to accommodate it).

The next day, unmould the cream, which will have shrunk and become more solid.

Rinse the berries and remove their leaves and stalks. Slice each in half and put them in a glass or china bowl. Squeeze over the orange juice. Cut the passion fruit in half and squeeze over the seeds and juice. Chill for two hours, but no longer, as the berries are inclined to go 'fluffy' if they soak too long.

Serve the bowl of strawberries with the mound of cream, letting everyone spoon the fruit over the cream as they wish.

A high-summer jam to serve warm

There are two kinds of jam: the sort you use to preserve a glut of berries to last you through the grey days of winter and the sort for more immediate consumption. The advantage of the latter is that it is not required to have any shelf life and so can be less sweet. The most luscious jams, by which I mean plum, gooseberry, greengage, blackcurrant and apricot, all have the advantage of a bite of acidity to the raw fruit, resulting in a jam that is rarely oversweet. The strawberry lacks that essential piquancy, which is why most strawberry jams are so tongue-numbingly sweet, and no doubt why they are so popular.

Mid to late summer, when the roses are almost over, the bees are getting lazy, the lawn worse for wear and the raspberries almost red enough to pick, is when strawberry prices relax and we can turn our mind to jam. Pots and pots of it, for breakfast toast and afternoon tea, ladled from jars using spoons with sticky handles, spread on to floury scones and sandwiched between homemade sponges, their surfaces sparkling with caster sugar.

The jam I make is high on fruit, low on the sweet stuff. I bring it to the table still warm from the stove, a pretty dish of it with a faint pink froth on its brow. It won't keep. It is not meant to.

strawberries – 750g
granulated sugar – 100g
a squeeze of lemon juice

Rinse and hull the strawberries, but don't dry them. Pile them into a stainless steel or enamel pan with the sugar and lemon juice. Crush the fruit with your hands or a potato masher, then place the pan over a low to medium heat. Cook, stirring occasionally, for fifteen to twenty minutes, spooning off the pink froth as you go. The jam should be thick enough to fall slowly from the spoon, like syrup, but nowhere near thick enough to set.

Pour into a bowl and serve with scones (where it will drip down your fingers) or slices cut from a sponge cake, or spoon over goat's yoghurt, or stir into a mess of whipped cream and crumbled meringue.

Strawberries, passion fruit and mint

You will need a couple of passion fruit for each portion of strawberries. Check that the passion fruit are ripe, by which I mean heavily wrinkled. Hull the strawberries and cut them in half or even quarters, depending on their size. Halve the passion fruit and squeeze their juice and seeds into a bowl. Very finely chop a couple of mint leaves per person and stir them into the passion fruit, then add the strawberries and gently toss them about a bit. Cover with a plate and leave for at least twenty minutes, an hour if you can. Serve lightly chilled.

Strawberries, orange and orange-flower water

The merest breath of orange blossom here. It is a good wheeze for berries that prove less interesting than they appeared in the shop.

> *enough for 4*
> strawberries – 4 handfuls
> oranges – 3
> orange-flower water

Rinse the berries and remove their leaves and stalks. Slice each in half and put them in a glass or china bowl. Peel and slice the oranges, saving any escaping juice and adding it to the berries with the orange slices. Shake over the orange-flower water – you need just the merest drop (believe me, just a drop is heavenly, too much and it will taste like soap).

Chill for two hours, but no longer, as the berries are inclined to go 'fluffy' if they soak for too long.

A traditional strawberry jam

Again a fairly light set. I keep this in the fridge, which thickens the jam slightly.

> strawberries – 1kg
> granulated sugar – 800g
> the juice of a large lemon

Wash and hull the berries. Keep the small ones whole and halve or even quarter the large ones. Put them into a stainless steel pan with the sugar and lemon juice and bring to the boil. Boil rapidly for fifteen minutes or until the fruit is looking soft and translucent.

Skim off the pink froth that appears on the top, then spoon into sterilised jars, seal (see below) and leave to cool.

A few notes: It is essential to prepare the jars correctly if the jam is to keep. You can either warm the thoroughly washed jars in a cooling oven, thereby sterilising them, or you can immerse them in boiling water for ten minutes. Either way they must be both scrupulously clean and warm when you pour the jam in. Seal the jam with a disc of waxed paper or greaseproof. The transparent jam covers that can be bought in kitchenware shops and supermarkets should be applied whilst the jam is warm so that they shrink tightly over the top of the jar.

Strawberries and cream

Summer is shot through with elegant culinary marriages: white-tipped radishes and ice-cold butter, stewed pale gooseberries and lacework elderflowers, ripe melon and prosciutto, mozzarella and sun-warmed tomatoes, salmon and crisp, dewy cucumber. There is also strawberries and cream.

Of course, you can slice the fruit and pour cream over it. But listen, I have a better idea. You pick the smallest, ripest berries you can lay your fingers on, crimson right through to their little hearts. You hull them, put them in a bowl, then crush them with a fork. The flesh should retain some sort of texture rather than be reduced to a purée or a puddle. Mellow the flavour with a drip or two of balsamic vinegar. Stir in the merest dribble of golden cream. Fiddle no further. I think you owe this one a teaspoon.

Strawberry tarts

Strawberries, pastry and cream. A threesome made in heaven.

makes 6

for the crust
butter – 100g
caster sugar – 2 tablespoons
shelled pistachios – 100g, finely ground
an egg yolk
plain flour – 200g

for the filling
double cream – 250ml
vanilla extract
strawberries – approximately 8 small berries per tartlet
a little icing sugar or melted dark chocolate

You will need six tartlet tins with removable bases, about 8cm in diameter.

Cream the butter and sugar till pale and smooth. Add the ground pistachios, mix in the egg yolk and then the flour. Add a little water if necessary to make a firm but rollable dough.

On a floured board, roll the dough into a short, fat sausage the circumference of the tartlet tins. Wrap in greaseproof paper or cling film and refrigerate for a good twenty minutes. Set the oven at 200°C/Gas 6.

Cut the pastry into thin discs and place them in the tartlet cases, pushing them gently into the corners. Use greaseproof paper to line each pastry case, fill with baking beans, then bake for fifteen minutes or so, till the tartlet cases are pale biscuit colour. Remove the paper and baking beans and return to the oven for five minutes to dry them out. Let them cool a little before removing from the tartlet cases.

Gently whip the cream till it will just about hold its shape, adding the tiniest drop of vanilla extract as you go. It should be billowy and voluptuous rather than stiff. Divide between the tartlet cases. Add the strawberries, together with a dusting of icing sugar or a trickle of melted dark chocolate.

Walnuts

Christmas descends on this old house like a veil of spun sugar. A tree of snow-white lights and resinous scent, church candles in the smoke-stained fireplaces and bejewelled tartlets of candied peel and crushed walnuts in the oven. I drag bundles of holly and mistletoe home from the farmers' market and trails of ivy from the garden walls. There are bowls of crimson pomegranates and walnuts in their shells. Where the chestnut is the nut of damp, smoky autumn afternoons, the walnut is the Christmas nut, decorating fruit bowls and cheeseboards till well into the New Year.

My earliest acquaintance with the walnut was both sinister and sweet. First as the black, pickled nuts like lumps of decaying fungi passed around the table by my father to sharpen up slices of cold roast beef, and then as the buried treasure at the bottom of a Walnut Whip. The pickled walnut still has its faithful fans but gone are the days when the milk chocolate confection had half a walnut in its base as well as a proud one on top.

The meat of the freshly shelled walnut revels in sour or bitter company: preserved in vinegar; scattered in a salad with watercress, chicory or rocket; offered alongside chunks of pomegranate after a meal; or cloaked in darkest chocolate. Eaten too late after harvesting or stored in sunlight, the sweet nut can take on a bitterness all of its own – a quality that has done little to win it any friends.

Fresh, locally grown walnuts are few and far between. The trees are generally too large for domestic gardens and most are found on farms or in parks. Most of those in our shops come from France or Iran. The ones with pale skins are the sweetest, their young flesh briefly mild and, like young hazelnuts, almost milky in taste. As the nuts age, their skin darkens and bitterness becomes a distinct possibility.

The Middle East and Turkey have walnut sauces for fish and game, while Greece excels in pastries made from the nut. Even though we can grow them here, we have no famous traditional dishes based on the walnut, save the pickled walnut, a dark and interesting ketchup and the long-lamented Fuller's walnut cake, a commercial gateau of walnut cream and crunchy, nut-flecked sponge with faintly lemon-scented icing. A cake that still has a following, thirty years after its demise, and which, like the Abbey Crunch biscuit, is long overdue for a revival.

I tend to take my walnuts early in the season whilst they are still pale and young. I toast them, then toss them amongst winter salads, tuck them into crisp ribbons of coleslaw, and grind them coarsely to add a nubbly texture to a cake. Most are eaten as a naked nut, along with the other Christmas fruits – figs, dates and mandarins.

The occasional tree appears in the wild here despite it being native to a plain from the Balkans to southwest China. The world's most prolific producer is California, and an ancient 700-acre orchard in the small village of Shahmirzad in Iran. We are lucky that this nut, unlike the Brazil, the pecan and the almond, will ripen in our climate. The word itself is derived from *wealhhnutu*, meaning 'foreign nut' (it came to us via France and Italy). Round and crinkly shelled, this is the nut of feasting and it appears throughout the art world in sumptuous displays of grapes, quinces, pomegranates and pears, mostly from the brushes of the Dutch masters. For me, it is something to share a plate with a pear or a piece of Appleby's Cheshire or true Caerphilly, or to be dipped into dark chocolate and eaten with vanilla ice cream.

The nut we see here most often is the Persian species, celebrated for its generous size and thin shell (some of the black variety are all but impossible to crack). You can shatter the Persian shells by squeezing two together in the palm of your hand. They can be harvested here as early as September, when the shells are still green, resembling spineless conkers. In this state the nuts within are creamy white in colour, crisp, but softer than the dried nut; a treat with the first of the season's apples.

The British are partial to these young, green walnuts. I have rarely seen these – or 'wet walnuts', as they are most often known – on sale anywhere else. It is at this point in their life, when the 'meat' of the nut is the colour of sour milk, that the walnuts are used for pickling and in gritty sauces for game and in particular pheasant.

The Armenians preserve the juiciest of them in a thick sugar syrup, eating them by the teaspoonful. In Italy, those that don't end up in a sauce for pasta may be used to flavour the liqueurs Nocino and Nocello.

Those who wait for Santa's stocking before getting the nutcrackers out are missing a trick. By Christmas the nuts are starting to dry out and, though still good, have lost a bit of the spring in their step. Obsessive I may be (and I am) but surely I'm not the only one who attempts to winkle the nut out of its shell in one piece. Even a corner broken is regarded as a failure. Worse, I like to extract those dry, sharp wings that wedge themselves between the two halves of the nut whilst keeping the kernel intact. One of life's little rituals, like trying to maintain an unbroken length of peel when paring a Bramley for a pie, or sucking a Murray mint all the way till it disappears without crunching.

The shells, when ground, are used as an environmentally sound abrasive to scale, clean and polish everything from soft metals and stone to aircraft engines. They form a useful part in the manufacture of dynamite, paint, exfoliators and much else besides. The husks that so easily stain the hands when you pick the fresh nuts are used as a natural dye. Left whole, an empty walnut shell makes a charming, fairytale receptacle for holding a special, tiny gift. (Think ring.)

The wood, much prized by carpenters, gunsmiths and furniture makers, is dark, dense and tightly grained. My kitchen drawers are lined with kiln-dried walnut heartwood, each tobacco-coloured compartment holding a knife, a ladle or a measuring cup. The outer wood of the tree is the colour of pale honey.

A walnut tree in the garden

You will need as much patience as space. Many take a decade or more to fruit, and some trees can grow to immense specimens of 30 metres, far too big for the average domestic garden. They also exude a protective compound – juglone – that is poisonous to many garden vegetables, including tomatoes and apples. Horses, too. Not much will grow under a walnut tree. There are several species of this hardy tree, but it is *Juglans regia* that is most often grown for its nuts. Many species have shells too hard to crack.

Unless you are picking them 'wet' in July and August for pickling or simply to munch raw, the nuts are ready to harvest from October onwards, when their hulls split or they start to fall off the tree. They are ready when the papery tissue between the kernel and the shell has turned pale brown. The outer cases should be easy to remove, but wearing gloves will stop your fingers turning brown.

Drying the nuts is essential if you are to store them. You can do this in a single layer in a warm, dry place for a couple of weeks, or do it more quickly over a radiator.

Varieties

A few specialist nurseries can provide young trees, carefully chosen from the hundreds of varieties available to suit our climate and to fruit within four years or so. Just in case you have the space and time, and the kindness, to plant a tree that is more for the next generation than our own, I list a few of the nut-bearing varieties available.

Franquette A traditional French variety, slow growing but very high quality nuts.
Red Danube A rare red variety from Germany.
Lara French, reliable and of 'moderate vigour'.
Buccaneer Vigorous and early. Apparently good for pickling.
Fernor A new French variety that has especially light-coloured kernels.

Walnuts in the kitchen

Those cooks who possess neither a walnut tree in their garden nor a post-Christmas glut of whole nuts are likely to buy their nuts ready shelled. It is worth looking out for those that are light in colour. They will probably be younger and less inclined to the bitterness that can occasionally develop as the nuts darken and dry. An effective way to remove any hint of bitterness is to soak them in boiling water for ten minutes. For a recipe where the nuts are the point – a sauce with lemon juice and garlic or a walnut cake, for instance – this might not be a bad habit to get into.

Nuts like salt. It brings out their sweetness. I grind over a little sea salt and toast my walnuts till they just start to colour – no more than a single shade on a decorator's colour card – then eat them while they are still hot. I tuck them into salads at this point too, the most successful being anything involving bitter leaves such as watercress or chicory.

The most famous walnut salad is the Waldorf, named for the New York hotel on whose menu it first appeared in the early 1890s. Legend has it that the restaurant's maître d'hôtel, Oscar Tschirky, first made the salad, a crunchy mixture of celery, apple and mayonnaise, without the now-synonymous walnuts. They were added by the time the recipe first appeared in print. Another worth making is one with 'rabbit ears' of crisp white chicory, Roquefort cheese and walnuts. This is an absolute gem. Crackling salad leaves, salty cheese, toasted walnuts and a mustard dressing – it is hard to think of a salad I would rather start my dinner with. I make an alternative with grated pecorino and a very mustardy dressing. It looks cool and elegant but packs a punch. I know of no better use for a walnut.

Most of the kernels not used in a sauce or salad tend to end up in a cake. My own favourite coffee and walnut aside, the nut is most common in a teabread, perhaps with golden sultanas, dark cherries and a smidgen of allspice. Something to slice and butter. I also make a coarse, less sweet cake with breadcrumbs in lieu of flour. The gravelly texture is softened with a silky frosting scented with orange blossom.

Shallow tarts of walnuts and honey are good for mid morning, as are similar affairs with a little bitter chocolate to take the edge off the sweetness. Walnut biscuits, thin and crisp, are an excellent choice for mild cheeses. A few chopped nuts in a crumble topping can be pleasing if you can keep them from burning. A walnut that sits proud is likely to brown a little too quickly. Most successful of all, perhaps, is to include the roughly chopped nuts in a loaf for cheese. A few tobacco-coloured raisins might be welcome too. Thickly sliced, it is the bread for a young and chalky goat's cheese or a melting Camembert. A few sprigs of rosemary needles, finely chopped, will add an aromatic edge.

The walnut has another string to its bow in the shape of its golden oil. This has a curious affinity with tomatoes, peaches and apricots. Trickle a little oil over a grilled peach and you have a piece of poetry on a plate. I like a mayonnaise finished with it (use groundnut for the bulk, then add a little walnut near the end). A walnut oil mayonnaise comes into its own with a plate of cold, salt-encrusted roast pork and its chewy crackling.

This is not an oil for the frying pan or roasting tin, where its flavour will disappear further with each degree of heat. It burns easily too, as do the nuts themselves. I keep it for salad dressings – it is extraordinary as a balm for a plain salad of soft green lettuce leaves and exciting when spiked with lemon juice and black pepper for a chicory and walnut salad. The oil's warm, earthy quality has an affinity with pomegranate seeds, grapes and fennel.

Walnuts and...

Chocolate Like most nuts, the walnut is exceptionally happy in the company of chocolate, particularly the darker types around 70 per cent cocoa solids. I have occasionally included them in the filling for a chocolate tart, the cream in a roulade and as a secret treat at the bottom of a pot of chocolate mousse.

Maple syrup The flavours flatter one another – a trickle of the syrup over a walnut cake being a good example.

Honey The halved kernels can be stored in honey as a sweetmeat, to be eaten with long spoons and perhaps a little sharp yoghurt. Thick honey and walnuts make an exceptional filling for an autumn tart, and both make good partners for goat's cheeses.

Pears Include walnuts in the poaching syrup for pears; add the crushed nuts to cream cheese and use it to stuff the halved pears; introduce a few nuts to the filling of a pear tart.

Cheeses The walnut is a pleasing partner for almost any cheese you can think of. The obvious choices are the milder blues, but goat's and sheep's milk cheeses, and the firm British varieties such as the Cheddars and Cheshires, can produce happy marriages.

Caramel Coat the lightly toasted kernels in crisp caramel for a more fragile version of nut brittle. I sometimes pass them round with coffee after dinner.

Celery Match the two in salads, especially with Russet apples, or add the toasted and salted nuts to a celery soup.

Peaches A walnut stuffing, made with the coarsely ground nuts, soft cream cheese such as mascarpone and a little honey, can be used with halved peaches and baked till the filling has melted and the fruit is soft.

Figs Include a handful of nuts in a dish of baked figs with honey; work them into a fig and pomegranate salad; offer them together as a simple dessert.

* Most walnuts don't need nutcrackers. The point of a knife, inserted into the fat end of the shell, should be enough to open them with a flip of the wrist. For a tough nut, I resort to the oyster opener.
* The high level of unsaturated fat in walnut oil assures that it will not keep well. I store this oil in the fridge.
* Oil from tropical regions has been found to be higher in saturated fats than that produced from nuts grown in a temperate climate.
* English walnuts will keep in the shell for several months in a cool, dry place.
* Shelled walnuts store best in an airtight container.

A simple salad of leaves and new walnuts

Sometimes, you just cannot beat a simple green salad with masses of spankingly fresh leaves and a mild, nutty dressing.

Walnuts

1170

enough for 4 as a side salad
salad leaves (butterhead lettuce, Cos, oakleaf, frisé, etc.) – 8 handfuls
shelled new walnut halves – a couple of handfuls

for the dressing
tarragon vinegar – 2 teaspoons
French mustard – a level teaspoon
sunflower oil – 2 tablespoons
walnut oil – 3 tablespoons

Put the tarragon vinegar in a jar to which you have a tight-fitting lid. Add the mustard, a grinding of salt and black pepper, then the oils. Screw on the lid and shake hard to mix.

Wash and dry the salad leaves. Gently toss with some of the dressing. Don't overdress; each leaf should just be moist, no more. Toss with the new walnuts, untoasted and unskinned.

A 'new' Waldorf salad

The classic salad is simply chopped celery, apples and walnuts bound with mayonnaise. Some like its mildness and slightly sticky texture. I prefer the classic ingredients brought together in a somewhat lighter dressing, with more bite to it than the usual recipe. A good one for accompanying a punchy cheese, slices of smoked mackerel or cold meats such as speck.

enough for 2 as a side salad
large, sweetish apples, preferably russet – 3
large celery sticks – 2
walnut halves – 12

for the dressing
crème fraîche – 2 tablespoons
chopped parsley – 2 tablespoons
chopped mint – 2 tablespoons
mayonnaise – 150ml

To make the dressing, mix all the ingredients in a bowl. Roughly chop the apples, celery and walnuts and toss them with the dressing.

A salad of chicory, pecorino and new walnuts

enough for 2
medium-sized chicory heads – 4
new walnuts in their shell – 8
chopped flat-leaf parsley – 2 tablespoons
grated pecorino or Parmesan – 4 heaped tablespoons

for the dressing
Dijon mustard – 1 tablespoon
white wine vinegar – 2 teaspoons
walnut oil – 1 tablespoon
groundnut oil – 2 tablespoons

Trim the chicory, removing any leaf that isn't utterly white and perfect.
Separate the leaves, rinse and pat dry carefully, then put them in a
salad bowl.

Crack the walnuts, remove the nuts from their shells and season
lightly with salt. Toast them briefly under a hot grill or in a small pan over
a moderate heat. Keep your eye on them all the time, they burn within
seconds. They should be barely coloured.

Put the mustard, vinegar, walnut and groundnut oils in a blender with
a little salt and pepper and whiz for a few seconds. Pour the dressing into
the salad bowl, then add the nuts, chopped parsley and grated cheese.
Toss the salad gently and serve immediately.

A salad of marinated goat's cheese, figs and pomegranate

A classy little starter this, full of crisp leaves and fresh tastes.

> *enough for 4*
> small goat's cheeses – 4
> bushy sprigs of thyme – 4
> black peppercorns – 12, lightly crushed
> bay leaves – 4
> olive oil – 150ml
> walnut oil – 100ml
> salad leaves – 4 large handfuls
> a large pomegranate
> figs – 4
> red wine vinegar – 2–3 tablespoons
> walnut halves – 24

Cut each cheese in half horizontally. Put the discs of cheese in a flat dish, sitting snugly, then tuck in the sprigs of thyme, the lightly crushed peppercorns and the bay leaves. Pour over the oils, cover with cling film and leave in a cool place overnight.

Rinse and dry the salad leaves. Halve the pomegranate and pick or knock out the seeds. Mind the bitter pith, you want just the jewel-like seeds. Cut a cross in the top of each fig and press its shoulders with your fingers and thumbs so that it opens out like a flower (actually I think they more resemble baby birds singing in their nest).

Pour the oil from the cheeses into a bowl, holding them in place with a spatula. Add a little salt and the vinegar to the oil, whisking lightly to give a sharp dressing. Taste as you go, adding more or less vinegar depending on its acidity. Toast the walnuts in a hot, dry non-stick pan.

Divide the salad leaves between four plates. Lay two slices of cheese on each plate, one fig, a scattering of pomegranate seeds and the hot walnuts. Spoon over a little of the dressing.

Penne, walnuts, Gorgonzola and sage

Supper in ten minutes; what more could anyone ask on a cold midweek night in midwinter? The flavour here is deliberately mild and soothing (the exact opposite of a puttanesca). The pasta coheres gently with the sauce rather than swimming in it. I usually make a chicory salad to follow, something crisp and slightly bitter. Even then, all I want to do is drop off to sleep afterwards. That's what creamy pasta recipes are for.

enough for 2
penne or other small, tubular pasta – 300g
creamy Gorgonzola – about 300g
double cream – 100ml
walnuts – a dozen or more, young and freshly shelled
sage leaves – about 6 will do

Put the pasta on to cook in a deep pan of generously salted boiling water. Test it throughout the cooking, but it should be ready after about nine minutes. I like my pasta to have a bit of bite. Drain the pasta in a colander, reserving a couple of tablespoonfuls of the cooking water.

Put the empty pan immediately back on the stove and turn the heat down low, then add the cheese, cream and the reserved cooking water. Stir for a minute or less, till the cheese starts to melt and you have an impromptu sauce. Tip the pasta back into the pan with the walnuts and sage leaves, then tip on to warm plates.

Vanilla walnut sundae

It was Stephen Fry who I feel discovered the best possible use for this particular nut. On visiting a world-famous Vermont ice-cream manufacturer, he was encouraged to come up with his own 'flavor'. It was a stroke of typical Fry genius that led him to woo the assembled crew with a simple mixture of vanilla ice cream, bitter chocolate and toasted walnuts. Never has a recipe made me leave my seat so quickly and head for the kitchen. Simple, perfect.

Fig and walnut cake

A big family cake made in much the same way as carrot cake.

Serves 8 (at least)
soft dried figs – 250g
shelled walnuts – 100g
eggs – 3
golden caster sugar – 65g
light muscovado sugar – 65g
groundnut oil – 200ml
flour – 250g
baking powder – a gently heaped teaspoon
ground cinnamon – a teaspoon
a pinch of ground nutmeg
yoghurt – 100ml
a drop or two of vanilla extract

for the icing
cream cheese – 250g
mascarpone – 200g
softened butter – 50g
a drop or two of vanilla extract
icing sugar – 150g

Set the oven at 180°C/Gas 4. Line the base of two 20cm cake tins with a piece of lightly buttered or oiled baking parchment. Roughly chop the figs and walnuts. The nuts should be chopped slightly finer than the fruit.

Mix the eggs, sugars and oil using an electric mixer and beat till pale and fluffy. Sift the flour with the baking powder, cinnamon, nutmeg and a pinch of salt. Add the yoghurt to the cake mixture, alternating with the flour and spices. Stir in the vanilla, the figs and the walnuts.

Divide the mixture between the two lined baking tins and bake for thirty-five to forty minutes until firm like a fruit cake. Remove from the oven, leave to settle for a few minutes then run a palette knife around the edges and carefully turn on to a cooling rack. Remove the paper from each cake.

Make the icing. Beat the cream cheese, mascarpone, butter and vanilla till smooth then beat in the icing sugar. Spread a layer on the base of one of the cakes, place the other cake on top then move to a cake stand or plate. Spread the remaining butter cream over the top and sides of the cake.

Walnut, chocolate and honey tart

Dense, sweet and crumbly. A tart for serving with coffee. Also good cold in a lunchbox.

enough for 6–8

for the crust
butter – 150g
plain flour – 200g
a large egg, beaten

for the filling
butter – 150g
set honey – 180g
light muscovado sugar – 180g
double cream – 80ml
a drop or two of vanilla extract
dark chocolate – 140g, roughly chopped
walnuts – 220g, roughly chopped

crème fraîche, to serve

To make the pastry, cut the butter into pieces and rub into the flour with your fingertips, then mix in the egg to give a firm dough. Roll out and use to line a 22–24cm shallow tart tin. Leave to rest in the fridge for a good twenty minutes. Set the oven at 200°C/Gas 6.

Cover the pastry case with baking paper and fill with dried or ceramic baking beans. Cook in the preheated oven for about ten minutes, till the pastry is lightly biscuit coloured. Carefully remove the paper and beans and return the pastry case to the oven for five minutes, until dry to the touch.

For the filling, melt the butter in a small pan, add the honey and sugar and then pour in the cream and a couple of drops of vanilla extract. Boil hard for two minutes, then remove from the heat and lightly fold in the roughly chopped chocolate and walnuts. Pour the filling into the tart case.

Turn the oven down to 190°C/Gas 5 and bake for twenty minutes or until golden. Remove and leave to cool for a good half hour before serving with crème fraîche.

Classic coffee and walnut cake

I thought long and hard before including this cake here. The recipe is in my 2005 book, *The Kitchen Diaries*, and initially I didn't want to repeat it. What is more, it wasn't a recipe I wanted to tinker with or alter in any way. But I also feel that a chapter dedicated to the walnut is incomplete without such a classic recipe. So here it is again. It is more than my 'dessert' island dish, it is the cake I want on my lips as I leave this world. Fat chance.

enough for 8–10
butter – 175g
golden caster sugar – 175g
large eggs – 3
self-raising flour – 175g
baking powder – 1 teaspoon
instant coffee granules – 2 teaspoons
walnut pieces – 65g

for the butter cream
butter – 200g
icing sugar – 400g
instant coffee granules – 2 teaspoons
walnut pieces – 60g

You will need two 20cm loose-bottomed sponge tins. Line the base of the tins with baking parchment. Set the oven at 180°C/Gas 4.

Beat the butter and caster sugar till light, pale and fluffy. You could do this by hand but it is far easier and, frankly, better with an electric mixer. Crack the eggs into a bowl, break them up with a fork, then add them a little at a time to the butter and sugar, beating well after each addition.

Mix the flour and baking powder together and gently mix into the butter and sugar, either with the mixer on a slow speed or by hand, with a large metal spoon. Dissolve the coffee granules in a tablespoon of boiling water, then stir them into the mixture. Chop the walnuts and fold them in gently.

Divide the cake mixture between the two tins, smooth the top lightly and bake for twenty to twenty-five minutes. I have noticed mine are pretty much consistently done after twenty-three minutes. Remove from the oven and leave to cool.

To make the butter cream, beat the butter with an electric beater till soft and pale, then add the icing sugar and beat till smooth and creamy. Stir a tablespoon of boiling water into the coffee granules then mix it into the buttercream. Fold in the walnut pieces.

As soon as the cake is cool, turn one half of it upside down on a plate or board, spread it with a good third of the butter cream, then place the second cake half on top. Spread the remaining butter cream on top and round the sides.

A raisin and walnut loaf for pears and cheese

Two thick slices cut from a warm wholemeal loaf studded with walnuts; a golden, washed-rind cheese and two crisp, grainy pears, all set out on a thin beech board. It's a perfect Saturday lunch, and one worth making a loaf for. Apples too, appreciate the nutty, chewy quality of a fruit loaf.

makes 2 small loaves
strong wholemeal flour – 250g
strong white flour – 250g
fresh yeast – 40g
black treacle – a tablespoon
salt – a gently heaped teaspoon
warm water – 350ml
juicy raisins – 250g
shelled walnut halves – 50g

Put the flours into a large bowl (or the bowl of a food mixer) and crumble in the fresh yeast. Add the treacle and the salt, then mix in the water with a wooden spoon (or the beater attachment of the food mixer). Keep mixing till all is smooth and there are no lumps of yeast. Turn the dough out on to a generously floured surface and knead for three or four minutes. I am never too fussy about my kneading method, and find simply working the dough with my hands until it feels springy and alive, moist but not sticky, does the trick.

Flour the bowl and return the kneaded dough to it. Cover with a clean cloth and leave in a warm place for an hour. It should have risen to almost twice its size.

Turn the dough out on to the floured surface again and push the raisins and walnuts into it, kneading lightly as you go. Cut the dough in half and form into two balls. Place on a floured baking sheet and leave to prove once again for an hour until nicely risen. Set the oven at 220°C/Gas 8.

Bake the loaves for twenty-five minutes, then allow to cool on a wire rack.

Walnut cardamom cake with orange-flower frosting

With a texture I can only describe as 'scrunchy', this simple, shallow cake has masses of walnut flavour. It is mercifully less sweet than the majority of cakes, good for tea or perhaps something to eat with coffee. A cake for nut fans.

enough for about 8
eggs – 6
caster sugar – 150g
shelled walnuts – 250g
fresh white breadcrumbs – 75g
green cardamom pods – 5
the grated zest and juice of a large orange

for the frosting
the juice of a mandarin or clementine
the juice of half a lemon
icing sugar – 175–250g
orange-flower water (optional) – a couple of drops

Line a square 22cm cake tin with very lightly oiled baking paper. Set the oven at 180°C/Gas 4.

Separate the eggs. Put the yolks and sugar into an electric mixer fitted with a whisk attachment and beat till thick, pale and light. This is likely to take a good five or ten minutes.

Chop the walnuts. They should be neither roughly chopped nor finely ground but somewhere in between, rather like fine gravel, so that the texture of the finished cake is both sponge-like and chewy. Mix them with the breadcrumbs. Crack open the cardamom pods, discard the papery cases, then crush the black seeds finely using a pestle and mortar. Add them to the nuts together with the grated orange zest and juice.

Beat the egg whites till stiff. Gently fold the nut mixture into the egg yolks and sugar, then incorporate the beaten egg whites. I do this with a large metal spoon, gently but firmly folding the egg whites in, scooping right down to the base of the mixture. It is essential to mix thoroughly but not to overmix, so that the mixture stays light.

Tip the mixture tenderly into the cake tin, using a rubber spatula so as not to waste a drop, then bake for thirty minutes, until firm in the middle. A skewer, pierced in the middle of the cake, should come out without any uncooked mixture on it. Leave to settle in the tin for fifteen minutes before turning the cake out on to a cooling rack and carefully peeling off the paper.

Make the frosting: put the fruit juice into a small bowl and stir in enough icing sugar, with a drop or two of orange-flower water, to give a smooth mixture just thick enough to pour. Smooth it over the top of the cake, allowing it to run down the sides here and there. Leave to set before serving.

Walnut maple sugar biscuits

Crumbly cookies, sweet with the warm, honeyed flavour of maple sugar and tart with dried cranberries. Maple sugar is extraordinarily difficult to find in Britain. I include the recipe for American and Canadian readers and those lucky enough to get hold of this warm and buttery sugar. You could use light brown sugar if the maple variety eludes you.

If you feel the family cannot cope with thirty biscuits at once (they don't keep well), freeze any remaining mixture in a takeaway-type carton for another day.

makes about 30
maple sugar – 80g, plus a little extra for dusting
salted butter – 150g, cut into cubes
a large egg
self-raising flour – 75g
ground almonds – 100g
shelled walnuts – 75g
dried cranberries – 75g

Set the oven at 190°C/Gas 5. Put the sugar, butter and egg into a mixing bowl and cream together till quite smooth. You really don't need to be terribly thorough about this, but even so you will find a hand-held electric whisk much less trouble than doing it with a wooden spoon. Stir in the flour and ground almonds, roughly chop the walnuts and add those along with the dried cranberries, folding them in with a spoon until everything is well mixed.

Take walnut-sized lumps of the mixture in your fingers and roll them gently in a little more maple sugar, then place them on a non-stick baking sheet, pushing them down gently with the back of a spoon. They will be all the more interesting for being left knobbly and rough hewn. A centimetre on each side of them will allow them to spread without touching the next. Bake for ten to twelve minutes, then remove and leave to cool a little before transferring carefully to a cooling rack.

Warm Christmas tartlets of candied peel and walnuts

A fragile alternative to the mince pie, rich with peel and spice. I like to serve these warm, with a jug of cream.

makes 18

for the pastry
cold butter – 150g
plain flour – 300g

for the filling
golden syrup – 200g
walnuts – 100g
candied orange and lemon peel – 50g
dried cranberries – 50g
mixed spice – a pinch
soft amaretti – 4 (or 90g cake crumbs)
an egg, lightly beaten

You will need eighteen jam tart or shallow bun tins, 7.5cm in diameter and 1cm deep.

For the pastry, cut the butter into small pieces and rub it into the flour with your fingertips until it resembles fine breadcrumbs. You can add a tiny pinch of salt if you want to. Drizzle in a very small amount of water – I would start with just a teaspoon or two – bringing the mixture together to form a soft, but not sticky, rollable ball. Pat the pastry into a fat sausage the same diameter as your tart tins, cover with cling film and chill for twenty minutes. This will give the pastry time to rest, making it less likely to shrink when it's in the oven.

Set the oven at 180°C/Gas 4. Warm the syrup in a small pan set over a low heat. Add the walnuts, roughly chopped, the finely diced peel, the cranberries and the spice, then crumble in the amaretti or cake crumbs. Remove the pan from the heat, leave to cool for five minutes, then quickly and lightly stir in the beaten egg.

Cut the roll of pastry into 18 thin slices and use them to line the tart tins. Trim the edges with a small knife. Divide the mixture between the tartlet cases – you don't want to overfill them – then bake until golden and bubbling, about fifteen to twenty minutes.

The finished tarts are very fragile, so allow them to cool a little before attempting to remove them from their tins. Serve with cream.

White currants

A white currant bush is beautiful enough to have around even if you choose to leave its fruit for the birds. From the first acid-green buds that open in March to the frilled swags of diminutive white flowers that fall from the branches in lacy trusses in July, this is a sensational shrub. The fact that it has rows of berries with which to make a fairytale fruit tart or to toss with golden raspberries or wild blackberries is almost irrelevant.

My initial love for this berry comes from sitting, as an eleven year old, amongst its electric-green leaves and glassy white berries in early summer. A group of bushes hung with cascading fruit is a magical place for a child to hide. As the sun streams through the lime-green leaves and transparent fruit, it creates an enchanted place from which to view the world.

The fruit makes a good open tart. The sparkling tartness is a credible contrast to the sweet, buttery crust. The filling must not overpower, like a true custard or pastry cream might. Better is probably a mixture of mascarpone and softly whipped cream or a layer of fromage blanc. Perhaps best of all are the little paper-wrapped cream cheeses called Petit Suisse. Good luck in finding those.

Some would suggest that there are better uses of your outdoor space. It would be difficult to disagree. Yet what other bush can offer such delicate charms, such pretty fruit, such brief, teasing pleasure? It is as if you have found and opened up a secret Victorian jewel box, and every working vegetable garden needs a little romance amongst the potatoes.

White currants in the garden

A white currant bush needs little attention, save a quick pruning after fruiting to remove any weak branches and keep the tree in shape. Take all the branches back a few centimetres each autumn with secateurs. The birds are less interested in this than the red, so netting is relatively unnecessary. The bushes will thrive in rich soil but can take a little shade. Mine does. Expect flowers in early May and trusses of ripe fruit from late June.

Varieties

There are nineteen varieties in the National Fruit Collection, including the poetically named old Bar-le-Duc à Fruits Blancs, Verriere Blanche, Weisse Aus Juterbog and the White Antagonist and White Transparent from the 1940s. Versailles Blanche – the one I grow – and the relatively new White Pearl are the most popular in nurseries now and probably the only ones you will be offered.

I must mention that there is also a rare and special pink currant that I would dearly love to grow, a fruit of such exquisite beauty that it charms all who see it. The flesh is pink, the skin translucent. The names alone seduce: Couleur de Chair, Gloire de Sablons and Rosa Hollandische, all of which first appeared in 1958. An earlier variety, the October Currant, is a survivor from the early 1920s. I long to get hold of a bush or two.

White currants in the kitchen

A salad of grey lentils and transparent currants is as understated and graceful as a dish of food could be. Even more so if you offer it in the sombre colours of a grey or jade-green bowl. The contrast of nutty lentils and sharp berries that burst in the mouth is extraordinary.

The season is fleeting, and the only possibility of preserving these rare fruits is in a fruit jelly, the white substituted for the more usual red. They will freeze, but emerge curiously foggy, without their characteristic glass-like clarity. Red and white currants are interchangeable. Anything you can do with a red you can do with a white. The latter tends to be more intriguing; a lot of people have never seen them, and they have, arguably, a subtler flavour. I have a fancy to make a white summer pudding of currants and golden raspberries. One day, I shall. And I will eat it in the garden, by moonlight.

White currants and...

Golden raspberries A dessert of such purity and simplicity, like a dish of precious jewels.

Lentils Dark green or brown lentils have an earthy note that makes a successful and unusual marriage with the astringent edge of the little currants.

Cream cheese The more lactic dairy products, such as curd cheeses, fromage frais and soft, fresh desserts like Les Cremets, have a mild acidity that only enhances the currants' flavour. Petit Suisse, the soft fresh cheese sold in tiny paper wrappings, in particular.

Blackberries A rather beautiful combination for lovers of tart, refreshing fruit salads.

A tart of fromage frais and white currants

A year after planting, I picked my first decent crop of Versailles Blanche currants. I wanted to celebrate their delicate beauty and translucency. I could, I suppose, have set them in a golden jelly (elderflower, perhaps, or Sauternes), turned them into a conserve or mixed them with another suitable fruit. Instead they became a fruit tart, their sharpness taken further with a light filling of strained yoghurt and fromage frais. I picked a sweet crust to support them, to balance the bracing freshness of the rest of the ingredients.

enough for 8

for the filling
fromage frais – 500g
plain yoghurt – 450g
icing sugar – 3 lightly heaped tablespoons, plus more for dusting
the grated zest of a small orange
white currants – 450g

for the crust
butter – 75g
lemon, orange or ginger biscuits – 300g

Mix the fromage frais and yoghurt. Line a colander or sieve with white muslin or a new J-cloth. Pour the mixture into the sieve, place the whole thing on a shallow dish to catch the drips and put it in the fridge (you may well have to take a shelf out to fit it in). Leave overnight.

To make the crust, melt the butter. Crush the biscuits to a coarse, open crumb, then mix them with the melted butter. Tip them into a loose-bottomed tart tin, about 22cm in diameter, then smooth them in, pushing them into the corners with your fingers. Chill for twenty minutes.

For the filling, tip the strained cheese mixture out of the muslin into a bowl. Stir in the icing sugar and grated orange zest. Smooth the filling into the chilled tart crust. Pull the currants from their stalks and pile them on top of the tart filling. Dust generously with icing sugar. Leave for a few minutes before slicing.

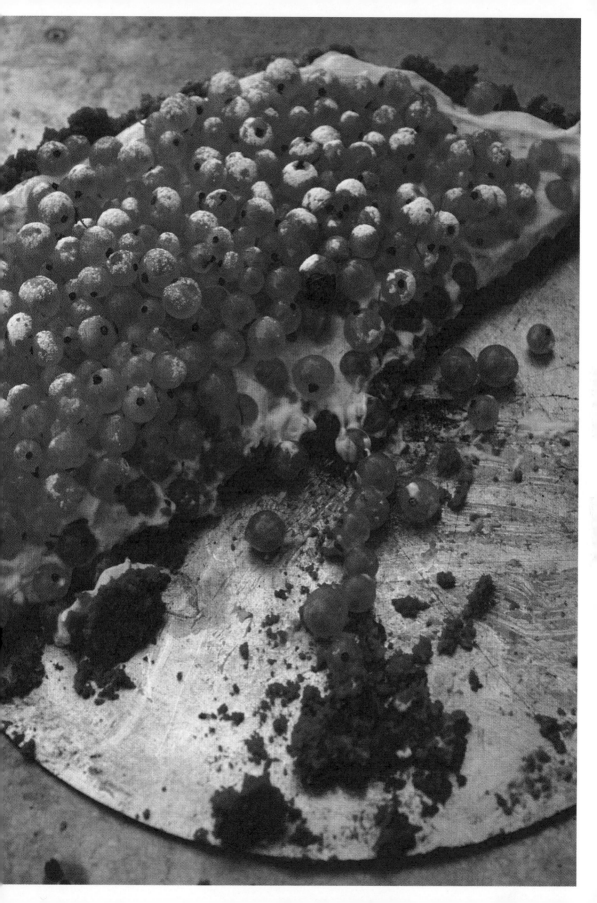

An elegant compote

You can use this for redcurrants, too. I wouldn't want to destroy its
simplicity by serving it with cream, but a nice, crisp biscuit would
be welcome.

> *enough for 2–3*
> caster sugar – 100g
> water – 300ml
> white currants – 250g

Make a light syrup with the sugar and water by bringing them slowly to
the boil in a small pan, then leaving to bubble for three or four minutes.
Remove the currants from their stems and tip them into the warm syrup.
Turn off the heat immediately and leave the currants be while they cool
down. You could serve them warm or thoroughly chilled; they are delicious
either way. A dessert of tender elegance.

A midsummer dessert of quiet perfection

A small plate or saucer. A tenderly unwrapped Petit Suisse cheese or
chalk-white fromage frais. A palmful of white currants scattered over the
surface. A trickle of double cream. An ivory and white dessert of utter charm
and purity.

A salad of lentils and white currants

The first mention of lentils with fresh currants was in *Real Fast Food*.
I used red then, but at the time suggested using white if you could get hold
of them. I am honestly not sure where the idea came from, I only know it
was something I made a lot at one time, and I still find the mixture of the
sharp fruit with the nutty, bland lentils an invigorating one. This is a side
dish, and one that I would use to accompany a cold roast – particularly
lamb, pork, salmon or guinea fowl. You could make a deeper-flavoured
dressing if you like, but the flavour of the white currants would be lost.

enough for 2 as a side dish
small green lentils – 175g
olive oil – 3 tablespoons
white wine vinegar – a tablespoon
white or red currants – 125g
a few mint sprigs
parsley – a small bunch

Wash the lentils in a sieve under running water. Lentils are invariably dusty.
Cook them in boiling, lightly salted water for twelve to fifteen minutes, till
they are tender but retain a nutty bite. They shouldn't be soft. Drain and
place in a bowl. Dress while they are still warm with the olive oil, vinegar
and some salt and pepper.

Top and tail the currants and add them to the lentils. Remove the leaves
from the mint and parsley, then add them, chopped or whole. Stir the salad
gently, so as not to crush the little white jewels.

A few other good things: medlars and sloes

The garden's yew and box hedges went in as soon as the ground was dug. Even before the fruit trees. The idea was to break up the long, thin space into small 'rooms' and to enclose and protect the vegetable and fruit beds. Having spent much of my childhood in farming country, I learned to appreciate this ancient form of partitioning and marking the land. The tearing out of traditional hedges in the name of farming efficiency is undoubtedly one of the most destructive acts of vandalism this country has seen. So many of the hedges of my childhood, alive with hawthorn and hazel, with blackbirds and voles, hedgehogs, wild roses and cherries and the inevitable rowans with their scarlet-orange berries, are gone.

Now well established, the hedges here in this garden are principally of box and yew. I wish I had thought to include more variety – a sloe bush or two, a wild rose, the creamy white froth of hawthorn that so entranced me as a child on the long, long walk to school. But what mattered at the time was a rich, dark green background against which the white blossom of the damsons, plums, apples and pears would be at their most beautiful. The appearance of a wild plum in the midst of one of the yew hedges has brought much joy. Blackbirds nest in the hedges each spring and I fancy they are the same pair. They are here again now, as I write, darting in and out with titbits for their young.

Each autumn, just as the frosts start threatening, I go to friends who know where there are sloes to pick. We come back with bags-full, with which to make bottles of crimson gin, and a few rose hips for jelly.

There is a medlar here too, standing amongst the rhubarb and gooseberries. These are the trees that live in old gardens, farmyards and, occasionally, country lanes. Mine gives me enough for one, maybe two, jars of aromatic jelly a year. But that is all I ask of it.

The medlar

The quaint, hopelessly crooked medlar tree was planted for the same reason I insisted on having a quince, a mulberry and a cobnut in the garden – I was taken by the romance and mystery of it. There is something enchanting about the idea of growing a fruit that you rarely see in the shops, that appears only in very old recipe books, and that came shot through with visions of medieval walled gardens and monastery kitchens. How could anyone resist?

Five years on, the quince and mulberry are doing well but the medlar has been spectacular since day one, giving white, gardenia-like blossom in spring, followed by a hundred or more fruits hidden amidst the rust and golden leaves each autumn. Some years, such as 2009, the blossom is rose-coloured, others, like 2010, perfectly white. I can't recommend it enough for someone looking for an interesting, decorative, edible fruit tree for a small garden.

But what on earth do I do with the fruit that smells of rancid wine and resembles nothing so much as a cat's bottom? (Cat's arse was, somewhat appropriately, the medieval name for this fruit.) The only recipes I could find were for jelly, and until recently I was not a preserving kind of guy (the term jelly bag, like piping bag, usually sends me running for the hills). The idea of baking them appealed less, even with the promise of scooping their flesh out and mixing it with sugar and cream. Medlar cheese sounded like a bridge altogether too far. But then I thought of the glistening amber jelly quivering on the same fork as hot roast pork and a nib of crackling or a slice of cold, rose-pink pheasant and thought I'd give it a go. Anyway, in reality a jelly bag is only a fiver from a kitchen shop and it sleeps quietly in the airing cupboard next to the hot water bottle for the rest for the year.

Picked unripe and hard, the fruits need to be bletted, in other words left to soften, before you use them. History dictates that you should do this by burying them in sawdust, but piling them on a plate in the kitchen works well enough for me. This is a fruit you look at, wondrously, at the farm shop, buy in a fit of enthusiasm and intrigue, then promptly leave in the bottom of the fridge till you find them, rotted to a pulp, a month later.

Making medlar jelly sounds like someone has too much time on their hands, but I wanted to taste the fruits of the most beautiful tree in my garden, the one that always comes up trumps for me. I wanted to find a use for them beyond piling them on the table for the appropriate autumnal oohs and aahhs.

Once they have softened, you bring them to the boil with water and sugar, squash them a little (too much will make the jelly cloudy), then strain the result through a jelly bag, boil it with sugar and pour into jars. I would imagine a pair of tights might work too, but I can't pretend I have tried it. Sir Harry Luke's book *The Tenth Muse* (Putnams, 1954) mentions that, curiously, Worcestershire sauce is worth adding to the preserve, but I tend to make it without any intrusion, to get the true flavour.

My medlar is the Nottingham variety, though for no other reason than I liked the shape of the tree – which looked bent and ancient from the start. The Dutch variety offers larger fruit, but can take up rather more room than most small gardens can spare.

Medlar jelly

A bronze-coloured preserve for eating with cold roast meat. If you have no firm medlars, only 'bletted' ones, then you can still make a perfectly good jelly.

makes 1 jar
bletted medlars (see below) – 800g
firm medlars – 200g
water – 1.2 litres
lemons – 2
sugar

Make sure the medlars are well bletted and remove any leaves. Cut each fruit in half and drop into a heavy-based saucepan. Pour over the water. Cut the lemons into six pieces and add them to the fruit. Bring to the boil, then turn the temperature down so that the liquid simmers gently, partially cover with a lid and leave to cook for an hour. Take care that the liquid doesn't evaporate, and give the fruit an occasional squash with a wooden spoon. Avoid the temptation to stir or mash the fruit, which will turn the finished jelly cloudy.

Pour the fruit and its liquid into a jelly bag suspended over a large jug or bowl (I hang mine from the taps over the sink). Let the juice drip into the jug, giving it the occasional squeeze, till it has all dribbled through.

Put the juice back into a clean saucepan and boil for four minutes, then add an equal amount of sugar (this is likely to be about 500g or 2 cups). When the sugar has dissolved, pour the mixture into clean, warm jars and seal. I use Kilner jars with rubber seals. Leave to cool.

To blet medlars

Medlars are usually bought rock hard and have to be softened. Pull them off their leaves and place the whole fruits on a shallow plate. Don't pile them up. Leave them at cool room temperature for a week or two till they turn deep brown and are soft, almost squashy, to the touch. They are then ready to cook.

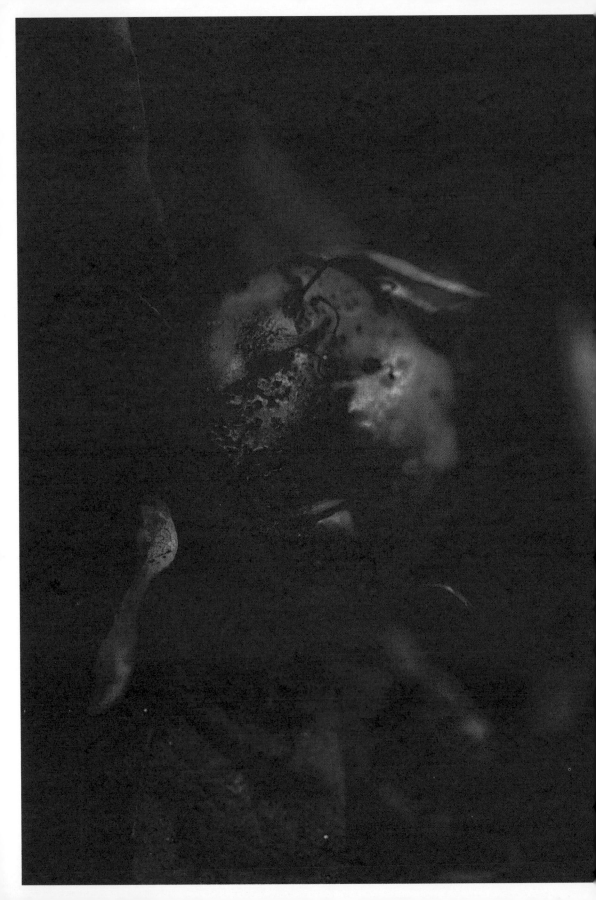

Roast partridge, juniper, thyme and medlar gravy

enough for 4
young, plump partridges – 4
thyme – 6 bushy little sprigs
juniper berries – 12
butter – 50g
thin rashers of green bacon – 8
pears – 2
a squeeze of lemon juice
a glass of vermouth or white wine
medlar jelly – 3 tablespoons

I always check the birds all over for any stray feathers or bits of shattered bone before I start. Set the oven at 220°C/Gas 7.

Pull the leaves from the thyme branches and mash them with the juniper berries, butter and a hefty pinch of sea salt and black pepper, using a pestle and mortar. Reserve a tablespoon for cooking the pears, then spread the butter all over the birds, but particularly on their breasts.

Lay each rasher of bacon flat on a chopping board, then stretch with the flat of a knife blade to give a longer, thinner rasher. Wrap the rashers round the birds and place in a roasting tin.

Cut the pears into thick slices, core them, toss them in a little lemon juice and cook briefly in the reserved herb butter in a shallow non-stick pan. When both sides are pale gold, transfer them to the roasting tin. Roast for twenty minutes, then peel off the bacon, setting it aside if it is crisp enough or leaving it in the roasting tin if not. Return the birds to the oven for a further ten minutes' roasting.

Remove the birds and pears from the tin and leave to rest in a warm place, covered with foil. Put the roasting tin over a low to moderate heat, pour in the vermouth or white wine and leave to bubble for a few minutes, then add the jelly, stirring until it has dissolved. Correct the seasoning, then serve the birds, pouring over the medlar gravy from the pan.

The blackthorn and its fruit

I am a winter person, never happier than on a clear, frosty morning. The ash-grey branches of bare trees against a crisp sky; cinnamon leaves and blood-red hips still holding on to charcoal twigs; a kitchen that smells of juniper. This is my time, just as others long for the dog days of summer.

Spotting a blackthorn hedge dotted with tiny sloes, or finding punnets of the fruit for sale on a frozen November morning at the farmers' market, is even more exciting for me than a field full of asparagus in May. Sloes make me want to get out the gin bottle. Hard to think that such a velvet-throated drink as sloe gin could come from so sour and impenetrable a fruit. Even the stones within are tough. Crows and hawfinches are the only birds with beaks strong enough to crack them.

The blackthorn, or sloe, is native to Europe, and widespread throughout the country. Although the names are interchangeable, blackthorn is most often used to describe the bush, while the term sloe is generally kept for the fruit. If allowed to grow into a tree, the blackthorn can reach four metres in height, though most are found as part of a mixed hedgerow.

The creamy-white blossom appears in early spring and brings a soft froth to hedges up and down the country. You can make a syrup from the blossom, though I have yet to try it. The result is said to taste of almonds. The fruit itself is beautiful, smaller and darker than a damson, and bullet hard. Its bitterness will leave your mouth numb.

Whilst for many, the wood of the blackthorn is still a preferred choice for making a shillelagh, the principal use of the fruit is the gorgeous drink, sloe gin. The glowing-red drink is without question my favourite cold-weather tipple. Many a bitterly cold winter's night I have sat with a candle burning in the hearth and a bottle of this glorious red liqueur at my side. It is made easily enough by pricking or bashing the fruit and leaving it to steep for a few weeks in a bottle with gin or vodka.

Pricking the sloes so that the alcohol can absorb their juice is a job I enjoy, and choose to do with a needle stuck into a cork. A mention of this in print once brought hundreds of emails from readers telling me of their 'quick' way that involved putting the fruits in the freezer, then hitting them with a bottle or a hammer instead. Yes, I could have done that, but they had missed my point entirely that for me the task is not about speed, it is something I like to take pleasure in, slowly working my way through a colander of inky-blue fruits one by one. I found it odd and somehow sad that even the calmest and most ancient of kitchen pleasures had to be reduced to something to be 'done and dusted' as quickly as making a pot noodle.

Sloe gin

Pricking the diminutive fruits with a needle is less fiddly than it sounds –
a job to do on a damp Saturday afternoon. The jars, filled with sugar, gin
and fruit, need turning regularly till the sugar has dissolved, then tucking
away in a dark corner for a couple of months while the magic gets to work.
Christmas seems an appropriate time to break open a jar. I can rarely wait
that long.

> sloes (or damsons) – 900g
> caster sugar – 700g
> gin – around 1.5 litres

Wipe the sloes, discarding any that are squashy or bruised. Prick the fruit
all over with a needle and put them into glass preserving jars, layering them
with the sugar. Fill each jar just over half full. Pour enough gin over the fruit
to fill the jars, keeping the gin bottles for later. Seal them, then leave in a
cool, preferably dark place for about three months. Turn the jars over from
time to time – I do it every few days – or give them a respectful shake. Filter
the gin through a muslin-lined funnel into the reserved gin bottles. Seal and
store in the cool, where it will keep for several months.

Roast duck with apples and sloe gin

A wild duck such as a mallard is enough for two – just. You will also need some roast or mashed potatoes or pumpkin and some vegetables too.

> *enough for 4*
> wild duck – 2
> an onion
> butter – about 50g
> juniper berries – 10
> small, sharpish dessert apples – 4
> sloe gin – a wine glass
> stock – a wine glass

Set the oven at 220°C/Gas 7. Put the birds in a roasting tin, not too close together. Peel the onion, cut into quarters and stuff each of the birds with two of the pieces. Rub a thin layer of butter over the birds, then tuck a small knob of butter inside each. Using a pestle and mortar, crush the juniper berries with a little coarse sea salt and half a dozen black peppercorns. Rub the mixture over the ducks.

Score the skin of the apples around the middle and tuck them into the tin. Roast for fifteen minutes, then turn the heat down to 180°C/Gas 4 and continue roasting for twenty to thirty minutes, or until the skin of the birds is a fine colour and lightly crisp. Lift out the ducks and put them in a warm place to rest. Put the roasting tin over a moderate flame, pour in the sloe gin and stock and stir with a wooden spoon to dissolve any pan-stickings into the liquid. Season with salt and pepper and leave to bubble for a good couple of minutes. When the sauce has started to thicken slightly, pour into a small hot jug.

Cut the birds in half and place a half on each of four warmed plates, together with an apple. Stir the gravy and pour it over.

Baked fruits with sloe gin

The marriage of fruits and sloe gin produces a heady dessert with glowing, garnet juices. You really don't need cream, and don't even think of making custard. If you can't make your own sloe gin (sloes are not exactly something you can pick up at the supermarket), the website www.bramleyandgage. co.uk will send a bottle of their gorgeous liqueur by post.

enough for 4
plums, rhubarb, apricots, damsons or peaches – 700g
sugar – 100g
sloe gin – 8 tablespoons
water – 2 tablespoons

Set the oven at 180°C/Gas 4. Put the fruit in an ovenproof dish, cutting it in half or into thick pieces no bigger than will comfortably sit in a spoon. Scatter the sugar over evenly, then pour in the sloe gin and water. Place the dish in the oven, covered with a lid or foil if you wish, and bake for forty minutes or so (much will depend on the type of fruit you are using), till the fruit is starting to burst.

Remove from the oven and leave to cool a little. I think this is best eaten warm rather than hot, though it is also very good chilled.

A note on the type

Claude Garamond (c. 1480–1561) cut type for the Parisian scholar-printer Robert Estienne in the first part of the sixteenth century, basing it on the type cut by Francesco Griffo for Venetian printer Aldus Manutius in 1495. Garamond refined his typeface in later versions, adding his own concepts as he developed his skills as a punchcutter.

Adobe Garamond, the type used in *Tender*, was designed by Robert Slimbach in 1989. The roman weights were based on the true Garamond, and the italics on those of punchcutter Robert Granjon. This font has been expanded to include small caps, titling caps, expert fonts, and swash caps, which were typical in the fifteenth and sixteenth centuries.